U0687026

新东方ACT课程指定用书

ACT

写作教程

新东方教育科技集团国外考试推广管理中心　编著

素材

海豚出版社
DOLPHIN BOOKS
中国国际出版集团

图书在版编目（CIP）数据

ACT写作教程 / 新东方教育科技集团国外考试推广管
理中心编著. — 北京：海豚出版社，2018.7
ISBN 978-7-5110-4214-9

Ⅰ.①A⋯　Ⅱ.①新⋯　Ⅲ.①英语—写作—高等学校
—入学考试—美国—自学参考资料　Ⅳ.①H315

中国版本图书馆CIP数据核字（2018）第112637号

ACT写作教程

新东方教育科技集团国外考试推广管理中心　编著

出　版　人	蔡剑峰
责任编辑	慕君黎　梅秋慧
特约编辑	田玉肖
封面设计	王　嵩
责任印制	于浩杰　蔡　丽
出　　版	海豚出版社
网　　址	http://www.dolphin-books.com.cn
地　　址	北京市西城区百万庄大街24号
邮　　编	100037
电　　话	010-68325006（销售）　010-68996147（总编室）
邮　　箱	dywh@xdf.cn
印　　刷	三河市良远印务有限公司
经　　销	新华书店及网络书店
开　　本	787mm×1092mm　1/16
印　　张	24.25
字　　数	429千字
版　　次	2018年7月第1版　2018年7月第1次印刷
标准书号	ISBN 978-7-5110-4214-9
定　　价	78.00元

目录

CONTENTS

教育类素材

Reference Article 1: The Benefits of Multilingual Education
多语言教学的益处

素材简介： 语言既是交流工具，也是文化沟通的桥梁。大多数美国人说两门语言。掌握两门语言对于科技的发展和文化的传承都具有重要意义。用英语教授数学和科学可以让学生和全球科学界受益，用小语种教授人文可以增强人们的文化认同。

Language is a bridge between cultures as much as it is a tool for communication. The complex role of language has led to controversy over whether it is better to provide education in a minority language (a language spoken by the minority of a population) or simply educating students in the dominant language of a given region. There is no one-size-fits-all solution to the problem: 20 percent of the population of the United States speak a language at home other than English, 56 percent of Europeans are bilingual, and it is believed that over half of the entire world's population is bilingual.

Given the growing size of the bilingual population, students should receive bilingual education starting in elementary school, in which humanities and social studies are taught in one of the country's minority languages, and math and the sciences are taught in the dominant language. After establishing fluency in both languages, from middle school onwards, students would be taught their classes in the dominant language—in preparation for college admissions or job searches, depending on their intended career—in addition to one literature class continued to be taught in a minority language. This ensures that students are more skilled and maintain a competitive edge when applying to colleges or for jobs, and that students retain their newly acquired command of their minority language.

Teaching math and sciences in English benefits both students and the global scientific community. It equips students with a universal tool with which to contribute to future scientific research. For example, schools in the Philippines teach Filipino history in Tagalog, but math and science in English. In an increasingly competitive global economy, allowing foreign students to learn technical subjects in English may even give the U.S. an edge in attracting the best and brightest from a global pool of talent.

Furthermore, teaching humanities classes in the minority language would benefit both students and their local communities. Studying their minority language in a cultural context would not only enrich students' cultural identities, but it would also cultivate their social relationships with people of similar cultures. Furthermore, the linguistic preservation and revitalization that comes with teaching literature or history in a minority language would be valuable to any community. For example, in Hebrew day schools in the United States, the *Old Testament* is taught in Biblical Hebrew while Israeli history is taught in modern Hebrew. Teaching ethnically relevant subjects in the most appropriate language is more likely to capture the subtleties that may only be aptly expressed in that language.

In a globalized society, it is more important now than ever to both be communicative in the dominant language common across global communities, as well as to preserve one's cultural identity by retaining or learning one's minority language. A bilingual education would prepare students for future professions, enrich their connection with their cultural heritage, and enhance their social experiences. (491 words)

(Excerpted from *https://thetech.com/2013/10/29/trent-v133-n49*)

Reference Article 2: Specialist vs. Generalist: Who Wins?
专才和通才：谁更有优势？

素材简介： 专才是把所有的精力和技能发展放在一个专业上面，达到精通的程度；通才擅长很多方面，但是都没有达到精通的程度。专才和通才各有优势，但是将二者结合才是最佳的成功秘诀。

Many fields with a great amount of depth, like web design and development, have a split of service providers. Some offer specialized services while others focus on a more general area. Having done both myself, I think there are merits (and detriments) to each, although I certainly have my own opinion about what works best! But before we get into that, let's take a look at the match up.

The Specialist
The specialist focus all of their effort, including skill development, on that one specialty. Some pros of being a specialist include:

- They are experts in their specialty.
- They know the work inside and out, upside and down.
- They may have an easier time selling their services once they find their market.
- They can charge more.
- Their work process is streamlined.

OK, flip it over. Some cons:

- They have no "filler" services to pick up the slack when work slows.
- Their market may be too narrow for consistent income.
- They probably have to turn down or outsource a lot of work.
- They limit their ability to expand their business.
- They risk going out of business if their specialty becomes obsolete.

The Generalist
Generalists may be very good at doing many things, but typically are not at the same expert level as specialists at any one service.

The pros:

- They are able to market to a broader audience.
- They have more services to offer current and past clients in order to generate additional work.
- They can easily add, remove and update service offerings to match the market.
- They have broad peripheral knowledge, which may be enough for some clients.
- They can provide clients with alternatives if one solution is not a fit.

The cons:

- They probably have to turn down or outsource specialized work.
- They have more to juggle in terms of project management.
- Their rates may be lower.

There are advantages to being in both groups, but I think the only way to be truly successful is by being a little of both. You can be a specialist, but in order to be able to develop a profitable business (of course, depending on what your specialty is), you may need to be able to supplement your specialty services with some add-on services that may not be exactly in line with your focus. On the generalist side, you can't just do everything mediocre. You can offer a lot of services, but you need to do all of them well and some of them perfectly. If you're not at least doing them well, it may be time to consider not offering those services. (439 words)

(Excerpted from *https://www.sitepoint.com/specialist-vs-generalist-who-wins/*)

Reference Article 3: Value of Education
教育的价值

素材简介： 在经济萧条时期，下岗工人会回到大学接受培训或学习新的技能，从而能再次进入竞争激烈的职场。为了提高大学的教学质量，政府给予了公立和私立高校很多财政支持。公众对政府慷慨的教育预算意见不一，有些人认为这可以使更多人接受教育，另一部分人则表示这只是在"批量生产文凭"。何种形式的教育更重要？政府应该如何分配预算？这些问题值得我们思考。

Citizens recognize the value of education, particularly during times of economic turmoil, which create an environment rampant with job insecurity. Each of the twelve districts within the Federal Reserve banking system is obligated to assess the requirements for its community in preparation for its meetings with the Board of Governors under the Federal Reserve, where members meet to discuss the state of the economy and decide about making adjustments that could assist in stabilizing the economy. Through these surveys, the Board of Governors has become aware that typical cultural behavior during times of economic turmoil results in displaced workers returning to community colleges after becoming unemployed, so they may become retrained or skilled in a new trade and effectively re-enter the workforce. In 2010, an article from *Economic Review* examined the number of people within the tenth district of the Federal Reserve who enrolled into community colleges as observed by the Federal Reserve Bank of Kansas City, stating, "The recent recession and now the recovery have caused enrollment at many community colleges to soar as unemployed workers retrain for new occupations..." The article further discusses the importance of educational institutions (particularly during and after times of economic hardship), and the need for one to educate oneself so a person may be capable of re-entering the new workforce saying, "In the Tenth District, the importance of community colleges is likely to rise even further as the economy continues to evolve and industries demand workers with new skills." This new and improved workforce will pose difficult challenges to those re-entering the workforce because the job market has suffered forced alteration to survive in such a competitive era. Many workers may have been displaced for significant periods of time, and will require tutoring regarding the skills demanded for the enhanced job market. Fortunately, community colleges and trade schools provide these desperately needed services to aid in the retraining process.

Another fortunate aspect for American citizens' continued educational growth includes the government's expressed support of the schooling system via subsidized education programs. The government accounts for the funding of education programs in its annual budget. An article in the *Journal of Higher Education* remarked, "The federal government is an important part of higher education governance and finance. Federal decisions affect many aspects of how universities operate. The federal government spent approximately $66 billion on public and private higher education in the year 2005, making it a one-third contributor to the total budget of higher education in the U.S." By providing financial support to the different tiers of the education system, the federal government makes schools better able to provide a good education for their students.

In addition, the student aid allocation of these funds allows students, who would otherwise be incapable of affording education post-high school, an opportunity to achieve higher learning and, hopefully, a better quality of life. While many people believe that such subsidization is necessary for America to continue asserting itself as a leader in the international sense, some view the use of subsidization of the education system as ineffective and contradictory to that same effort. Perhaps not every citizen should reach for goals in the higher education realm, and should rather focus on filling blue collar jobs within the U.S. One article from *Independent Review* addresses this topic noting the following:

> During the past half-century, the conventional view of American education has held that the nation needs more college graduates and that increasing the rates of college attendance and completion should be a national goal, advanced and subsidized by the federal government... This idea has reshaped higher education in the United States in a very short historical period, turning what was a guild-like activity into an industry for mass-producing credentials.

Bankston emphasizes that over the last century America has instilled increased expectations for its people to thrive through higher education. However, later in the article he also examines the notion that because the U.S. government subsidizes higher education programs, ultimately providing an elevated level of education for the masses, the country's citizens are not meeting the demands of the workforce and the overall economy. The question then becomes, "We agree education is important, but which forms of education are the most important, and how do we specifically support those different areas of education in the budget?" (734 words)

(Excerpted from *http://www.athens.edu/business-journal/spring-2013/the-value-of-education-in-todays-american-society-a-glimpse-into-the-current-way-america-supports-the-educational-system/*)

Reference Article 4: The Link Between Sports and Academic Performance
体育运动与学业成绩之间的联系

素材简介： 参加体育运动的人既能保持健康，也能够在智力测试中表现更好。如果久坐不动的人突然开始锻炼增强身体素质，他的海马区（负责记忆和学习）、额叶和颞叶会更活跃。有些人质疑体育和学习之间的正相关关系，因为很多大学生运动员的学习成绩不是很好。作者进行反驳，这是因为大学生运动员把更多精力放在体育运动上。总体而言，运动有助于提高学习成绩。

Studies have consistently demonstrated that physically active people remain healthier and are able to perform better on tests of cerebral or intellectual ability. Some studies even indicate that the results are sharp and immediate—even a quick 5-minute walk can yield immediate results.

Most studies show that the more exercise one gets, the higher one's mental faculties and cerebral performance. Yet, the picture is somewhat more complicated when it comes to college students who are also serious athletes. When these high-level athletes have to stay in shape, attend practices, travel to meets or games away from home, and still fulfill all the requirements of other college students, things can get tricky, and the measure of academic performance is no longer just a grade on a single exam.

While some college athletes experience difficulty balancing the responsibilities of their sport with the responsibilities of their academics, many student athletes actually find that the high degree of organization required to accomplish both leads them to be highly successful in both areas.

Scientific Correlation Between Physical Exercise and Achievement

In general, it has been scientifically demonstrated time and again that physical exercise is tightly correlated with mental acuity. A 2010 article in the *Washington Post* cited John J. Ratey, a Harvard University psychiatrist who synthesized volumes of research for his intriguing 2008 Book *Spark: The Revolutionary New Science of Exercise and the Brain*. In his book, Ratey describes taking MRI scans of the brains of sedentary people who have suddenly improved their fitness—and increased volume in the hippocampus and frontal and temporal lobes, the regions of the brain associated with cognitive functioning. The hippocampus in particular is associated with memory and learning.

Moreover, a recent article of the BBC (British Broadcasting Corporation) cited a university study carried out on about 5,000 children and adolescents, which found likes between exercise and exam success in English, mathematics and science and discovered an increase in performance for every extra 17 minutes boys exercised, and 12 minutes for girls. The study was carried out by the universities of Strathclyde and Dundee, and found physical activity particularly beneficial to girls' performance at science; the author said this could be a chance finding or reflect gender differences in the impact of physical activity on the brain. Overall, though, children who carried out regular exercise, not only did better academically at 11 but also at 13 and in their exams at 16, the study suggested.

In the studies examined by the Centers for Disease Control and Prevention (CDC) report, "increased time in physical education appears to have a positive relationship or no relationship with academic achievement. Increased time in physical education does not appear to have a negative relationship with academic achievement. Eleven of the 14 studies found one or more positive associations between school-based physical education and indicators of academic performance; the remaining three studies found no significant associations."

A Complex Picture: Elite-Level Athletes in College Sports

While universities across the country offer a large number of collegiate sports for students, only a handful get wide recognition. Often those big-business sports—mostly football and basketball—feature students who sometimes having difficulty making the academic cut, for various reasons. For this reason, sometimes sports have gotten a bad rap as a negative factor in college academic performance. Yet this may be an unrelated issue—some students' mediocre grades may simply reflect those students' sharper focus on excelling in sports than in academics—which is not surprising in sports that offer the possibility of professional recruitment post-college.

Yet grades and GPAs averages are not always the only measure of academic success. Many student athletes work hard to find a balance between their responsibilities. While some students may not have personal responsibilities, athletics, or the need to earn a living outside their studies, and post straight A's, other students may have any or all of these other responsibilities and yet manage to post 3.9 GPAs throughout college. With all those responsibilities outside the classroom, no one could deny that 3.9 to be an impressive achievement. In short, while there are no comprehensive data that compare student athletes' grades to those of their non-athlete peers, it is clear that the difference really comes down to personal drive, determination, and ability to organize and balance.

Getting Some Exercise Means Getting More Done

Ultimately, countless health benefits are brought on by physical activity—be it devotion to practicing an individual sport, team sports pick-up games, the weekend trip to the gym, or simply a daily walk around the block. When we take care of our bodies, our minds follow the positive pattern, and we are able to be the best we can be at academics—and beyond. (785 words)

(Excerpted From *https://www.fnu.edu/the-link-between-sports-and-academic-performance/*)

Reference Article 5: Education Dept. Could Scale Back Help on Loans
教育部要减少免除学生贷款的金额

素材简介： 数以十万计的学生被已关停的学校欺骗，所以奥巴马政府取消了这部分学生的共计 5.5 亿美元的贷款。但特朗普政府并不完全赞同该政策，决定只取消部分贷款。这引起了学生和其他人士的不满。

The Education Department is considering only partially forgiving federal loans for students defrauded by for-profit colleges, according to department officials, abandoning the Obama administration's policy of erasing that debt.

Under President Barack Obama, tens of thousands of students deceived by now-defunct for-profit schools had over $550 million in such loans canceled.

But President Donald Trump's education secretary, Betsy DeVos, is working on a plan that could grant such students just partial relief, according to department officials. The department may look at the average earnings of students in similar programs and schools to determine how much debt to wipe away.

The officials were not authorized to publicly comment on the issue and spoke on condition of anonymity.

If DeVos goes ahead, the change could leave many students scrambling after expecting full loan forgiveness, based on the previous administration's track record. It was not immediately clear how many students might be affected.

A department spokeswoman did not immediately respond to a request for comment Saturday. But the Trump team has given hints of a new approach.

In August, the department extended its contract with a staffing agency to speed up the processing of a backlog of loan forgiveness claims. In the procurement notice, the department said that "policy changes may necessitate certain claims already processed be revisited to assess other attributes." The department would not further clarify the meaning of that notice.

DeVos' review caused an outcry from student loan advocates, who said the idea of giving defrauded students only partial loan relief was unjustified and unfair because many of their classmates had already gotten full loan cancellation. Critics say the Trump administration, which has ties to the for-profit sector, is looking out for industry interests.

Earlier this year, Trump paid $25 million to settle charges his Trump University misled students.

"Anything other than full cancellation is not a valid outcome," said Eileen Connor, a litigator at Harvard University's Project on Predatory Student Lending, which has represented hundreds of defrauded students of the now-shuttered Corinthian Colleges. "The nature of the wrong that was done to them, the harm is even bigger than the loans that they have."

"Even more importantly, it is completely unfair that a happenstance of timing is going to mean that one student who's been defrauded is going to have full cancellation and the next is not," Connor said.

Jennifer Wang, an expert with the Institute of College Access and Success, said the Obama administration was providing full loan cancellations to students.

"It would be totally different from what was happening under the last administration," Wang said. "It's not equitable; it's not fair for students. If she provides partial relief, it's that she only cares what's fair for schools and not students." (453 words)

(Excerpted from *https://www.pbs.org/newshour/education/ap-sources-education-dept-could-scale-back-help-on-loans*)

Reference Article 6: Mark Emmert Says Public Losing Confidence in NCAA
公众对全国大学生体育协会失去信心

素材简介: 调查显示公众对全国大学生体育协会正在失去信心,最近曝光的关于学校篮球队中普遍存在的犯罪行为更是加重了公众对协会的负面印象。这件事情引起了协会主席马克·艾默特的高度重视,他强调必须解决这个问题;同时,他认为协会这种运营模式还是应该继续的,不应该因为这些事件和负面评价就取消全国大学生体育协会而另立其他部门。

The American public is losing confidence in the governance of collegiate athletics, NCAA president Mark Emmert said Monday.

The latest information reflects growing public negativity after the uncovering by the FBI of alleged widespread criminal activity in college basketball. Ten people, including four assistant coaches at Power 5 schools, were arrested on Sept. 26 and charged with fraud and corruption for their role in attempting to use illegal payments to steer NBA-bound prospects toward sports agents, financial advisers and apparel companies.

Emmert said the revelations create doubt around two key notions at the heart of the NCAA mission. "What kind of business are we in?" he asked, "and how do we govern?"

"The NCAA members, my staff and those schools have got to get our arms around it fast," Emmert said. "I don't think this is some little blip that's going to go away over time. This is a real question of whether or not the universities and colleges, through the association, can manage their affairs."

Former U.S. Secretary of Education Arne Duncan said the "legitimacy, integrity and even the relevancy" of the NCAA is stake.

Through the creation of the Commission on College Basketball, directed by former U.S. Secretary of State Condoleezza Rice and on which Emmert sits, the sport must undergo a major shift over the next year, Emmert said.

Emmert said he hears questions often. Where is the investigation headed? How many schools will it involve? He said he doesn't know the answers. But the eventual size of the scandal matters little, Emmert said.

"It's disgusting enough as it is," he said. "And we ought to recognize that we own that. That's part of us. When we see a coach, an assistant coach, making $200,000-$300,000 per year, taking a $10,000 bribe to throw some kid under the bus by steering him and his family to an disreputable financial adviser, you've got to be just sick to your stomach."

Emmert said he's confident that the NCAA governance model will survive, in part because no better alternative exists. If university leaders dissolved the NCAA, they would need another organization to direct college sports.

"Curiously, when I travel around the world," Emmert said, "they all want to emulate our model, because they hate their model. And they all think that having education and athletics linked together is part of the secret sauce of America.

"Having said that, we've got to find a way to avoid having to careen from crisis to crisis."

The NCAA won't conduct its own investigations until the feds are finished, he said, so as not to accidentally complicate the government's work. But new proposals regarding shoe companies, agents, advisers and the NBA will be addressed by Rice's commission.

"I think the NCAA has a great opportunity," Robinson said. "We should be doing a better job of presenting these kids with the opportunity to come to college." (480 words)

(Excerpted from *http://www.espn.com/college-sports/story/_/id/21227671/ncaa-president-mark-emmert-says-public-losing-confidence-governance-collegiate-athletics*)

Reference Article 7: Specialists or Generalists: What Do Employers Really Want? 雇主真正想要的是什么？

素材简介： 现在，一半以上具有专业技能的员工认为自己的工作大多需要通才的技能。如果这种想法继续蔓延，英国将会在全球经济竞争中处于劣势。多种原因促成这些拥有专业技能的人向通才方向发展。首先，很多工作涉及的范畴广泛。其次，很多人步入职场是先广泛尝试不同的工作，然后再确定具体岗位。最后，越是向上晋升，越需要多方面技能。

More than half of employees with specialist skills now consider their job to be mostly generalist despite the fact that they were employed for their niche skills, according to recent survey.

Oliver Watson, managing director at Page Group, who undertook the research, says, "If this trend continues, we risk creating a generation of generalists, which will undoubtedly hinder individuals' career development and ultimately damage the UK's ability to compete effectively in a global economy."

So when you're looking for a new role, is it better to be a generalist or a specialist?

Generalists tend to have a broad range of skills and experience across a range of disciplines within their field, while specialists invest time and effort in becoming the go-to person in a certain niche.

Traditionally, people have been advised to steer clear of appearing too "general" on their CV. "Usually, specific skills are valued more because they are more difficult to teach," says Nannette Ripmeester, founder of Expertise in Labour Mobility.

Some experts now believe that may be about to shift as organizations try to do more with less. In the Page Group survey, 23% of people said the economic climate was responsible for their role becoming more generalist, and Ripmeester agrees. "There's a cutback in people but the work isn't getting less, so lots of people are doing things that are not entirely part of their job," she says.

For those starting out in their careers, being a generalist may also provide them with the opportunity to test their options before specializing. Dominic Wyld, head of graduate business at Guardian Jobs, says, "Having a range of different experiences and skill sets can allow employees to identify what their ideal role would be over time, and then look for specialist jobs. For example, the traditional graduate recruitment model at most large organizations would be for them to work in a number of different areas of the company before being identified as a specialist in one particular area."

At the opposite end of the career ladder, more generalist skills are also useful. Among the survey respondents, 60% thought their boss was a good generalist, and transferable skills—such as people management and leadership—are often associated with more senior roles.

Ripmeester says, "It's a given fact that the higher up the career ladder you go, the more general and managerial skills you need. If you are able to practice those and show that you excel at them early on, it could catapult your career to a different level."

Ultimately, supplementing your broad base of skills with a sprinkling of expert knowledge is your best bet. "This is a struggle for some personalities as some people like to deep dive into areas," says Pellowe. (456 words)

(Excerpted from *https://www.theguardian.com/careers/careers-blog/specialist-generalist-what-do-employers-want*)

Reference Article 8: Why Being a Generalist Is Better Than Being a Specialist? 为什么成为通才比成为专才好？

素材简介： 当今的经济环境需要的是通才。通才善于学习新的事物，能够不拘小节地看到全局的发展，能够同时处理不同的问题，并且具有很高的决策力。未来之所以属于通才们，原因如下：经济全球化的发展，时间利用率高，合理利用资源，团队合作能力强。

The competition in every industry is soaring towards the sky with each passing day, and in order to make your mark, you need to highlight your strongest points. That's why people introduce themselves as specialists or 'domain experts'. In today's scenario, the world is overflowing with specialists in every possible field one can imagine. You may find it hard to believe, but being a generalist instead of an expert can be a really smart move.

WHAT EXACTLY GENERALISTS DO

If you want to call yourself a generalist, the first quality you need to acquire is to develop a keenness for learning new things. A generalist should be able to adapt quickly according to the demands of the circumstances he's facing at that particular moment. There are many instances when generalists are asked to act like specialists in order to achieve certain goals. Specialists show stringency in their thought process. They are usually not capable of visualizing the big picture since their focus is to grow in only their own field of expertise, which can make them less of a team player. Generalists on the other hand can handle different situations and circumstances at the same time. Their decision making power is usually superior and they always try to find universal solutions to their problems.

WHY THE FUTURE BELONGS TO THE GENERALISTS

There are several reasons why generalists will soon be considered as an integral part of the corporate world—RISE OF GLOBAL PLATFORMS—The world is now interconnected like never before and in such a scenario, only the generalists can help a corporation understand developments which may not be directly related to their core area of expertise but may affect them in several other ways.

LESS WASTAGE OF TIME—While a specialist would like to solve a problem by applying a more mechanical solution to it, a generalist could solve it in a much smaller timeframe by offering a diversified opinion.

BETTER UTILIZATION OF RESOURCES—Since generalists are skilled at adapting to different environments, they can ensure better utilization of resources. They do not have a restricted mindset which helps them in discovering alternative resources at any given point of time.

TEAM PLAYERS—Generalists have the talent of juggling several sets of teams at the same time and a generalist manager can bring a strong sense of team spirit in a corporate environment. (405 words)

(Excerpted from *http://businessadviser.co/generalist-better-specialist/*)

Reference Article 9: Education Is Worth the Investment
教育值得投资

> 素材简介：2013 年，高校毕业生和非高校毕业生的收入差距到达了最高点。据调查分析，四年制大学毕业生的收入比没有文凭的人每小时高出 98%。虽然学生需要支付学费，但是这部分费用并没有给学生带来很大的经济负担。教育值得投资，我们必须认识到教育的意义。

There is no greater financial investment in one's future than a college degree. While this view point has its critics, the reality is the value of a degree has never been greater.

Despite public questions about a degree's worth, the pay gap between college graduates and those without a degree reached a high in 2013, even with the slow recovery from the most severe recession in seventy-five years.

According to new data, based on an analysis of Labor Department statistics by the Economic Policy Institute, Americans with four-year college degrees are not only equipped for a fulfilling adult and professional life but made 98 percent more an hour on average than those without a degree. And, the wage gap is only increasing, up from 89 percent five years ago, 85 percent a decade earlier, and 64 percent in the early 1980s.

College graduates are not excluded from this reality. The vast majority with degrees in the humanities and social sciences are employed, and at salaries significantly higher than those having earned only a high school diploma.

Putting the cost of college in perspective, 30 percent of students are earning their degrees at institutions with annual tuitions from $6,000 to $9,000, often at regional campuses like mine where tuition is at the low end of the range. Students attending universities where tuition exceeds $45,000 only account for 3 percent of undergraduates nationwide.

When it comes to financing even an affordable degree, Finaid.org recommends educational debt should not exceed more than salary a graduate earns in his or her first year of employment.

Students nationwide are keeping this in mind, and making smart financial choices. The National Center of Education Statistics found more than one-third of graduates have no debt, while 12 percent owe $1,000 to $10,000. Professional school graduates owing $100,000 account for only one percent. Indiana University's Financial Literacy initiative, for example, has helped to reduce student borrowing at my campus by 25 percent in the last year.

Regional, public campuses, like Indiana University Northwest, play a critical role in creating access to higher education, ensuring that all students have an opportunity to invest in their future through personal, affordable and life-changing education.

I am proud to be Chancellor at an institution where nearly 50 percent are under-represented students, and one-third are aged 26 or older. Our camps serves the students who might not otherwise be provided with an opportunity to earn a degree that brings a more financially secure and rewarding life.

Unless the diverse students of our nation see the value in a degree, and have the opportunity to succeed academically and complete their degrees, none of the nation's goals for increasing numbers of college graduates are attainable, or even meaningful. (461 words)

(Excerpted from *https://www.huffingtonpost.com/william-j-lowe/education-is-worth-the-in_b_5767518.html*)

Reference Article 10: A New Wrinkle on School Uniforms
校服

素材简介： 有家长担心学校强制穿校服会扼杀学生个性，孩子对政策的遵守体现的是屈从权威。但是，穿校服其实有很多好处，比如可以帮助学生减轻挑选衣服的负担。而且，即使学生想表达自己的个性和观点，也不一定非要通过穿衣体现出来。

Dear Carolyn: I have three kids in public school, one is a high school freshmen and twins are in seventh grade. When they returned to school after winter break, it was announced that public schools would now require uniforms.

The uniforms are fairly basic, khaki or black plants or skirts, with a few solid colored shirts as options. My kids and their friends are shockingly okay with this shift and don't seem to care at all.

I think this is really boring. The clothes we wear say a lot about individuality and personality. Imposing uniforms on public school students seems to be limiting them for no clear or good reason.

I am outraged about this, but what surprises me more is that my kids don't really seem to care. When I asked them why they didn't care, they all just said that they will wear the uniform and don't want me to make a big deal about it. There is a meeting on Tuesday to discuss this, and I very much want to bring up my opposition, but my kids asked me not to go to the meeting or speak up. I strongly feel these uniforms are a bad idea, but I want to respect my kids' wishes as well.

I'm also a little concerned I'm raising kids who will go along with authority perhaps a little too well.

—**Uniform Disgust**

Uniform Disgust: Why does it have to be that they're "go[ing] along with authority"? Maybe they're relieved at having the fashion pressure removed. Maybe their school environment was label-competitive or trend-snarky, or some kids push hard against the boundaries of taste. Especially at these ages, kids can be vicious about clothing choices, and the ones who lack the money or body conformity or social conformity to fit in can pay a heavy social price.

Whatever the case, "outraged" strikes me as an outsize reaction for someone not actually wearing the clothes.

Respect your kids' autonomy enough to stay out of it, please, and in the free time this gives you on Tuesday, give some thought to why you care so much.

And, not for nothing—wouldn't agreeing with you mean they're just deferring to your authority? Their standing up to you on this should fill you with hope on your kids' ability to know their own minds and choose their battles accordingly.

Re: School uniforms: I went to a school that required uniforms and loved it at the time—I never had to think about what to wear and never had the pressure of "expressing my individuality" via my clothing choices. Some of us HATE that.

I grew up to be as anti-authoritarian as can be, due to my parents' influence.

—Anonymous (490 words)

(Excerpted from *https://www.washingtonpost.com/lifestyle/style/carolyn-hax-a-new-wrinkle-on-school-uniforms/2017/06/08/62f8b750-47df-11e7-a196-a1bb629f64cb_story.html?utm_term=.d27753488ebe*)

工作类素材

Reference Article 1: Passion for Your Job? If Not, It's Attainable
对工作的激情是可以培养出来的

> **素材简介：** 激情对工作确实重要，但不是做好工作的唯一前提。研究人员调查了两种存在于雇员中的思维方式对工作期望、选择和产出的影响。这两种思维方式分别是做自己感兴趣的工作（fit theory）和逐渐在工作中培养兴趣（develop theory）。结果发现，这两种思维方式的员工都能有效地完成工作任务。

People who have not found their perfect fit in a career can take heart: There is more than one way to attain passion for work.

Contrary to popular wisdom, a love-at first-sight experience is not necessary when evaluating a potential job, according to a new University of Michigan study. "The good news is that we can choose to change our beliefs or strategies to cultivate passion gradually or seek compatibility from the outset and be just as effective in the long run at achieving this coveted experience," said Patricia Chen, a doctoral psychology student and study's lead author.

The dominant mentality in America is the belief that passion is attained through finding a fit with the right line of work, or "following one's passion." An alternative mindset is that passion can be cultivated over time as one gains competence in a line of work.

Researchers examined people's expectations, choices and outcomes associated with each of these two mindsets—termed as the "fit theory" and "develop theory." They found that both mentalities are similarly effective at achieving vocational well-being. "What differs is how they motivate people to get to this outcome," Chen said.

People with the fit theory tend to select vocations that they enjoy from the outset—an indication of compatibility that is important to them. In contrast, people with the develop theory prioritize an immediate vocational fit less, but focus on cultivating passion and fit over time. "Thus, they are more likely to prioritize vocational characteristics other than immediate enjoyment, such as pay," Chen said.

The findings, which appear in the recent issue of Personality and Social Psychology Bulletin, offer assurance to those who have not—or have yet—to find what they are passionate about: If you can't discover your passion, you can learn to develop it. (303 words)

(Excerpted from *https://www.sciencedaily.com/releases/2015/08/150821111042.htm*)

Reference Article 2: Job Passion or Money? Why Not Both?
找工作到底是情怀重要还是钱重要？

素材简介： 大学生在真正进入职场之前很难对未来的工作有一个合理的预期，本文探讨了影响工作预期的一个很重要的因素：钱。以工资待遇来评判工作合适与否无可厚非，但是如果这份工作无法满足你的工资期望怎么办？本文的建议是，要么跳槽，要么降低自己的预期。

For college students, possessing a realistic expectation of their career at a company is extremely difficult because they have never worked in the corporate world before. Sure, many college students have had internships and part time jobs before, but it is not the same as being in a full-time career.

There are many things that college students can do to gain a more realistic expectation of the factors affecting their careers. This blog will cover one of the most important factors affecting the expectations of their careers: MONEY.

When it comes to choosing a career from a list of job offers, many people resort to a mindset of "choose the job that pays the most!" This is not a bad instinct by any means. But is that job paying its employees enough to fulfill their expectations of the type of lifestyles they envisioned for themselves after college? If not, even the highest paying career is not enough to satisfy these employees' expectations.

What can college students do to have a more realistic expectation of their lifestyle and how much money they should make after college?

They can begin by looking at their current lifestyle. If college students have accustomed themselves to a spend-heavy lifestyle in college (or vice versa and not spend much at all), they will likely live a similar lifestyle when they enter their careers. This is because students have grown accustomed to their lifestyles. Even if their parents, student loans, or scholarships covered the tab on many of the expenses that they are going to have to pay for now, students (and all people for that matter) have a difficult time changing their habits. To prove this point, checkout the ESPN 30 for 30 documentary Broke which details the amount of former professional athletes that could not change their lifestyles after retiring and are now bankrupt.

Fortunately for college students, there is an awesome cost of living calculator on Nerdwallet which details the cost of living change from one city to another. By using this website college students are able to calculate their annual living, food, entertainment, and transportation expenses currently. They then can get a really good idea of how much they will spend annually on their lifestyles after college by comparing it to the costs associated with other cities where they wish to live. College students then have to factor in taxes and the amount of money they want to save annually in order to derive the minimum starting salary they need to achieve to live the current lifestyle they are living.

What if the minimum starting salary a student needs to have exceeds the amount of money they have been offered in their job offers? There are 2 options at this juncture. Either the student needs to find job offers for more money, or he needs to realign his expectations of his lifestyle to meet a more realistic expectation. When expectation meets reality, satisfaction occurs. (494 words)

(Excerpted from *http://www.linkedin.com/pulse/job-passion-money-why-both-garrett-mintz*)

Reference Article 3: The Solution to (Nearly) Everything: Working Less
解决一切的办法：少工作

素材简介： 减少工作时间可以解决很多问题。首先，短的工作周可以有效减少碳排放，缓解气候问题。其次，短的工作周能避免过度劳累导致的失误。此外，减少工作时间有助于实现男女同工同酬和不同年龄层的同工同酬。

In 2000, countries such as the UK and the US were already five times as wealthy as in 1930. Yet as we hurtle through the first decades of the 21st century, our biggest challenges are not too much leisure and boredom, but stress and uncertainty.

What does working less actually solve, I was asked recently. I'd rather turn the question around: Is there anything that working less does not solve?

Take climate change. A worldwide shift to a shorter working weak could cut the carbon-dioxide emitted this century by half. Countries with a shorter working week have a smaller ecological footprint. Consuming less starts with working less—or, better yet—with consuming our prosperity in the form of leisure.

Overtime is deadly. Long working days lead to more error: tired surgeons are more prone to slip-ups and soldiers who get too little shut-eye are more prone to miss targets. Overworked managers often prove to have played a role in disasters. It is no coincidence that the financial sector, which triggered the biggest disaster of the past decade, is absolutely groaning with people doing overtime.

Furthermore, countries with shorter working weeks consistently top gender-equality rankings. The central issue is achieving a more equitable distribution of work. Not until men do their fair share of cooking, cleaning and other domestic labour will women be free to fully participate in the broader economy. Take Sweden, a country with a truly decent system for childcare and paternity leave—and the world's smallest work-time disparity between men and women.

Besides distributing jobs more equally between the sexes, we also have to share them across the generations. Older people increasingly want to continue working even after hitting pensionable age. But while thirty somethings are drowning in work, family responsibilities and mortgages, seniors struggle to get hired, even though some working has proven health benefits. Young workers who are just entering the labour market may well continue working into their 80s. In return, they would put in not 40 hours a week for all those years, but perhaps just 20-30.

And then there is the issue of economic inequality. The countries with the biggest disparities in wealth are precisely those with the longest working weeks. While the poor are working longer hours just to get by, the rich are finding it ever more "expensive" to take time off as their hourly rates rise. Nowadays excessive work and pressure are status symbols. Time to oneself is sooner equated with unemployment and laziness, certainly in countries where the wealth gap has widened.

It doesn't have to be this way. We have the ability to cut a big chunk off our working week. Not only would it make all of society a whole lot healthier, it would also put an end to untold piles of pointless and even downright harmful tasks. A universal basic income would be the best way to give everyone the opportunity to do more unpaid but incredibly important work, such as caring for children and the elderly. (506 words)

(Excerpted from *https://www.theguardian.com/commentisfree/2016/apr/18/solution-everything-working-less-work-pressure*)

Reference Article 4: Vincent van Gogh and Passion for Your Career
梵高，激情与工作

素材简介: 梵高的名画《星夜》之所以广受喜爱和赞誉，并不是因为当时激发梵高创造的阴郁情绪，而是因为画中的星光给人们带来希望和热情。这份热情也激励着我在南非经济低迷的时候仍然坚持着自己的事业和对成功的渴望。我也同样用这份热情来激励我的员工。

"I would rather die of passion than of boredom." Vincent van Gogh who was born in 1853.

When I imagine passion as a work of art I think of the image of one of Van Gogh's most famous works—*Starry Night*. Perhaps one of the real reasons this work is so famous and appreciated today is not due to the negative emotions that may have initially inspired the artwork. Instead, my experience of the artwork is that it inspires strong feelings of hope, which I believe Van Gogh conveys through the bright lights of the stars that radiate over the night's dark landscape.

In this particular moment in South African history it is relatively easy to describe our economic climate as uncertain. I acknowledge that I am operating a business in a challenging environment. However, I don't allow the factors that are driving the economy, which I have no control over, to negatively influence my passion for my career or my desire to achieve.

I believe passion fuels desire and this belief is part of some of the ingredients I need for achieving success regardless of macro and micro economics. Being truly Passionate about what you are aiming to achieve this year requires:

- Intense enthusiasm that inspires your clients;
- Great spirit that is infectious to those around you;
- Strong desire to achieve results;
- Great emotion when you celebrate a single success;
- Exceptional service that creates client delight.

I often remind my sales people to consider the following: When you book an appointment do so with the enthusiasm. When your phone rings, answer with a smile so that the tonality of your voice is welcoming and inspiring. Prepare for all your appointments as if they were your first. You are the master of your skill and every client should experience your service in the same way I experience *Starry Night*. Your client should feel the immediate difference of dealing with a passionate professional like you as opposed to your competitor. A professional that, like the bright lights of the stars in *Starry Night*, confidently guides and radiates the path to finding or selling their most prized possession—their home. (369 words)

(Excerpted from *http://www.linkedin.com/pulse/vincent-van-gogh-passion-your-career-nelson-ferreira*)

Reference Article 5: Audrey Hepburn
奥黛丽·赫本

> **素材简介：** 赫本最初的梦想是成为一名芭蕾舞者，但是由于她的身高和体形并不具备成为一位优秀舞者的素质，而且开始专业训练的时间比较晚，所以她必须放弃这个梦想。随后她在合唱团工作过。但最后被导演发掘成为一名演员，随着几部著名影片的上映，她的演员生涯大获成功。

In 1945, Winja Marova referred Hepburn to Sonia Gaskell's Ballet Studio '45 in Amsterdam, where Hepburn studied ballet for three more years. Gaskell believed that Hepburn had something special; especially the way she used her doe eyes to captivate audiences. Gaskell introduced Audrey to Marie Rambert of Ballet Rambert in London, a company performing night revues in London and international tours. Hepburn auditioned for Rambert and was accepted with scholarship in early 1948. By October, Rambert told Hepburn that she did not have the physique to become a prima ballerina for she was too tall (Hepburn was 5'7"). Plus, Hepburn didn't compare to the other dancers since she had begun serious training too late.

Devastated that her dream was over, Hepburn tried out for a part in the chorus line in High Button Shoes, a zany play at London's Hippodrome. She got the part and performed 291 shows, using the name Audrey Hepburn. Afterward, Cecil Landeau, producer of the play *Sauce Tartare* (1949) had spotted Hepburn and cast her as the girl walking across the stage holding up the title card for each skit. With her impish smile and large eyes, she was cast at higher pay in the play's sequel, *Sauce Piquant* (1950), in a few comedy skits. In 1950, Audrey Hepburn modeled part time and registered herself as a freelance actress with the British film studio. She appeared in several bit parts in small movies before landing the role of a ballerina in *The Secret People* (1952), where she was able to show off her ballet talent.

In 1951, the famed French writer Colette was on the set of *Monte Carlo Baby* (1953) and spotted Hepburn playing the small part of a spoiled actress in the movie. Colette cast Hepburn as Gigi in her musical comedy play Gigi, which opened on November 24, 1951, on Broadway in New York at the Fulton Theater. Simultaneously, director William Wyler was looking for a European actress to play the lead role of a princess in his new movie, *Roman Holiday*, a romantic comedy.

Executives in the Paramount London office had Hepburn do a screen test. Wyler was enchanted and Hepburn got the role. Gigi ran until May 31, 1952, earning Hepburn a Theatre World Award and plenty of recognition. (391 words)

(Excerpted from *https://www.thoughtco.com/audrey-hepburn-1779791*)

Reference Article 6: Founder of Apple Inc. (Steve Jobs)
苹果公司创始人（史蒂夫·乔布斯）

> **素材简介：** 乔布斯的灵感受多领域的影响，而他的敏锐的美学素养是他能够拥有 450 多项专利的主要原因。他的很多专利都是设计专利（design patent），而不是发明专利（utility patent），也就是说，他参与的是产品的设计而非发明。

Jobs's design aesthetic was influenced by the modernist architectural style of Joseph Eichler, by the industrial designs of Braun's Dieter Rams, and by Buddhism. In India, he experienced Buddhism while on his seven-month spiritual journey, and his sense of intuition was influenced by the spiritual people with whom he studied.

According to Apple cofounder Steve Wozniak "Steve didn't ever code. He wasn't an engineer and he didn't do any original design…" Daniel Kottke, one of Apple's earliest employees and a college friend of Jobs's, stated that "Between Woz and Jobs, Woz was the innovator, the inventor. Steve Jobs was the marketing person."

He is listed as either primary inventor or co-inventor in 346 United States patents or patent applications related to a range of technologies from actual computer and portable devices to user interfaces (including touch-based), speakers, keyboards, power adapters, staircases, clasps, sleeves, lanyards and packages. Jobs's contributions to most of his patents were to "the look and feel of the product." His industrial design chief Jonathan Ive had his name along with him for 200 of the patents. Most of these are design patents (specific product designs; for example, Jobs listed as primary inventor in patents for both original and lamp-style iMacs, as well as PowerBook G4 Titanium) as opposed to utility patents (inventions). He has 43 issued US patents on inventions. The patent on the Mac OS X Dock user interface with "magnification" feature was issued the day before he died. Although Jobs had little involvement in the engineering and technical side of the original Apple computers, Jobs later used his CEO position to directly involve himself with product design.

Even while terminally ill in the hospital, Jobs sketched new devices that would hold the iPad in a hospital bed. He also despised the oxygen monitor on his finger and suggested ways to revise the design for simplicity.

Since his death, the former Apple CEO has won 141 patents, more than most inventors win during their lifetimes. Currently, Jobs holds over 450 patents. (335 words)

(Excerpted from *http://www.linkedin.com/pulse/founder-apple-inc-steve-jobs-web-design-media*)

Reference Article 7: Michelangelo
米开朗琪罗

素材简介： 米开朗琪罗凭借着对于艺术的领悟和技能，在多重领域都取得重要的成就，成为文艺复兴时期的杰出人物。他不止在一个领域专精，而是在三个领域（绘画、雕塑、建筑）都很卓越。

Michelangelo di Lodovico Buonarroti Simoni was an Italian sculptor, painter, architect, and poet of the High Renaissance born in the Republic of Florence, who exerted an unparalleled influence on the development of Western art. Considered to be the greatest living artist during his lifetime, he has since been described as one of the greatest artists of all time. Despite making few forays beyond the arts, his versatility in the disciplines he took up was of such a high order that he is often considered a contender for the title of the archetypal Renaissance man, along with his rival and fellow Florentine Medici client, Leonardo da Vinci.

A number of Michelangelo's works of painting, sculpture, and architecture rank among the most famous in existence. His output in every field of interest was prodigious; given the sheer volume of surviving correspondence, sketches, and reminiscences taken into account, he is the best-documented artist of the 16th century.

He sculpted two of his best-known works, the *Pietà* and *David*, before the age of thirty. Despite holding a low opinion of painting, Michelangelo also created two of the most influential frescoes in the history of Western art: the scenes from *Genesis* on the ceiling of the Sistine Chapel in Rome, and *The Last Judgment* on its altar wall. As an architect, Michelangelo pioneered the Mannerist style at the Laurentian Library. At the age of 74, he succeeded Antonio da Sangallo the Younger as the architect of St. Peter's Basilica. Michelangelo transformed the plan so that the western end was finished to his design, as was the dome, with some modification, after his death.

Michelangelo was unique as the first Western artist whose biography was published while he was alive. In fact, two biographies were published during his lifetime; one of them, by Giorgio Vasari, proposed that his work transcends that of any other artist, living or dead and is "supreme in not one art alone but in all three".

In his lifetime, the master was often called Il Divino ("the divine one"). One of the qualities most admired by his contemporaries was his terribilità, a sense of awe-inspiring grandeur. The attempts by subsequent artists to imitate Michelangelo's impassioned and highly personal style resulted in Mannerism, the next major movement in Western art after the High Renaissance. (381 words)

(Excerpted from *https://en.wikipedia.org/wiki/Michelangelo*)

Reference Article 8: Coco Chanel
可可 · 香奈儿的情怀和商业结合

> **素材简介：** 香奈儿是个成功的艺术家，也是商人。她的服装设计把女性从紧身胸衣的束缚中解放出来。除了在服装上的成就外，香奈儿在珠宝、包和香水领域也非常成功。她的成功离不开她的决心、抱负和旺盛的精力。

Gabrielle Bonheur "Coco" Chanel (19 August 1883 – 10 January 1971) was a French fashion designer and businesswoman. She was the founder and namesake of the Chanel brand. Along with Paul Poiret, Chanel was credited in the post-World War I era with liberating women from the constraints of the "corseted silhouette" and popularizing a sporty, casual chic as the feminine standard of style. A prolific fashion creator, Chanel extended her influence beyond couture clothing, realising her design aesthetic in jewellery, handbags, and fragrance. Her signature scent, Chanel No.5, has become an iconic product. She is the only fashion designer listed on *TIME* magazine's list of the 100 most influential people of the 20th century. Chanel designed her iconic interlocked—CC monogram, meaning Coco Chanel, using it since the 1920s.

Chanel was known for her lifelong determination, ambition, and energy which she applied to her professional and social life. She both achieved financial success as a businesswoman and catapulted to social prominence in French high society, thanks to the connections she made through her work. These included many artists and craftspeople to whom she became a patron.

Her social connections appeared to encourage a highly conservative personal outlook. Rumors arose about Chanel's activities in the course of the German occupation of France during World War II, and she was criticised for being too comfortable with the Germans but never thoroughly investigated. One of Chanel's liaisons was with a German diplomat, Baron (Freiherr) Hans Günther von Dincklage (de). After the war ended, Chanel was interrogated about her relationship with von Dincklage, but she was not charged as a collaborator. After several years in Switzerland after the war, she returned to Paris and revived her fashion house. In 2011, Hal Vaughan published a book on Chanel based on newly declassified documents of that era, revealing that she had collaborated with Germans in intelligence activities. One plan in late 1943 was for her to carry an SS separate peace overture to British Prime Minister Winston Churchill to end the war. (336 words)

(Excerpted from *https://en.wikipedia.org/wiki/Coco_Chanel*)

Reference Article 9: Be Yourself. The 2 Things College Students Should Know about Personality on the Job
性格与工作

> **素材简介：** 李小龙曾说过，坚持做自己，相信自己，不要模仿他人。这种观点同样适用于职场当中。你不需要把自己伪装成你认为雇主喜欢的样子，因为即使你因此被雇用了，在未来的工作和与同事的相处中你也会感到太多压力。而如果你真实做自己，你会越来越自信，这会让你游刃有余。

Bruce Lee, the martial actor, once said, "Always be yourself, express yourself, have faith in yourself, do not go out and look for a successful personality and duplicate it." Lee's sentiment about being yourself is something everyone should keep in mind. Straining yourself to be somebody you are not creates immense amounts of unneeded stress. This is especially true for college students pursuing their careers.

1. You are not a machine that needs to fit the specs of what you think an employer wants.

For college students pursuing their careers, thinking that you can be yourself and get a job can be a difficult notion to grasp, as getting a job can be quite difficult. It is easy to assume that catering your personality to what you think an employer wants would make you more hirable. But if you are able to land a job because you have catered your personality to what you think the employer wants, how long can you maintain that personality? How will being this different affect your relationship with your coworkers?

2. Putting on an alternate personality for your career will not last nor be satisfying.

Portraying a persona of somebody that you are not is difficult to maintain and will not be sustainable in the long run. More importantly, it is not enjoyable. What most college students do not understand is that an employer would rather hire somebody that can enjoy their work and thrive than somebody that is straining themselves to try and fit the mold that they think the employer wants. This is because employers know that happy employees tend to be more engaged and stay longer than those who are unhappy.

How awesome would it be if a company would hire you for who you are? This does not have to be a situation reserved for the extremely lucky. If you are yourself in the interview process, you can feel free to be yourself when you work. Similar to dating, if you put on this façade during the first few dates that you will do all of these marvelous things as a relationship partner that you won't actually do or want to do, it will lead to dissatisfaction for both you and your partner. On top of that, your partner may not even want all of these marvelous promises that you have made and not continue the relationship.

How important is it to be yourself during the interview process and in your career? Extremely important!

When you feel free to be yourself, express yourself, and have faith in yourself in your career, you can begin to develop a level of comfortability on the job that breeds confidence. Comfortability and confidence are major aspects to building proficiency and happiness in your career.

Ultimately, choose a career that you can be yourself in. Nobody can be you better than you can. (484 words)

(Excerpted from *https://www.huffingtonpost.com/entry/be-yourself-the-2-things-_b_9516214.html*)

Reference Article 10: Personality and Extra-Role Performance
性格与工作表现

> **素材简介：** 在机构或企业中，员工在做好本职工作外所做的额外的工作叫作 extra-role performance，包括积极表现（OCB）和消极表现（CWB）。经研究发现，责任心（conscientiousness）是决定员工具有 OCB 还是 CWB 的一个重要人格。高责任心的人会对同事和企业的发展起到积极作用，低责任心的人则起到消极作用。

Every employee in your organization (hopefully) performs his or her formal work tasks. In fact, possibly the largest body of knowledge in applied organizational research has been the study of factors that are related to the performance of such tasks. However, task performance is not everything! Beyond task performance is another topic of importance: extra-role performance. Extra-role performance is consisted of employee behaviors that are not part of a formal job description. These can include organizational citizenship behaviors (OCB—voluntary behaviors that go above and beyond formal duty to help individuals or the organization) and counterproductive work behaviors (CWB—behaviors that are harmful to the organization). OCBs include behaviors like staying late to help a coworker or taking the time to onboard new employees, while CWBs include behaviors like stealing, skipping work, or sexual harassment. These behaviors have the potential to greatly affect the well-being of an organization and its members.

Recently, researchers have looked at the role of personality in the display of OCB and CWB at work. They found that one personality trait has a particularly strong relationship with these behaviors, and trait is conscientiousness. One of the Big Five personality traits (along with extraversion, openness to experience, agreeableness, and emotional stability), conscientiousness can be defined as the tendency to aim for achievement, act dutifully and deliberately, and have strong self-discipline. Of all of the Big Five traits, conscientiousness has the strongest links with positive job outcomes. For example, it is predictive of:

- job performance (across all categories of jobs)
- teamwork
- reliability
- getting along with coworkers
- job dedication

So how does conscientiousness relate to OCB and CWB? A recent study (Bowling, 2010) found that conscientiousness plays a large role in the performance of positive extra-role behaviors such as OCB. Although behavior is mostly the result of a combination of environment and personal disposition, this is an important finding in that organizations can accurately use this type of research to make selection decisions, especially if they are actively trying to change culture or create a more positive work environment. The findings indicated that high conscientiousness individuals are more likely to engage in OCB, while low conscientiousness was connected to

CWB, especially when job satisfaction was low. Here are some practical implications associated with these findings:

- Organizations that want to increase OCB and decrease CWB can do so by using a selection system that screens out individuals that are low on conscientiousness (note—personality measures should also be combined with other tools like interviews in any selection procedure).
- Improving job satisfaction (by acting on the results of the most recent employee survey, for example) will also increase OCB and decrease CWB, especially among employees with average and low conscientiousness. (449 words)

(Excerpted from *http://www.scontrino-powell.com/2011/personality-and-extra-role-performance/*)

社会进步类素材

Reference Article 1: Emancipation of Enslaved Africans
非洲奴隶的解放

素材简介： 英国的威廉·韦伯福斯议员引领了解放非洲黑奴的运动。尽管他面对来自于其他议员、庄园主和奴隶主的激烈反对和攻击，但是他仍然坚守和捍卫自己纯正的宗教理念：每个人都是被上帝平等地创造的。威廉·韦伯福斯议员为了解放黑奴而无私奉献了一生，最终在去世前三天见证了奴隶制的废除。

The hopes of the abolitionists notwithstanding, slavery did not wither with the end of the slave trade in the British Empire, nor did the living conditions of the enslaved improve. The trade continued, with few countries following suit by abolishing the trade, and with some British ships disregarding the legislation. Wilberforce worked with the members of the African Institution to ensure the enforcement of abolition and to promote abolitionist negotiations with other countries. In particular, the US had abolished the slave trade in 1808, and Wilberforce lobbied the American government to enforce its own prohibition more strongly.

The same year, Wilberforce moved his family from Clapham to a sizable mansion with a large garden in Kensington Gore, closer to the Houses of Parliament. Never strong, and by 1812 in worsening health, Wilberforce resigned his Yorkshire seat, and became MP for the rotten borough of Bramber in Sussex, a seat with little or no constituency obligations, thus allowing him more time for his family and the causes that interested him. From 1816 Wilberforce introduced a series of bills which would require the compulsory registration of slaves, together with details of their country of origin, permitting the illegal importation of foreign slaves to be detected. Later in the same year he began publicly to denounce slavery itself, though he did not demand immediate emancipation, as "They had always thought the slaves incapable of liberty at present, but hoped that by degrees a change might take place as the natural result of the abolition."

In 1820, after a period of poor health, and with his eyesight failing, Wilberforce took the decision to further limit his public activities, although he became embroiled in unsuccessful mediation attempts between King George IV, and his estranged wife Caroline of Brunswick, who had sought her rights as queen. Nevertheless, Wilberforce still hoped "to lay a foundation for some future measures for the emancipation of the poor slaves", which he believed should come about gradually in stages. Aware that the cause would need younger men to continue the work, in 1821 he asked fellow MP Thomas Fowell Buxton to take over leadership of the campaign in the Commons. As the 1820s wore on, Wilberforce increasingly became a figurehead for the abolitionist movement, although he continued to appear at anti-slavery meetings, welcoming visitors, and maintaining a busy correspondence on the subject.

The year 1823 saw the founding of the Society for the Mitigation and Gradual Abolition of Slavery (later the Anti-Slavery Society), and the publication of Wilberforce's 56-page *Appeal to the Religion, Justice and Humanity of the Inhabitants of the British Empire in Behalf of the Negro Slaves in the West Indies*. In his treatise, Wilberforce urged that total emancipation was morally and ethically required, and that slavery was a national crime that must be ended by parliamentary legislation to gradually abolish slavery. Members of Parliament did not quickly agree, and government opposition in March 1823 stymied Wilberforce's call for abolition. On 15 May 1823, Buxton moved another resolution in Parliament for gradual emancipation. Subsequent debates followed on 16 March and 11 June 1824 in which Wilberforce made his last speeches in the Commons, and which again saw the emancipationist outmaneuvered by the government. (534 words)

(Excerpted from *https://en.wikipedia.org/wiki/William_Wilberforce*)

Reference Article 2: Mahatma Gandhi
圣雄甘地

素材简介： 圣雄甘地是印度的精神领袖，是一位有远见、有社会责任感、博爱和正直的国家灵魂人物。他因为高尚的人品被印度人民尊称为圣雄。他所引领的非暴力不合作运动不仅帮助印度脱离了英国的殖民并赢得了独立，而且也激励了其他国家的民权领袖选择非暴力反抗来改良社会的不公。

Mohandas Karamchand Gandhi was the leader of the Indian independence movement against British rule. Employing nonviolent civil disobedience, Gandhi led India to independence and inspired movements for civil rights and freedom across the world. He is unofficially called the Father of the Nation.

Gandhi famously led Indians in challenging the British-imposed salt tax with the 400km (250 mi) Dandi Salt March in 1930, and later in calling for the British to Quit India in 1942. He was imprisoned for many years, upon many occasions, in both South Africa and India. He lived modestly in a self-sufficient residential community and wore the traditional Indian dhoti and shawl, woven with yarn hand-spun on a charkha. He ate simple vegetarian food, and also undertook long fasts as a means of both self-purification and political protest.

Gandhi's vision of an independent India based on religious pluralism, however, was challenged in the early 1940s by a new Muslim nationalism which was demanding a separate Muslim homeland carved out of India. Eventually, in August 1947, Britain granted independence, but the British Indian Empire was partitioned into two dominions, a Hindu-majority India and Muslim-majority Pakistan. As many displaced Hindus, Muslims, and Sikhs made their way to their new lands, religious violence broke out, especially in the Punjab and Bengal. Eschewing the official celebration of independence in Delhi, Gandhi visited the affected areas, attempting to provide solace. In the months following, he undertook several fasts unto death to stop religious violence. The last of these, undertaken on 12 January 1948 when he was 78, also had the indirect goal of pressuring India to pay out some cash assets owed to Pakistan. Some Indians thought Gandhi was too accommodating. Among them was Nathuram Godse, a Hindu nationalist, who assassinated Gandhi on 30 January 1948 by firing three bullets into his chest. Gandhi's birthday, 2 October, is commemorated in India as Gandhi Jayanti, a national holiday, and worldwide as the International Day of Nonviolence.

In April 1893, Gandhi aged 23, set sail for South Africa to be the lawyer for Abdullah's cousin. He spent 21 years in South Africa, where he developed his political views, ethics and politics.

Immediately upon arriving in South Africa, Gandhi faced discrimination because of his skin color and heritage, like all people of color. He was not allowed to sit with European passengers in the stagecoach and told to sit on the floor near the driver, then beaten when he refused; elsewhere he was kicked into a gutter for daring to walk near a house, in another instance thrown off a train at Pietermaritzburg after refusing to leave the first-class. He sat in the train station, shivering all night and pondering if he should return to India or protest for his rights. He chose to protest and was allowed to board the train the next day. In another incident, the magistrate of a Durban court ordered Gandhi to remove his turban, which he refused to do. Indians were not allowed to walk on public footpaths in South Africa. Gandhi was kicked by a police officer out of the footpath onto the street without warning. (520 words)

(Excerpted from *https://en.wikipedia.org/wiki/Mahatma_Gandhi*)

Reference Article 3: David C. Korten
大卫·科尔顿

素材简介: 大卫·科尔顿是前哈佛商学院的教授，在发展中国家生活了 30 年，帮助贫穷的国家发展经济，他的亲身经历，见证了跨国公司通过推行全球化，对贫穷国家和人民的财富洗劫和生活带来的苦难，早在 1995 年他的著作《当企业统治世界》就表达出他对跨国企业统治世界给人类社会所带来的各种灾难的担忧。他创办了《Yes!》杂志和反战的老兵组织，对推动社会进步、维护世界和平和呼吁民主作出积极的贡献。

David C. Korten (born 1937) is an American author, former professor of the Harvard Business School, political activist, prominent critic of corporate globalization, and "by training and inclination a student of psychology and behavioral systems". His best-known publication is *When Corporations Rule the World* (1995 and 2001). In 2011, he was named an Utne Reader visionary.

Early life and career
David Korten was born in Longview, Washington, in 1937 and is a 1955 graduate of its R. A. Long High School. He received a master of business administration and Ph.D. from the Stanford University Graduate School of Business. He said, "My early career [after leaving Stanford in 1959]

was devoted to setting up business schools in low-income countries—starting with Ethiopia." He served during the Vietnam War as a captain in the United States Air Force, undertaking U.S.-based teaching and organizational duties; and for five and a half years was a visiting professor in the Harvard Business School. While at Stanford in the 1950s, he married Frances Fisher Korten, with whom he now lives on Bainbridge Island near Seattle, Washington.

David Korten in conversation with Silver Donald Cameron about his work

Korten served for five and a half years as a visiting associate professor of the Harvard University Graduate School of Business where he taught in Harvard's middle management, M.B.A., and doctoral programs.

He also served as the Harvard Business School adviser to the Nicaragua-based Central American Institute of Business Administration. He subsequently joined the staff of the Harvard Institute for International Development, where he headed a Ford Foundation-funded project to strengthen the organization and management of national family planning programs.

In the late 1970s, Korten moved to Southeast Asia, where he lived for nearly fifteen years, serving as a Ford Foundation project specialist and, later, as Asia regional adviser on development management to the United States Agency for International Development (USAID), which involved him in regular travels to Pakistan, India, Bangladesh, Sri Lanka, Thailand, Indonesia, and the Philippines.

Korten has written that he became disenchanted with the official aid system and devoted his last five years in Asia to "working with leaders of Asian non-governmental organizations on identifying the root causes of development failure in the region and building the capacity of civil society organizations to function as strategic catalysts of national- and global-level change". He formed the view that the poverty, growing inequality, environmental devastation, and social disintegration he was observing in Asia also was being experienced in nearly every country in the world, including the United States and other "developed" countries. He also concluded that the United States was actively promoting—both at home and abroad—the very policies that were deepening the resulting global crisis.

He returned to the U.S. in 1992 and has assisted in raising public consciousness of the political and institutional consequences of economic globalization and the expansion of corporate power at the expense of democracy, equity, and environmental protection.

Korten is co-founder and board chair of the Positive Futures Network, which publishes the quarterly *YES! Magazine.* He is also a founding board member, emeritus, of the Business Alliance for Local Living Economies, a former associate of the International Forum on Globalization, and a member of the Club of Rome. (537 words)

(Excerpted from *https://en.wikipedia.org/wiki/David_Korten*)

Reference Article 4: Noam Chomsky
诺姆·乔姆斯基

> **素材简介:** 诺姆·乔姆斯基被评为全世界拥有最高智慧的十位学者之一。他是全世界著名的语言学家、哲学家、认知领域的科学家、历史学家以及社会评论家、政治活动家。他写过的纪实作品超过 100 本，观点非常犀利，对引发人对社会问题的思考、推动社会进步作出惊人的贡献。

Avram Noam Chomsky is an American linguist, philosopher, cognitive scientist, historian, social critic, and political activist. Sometimes described as "the father of modern linguistics," Chomsky is also a major figure in analytic philosophy and one of the founders of the field of cognitive science. He is the author of over 100 books on topics such as linguistics, war, politics, and mass media. Ideologically, he aligns with anarcho-syndicalism and libertarian socialism. He holds a joint appointment as Institute Professor Emeritus at the Massachusetts Institute of Technology (MIT) and laureate professor at the University of Arizona.

Born to middle-class Ashkenazi Jewish immigrants in Philadelphia, Chomsky developed an early interest in anarchism from alternative bookstores in New York City. At the age of 16 he began studies at the University of Pennsylvania, taking courses in linguistics, mathematics, and philosophy. From 1951 to 1955 he was appointed to Harvard University's Society of Fellows, where he developed the theory of transformational grammar for which he was awarded his doctorate in 1955. That year he began teaching at MIT, in 1957 emerging as a significant figure in the field of linguistics for his landmark work Syntactic Structures, which remodeled the scientific study of language, while from 1958 to 1959 he was a National Science Foundation fellow at the Institute for Advanced Study. He is credited as the creator or co-creator of the universal grammar theory, the generative grammar theory, the Chomsky hierarchy, and the minimalist program. Chomsky also played a pivotal role in the decline of behaviorism, being particularly critical of the work of B. F. Skinner.

An outspoken opponent of U.S. involvement in the Vietnam War, which he saw as an act of American imperialism, in 1967 Chomsky attracted widespread public attention for his anti-war essay "The Responsibility of Intellectuals". Associated with the New Left, he was arrested multiple times for his activism and placed on President Richard Nixon's Enemies List. While expanding his work in linguistics over subsequent decades, he also became involved in the Linguistics Wars. In collaboration with Edward S. Herman, Chomsky later co-wrote an analysis articulating the propaganda model of media criticism, and worked to expose the Indonesian occupation of East Timor. Additionally, his defense of unconditional freedom of speech—including for Holocaust deniers—generated significant controversy in the Faurisson affair of the early 1980s. Following his retirement from active teaching, he has continued his vocal political activism, including opposing the War on Terror and supporting the Occupy movement.

One of the most cited scholars in history, Chomsky has influenced a broad array of academic fields. He is widely recognized as a paradigm shifter who helped spark a major revolution in the human sciences, contributing to the development of a new cognitivistic framework for the study of language and the mind. In addition to his continued scholarly research, he remains a leading critic of U.S. foreign policy, neoliberalism and contemporary state capitalism, the Israeli–Palestinian conflict, and mainstream news media. His ideas have proved highly significant within the anti-capitalist and anti-imperialist movements, but have also drawn criticism, with some accusing Chomsky of anti-Americanism. (512 words)

(Excerpted from *https://en.wikipedia.org/wiki/Noam_Chomsky*)

Reference Article 5: Nicolaus Copernicus
尼古拉斯·哥白尼

> **素材简介：**尼古拉斯·哥白尼是一个多才多艺的科学家、天文学家、数学家、宗教学家和学者。他提出的日心说颠覆了地心说。虽然因此受到政治迫害，但是他捍卫了科学的真理。对人类更好地认识宇宙作出了巨大的贡献。

Astronomer Nicolaus Copernicus was instrumental in establishing the concept of a heliocentric solar system, in which the sun, rather than the earth, is the center of the solar system.

Background and Education

Famed astronomer Nicolaus Copernicus (Mikolaj Kopernik, in Polish) came into the world on February 19, 1473. The fourth and youngest child born to Nicolaus Copernicus Sr. and Barbara Watzenrode, an affluent copper merchant family in Torun, West Prussia, Copernicus was technically of German heritage. By the time he was born, Torun had ceded to Poland, rendering him a citizen under the Polish crown. German was Copernicus's first language, but some scholars believe that he spoke some Polish as well.

During the mid-1480s, Copernicus's father passed away. His maternal uncle, Bishop of Varmia Lucas Watzenrode, generously assumed a paternal role, taking it upon himself to ensure that Copernicus received the best possible education. In 1491, Copernicus entered the University of Cracow, where he studied painting and mathematics. He also developed a growing interest in the cosmos and started collecting books on the topic.

Established as Canon

By mid-decade, Copernicus received a Frombork canon cathedral appointment, holding onto the job for the rest of his life. It was a fortunate stroke: The canon's position afforded him the opportunity to fund the continuation of his studies for as long as he liked. Still, the job demanded much of his schedule; he was only able to pursue his academic interests intermittently, during his free time.

In 1496, Copernicus took leave and traveled to Italy, where he enrolled in a religious law program at the University of Bologna. There, he met astronomer Domenico Maria Novara—a fateful encounter, as the two began exchanging astronomical ideas and observations, ultimately becoming housemates. Historian Edward Rosen described the relationship as follows: "In establishing close contact with Novara, Copernicus met, perhaps for the first time in his life, a mind that dared to challenge the authority of [astrologist Claudius Ptolemy] the most eminent ancient writer in his chosen fields of study."

In 1501, Copernicus went on to study practical medicine at the University of Padua. He did not, however, stay long enough to earn a degree, since the two-year leave of absence from his canon position was nearing expiration. In 1503, Copernicus attended the University of Ferrara, where he took the necessary exams to earn his doctorate in canon law. He hurried back home to Poland, where he resumed his position as canon and rejoined his uncle at an Episcopal palace. Copernicus remained at the Lidzbark-Warminski residence for the next several years, working and tending to his elderly, ailing uncle and exploring astronomy.

Heliocentric Solar System

Throughout the time he spent in Lidzbark-Warminski, Copernicus continued to study astronomy. Among the sources that he consulted was Regiomontanus's 15th-century work Epitome of the Almagest, which presented an alternative to Ptolemy's model of the universe and significantly influenced Copernicus's research.

Scholars believe that by around 1508, Copernicus had begun developing his own celestial model, a heliocentric planetary system. During the second century A.D., Ptolemy had invented a geometric planetary model with eccentric circular motions and epicycles, significantly deviating from Aristotle's idea that celestial bodies moved in a fixed circular motion around the earth. In an attempt to reconcile such inconsistencies, Copernicus's heliocentric solar system named the sun, rather than the earth, as the center of the solar system. Subsequently, Copernicus believed that the size and speed of each planet's orbit depended on its distance from the sun. (584 words)

(Excerpted from *https://www.biography.com/people/nicolaus-copernicus-9256984*ps://en.wikipedia.org/wiki/Thomas_Jefferson)

Reference Article 6: Nikola Tesla
尼古拉·特斯拉

素材简介：尼古拉·特斯拉是人类历史上的一位奇才，天赋异禀，他每天睡眠只有两个小时，发明了近 700 样东西，比如发动机、电动汽车、交流电、直升机、无线电等，为人类社会的科技进步作出非凡的贡献。他一生没有追求财富或者名声，甚至没有结婚，生活的全部只是为了对人类社会作出贡献。

Inventor Nikola Tesla contributed to the development of the alternating-current electrical system that's widely used today and discovered the rotating magnetic field (the basis of most AC machinery).

Who Was Nikola Tesla?

Nikola Tesla (July 10, 1856 to January 7, 1943) was an engineer known for designing the alternating-current (AC) electric system, which is still the predominant electrical system used across the world today. He also created the "Tesla coil," which is still used in radio technology. Born in what is now Croatia, Tesla came to the United States in 1884 and briefly worked with Thomas Edison before the two parted ways. He sold several patent rights, including those to his AC machinery, to George Westinghouse.

Nikola Tesla's Inventions

Throughout his career, Tesla discovered, designed and developed ideas for a number of important inventions—most of which were officially patented by other inventors—including dynamos (electrical generators similar to batteries) and the induction motor. He was also a pioneer in the discovery of radar technology, X-ray technology, remote control and the rotating magnetic field—the basis of most AC machinery. Tesla is most well-known for his contributions in AC electricity and for the Tesla coil.

AC Electrical System

Tesla designed the alternating-current (AC) electrical system, which would quickly become the preeminent power system of the 20th century and has remained the worldwide standard ever since. In 1887, Tesla found funding for his new Tesla Electric Company, and by the end of the year he had successfully filed several patents for AC-based inventions.

Tesla's AC system soon caught the attention of American engineer and businessman George Westinghouse, who was seeking a solution to supplying the nation with long-distance power. Convinced that Tesla's inventions would help him achieve this, in 1888 he purchased his patents for $60,000 in cash and stock in the Westinghouse Corporation.

As interest in an AC system grew, Tesla and Westinghouse were put in direct competition with Thomas Edison, who was intent on selling his direct-current (DC) system to the nation. A negative-press campaign was soon waged by Edison, in an attempt to undermine interest in AC power. Unfortunately for Thomas Edison, the Westinghouse Corporation was chosen to supply the lighting at the 1893 World's Columbian Exposition in Chicago, and Tesla conducted demonstrations of his AC system there.

Hydroelectric Power Plant

In 1895, Tesla designed what was among the first AC hydroelectric power plants in the United States, at Niagara Falls. The following year, it was used to power the city of Buffalo, New York—a feat that was highly publicized throughout the world and helped further AC electricity's path to becoming the world's power system.

The Tesla Coil

In the late 19th century, Tesla patented the "Tesla coil," which laid the foundation for wireless technologies and is still used in radio technology today. The heart of an electrical circuit, the Tesla coil is an inductor used in many early radio transmission antennas. The coil works with a capacitor to resonate current and voltage from a power source across the circuit. Tesla himself used his coil to study fluorescence, x-rays, radio, wireless power and electromagnetism in the earth and its atmosphere.

Tesla Motors & the Electric Car

In 2003, a group of engineers founded Tesla Motors, a car company named after Nikola Tesla dedicated to building the first fully electric-powered car. Entrepreneur and engineer Elon Musk contributed over $30 million to Tesla in 2004 and serves as the company's co-founder CEO. In 2008, Tesla unveiled its first electric car, the Roadster. A high-performance sports vehicle, the Roadster helped changed the perception of what electric cars could be. In 2014, Tesla launched the Model S, a lower-priced model that, in 2017, set the Motor Trend world record for 0 to 60 miles per hour acceleration at 2.28 seconds. Tesla's designs showed that an electric car could have the same performance as gasoline-powered sports car brands like Porsche and Lamborghini. (649 words)

(Excerpted from *https://www.biography.com/people/nikola-tesla-9504443*)

Reference Article 7: Poverty and Obligation
贫穷和义务

素材简介： 根据美国人口调查局的报告，美国无法支付且没有拥有医疗保险的人在 2009 年达到了 4900 万之多，生活在贫困线以下的人高达 15.1%。很多家庭饿着肚子入睡。诺贝尔经济学奖的得主约瑟夫·斯蒂格利茨在《不平等的代价》一书中谈到，就算是能每周工作 40 小时的人，如果只有每小时 8.5 美金的收入，那么一年的收入除去社保、医疗保险、车险、房租等，一个家庭每天每人可以花费的钱不到 3 美金。

More depressing news from the home office in Washington DC. The US Census Bureau this week released its report *Income, Poverty, and Health Insurance Coverage in the United States: 2010*. Despite the sexy title, the report provides some rather grim reading. Everybody who is not living in a cave (or is not the CEO of a major corporation) knows that we are in economic trouble. Household income is down by 2.3%. The number of people without health insurance is now at 49.9 million (statistically the same as in 2009). However, the most disturbing statistic is the poverty rate. According to the report, the percentage of Americans living below the poverty line last year (15.1%) was the highest percentage since 1993, and the number of Americans living in poverty in 2010 is the largest number in the 52 years for which the poverty estimates have been published.

To restate, 46.2 million Americans are living below the poverty line. The poverty line for a family of four last year was $22,314. To put this in perspective, the living wage in Los Angeles— the amount a family of four has to make so that they can afford food, child care, medical care, housing and transportation is $70,860. That would be almost $50,000 more than the poverty line if you lived in the city of dreams.

So let's take a step back and ask the larger theoretical and ideological question. Is the support of the poor an obligation on society, and therefore should be enacted through the government by way of taxation? Or, is the support of the poor not a government obligation but, rather an individual's obligation and perhaps a sign of personal virtue? Should the government be in the business of poverty relief?

Torah has a lot to say about poverty. Every person is commanded to support the poor. Every farmer is commanded to leave a corner of his field for the hungry to harvest. The grain that falls on the ground during harvest is also to be left for the poor. If you lend money to a poor person you must take special care not to take advantage of him.

However, all this is personal. According to the Torah, I have an obligation to support poor people that I meet. I have an obligation to leave the corners of my field for the poor. This is fine if you are the poor guy in a rural area with lots of farms (think the Central Coast of California or the Galilee). You would definitely not starve to death, and you would be able to gather enough to provide for your family. (This is the context of *The Book of Ruth*.) However, what if you live in Los Angeles, or Jerusalem. Urban areas have many more poor people and far fewer agricultural resources. This is not a matter of personal virtue but legal, moral and religious obligation.

This is where we are today. At the moment when there are more poor people in the United States than at any time since these statistics were recorded; at the moment when there are fewer jobs to be had by those poor people, fewer sources of revenue; at this moment there is a growing sentiment to back off of our obligations to the needy amongst us. This is the choice that is before us. Do we choose to be a society in which poverty relief is recognized as a moral and therefore also a legal obligation? Or do we elevate private acquisition and ownership to a religious level? (600 words)

(Excerpted from *http://www.justice-in-the-city.com/poverty-and-obligation/, Sep 16, 2011*)

Reference Article 8: 1.5 Billion People Living in Absolute Poverty Makes Its Eradication Humankind's Most Significant Challenge
15 亿人生活在绝对贫困中，消灭它是人类面临的最大挑战

素材简介：联合国在帮助全世界的穷人摆脱贫困方面作出了杰出的贡献，但是地球上仍然有 15 亿人生活在极度的贫困中。帮助这部分人群摆脱贫困是这个时代的人面临的最大挑战。

With nearly 1.5 billion people still living in absolute poverty, eradication efforts had not succeeded, and it remained the most significant challenge facing humankind, delegates in the Second Committee (Economic and Financial) said today.

"At the rate of decline observed from 1990 to 2005, it would take another 88 years to eradicate extreme poverty," said Nepal's representative, speaking for the Group of Least Developed Countries, as the Committee considered the eradication of poverty, women in development, human-resource development and related issues. Citing "alarming" figures from the Secretary-General's report on the issue, he urged the international community to make substantive and tangible progress towards eradicating poverty and hunger. "International support is not a choice but a compulsion," he added.

India's representative said her country's Government had launched large-scale socio-economic programs and interventions to reduce poverty, fight malnutrition and hunger, reduce infant mortality, and promote health and gender empowerment. Such initiatives had helped to lift about 180 million people out of poverty since 1990, though India would remain home to the largest number of the global poor, she said. Poverty-reduction strategies in developing countries must focus on agriculture and rural development as most of their people were dependent on agriculture.

Reinforcing that point, Myanmar's representative noted that 70 per cent of her country's population lived in rural areas and comprised the largest element of the workforce. That had led to a focus on boosting agricultural production as the engine of national economic development. The Government had also sought ways to ease the crises faced by farmers, including tax exemptions for agricultural exports, establishing a rice fund to help farmers and drafting legislation to contribute not only to poverty alleviation, but also to small- and medium-sized enterprises.

Sudan's representative said his country had responded to the world food crisis by strengthening "green" efforts to stimulate agricultural development. Noting that drought, desertification and climate change were jeopardizing agricultural production, he said Sudan's national policies were aimed at ensuring the recovery of its agricultural sector while also working in an environmentally sustainable manner. However, external debt weighed heavily on the country, and it was not possible to reduce poverty to the extent of meeting the relevant Millennium Development Goal. With a national debt of $38 billion, and despite reforms adopted since 1997, the country's lack of access to debt-exemption mechanisms frustrated its efforts to reduce the burden, he said.

A number of other countries outlined their progress in closing the "gender gap" and working to empower women. Ukraine's representative pointed out that women and girls formed a disproportionally large share of the poor in many countries, and that poverty differed between women and men, girls and boys. Removing formal and informal barriers to education, while introducing social-protection measures and gender-responsive labour laws and policies, would all contribute to more constructive participation by women in the labour market, and would have a positive effect on overall economic growth. "Gender equality is smart economics," she said.

The observer for the International Labour Organization (ILO) noted the important link between migration and development, illustrated most clearly by remittances. The 214 million international migrants worldwide had accounted for $325 million of money flowing to developing countries in 2010. Migration's potential for human resources development was high, helping the transfer of skills and knowledge, circular and temporary migration, and the potential for "brain gain". She encouraged States to pay attention to developing the skills of migrants, particularly in destination countries. Still, the "brain drain" was a considerable concern for some States and losing skilled workers was particularly damaging when it disproportionately affected certain professions, including health workers and educators, she said. (601 words)

(Excerpted from *un. org, Sixty-sixth General Assembly, Second Committee*)

Reference Article 9: Is Helping the Poor a Moral Obligation?
帮助穷人是一种道德义务吗？

素材简介： 世界银行主席金墉宣布了在 2030 年以前消除极度贫困的计划。全世界有多于 8 亿 7000 万的人每天饿着肚子睡觉，由于没有食物，每年有 6900 万年龄小于 5 岁的孩子死于饥饿。帮助穷人是人类的道德义务。

The President of the World Bank, Jim Yong Kim, recently announced the goal of eliminating extreme poverty by the year 2030. Kim noted that there are 1.3 billion people living in extreme poverty, 870 million who go hungry every day, and 6.9 million children under 5 who die every year as a result. Kim concluded that helping the poor is "a moral imperative."

Moral imperatives establish duties and obligations. If Kim is right that there is a duty to help the poor, then it is wrong not to help them. If there is a duty to help the poor, we should feel guilty when we are not helping them.

Billions of people live on less than $2.50 per day—what we pay for a café latte or an ice cream treat. Should we feel guilty for indulging in such luxuries while children die of deprivation?

Most of us don't feel guilty as we spend money on trivial luxuries. Perhaps we're morally clueless. It is easy to ignore suffering that is hidden in distant places. But the more plausible explanation is that people don't agree with Kim that helping the poor is a moral imperative.

We think it would be nice to help the impoverished. But charity is not obligatory. We might also think that global poverty is simply not our own fault. If we've done nothing wrong, then we should not feel guilty or blameworthy.

Most people would agree that there is a duty to help those whom we've wronged or harmed. If I am riding on someone else's back, I have an obligation to get off his back. If I am somehow contributing to the problems of the poor, then I might be blamed for their plight.

But are middle-class Americans riding on the backs of the global poor?

We do benefit from cheap consumer goods and resources that are produced and extracted by the world's working poor. Your clothes, for example, were most likely made by poor people working in dangerous conditions. In November, a garment factory burned down in Bangladesh. Clothing was manufactured there for American brands. More than 100 people died in the fire. According to *The New York Times*, the minimum wage for workers in that factory was about $40 per month—just over $1 per day.

The clothes we wear are manufactured by poor people, who may die as a result of dangerous working conditions. Does that create an obligation on our part? Or is that just the result of free market economics?

Thomas Pogge, an ethics professor from Yale, discussed this question last week in San Francisco at a meeting of the American Philosophical Association. Pogge received a prize for an article where he argues that the international system unjustly violates the human rights of the world's poor.

Pogge thinks that injustices in the global economic structure create an obligation to the poor. He admits that failing to save people is not as bad as killing them. But Pogge claims that we are not simply failing to save the poor. Instead, he claims, the international system is rigged against them.

From Pogge's perspective, we are riding on backs of the global poor, actively contributing to their poverty. Affluent nations extract profit and resources from poor countries, while poor countries cannot overcome the headwind created by international systems. We should get off their backs and compensate them for their predicament.

It might be that if we did not purchase products manufactured in foreign sweatshops, we would further impoverish the global poor. It might also be that donations to the poor cause dependency and corruption.

Those practical concerns do not weaken the moral claim that we have an obligation to the poor. We need to be careful and strategic as we readjust global economic priorities. But the President of the World Bank appears to agree with the ethics professor that there is a moral obligation to create a world free of poverty. (657 words)

(Excerpted from *http://www.plannedscape.net* , by Andrew Fiala, Fresno Bee, Friday, Apr. 05, 2013)

Reference Article 10: Thomas Jefferson's Political and Social Views
托马斯·杰弗逊的政治和社会观点

素材简介： 托马斯·杰弗逊把自己的民主思想写入了宪法，居民应该拥有生命、自由和追求幸福的不可被剥夺的权利。对于托马斯·杰弗逊来说，宪法的基础就是去捍卫居民自由和权利。

Society and government

According to Jefferson's philosophy, citizens have "certain inalienable rights" and "rightful liberty is unobstructed action according to our will, within limits drawn around us by the equal rights of others". A staunch advocate of the jury system to protect people's liberties, he proclaimed in 1801, "I consider [trial by jury] as the only anchor yet imagined by man, by which a government can be held to the principles of its constitution." Jeffersonian government not only prohibited individuals in society from infringing on the liberty of others, but also restrained itself from diminishing individual liberty as a protection against tyranny from the majority. Initially, Jefferson favored restricted voting to those who could actually have free exercise of their reason by escaping any corrupting dependence on others.

He was convinced that individual liberties were the fruit of political equality, which were threatened by arbitrary government. Excesses of democracy in his view were caused by institutional corruptions rather than human nature. He was less suspicious of a working democracy than many contemporaries. As president, Jefferson feared that the Federalist system enacted by Washington and Adams had encouraged corrupting patronage and dependence. He tried to restore a balance between the state and federal governments more nearly reflecting *The Articles of Confederation*, seeking to reinforce state prerogatives where his party was in a majority.

Jefferson was steeped in the British Whig tradition of the oppressed majority set against a repeatedly unresponsive court party in the Parliament. He justified small outbreaks of rebellion as necessary to get monarchial regimes to amend oppressive measures compromising popular liberties. In a republican regime ruled by the majority, he acknowledged "it will often be exercised when wrong". But "the remedy is to set them right as to facts, pardon and pacify them". As Jefferson saw his party triumph in two terms of his presidency and launch into a third term under James Madison, his view of the U.S. as a continental republic and an "empire of liberty" grew more upbeat. On departing the presidency in 1809, he described America as "trusted with the destines of this solitary republic of the world, the only monument of human rights, and the sole depository of the sacred fire of freedom and self-government".

Democracy

Jefferson considered democracy to be the expression of society, and promoted national self-determination, cultural uniformity, and education of all males of the commonwealth. He supported public education and a free press as essential components of a democratic nation.

Beginning with Jefferson's electioneering for the "revolution of 1800", his political efforts were based on egalitarian appeals. In his later years, he referred to the 1800 election "as real a revolution in the principles of our government as that of '76 was in its form", one "not effected indeed by the sword...but by the...suffrage of the people." Voter participation grew during Jefferson's presidency, increasing to "unimaginable levels" compared to the Federalist Era, with turnout of about 67,000 in 1800 rising to about 143,000 in 1804.

At the onset of the Revolution, Jefferson accepted William Blackstone's argument that property ownership would sufficiently empower voters' independent judgement, but he sought to further expand suffrage by land distribution to the poor. In the heat of the Revolutionary Era and afterward, several states expanded voter eligibility from landed gentry to all propertied male, tax-paying citizens with Jefferson's support. In retirement, he gradually became critical of his home state for violating "the principle of equal political rights"—the social right of universal male suffrage. He sought a "general suffrage" of all taxpayers and militia-men, and equal representation by population in the General Assembly to correct preferential treatment of the slave-holding regions. (611 words)

(Excerpted from *https://en.wikipedia.org/wiki/Thomas_Jefferson*)

个人选择类素材

Reference Article 1: Why Failure Is Good for Success?
失败对于成功的重要性，人们应该重新看待失败

素材简介： 本文针对大多数人忽视、逃避甚至厌恶失败的事实，提出：1. 最伟大的成功都是最艰难的；2. 失败是成功的必经之路。作者通过论证失败的价值，并列举不同领域经过失败取得成功的人物和事例，呼吁人们重新看待失败，对人生提出更高的要求。

The sweetest victory is the one that's most difficult. The one that requires you to reach down deep inside, to fight with everything you've got, to be willing to leave everything out there on the battlefield—without knowing, until that do-or-die moment, if your heroic effort will be enough. Society doesn't reward defeat, and you won't find many failures documented in history books.

The exceptions are those failures that become steppingstones to later success. Such is the case with Thomas Edison, whose most memorable invention was the light bulb, which purportedly took him 1,000 tries before he developed a successful prototype. "How did it feel to fail 1,000 times?" a reporter asked. "I didn't fail 1,000 times," Edison responded. "The light bulb was an invention with 1,000 steps."

Unlike Edison, many of us avoid the prospect of failure. In fact, we're so focused on not failing that we don't aim for success, settling instead for a life of mediocrity. When we do make missteps, we gloss over them, selectively editing out the miscalculations or mistakes in our life's résumé. "Failure is not an option," NASA flight controller Jerry C. Bostick reportedly stated during the mission to bring the damaged Apollo 13 back to Earth, and that phrase has been etched into the collective memory ever since. To many in our success-driven society, failure isn't just considered a non-option—it's deemed a deficiency, says Kathryn Schulz, author of *Being Wrong: Adventures in the Margin of Error*. "Of all the things we are wrong about, this idea of error might well top the list," Schulz says. "It is our meta-mistake: We are wrong about what it means to be wrong. Far from being a sign of intellectual inferiority, the capacity to err is crucial to human cognition."

When we take a closer look at the great thinkers throughout history, a willingness to take on failure isn't a new or extraordinary thought at all. From the likes of Augustine, Darwin and Freud to the business mavericks and sports legends of today, failure is as powerful a tool as any in reaching great success. "Failure and defeat are life's greatest teachers [but] sadly, most people, and particularly conservative corporate cultures, don't want to go there," says Ralph Heath, managing partner of Synergy Leadership Group and author of *Celebrating Failure: The Power of Taking Risks, Making Mistakes and Thinking Big*. "Instead they choose to play it safe, to fly below the radar, repeating the same safe choices over and over again. They operate under the belief that if they make no waves, they attract no attention; no one will yell at them for failing because they generally never attempt anything great at which they could possibly fail (or succeed)."

However, in today's post-recession economy, some employers are no longer shying away from failure—they're embracing it. According to a recent article in *BusinessWeek*, many companies are deliberately seeking out those with track records reflecting both failure and success, believing that those who have been in the trenches, survived battle and come out on the other side have irreplaceable experience and perseverance. (516 words)

(Excerpted from *https://www.success.com/article/why-failure-is-good-for-success*)

Reference Article 2: About Walt Disney
动画大师华特·迪士尼

素材简介： 在迪士尼成名为全世界著名的动画大师之前，他经历了数次的失败，甚至一度被人认为"缺乏创造力"。但是他一直心怀远大抱负，要走进好莱坞，创造惊人的创世动画作品。在公司破产、生活窘迫、作品不被人认可之后，他甚至坚持在车库中创作出人们喜闻乐见的动画作品。为了关注更多人的生活品质，他建立了迪士尼乐园，给全世界的人们提供了一个美妙的乐趣之地。

During a 43-year Hollywood career, which spanned the development of the motion picture medium as a modern American art, Walter Elias Disney established himself and his product as a genuine part of American. A pioneer and innovator, and the possessor of one of the most fertile imaginations the world has ever known, Walt Disney, along with members of his staff, received more than 950 honors and citations from throughout the world, including 48 Academy Awards and 7 Emmys in his lifetime.

When visiting one of the many Disney amusement parks that exist today around the world, or watching the Disney movies, it's hard to believe how many times Walt Disney failed before succeeding. When Walt Disney was a young man, he was fired by a newspaper editor because "he lacked imagination and had no good ideas." Disney's next failure came in 1922 when he started his first film company. Along with a partner, he bought a used camera and made short advertising films and cartoons under the studio name Laugh-O-Gram. The company went bankrupt in 1923. Later, Disney was told that Mickey Mouse—who has become one of the world's most beloved animated characters—was a bad idea because women were afraid of mice. Several more of his businesses failed before the premiere of his movie "Snow White." Today, most childhoods wouldn't be the same without his ideas.

In 1965, Walt Disney turned his attention toward the problem of improving the quality of urban life in America. He personally directed the design on an Experimental Prototype Community of Tomorrow, or EPCOT, planned as a living showcase for the creativity of American industry. Said Disney, "I don't believe there is a challenge anywhere in the world that is more important to people everywhere than finding the solution to the problems of our cities. But where do we begin? Well, we're convinced we must start with the public need. And the need is not just for curing the old ills of old cities. We think the need is for starting from scratch on virgin land and building a community that will become a prototype for the future." Thus, Disney directed the purchase of 43 square miles of virgin land in the center of the state of Florida. Here, he master planned a whole new Disney world of entertainment to include a new amusement theme park, motel-hotel resort vacation center and his Experimental Prototype Community of Tomorrow. After more than seven years of master planning and preparation, including 52 months of actual construction, Walt Disney World opened to the public as scheduled on October 1, 1971. Epcot Center opened on October 1, 1982.

Walt Disney is a legend, a folk hero of the 20th century. His worldwide popularity was based upon the ideas which his name represents: imagination, optimism and self-made success in the American tradition. Walt Disney did more to touch the hearts, minds and emotions of millions of Americans than any other man in the past century. Through his work, he brought joy, happiness and a universal means of communication to the people of every nation. Certainly, our world shall know but one Walt Disney. (524 words)

(Excerpted from *https://d23.com/about-walt-disney/*)

Reference Article 3: Oprah Winfrey
脱口秀女王奥普拉·温弗瑞

素材简介： 女性励志领袖奥普拉，童年遭受强奸，她曾经吸烟、酗酒、吸毒，是个不折不扣的问题少女。少年时期接受教育，受到同龄人良好的影响，展露与生俱来的口才天赋。她担任《奥普拉脱口秀》主持人几十年，用亲身经历向广大观众展示如何努力摆脱逆境、收获成功人生的励志故事。

As a black, one of the most influential women, she has many glorious accomplishments: holding shares of Harper Entertainment Group, controlling more than 10 billion dollars in personal wealth, hosting TV talk show "Oprah," attracting 33 million viewers per week, and running 16 years of similar programs in the first row.

Oprah Winfrey was born in a small town in Mississippi. The difference is that with the other children, God did not give her a warm family—her parents are not married, and she was not well cared by parents. Winfrey has stated she was molested by her cousin, uncle, and a family friend, starting when she was nine years old, something she first announced to her viewers on a 1986 episode of her TV show regarding sexual abuse. In 1963, when she was 9 years old, she was raped by relatives; 13 years old, she was repeatedly raped and humiliated and left home, coming close to being sent to juvenile detention; 14 years old, she gave birth to a child died young...until the 80's on a firm footing, Oprah did have the courage to put this bitterly painful childhood made public, and to recognize those of her later life had a profound impact.

Oprah, after 14 years of age, living with her father, in his rigorous education, the Oprah had dull life, and finally began to glow color. 17 years old, she transformed into "Miss fire that Boswell", the same year won the "Miss Black Tennessee," the crown. Early 30s, in their own name alone, Oprah Winfrey's "Oprah Winfrey Show" undisputedly honored her "talk show queen."

Credited with creating a more intimate confessional form of media communication, she is thought to have popularized and revolutionized the tabloid talk show genre pioneered by Phil Donahue, which a Yale study says broke 20th century taboos and allowed LGBT people to enter the mainstream. By the mid-1990s, she had reinvented her show with a focus on literature, self-improvement, and spirituality. Though criticized for unleashing a confession culture, promoting controversial self-help ideas, and an emotion-centered approach, she is often praised for overcoming adversity to become a benefactor to others. From 2006 to 2008, her endorsement of Obama, by one estimate, delivered over a million votes in the close 2008 Democratic primary race. (383 words)

(Excerpted from *https://en.wikipedia.org/wiki/Oprah_Winfrey*)

Reference Article 4: Franklin D. Roosevelt
身残志坚的罗斯福总统

素材简介： 美国迄今在任时间最长的总统。身残志坚，即使坐在轮椅上，也用超人的胆魄带领美国人民走出经济大萧条。罗斯福用自身的励志经历向美国人民展示了坚强不屈的美国领袖品质，推行新政以提供失业救济与复苏经济，从经济危机的深渊中挽救了美国。

Franklin Delano Roosevelt, commonly known as FDR, was an American statesman and political leader who served as the 32nd President of the United States from 1933 until his death in 1945. A Democrat, he won a record four presidential elections and emerged as a central figure in world events during the mid-20th century. He directed the United States government during most of the Great Depression, implementing his New Deal domestic agenda in response to the worst economic crisis in U.S. history. As a dominant leader of his party, he built the New Deal Coalition, realigning American politics into the Fifth Party System and defining American liberalism throughout the middle third of the 20th century. His third and fourth terms were dominated by World War II. He is often rated by scholars as one of the three greatest U.S. Presidents, along with George Washington and Abraham Lincoln.

In 1921, Roosevelt contracted a paralytic illness, which left his legs permanently paralyzed. He attempted to recover from the illness. Roosevelt returned to public office by winning election as Governor of New York in 1928. He was in office from 1929 to 1933 and served as a reform governor, promoting programs to combat the economic crisis besetting the United States at the time. After the 1920 presidential election, Roosevelt sought to build support for a political comeback in the 1922, but his career was derailed by illness. While the Roosevelts were vacationing at Campobello Island, New Brunswick, in August 1921, Roosevelt fell ill and was left permanently paralyzed from the waist down.

Though his mother favored his retirement from public life, Roosevelt, his wife, and Roosevelt's close friend and adviser, Louis Howe, were all determined that Roosevelt continue his political career. Roosevelt convinced many people that he was improving, which he believed to be essential prior to running for public office again. He laboriously taught himself to walk short distances while wearing iron braces on his hips and legs by swiveling his torso, supporting himself with a cane. He was careful never to be seen using his wheelchair in public, and great care was taken to prevent any portrayal in the press that would highlight his disability. However, his disability was well known before and during his presidency and became a major part of his image. He usually appeared in public standing upright, supported on one side by an aide or one of his sons. (401 words)

(Excerpted from *https://en.wikipedia.org/wiki/Franklin_D._Roosevelt*)

Reference Article 5: Are We Facing Increasingly Complex and Challenging Problems? 我们现在是否面临更复杂、更具挑战性的问题?

素材简介: 本文讨论是否社会的问题越来越复杂和具有挑战性。作者通过讨论社会问题的改变和不变来回应讨论的话题。深层次的社会问题、越来越紧密的世界互联以及更加精进的科学研究都使得社会问题更加复杂。作者同时也承认基于人性的话题或者一些抽象话题至今依然未解。

In any sense that the problems we face are more complex and challenging that those which our predecessors faced merely an illusion—one that can be dispelled by way of knowledge and experience? The speaker believes so, although I disagree. In my view, the speaker unfairly generalizes about the nature of contemporary problems, some of which have no analog from earlier times and which in some respects are more complex and challenging than any problems earlier societies even confronted. Nevertheless, I agree that many of the other problems we humans face are by their nature enduring ones that have changed little in complexity and difficulty over the span of human history; and I agree that through experience and enlightened reflection on human history we grow to realize this fact.

I turn first to my chief point of contention with the statement. The speaker overlooks certain societal problems unique to today's world, which are complex and challenging in ways unlike any problems that earlier societies ever faced. Consider three examples. The first involves the growing scarcity of the world's natural resources. An ever-increasing human population, together with over-consumption on the part of developed nations and with global dependencies on finite natural resources, have created uniquely contemporary environmental problems that are global in impact and therefore pose political and economic challenges previously unrivaled in complexity.

A second uniquely contemporary problem has to do with the fact that the nations of the world are growing increasingly interdependent—politically, militarily, and economically. Interdependency makes for problems that are far more complex than analogous problems for individual nations during times when they were more insular, more self-sustaining, and more autonomous.

A third uniquely contemporary problem is an outgrowth of the inexorable advancement of scientific knowledge, and one that society voluntarily takes up as a challenge. Through scientific advancements we've already solved innumerable health problems, harnessed various forms of physical energy, and so forth. The problems left to address are the ones that are most complex and challenging—for example, showing the aging process, replacing human limbs and organs, and colonizing other worlds in the event ours becomes inhabitable. In short, as we solve each successive scientific puzzle we move on to more challenging and complex ones.

I turn next to my points of agreement with the statement. Humans face certain universal and time-less problems, which are neither more nor less complex and challenging for any generation than for preceding ones. These sorts of problems are the ones that spring from the failings and foibles that are part-and-parcel of human nature. Our problems involving interpersonal relationships with people of the opposite sex stem from basic differences between the two sexes. The social problems of prejudice and discrimination know no chronological bounds because it is our nature to fear and mistrust people who are different from us. War and crime stem from the male aggressive instinct and innate desire for power. We've never been able to solve social problems such as homelessness and hunger because we are driven by self-interest.

I agree with the statement also in that certain kinds of intellectual struggles—to determine the meaning of life, whether God exists, and so forth—are timeless ones whose complexities and mystery know no chronological bounds whatsoever. The fact that we rely on ancient teachings to try to solve these problems underscores the fact that these problems have not grown any more complex over the course of human history.

And, with respect to all the timeless problems mentioned above I agree that knowledge and experience help us to understand that these problems are not more complex today than before. In the final analysis, by studying history, human psychology, theology, and philosophy we come to realize that, aside from certain uniquely contemporary problems, we face the same fundamental problems as our predecessors because we face the same human condition as our predecessors whenever we look in the mirror. (650 words)

(Excerpted from *GRE CAT Answers to the Real Essay Questions*)

Reference Article 6: Michael Jordan
篮球巨匠迈克尔·乔丹

素材简介：乔丹，NBA 前职业篮球运动员，被称为"空中飞人"，NBA 历史上第一位拥有"世纪运动员"称号的巨星。他学生时代曾被认为身高不够不能进入校队，但是经过自己的刻苦训练，他凭借身高和实力一路飞跃，在他的篮球职业生涯中，总共获得 6 次 NBA 总冠军，成为全球篮球传奇。

Michael Jeffrey Jordan is an American retired professional NBA basketball player and businessman. Jordan played 15 seasons in the NBA for the Chicago Bulls and Washington

Wizards. His biography on the NBA website states: "By acclamation, Michael Jordan is the greatest basketball player of all time." Jordan was one of the most effectively marketed athletes of his generation and was considered instrumental in popularizing the NBA around the world in the 1980s and 1990s.

Jordan highlighted his athletic career by playing basketball, baseball, and football in high school. He tried out for the varsity basketball team during his sophomore year, but at 5'11" (1.80m), he was deemed too short to play at that level. Motivated to prove his worth, Jordan became the star of Laney's junior varsity squad, and tallied several 40-point games. The following summer, he grew four inches (10cm) and trained rigorously. Upon earning a spot on the varsity roster, Jordan averaged about 20 points per game over his final two seasons of high school play. Jordan quickly emerged as a league star at the University of North Carolina, entertaining crowds with his prolific scoring. His leaping ability, demonstrated by performing slam dunks from the free throw line in slam dunk contests, earned him the nicknames Air Jordan and His Airness.

Jordan is also known for his product endorsements. He fueled the success of Nike's Air Jordan sneakers, which were introduced in 1985 and remain popular today. Jordan also starred in the 1996 film *Space Jam* as himself. In 2006, he became part-owner and head of basketball operations for the then—Charlotte Bobcats, buying a controlling interest in 2010. In 2015, Jordan became the first billionaire NBA player in history as a result of the increase in value of NBA franchises. He is the third-richest African-American, behind Oprah Winfrey and Robert F. Smith. (306 words)

(Excerpted from *https://en.wikipedia.org/wiki/Michael_Jordan*)

Reference Article 7: Colonel Harland Sanders
肯德基创始人哈兰·山德士上校

素材简介： 山德士自创的炸鸡配方使得他的炸鸡在当地非常有名，但是 20 世纪 50 年代中期，由于政府新建的高速公路，他不得不出售他已经风生水起的餐厅。当时他已经 66 岁。但他觉得自己依然年轻，不需依靠政府救济，开车辗转各地兜售他的炸鸡配方。短短 5 年，他在美国及加拿大拓展 400 家店，这就是世界上餐饮加盟特许经营的开始。

Colonel Harland Sanders was an American businessman, best known for founding fast food chicken restaurant chain Kentucky Fried Chicken and later acting as the company's brand ambassador and symbol. His name and image are still symbols of the company.

By the age of seven, he was reportedly skilled with bread and vegetables, and improving with meat; the children foraged for food while their mother was away for days at a time for work. In 1930, the Shell Oil Company offered Sanders a service station in North Corbin, Kentucky, rent free, in return for paying them a percentage of sales. Sanders began to serve chicken dishes and other meals such as country ham and steaks. Sanders was commissioned as a Kentucky Colonel in 1935 by Kentucky governor Ruby Laffoon. His local popularity grew.

In July 1939, Sanders acquired a motel in Asheville, North Carolina. His North Corbin restaurant and motel was destroyed in a fire in November 1939, and Sanders had it rebuilt as a motel with a 140-seat restaurant. By July 1940, Sanders had finalized his "Secret Recipe" for frying chicken in a pressure fryer that cooked the chicken faster than pan frying. As the United States entered World War II in December 1941, gas was rationed, and as the tourists dried up, Sanders was forced to close his Asheville motel.

Sanders believed that his North Corbin restaurant would remain successful indefinitely, but at age 65 sold it after the new Interstate 75 reduced customer traffic. Left only with his savings and $105 a month from Social Security, Sanders decided to begin to franchise his chicken concept in earnest, and traveled the US looking for suitable restaurants. After closing the North Corbin site, Sanders opened a new restaurant and company headquarters in Shelbyville in 1959. Often sleeping in the back of his car, Sanders visited restaurants, offered to cook his chicken, and if workers liked it negotiated franchise rights.

Although such visits required much time, eventually potential franchisees began visiting Sanders instead. The company's rapid expansion to more than 600 locations became overwhelming for the aging Sanders. In 1964, then 73 years old, he sold the Kentucky Fried Chicken corporation for $2 million and he became a salaried brand ambassador. (370 words)

(Excerpted from *https://en.wikipedia.org/wiki/Colonel_Sanders*)

Reference Article 8: New Middle Class Embraces New Patterns of Spending
中国中产阶级的新型消费模式

素材简介： 随着生活水平的提高，中国中产阶级的消费模式在积极转型。人们不再只关注物质的形式，更加注重物质的品质，以切实提升生活的质量。他们有更加理性的消费观念，不会囿于传统消费模式的价值标榜，而是敢于忠于内心，丰富自己的生活经历。

Substance, not style, is seen as increasingly important to China's consumers. China's middle class is expanding at an unprecedented pace.

According to McKinsey & Co, by 2020 more than three-quarters of China's urban consumers will earn 60,000 yuan ($9,000; 7,700 euros; ￡6,800) to 229,000 yuan per year. That translates into nearly 400 million people who are considered by the consultancy to fall into the middle class category.

And thanks to a surging number of higher-paying jobs in the service and technology industries, 54 percent of them will be classified as "upper middle" class, meaning they have an annual income between 106,000 yuan and 229,000 yuan.

Beneath these figures are some significant shifts in consumption dynamics. Using income as the only indicator of spending habits allows some important information to slip through the cracks.

Research co-conducted by Chinese news service CBN Weekly and Japanese apparel brand Uniqlo uncovered the consumption pattern of the country's new middle class, who are able and willing to pay a premium for quality.

The survey, released in August, polled more than 12,000 respondents ages 20 to 45 across the relatively wealthy first-and second-tier cities. Minimum monthly income was set at 8,000 yuan.

Respondents showed a preference for products with good craftsmanship, with 84 percent favoring quality over price.

That said, more than 70 percent believe they shop more "rationally", meaning that despite loyalty to established brands, they are open to a variety of schools of thought and do not necessarily go for big-name items.

Jin Liyin, marketing professor at Shanghai-based Fudan University, attributes the changing attitude toward brands to the evolving benefit structure: from blatant status projection to more substance-driven consumption.

"Gone are the days when people used to define a life of good quality through possession of certain items or conspicuous logos," Jin says. "The new middle class see consumption not as a badge of honor but as a source of value."

Quality of life must be built around personal choices and filled with one's individual traits, the report says. Corporate social responsibility borne by brands will be factored in when consumers shop.

Meanwhile, this group of consumers is, more than ever, seeking emotional satisfaction through better taste or higher status. For instance, a store's ambience may serve as a catalyst for an impulse purchase, according to the research.

China's new middle class tends to place health high up the ladder of priorities. More than 70 percent said they would take up sports and adjust their daily routine to obtain a balance of work and rest.

To be more specific, 73 percent said they had set aside money in their budgets for sports apparel, workout facilities and organic food.

Also high on their radar are arts and leisure; two-thirds reported allocating more money for this sector. About 72 percent said they saw incremental growth in travel spending.

The increasing travel expenditure goes to more sophisticated and experiential activities, according to a report by consultancy Oliver Wyman, which said that overall trip spending surged—against a precarious drop in travel dedicated to shopping—when the Chinese went overseas last year.

"Chinese travelers continue to shift their spending toward more meaningful experiences, such as exquisite dining, extraordinary cultural journeys and even adventurous sports," says Hunter Williams, a partner at Oliver Wyman. (547 words)

(Excerpted from *http://africa.chinadaily.com.cn/weekly/2017-10/06/content_32906245.htm*)

Reference Article 9: The Tyranny of Things
人们的生活被物质所累

素材简介： 人们已经成为永不满足物欲主义的支持者，不停地买买买。但是过多的东西充斥在生活中，已经给人们的生活带来了巨大的负担和压力。作者呼吁人们"断舍离"，不要不理智地消费，不要被物质捆绑生活，要过简约化的生活，真正去关心重要的事情，并重新思考人与人之间的关系。

Two fifteen-year-old girls stood eyeing one another on first acquaintance. Finally one little girl said, "Which do you like best, people or things?" The other little girl said, "Things." They were friends at once.

I suppose we all go through a phase when we like things best; and not only like them, but want to possess them under our hand. The passion for accumulation is upon us. We make "collections," we fill our rooms, our walls, our tables, our desks, with things, things, things.

Many people never pass out of this phase. They never see a flower without wanting to pick it and put it in a vase, they never enjoy a book without wanting to own it, nor a picture without wanting to hang it on their walls. They keep photographs of all their friends and Kodak albums of all the places they visits, they save all their theater programmes and dinner cards, they bring home all their alpenstocks. Their houses are filled with an undigested mass of things, like the terminal moraine where a glacier dumps at length everything it has picked up during its progress through the lands.

But to some of us a day comes when we begin to grow weary of things. We realize that we do not possess them; they possess us. Our books are a burden to us, our pictures have destroyed every restful wall-space, our china is a care, our photographs drive us mad, our programmes and alpenstocks fill us with loathing. We feel stifled with the sense of things, and our problem becomes, not how much we can accumulate, but how much we can do without. We send our books to the village library, and our picture to the college settlement. Such things as we cannot give away, and have not the courage to destroy, we stack in the garret, where they lie huddled in dim and dusty heaps, removed from our sight, to be sure, yet still faintly importunate.

Then, as we breathe more freely in the clear space that we have made for ourselves, we grow aware that we must not relax our vigilance, or we shall be once more overwhelmed...

It extends to all our doings. For every event there is a "souvenir." We cannot go to luncheon and meet our friends but we must receive a token to carry away. Even our children cannot have a birthday party, and play games, and eat good things, and be happy. The host must receive gifts from every little guest, and provide in return some little remembrance for each to take home. Truly, on all sides we are best, and we go lumbering along through life like a ship encrusted with barnacles, which can never cut the waves clean and sure and swift until she has been scraped bare again. And there seems little hope for us this side our last port.

...

If we could but free ourselves once for all, how simple life might become! One of my friends, who, with six young children and only one servant, keeps a spotless house and a soul serene, told me once how she did it. "My dear, once a month I give away every single thing in the house that we do not imperatively need. It sounds wasteful, but I don't believe it really is... ." (555 words)

(Excerpted from *Elisabeth Woodbridge Morris's essay "The Tyranny of Things"*)

Reference Article 10: Is Gender-neutral Clothing the Future of Fashion? 中性风格穿衣会是未来的趋势吗?

素材简介: 服饰风格的流动性变得更强，性别在服饰上的体现开始不那么明显。知名服饰企业开始尝试弱化性别概念，提倡中性的穿衣风格。但是依然有声音支持性别在服饰上的体现，呼吁人们理性购衣，以适合自己作为标准，而不要一味地选择某种风格的衣服。

Gone are the days when skirts were just for women and trousers were just for men.

In 2017, gender no longer dictates the way people dress.

Fashion designers are combining men's and women's collections on the runway, John Lewis have abolished "girls" and "boys" labels on children's clothes, and more fashion brands are launching gender-neutral collections, one of these is streetwear-inspired label: Wildfang.

Following in the footsteps of H&M (who announced their unisex denim line in March), the forward-thinking brand is leading the way in gender-neutral fashion.

Their most recent project, The Future Is Fluid, reflects society's changing attitudes around gender expression and identity. Plus, 100 per cent of the profits go to LGBTQ causes.

The androgynous collection features a mixture of loose fitting suits, slogan T-shirts and tailored jackets that are neither overtly feminine nor masculine.

"Gender is a fairly restrictive concept," Wildfang CEO, Emma McIlroy tells *The Independent*.

"Historically, it has dictated what jobs people can do, how someone can act, how someone can dress and that limits someone's ability to truly self-express and reach their full potential.

"Gender-neutral clothing doesn't force someone into a box. It allows them to self-express exactly how they chose to."

McIlroy's progressive ideologies could be beneficial when applied to children's clothing, explained psychologist Dr. Christina Richards.

Initiatives like John Lewis' "allow children to express themselves fully and be all they can be— irrespective of sex," she said. However, gender therapist Dr. Christella Antoni, stresses the importance of not replacing one with the other.

"There is advantage to having clothes available that our more gender-neutral but this doesn't mean they should totally replace clothes for girls and clothes for boys," she told *The Independent*.

"In an ideal world gender-neutral clothes should exist alongside clothes for girls and clothes for boys," she said, adding that it would be wrong to force a child to wear clothes that they feel don't match their identity, whether that is strictly gendered or not.

"As for all matters relating to gender, the issue isn't simplistic," she added.

However, while brands are embracing this cultural subversion of gender norms, we still have a long way to go, Antoni notes.

"It's always been easier for women to cross the dressing stereotypes and much more difficult for men, which is more repressive, " she explained.

When British mode Agyness Deyn first came onto the sartorial scene in 2007, she became the poster child for androgynous fashion thanks to her tailored suits and trademark blonde buzzcut.

Hailed by fashion editors and photographers everywhere, she landed covers for *Vogue* and *Elle* and was cast in all of the top shows.

It wasn't until 2016 that an inverse phenomenon occurred, when Jaden Smith —son of Hollywood actor Will Smith—donned a skirt in Louis Vuitton's spring/summer 2016 campaign.

Now, a whole host of A-list celebrities are embracing so-called "feminine" fashion tropes.

There's Harry Styles in his Gucci boots, Zayn Malik in ladies' blouses—even Justin Bieber is impartial to women's skinny jeans.

If there was ever a clearer move towards gender fluidity in fashion, this is it. (513 words)

(Excerpted from *http://www.independent.co.uk/life-style/fashion/gender-neutral-clothing-fashion-future-male-female-women-wildfang-hm-a8017446.html.*)

科技创新类素材

Reference Article 1: Is Technology Really Making Us Less Social?
科技真的让我们更加不喜欢与人交流吗?

素材简介: 本文针对科技利弊，提出：1. 科技真的让我们更加不爱去社交了吗？ 2. 现代人习惯了网络社交，似乎已经遗忘如何在现实生活中与人交往。作者通过例证、列举场景和提出论点证明现代科技的确在毁灭人的生活。

We've all heard our parents say it, "Look up from your phone every once in a while", "Hey, talk to me don't text", "why are you being so anti-social on your phone?" Not only our cellphones, but also our laptops, televisions, creations like Facebook and other social media platforms. Are all of these inventions and enhancements in technology making us less social?

Some would say yes. People who lived before the day and age of technology would say people communicated more without these inventions. They ARE partially right. The only difference is their communication was face-to-face, ours is over the Internet or some other form of technology. When teens are looking at their phones instead of talking to their parents, usually they are talking to friends, or on social media sites such as Twitter, Facebook, and Instagram. All these are alternate forms of being social, just not face-to-face.

Keith N. Hampton, a Professor at Rutgers University of Communication and Information says technology is enriching our social relationships. Professor Hampton teaches "Yes, some things have changed—but maybe not as much as you might think. Consider 'what a strange practice it is...that a man should sit down to his breakfast table and, instead of conversing with his wife, and children, hold before his face a sort of screen on which is inscribed a world-wide gossip.' These words ring as true today as when they were written, in 1909. They were the observations of one of America's first and most renowned sociologists, Charles Cooley, about how morning delivery of the newspaper was undermining the American family. Thank goodness the scourge of the newsman is in decline."(Hampton). He has studied his students and colleagues and found the students have many more close relationships because of their cellphones and media usage than the older colleagues (Hampton).

In contrast, Professor Larry Rosen, a Psychologist from the University of California State, Dominguez Hills says the opposite. He holds that the multiple relationships we make online are not very fruitful; they aren't really close friends. He believes that technology has forced us to pay less attention to our real world communication and more to online communication. Professor Rosen says, "As a research psychologist, I have studied the impact of technology for 30 years among 50,000 children, teens and adults in the U.S. and 24 other countries. In that time, three major game-changers have entered our world: portable computers, social communication and smartphones. The total effect has been to allow us to connect more with the people in our virtual world—but communicate less with those who are in our real world." (Rosen). Rosen believes we need to put the phones down and technology away and stay focused on our real life communication, even if that means less communication altogether.

What do you think? Is technology making us less social? (462 words)

(Excerpted from *https://sites.psu.edu/siowfa15/2015/09/16/is-technology-really-making-us-less-social/*)

Reference Article 2: Technology Is Destroying the Quality of Human Interaction 科技阻碍人与人之间的交流

素材简介： 针对科技和交流，作者提出：1. 科技让现代人之间的交流不再真诚 。2. 人们打开社交网站或者手机应用，里面有非常多的好友，但是这种所谓的社交关系其实非常脆弱。

I had a terrible nightmare the other night. Instead of meeting for a quick cup of coffee, my friend and I spent 30 minutes texting back and forth about our day. After that, instead of going in to talk to my professor during his office hours, I emailed him from home with my question. Because of this, he never got to know who I was, even though he would have been a great source for a letter of recommendation if he had. I ignored a cute guy at the bus stop asking me the time because I was busy responding to a text. And I spent far too much time on Facebook trying to catch up with my 1000+ "friends," most of whom I rarely see, and whose meaning sadly seems to dispel even more as the sheer number of "connections" I've made grows.

This technological detachment is becoming today's reality.

Little by little, Internet and mobile technology seems to be subtly destroying the meaningfulness of interactions we have with others, disconnecting us from the world around us, and leading to an imminent sense of isolation in today's society. Instead of spending time in person with friends, we just call, text or instant message them. It may seem simpler, but we ultimately end up seeing our friends face to face a lot less. Ten texts can't even begin to equal an hour spent chatting with a friend over lunch. And a smiley-face emoticon is cute, but it could never replace the ear-splitting grin and smiling eyes of one of your best friends. Face time is important, people. We need to see each other.

There's something intangibly real and valuable about talking with someone face to face. This is significant for friends, partners, potential employers, and other recurring people that make up your everyday world. That person becomes an important existing human connection, not just someone whose disembodied text voice pops up on your cell phone, iPad or computer screen.

It seems we have more extended connections than ever in this digital world, which can be great for networking, if it's used right. The sad fact of the matter is that most of us don't. It's too hard to keep up with 1000 friends, let alone 200. At that point, do we even remember their names? We need to start prizing the meaning of quality in our connections, not sheer quantity.

Past evolutionary psychology research by British anthropologist and psychologist Robin Dunbar has revealed that people are actually limited to a certain number of stable, supportive connections with others in their social network: roughly 150. Furthermore, recent follow-up research by Cornell University's Bruno Goncalves used Twitter data to show that despite the current ability to connect with vast amounts of people via the Internet, a person can still only truly maintain a friendship with a maximum of 100 to 200 real friends in their social network.

While technology has allowed us some means of social connection that would have never been possible before, and has allowed us to maintain long-distance friendships that would have otherwise probably fallen by the wayside, the fact remains that it is causing ourselves to spread ourselves too thin, as well as slowly ruining the quality of social interaction that we all need as human beings.

So what are we doing with 3000 friends on the Internet? Why are we texting all the time? Seems like a big waste of time to me. Let's spend more time together with our friends. Let's make the relationships that count last, and not rely on technology to do the job for us. (604 words)

(Excerpted from *https://thebottomline.as.ucsb.edu/2012/01/technology-is-destroying-the-quality-of-human-interaction*)

Reference Article 3: Technology Trends Disrupting How We Communicate
科技趋势打乱了人们的交流方式

素材简介: 针对科技和人们的交流方式，作者提出：1. 科技改变了人们的生活方式。 2. 大数据现象 "入侵" 人们的生活，云共享对人们生活的改变。 3. 人们要如何面对。

As much as I love to get out and do public speaking, running a business can make it really hard to find the time to travel, deliver a presentation and keep up with the day to day operations. Especially without worrying about what you may be missing back at the office.

However, tomorrow I will be heading off to deliver a new presentation on technology disruption to a crowd of primarily B2B IT executives and as I prepared a presentation on disruption I couldn't help but think of the irony.

The focus of the presentation is set to be on how technology isn't just disruptive, but it is changing the way we communicate. In a world where our technology is so pervasive that we spend most of our time looking like this...

Big Data and Analytics: The word big data has been tossed around more in the last year than most people would like, but the reason people are talking about it is because it is such a big opportunity for improved marketing. Especially 1:1 messaging. For anyone using Facebook or Gmail they have probably noticed an eery correlation between what they have searched or talked about online and the advertisements they see in their stream. Am I right? This is a great example of Big Data disrupting the way brands can market to consumers. The trend however is much bigger than just advertising, it is an opportunity for brands to completely customize the human experience. With 90% of the world's data being created in the past 2 years it is without question that the information will continue to be managed, parsed and utilized by companies to better target and manage consumer interactions. With the rapid proliferation of wearable technologies the ability for us to create data in our offline lives is becoming completely intertwined with our online experience. Pretty soon our entire existence will be one big stream of data. Both interesting and scary!

Cloud: Last, but by no means least, the cloud has completely changed how accessible everything in our digital lives can be. Think about how our files, data, applications and security are all managed by the cloud? Whether we are talking about a corporate deployed private cloud or an individuals use of Office 365, Google Apps and Dropbox, the cloud has made us a lighter world as we can carry tablets or light appliance type PC's and never be without our "Stuff." This also invades our more traditional digital media assets such as our music, movies and photos. Anyone still have a big CD collection? Other than the collectors and hoarders, most of us would say we haven't bought a CD in years, but our music is still with us each and every day. On the business side our CRM solutions (SAP, Salesforce) and accounting packages (Quickbooks) have found their way to the cloud and our public application providers like those "Big Social Platforms" utilize cloud infrastructure as a service from companies like Softlayer and Amazon to deliver your applications on your mobile devices.

Communication as we know it is being disrupted. It lives at the center of our universe and has driven our lives both B2B and B2C to a simple common existence sometimes referred to as Peer to Peer (P2P). Social, mobile, big data and cloud have changed our lives, changed the way we communicate and will continue to revolutionize the business enterprise of the future. (573 words)

(Excerpted from *https://www.forbes.com/sites/danielnewman/2014/05/13/4-technology-trends-disrupting-how-we-communicate/#7a9c945b2529*)

Reference Article 4: Is Technology Creating a Family Divide?
科技让家庭支离破碎吗？

素材简介： 针对科技和家庭的关系，作者提出：1. 由于社交网站，孩子和家长缺乏交流。同时，家长在孩子面前也丧失了权威。2. 孩子把家长的询问视为一种干预。造成家长和孩子的冲突，部分原因也在于家长自己也在家庭时间中打电话、发消息、处理社交网络。

Nowhere is the impact of popular culture and technology on children's relationships more noticeable than in families. Both influences have contributed to a growing divide between the traditional roles that children and their parents play while, at the same time, blurring those same lines between parents and children. Over the past two decades, children who, for example, watch television, have received messages from popular culture telling them that parents are selfish, immature, incompetent, and generally clueless, for example, from *Malcolm in the Middle, Tool*

Time, *Family Guy*, *Two and a Half Men*, and *I Hate My Teenage Daughter*, not to mention reality TV shows such as *SuperNanny* and the *Housewives* franchise.

This divide has grown due to the increased use of technology among children in several ways. First, children's absorption in technology, from texting to playing video games, does by their very nature limit their availability to communicate with their parents. One study found that when the working parent arrived home after work, his or her children were so immersed in technology that the parent was greeted only 30 percent of the time and was totally ignored 50 percent of the time. Another study reported that family time was not affected when technology was used for school, but did hurt family communications when used for social reasons. Interestingly, children who spent considerable time on a popular social networkingsite indicated that they felt less supported by their parents.

Second, as digital immigrants, parents can struggle to gain proficiency and comfort with the new technology that their digital-native children have already mastered. This divergence in competence in such an important area of children's lives makes it more difficult for parents to assume the role of teacher and guide in their children's use of technology. Because of the lack of technological acumen on the part of many parents, they lack the authority, at least in the eyes of their children, to regulate its use. Due to parents' anxiety or apprehension about the use of technology, they may be unwilling to assert themselves in their children's technological lives. Because of their children's sense of superiority and lack of respect for parents' authority in these matters, children may be unwilling to listen to their parents' attempts to guide or limit their use of technology.

Third, computer and mobile technology have provided children with an independence in their communications with friends and others. Consider this. In previous generations, if children wanted to be in touch with a friend, they had to call them on the home phone which might be answered by a parent. Thus, parents had the opportunity to monitor and act as gatekeepers for their children's social lives.

Times have changed. New technology offers children independence from their parents' involvement in their social lives, with the use of mobile phones, instant messaging, and social networking sites. Of course, children see this technological divide between themselves and their parents as freedom from over-involvement and intrusion on the part of their parents in their lives. Parents, in turn, see it as a loss of connection to their children and an inability to maintain reasonable oversight, for the sake of safety and over-all health, of their children's lives. At the same time, perhaps a bit cynically, children's time-consuming immersion in technology may also mean that parents don't have to bother with entertaining their children, leaving them more time to themselves.

There is little doubt that technology is affecting family relationships on a day-to-day level. Children are instant messaging constantly, checking their social media, listening to music, surfing their favorite web sites, and watching television or movies. Because of the emergence of mobile technology, these practices are no longer limited to the home, but rather can occur in cars, at restaurants, in fact, anywhere there's a mobile phone signal.

It's not only the children who are responsible for the growing divide between parents and their offspring. Parents can be equally guilty of contributing to the distance that appears to be increasing in families. They are often wrapped up in their own technology, for example, talking on their mobile phones, checking email, or watching TV, when they could be talking to, playing with, or generally connecting with their children. (706 words)

(Excerpted from *https://www.psychologytoday.com/blog/the-power-prime/201303/is-technology-creating-family-divide*)

Reference Article 5: The American Obsession with Newness Is Suffocating Us. 美国人对新东西的追求让人窒息

素材简介： 针对美国人追求新东西的趋势，提出美国人追求快时尚，东西坏了就丢掉，不喜欢维修东西。作者觉得这样很不好，没有什么可以传承下去，于是开始自己修东西。

I have this beautiful hand-me-down jacket from the early eighties that my mother got when she went to Argentina to cover a story for NBC. It's an incredible soft brown suede jacket like none I've ever seen, but the zipper is broken and one of the sleeves is ripped along the seam. It's been broken and ripped for five years now and I haven't gotten it fixed. I certainly don't know how to fix it myself. Honestly, I've considered just giving it away instead of going through the hassle of schlepping it to a tailor and having it repaired.

What an awful instinct.

But this reaction to a defective item is all too common today. And, as a child of modern American culture, it's not surprising that I would rather just chuck and replace than take the time to care for a possession.

We, in America, have created and bought into a throw-away culture. Instead of problem-shooting or repairing long-lasting items, we discard them and purchase new ones. This generation, as hard-working, flexible, and adaptive as we have become, has a very different relationship with things than our parents and grandparents did.

My grandmother's silk dresses that she gave to me for fancy occasions still hold together, but that dress I bought for $30 recently is already unraveling in two places and is out of fashion. Marketing is now an enormous industry that tells us we need to spend our money as frequently as possible on affordable things with very short shelf lives.

Looking around my house, I started to ask myself, "Have I purchased anything yet in my home that I would want my child to have or my nieces or nephews to inherit?" I'm in my late twenties and the answer is a resounding no. I have some lovely furniture from my parents and in-laws, and my husband refinished some second-hand furniture, but I'm not sure I have actually bought anything I would be proud to pass on to another and be confident that the value was more than purely sentimental.

I regret this truth. We are called consumers now, because that's what we do continually: consume.

Not only are we told to buy more and more often, we are also more able to today than ever before. Or at least we are told that we are. I can't tell you how many letters I've gotten from banks offering me a credit card, and my credit score is far from perfect. If I hadn't been cautioned about the dangers of credit lines, I would be in some major debt right now. But many Americans fall into the trap of trying to keep up with the trends and continually purchase, throwing away the old and buying new things that will quickly lose their value, both to us and to the economy.

What if you committed to avoiding the fast fashion industry? How about learning to fix something instead of chucking it, or at least taking it to a professional who can?

I've made a commitment to do exactly this, and I'm already finding myself creating a personal style that is far more reflective of my priorities than what I was finding at fast fashion outlets. By choosing to care for the quality items I already own and refraining from buying the cute and trendy things that will look out of style in a few months, I will not only invest in more timeless items, but can also do my wallet a big favor. I think of it as asset investment. Yes, I have to take the time to bring that jacket to the tailor and yes, I have to buy some silver polish and other product care items, but I am choosing not to conform to the hottest fleeting style, no matter how much it's being pitched to me left and right. Plus, you can learn to improve or fix anything on YouTube these days, right? (663 words)

(Excerpted from *https://thetempest.co/2017/03/31/culture-taste/american-obsession-newness-suffocating*)

Reference Article 6: Your Smartphone Could Be Hacked Without Your Knowledge
手机很容易在你不知情的情况下被黑客入侵

素材简介：针对现在人人都用手机并使用手机上网的现状，作者提出：1. 手机很容易被黑，而且人们不容易注意到。2. 四个预防方法。

Not only can your smartphone be hacked, it can be done very easily without your knowledge. "At the end of the day, everything is hackable. What I am surprised about is that people sometimes forget that it's so easy to hack into these devices," said Adi Sharabani, the co-founder of mobile security company Skycure, who used to work for Israeli Intelligence.

Even if a malicious attacker cannot get into your phone, they can try to get the sensitive data stored inside, including contacts, places visited and e-mails.

Often, the hack or data breach occurs without the consumer's knowledge, according to Sharabani.

And it's not just consumers that criminals target.

Both Sharabani and McGeorge perform attack simulations for clients and find that these hacking demonstrations usually go undetected.

"It's usually very rare that a breach that originated through a mobile device or is just contained to a mobile device is likely to be detected by a corporation's incident response team," McGeorge said.

And Sharibani agrees. He says he's still waiting for someone to call him and say that their IT department identified the attack demonstration.

"No one knows," he said. "And the fact that organizations do not know how many of their mobile devices encountered an attack in the last month is a problem."

Despite the warning, "92 percent of people click continue on this screen," according to Sharabani. To protect yourself, be careful when connecting to free Wi-Fi and avoid sharing sensitive information.

Operating system flaws

Despite the best intentions of smartphone manufacturers, vulnerabilities are found which could let attackers in.

Experts advise you install operating system updates as soon as they are available. Once updates are released, hackers know about vulnerabilities and attempt to breach out-of-dates devices.

Malicious apps

Applications add functionality to smartphone, but also increase the risk of a data breach, especially if they are downloaded from websites or messages, instead of an app store. Hidden inside applications, even ones that work, could be malicious code that lets hackers steal data.

To protect yourself, McGeorge advises you limit the number of apps you install.

McGeorge also suggests you think about who the app developer is and if you really need the app.

Skycure's Sharabani suggests you look at the warning messages when installing applications.

"Read those messages that are being prompted to us that sometimes say, 'This app will have access to your email. Would you agree?'" He said.

Bottom line, according to Sharibani, there is no such thing as being 100 percent secure. But there are many ways to reduce the risk and make it harder for hackers to invade your smartphone.

In a statement sent by e-mail, an Apple spokesman said, "We've built safeguards into iOS to help warn users of potentially harmful content... We also encourage our customers to download from only a trusted source like the App Store and to pay attention to the warnings that we've put in place before they choose to download and install untrusted content."

And Google, which oversees Android said it also has added additional privacy and security controls. (543 words)

(Excerpted from *https://www.cnbc.com/2016/06/17/your-smartphone-could-be-hacked-without-your-knowledge.html*)

Reference Article 7: Are Video Games Addictive?
电子游戏会让人上瘾吗？

素材简介： 针对现代人越来越痴迷于电子产品和游戏，作者提出问题：游戏是否引发玩者上瘾并且分析游戏上瘾的原因和游戏上瘾的高发人群，教会读者如何避免。

In 2009, an Ohio court sentenced 17-year-old Daniel Petric to 23 years in prison for the fatal shooting of his mother. Petric had shot both his parents after they took away his copy of Halo 3. During his trial, the court was told that Petric had become addicted to the game after being left housebound following a jetski injury.

In 2011, Rebecca Colleen Christie was sentenced to 25 years in prison by a New Mexico court for allowing her 3 ½ year-old daughter to die of malnutrition while she spent hours playing World of Warcraft.

Is it possible to become addicted to video games?

While addiction remains a prime concern in most societies, whether drug addiction, alcohol addiction, gambling addiction, etc., becoming addicted to video games seems more controversial despite high-profile cases like the ones listed above. Media stories about extreme cases of video game addiction, especially online games, goes back to at least 1993 when Wired ran a story on MUDs (multi-user dungeons) and the players who become addicted to them.

Adolescents (particularly male adolescents) seem especially prone to video game addiction though identifying young people who are vulnerable can be difficult given how popular gaming is in people of all ages. Not only are people dealing with excessive stress and general unhappiness in their lives more likely to become addicted to video games, but gaming addicts are also more likely to be diagnosed with other disorders. These related diagnoses can include attention-deficit hyperactivity disorder (ADHD), depression, and anxiety.

But what other risk factors are associated with gaming addiction? Though researchers have looked at amount of time spent online as a risk for addiction, type of video game may be important as well. Not only are role-playing gamers more vulnerable to addiction but so are shooter and strategy gamers.

The motivation for playing also seems to be a factor in addiction. People who game for fun or socializing are less likely to become addicted than people who are caught up in the need for status or simply to escape from the problems in their lives. If you're dealing with real-life failure, escaping from that stress by playing games that give you a sense of victory or control over your life can be a helpful way of coping.

Actual studies looking at risk factors for video game addiction tend to be scarce. Among the outcomes of pathological gaming are depression, anxiety, social phobias and poorer performance in school.

But can social anxiety and other problems linked to excessive gaming be causing the problem or are the result of gaming addiction? A Dutch study of 543 gamers found that reduced social skills appeared to result in increased problem game behavior six months later though the opposite effect was not observed.

Socialization also appears to play a role in video game addiction. Children and adolescents who are well integrated into their class and who show good social skills are less likely to become problem game players. At-risk children are also more likely to have difficulty making friends or are less socially active. Results shown by Rehbein and Baier's research, as well as similar studies, suggest that children who are more socially isolated or who face problems in school or at home may use video games as a way of regaining control over their lives.

One surprising finding reported by Rehbein and Baier was that level of emotional support or supervision provided by parents did not play a significant role in video game addiction.

While most educational strategies aimed at preventing video game abuse involve having parents take greater responsibility over what their children are doing, this appears to be not that effective. Other recommended approaches, such as restricting time spent playing games and taking away X-boxes and other gaming devices don't appear to be very effective either (except possibly for children under the age of ten).

Getting away from problems in our lives by doing things that seem pleasurable or simpler to understand can be a potent lure for people in need, whether you are a child or an adult. (692 words)

(Excerpted from *https://www.psychologytoday.com/blog/media-spotlight/201308/are-video-games-addictive*)

Reference Article 8: How Technology Will Change the Future of Work? 科技将会如何改变未来的工作?

素材简介: 针对科技和未来工作的展望，作者提出：1. 科技会改变人们未来的工作方式的各方面。2. 这些科技虽然有很多好处，但是我们也不能掉以轻心。我们要教育下一代去适应以后的高科技环境。

It's estimated that some 65% of children entering primary schools today will likely work in roles that don't currently exist.

We expect the pace of change in the job market to start to accelerate by 2020. Office and administrative functions, along with manufacturing and production roles, will see dramatic declines accounting for over six million roles over the next four years. Conversely, business and financial operations along with computer and mathematical functions will see steep rises.

There is a central driver for many of these transformations, and it is technology.

Artificial intelligence, 3D printing, resource-efficient sustainable production and robotics will factor into the ways we currently make, manage and mend products and deliver services. The latter two have the potential to create jobs in the architectural and engineering sectors, following high demand for advanced automated production systems.

It's worth reflecting on how we could imagine a changed world like this.

Our future place of work might not be an open plan office, but interconnected workspaces not tied to one place, but many. They will be underpinned by virtual conferencing, complete and constant connection and portability.

Our working day will be fundamentally different. Leveraging big data, like real-time traffic information, could cut journey times, making the school run easier, and the morning commute more manageable. That is, if you have to commute: home-working will no longer be defined as a Friday luxury, but a more efficient way to work enabled by technology, taking the physical strain from megacities and regionalizing work locations.

Technology underpinning what futurologists have christened 'The Fourth Industrial Revolution' will enable disruptive business models to decentralize our economies as we move from value systems based on ownership to ones enabling access. Personally owned assets, from cars to spare bedrooms, will expand entrepreneurship, diversifying revenue streams. It's no fluke that within three years of trading, home-sharing platform Airbnb offers more rooms than some of the biggest hotel chains.

These disruptive business models will fundamentally reshape how we do business, both individually and as companies. For example, digitally enabling smallholder farmers can allow them to operate as a collective, transferring knowledge and sharing vital learnings with each other from proper crop irrigation technology to water efficiency. Cloud-based analytics hosted on BT's Expedite platform can assist in radically transforming such supply chains.

Critically, these very technologies might help us unlock the solutions to some of the biggest societal challenges we currently grapple with. The ICT underpinning these technologies, in consort with the transformational power of big data, could support smart systems that will help tackle climate challenges. Connected homes, factories and farms leveraging smart energy management systems could mean dramatically lower energy use, which would contribute to the decarbonisation of our economies.

And yet we must be vigilant. Not of technological change; we have the power and innovation to harness and use its power as we see fit. But of access to the connectivity and opportunity it brings.

What will be absolutely decisive is how we equip our children, our students and our colleagues to harness the power of this technology to transform our world for the better. That means ensuring the ICT skills of current school leavers are fit for the future. It means providing incentives for lifelong learning as the pace of technological advancement quickens. And it means reinventing the HR function, equipping it to continually assess and provide for the training needs of employees.

If we get this right the prize is clear. We have the potential to revolutionize the way we live and work and do it in a way that avoids the vicissitudes of previous industrial revolutions, creating new economic opportunities that, even as children, we would not have before imagined.

Lastly, we must use every tool within our armory to ensure the current and future generations are not left behind in the global digital skills race. (652 words)

(Excerpted from *https://www.weforum.org/agenda/2016/02/the-future-of-work/*)

Reference Article 9: Why Is Big Data So Dangerous?
大数据为什么很危险?

素材简介: 针对电脑、网络、智能手机的使用,越来越多的人的生活和大数据息息相关,作者持有谨慎的态度,提出:1. 大数据对于商业的挑战。2. 大数据会泄漏隐私,带来很多安全隐患。

Big Data is one of the most potentially dangerous and destructive new technologies to come about in the last century. While a new fighter jet or a new type of bomb can certainly wreck havoc, big data has the potential to insidiously undermine and subtly (and not-so subtly) change almost every aspect of modern life.

As you may know, I'm an advocate for big data. But I'm also an advocate for understanding the risks associated with it and taking the appropriate measures to counteract them.

I see the major risks of big data as follows.

It will challenge how businesses are run and the business models that will help them succeed. This is both good and bad. For some businesses, this underlying change will signal huge opportunity and trigger massive growth. For others who cannot adapt and change with the times, it will signal the beginning of the end. I predict we will see many more instances of upstart companies coming in and changing the entire dynamic of a particular field or market, the way Netflix disrupted video rentals and Uber has disrupted taxi service. Established "old school" businesses should wake up and take note. And these sorts of disruptions could have major potential economic implications.

Everything can be tracked and analysed. When I say everything, I mean everything. We have only scratched the surface of the data it is possible to collect about our lives, our businesses, our environment, our behaviours. I've written about some of the cool and frightening aspects of the Internet of Things, which will drive the big data generation going forward. And while it's great for a company to know exactly what's happening with its stock and products, where does it cross the line when they want to know everything about what their employees and customers are doing as well? Is it OK to track information about your children? Your health? Your buying habits? Your social interactions? And if it is permissable to track that information, under what circumstances? And who gets to access it? Who owns it? All these questions remain largely unanswered while the technology pushes ever forward.

Privacy problems and discrimination become rampant. Since everything about us can be tracked, it can also be used for nefarious purposes. Privacy law has not kept up with the technology and the types of data being collected. Who owns the data that is collected about you—you, or the company that collects it? The answer will determine how that data can be shared and used, whether it's about your buying habits online or more private matters. In addition, the more data we collect, the easier it is to parse down and use it to market (or not) to particular segments of the population, creating a new kind of discrimination. There are already accounts of data-driven discrimination happening; car insurance companies, for example, tend to penalise people who drive late at night, but that can impact otherwise safe drivers who happen to work a swing shift, and who tend to be lower-income to start with.

Finally, there is the danger from hacking and cyber crime. Having all our data somewhere in the cloud (or on the oceans) leaves it vulnerable to attacks and misuse. For every new security measure there is a hacker or criminal somewhere working on breaking it. And companies rarely take security as seriously as they should. In addition, I await with dread the first serious terrorist attack on our data or computer systems. Think of all the infrastructure, utilities, and vital information that relies on data and the cloud and then think about what a catastrophe it would be if it all went down at once. If that doesn't give you nightmares, I don't know what will

In short, big data is dangerous. We need new legal frameworks, more transparency and potentially more control over how our data can be used to make it safer. But it will never be an inert force. In the wrong hands big data could have very serious consequences. (676 words)

(Excerpted from *https://www.datasciencecentral.com/profiles/blogs/why-is-big-data-so-dangerous*)

Reference Article 10: Technology Makes Communication Less Personal, Says Business Psychologist
商业心理学家说，科技让人们的交流缺乏私密性

素材简介： 针对现代科技和人们的交流，作者提出：1. 人与人交流和科技对个体和集体的重要性。2. 人们越来越离不开科技，交流也越来越少，但是人们要学会如何权衡它们。

Business psychology trainer, author and teacher Rozaine Cooray is launching her book "From Crisis to Character" on November 12 in Colombo. Most of the articles were based on a column she writes for *The Business Times*. Here are excerpts of an interview with Ms. Cooray: What made you consider writing on workplace issues and the problems/concerns faced by both management/workers?

The question is, is WORK just a four-letter word? I always felt that work is much more than what we think it is. We spend close to 35 per cent-45 per cent of our time per day at work. For some of us this is even more, if you consider the amount of time we spend on the roads. Organizations are complex clusters of human beings who work towards a particular vision, mission and some set tasks. Even though not everyone understands the purpose behind their day to day work, what they do and how they do it make a difference, not only to the organization, but also to each and every individual employee.

My career, here in Sri Lanka and also abroad, entailed looking into both personal issues of the individual, organizational issues in the larger context, and how these two interact with each other to produce the final outcome. In my job, I get to hear, observe and study what really matters to people. I wanted to use these real life anecdotes and make it available to the public, so that more awareness could be raised amongst both employers and employees on psychology in the workplace.

Well that was the start, but what kept me going was the feedback given by my readers on in column in *The Business Times*, from organizational heads to young executives who are starting off their careers.

There's always much more to what we see behind performance, power, leadership, conflict, be it good or bad; there are certain dynamics that operate that need to be understood in order to optimize what we do. My focus has always been to encourage the reader to be more aware so that we can change the way we see things, to bring more meaning, engagement and fulfillment at work.

The subject of your specialty is not a familiar/popular field of study. Is this a new area of study/research that is gaining credence in the global context?

The field of Industrial/Organizational Psychology has been there for a long time and the first studies of Industrial/Organizational Psychology date back to the late 1800s, when scientists tried to understand the psychology behind advertising and worker efficiency. So no, it is not a new field, but the importance of it, is more and more highlighted in the workplace now in Sri Lanka than ever before.

Given the new age of technology and the ease of communication without meeting someone, what we see as a problem, is also the reality. As a result of technology, globalization, expansion of businesses, communication has inevitably become less personal. You may be in Sweden reporting to a boss in Sri Lanka, whilst working with a team of individuals scattered around Europe, working towards the same outcome. To a lesser degree of separation, in an organization, employees may sit side by side but still having very limited contact, due to over reliance on technology, preference of social media for breaks, or simply procedural reasons. Also, with the increasing workload, people may find themselves, absorbed to the computer, trying to finish their work, rather than interacting with their teams. But I must say that is this not the case all the time; there are instances when managers find it difficult to get employees to stop talking and to take their work more seriously.

This book talks about the importance of communication and technology, both, as it addresses both the modern day advantages and disadvantages that technology has introduced, not only to an organization but also to society as a whole. Technology has introduced a dynamic that has also altered how we raise kids, how we educate, how we train and do work, hence altering the expectations of the younger generations related to work. The businesses need to be more equipped in receiving the new millennial whose attitudes and values has been inherently altered due to exposure to technology at a very early age. The book discusses different generations that now work together to achieve the same goal. (730 words)

(Excerpted from *www.forte.lk or www.forteconsultancy.org*)

环保类素材

Reference Article 1: Massive Iceberg's Split Exposes Hidden Ecosystem
冰川大规模断裂，"隐身"的生态系统显形

素材简介： 生物学家们在南太平洋新发现的海域找到其中一个最大的冰山。当它移动到离威德尔海，就会暴露出海底已成为冰的 12 万年前的 5800 平方公里。如果研究人员能够很快地到达这个区域，他们就有机会在其中了解到导致它改变的原因，以及可以研究之前所存在的生态系统。

Biologists are racing to secure a visit to a newly revealed region of the Southern Ocean as soon as it is safe to sail there. One of the largest icebergs ever recorded broke free from the Larsen C ice shelf on the Antarctic Peninsula in July. As it moves away into the Weddell Sea, it will expose 5,800 square kilometres of sea floor that have been shielded by ice for up to 120,000 years. If researchers can get to the area quickly enough, they'll have the chance to study the ecosystem beneath before the loss of the ice causes it to change.

……

If the BAS proposal is successful, it will be the first time marine biologists have been able to explore such an ecosystem so soon after the break-up of the ice. Nearby sections of ice shelf, at Larsen A and Larsen B, broke away in 1995 and 2002, respectively. But it was several years before the ocean cleared of sea ice and biologists could safely visit the area. Gutt was first in with a detailed survey, leading a team of about 50 scientists on the German research vessel Polarstern in 2007. The group sampled hundreds of species in areas exposed by the break-ups at Larsen A and B, and saw signs of a unique ecosystem with more deep-sea species than elsewhere on the Antarctic continental shelf (J. Gutt et al. Deep-Sea Res. II 58, 74–83; 2011). But other species were already moving in, including fast-growing sea squirts, krill and minke whales. "By then, a lot had happened," says Linse.

Getting to the Larsen C exposed region before it starts to change is crucial, says Gutt, to see what a sub-ice-shelf ecosystem looks like. Video footage taken by geophysicists on a US Antarctic Program cruise at the Larsen B site in March 2005 had unexpectedly showed most of the sea floor covered with a white mat, which the team interpreted as a layer of sulfur-eating microbes, as well as large clams, which were also chemotrophic—that is, living on energy sources other than the Sun. It was the first report of a chemotrophic ecosystem in the Antarctic. But when the Polarstern arrived two years later, Gutt's team saw only dead clamshells and a layer of decaying plant matter and sediment.

One thing the researchers won't have to worry about is disturbance from commercial fishing fleets. The Larsen C region is the first area to be protected by a 2016 agreement by the multinational Commission for the Conservation of Antarctic Marine Living Resources (CCAMLR) to automatically designate any areas of ocean exposed by the collapse or retreat of ice shelves as a Special Area for Scientific Study. This prohibits commercial fishing—of the Antarctic toothfish, for example—for an initial period of two years.

Ice shelf break-up events could become much more common with climate change, says Andrea Kavanagh, director of the Pew Charitable Trusts' Global Penguin Conservation Campaign in Washington DC, and the CCAMLR protection will allow scientists to monitor how these changes affect wildlife. "It's really important to be able to separate the effects of fishing versus climate," she says.

Biologists will discuss research priorities for Larsen C and future exposed regions at a swiftly organized meeting at Florida State University's Coastal and Marine Laboratory in St Teresa on 18–19 November. Meanwhile, Linse's team is waiting to learn whether the BAS mission proposal will be approved, and monitoring the iceberg in satellite images. "We need the wind to blow the iceberg out a bit more and to blow the sea ice out of there," says BAS spokeperson Athena Dinar. (611 words)

(Excerpted from *https://www.scientificamerican.com/article/massive-icebergs-split-exposes-hidden-ecosystem1/*)

Reference Article 2: Major Companies Set Carbon-Slashing Goals
主要公司制定碳消减目标

素材简介： 根据联合国和环境组织发起的全球基于合作伙伴关系，包括耐克公司、盖璞公司和李维斯公司在内的品牌企业正在制定目标，以减少基于气候科学的温室气体排放量。并且宣布了对于一些主要的服装和数字技术公司如何制定基于气候科学的减少温室气体排放的目标。

Some major apparel and digital technology companies will set goals to cut their greenhouse emissions based on climate science, they announced today.

Brand-name businesses—including clothing companies Nike Inc., Gap Inc., Guess and Levi Strauss & Co., and tech firms Adobe Systems, Nokia Corp. and HP Inc.—are setting the goals as part of a partnership launched by the United Nations and environmental groups.

The initiative, Science Based Targets, prods companies to establish plans to slash heat-trapping gases from their operations to help stave off devastating global warming. It says more than 300 businesses have committed to the program, including 50 U.S. companies.

After joining, a company has two years to develop its targets, which Science Based Targets experts review. The group has approved 71 targets, including 41 this year, it said.

"This is becoming the new 'normal' in the business world, proving that a low-carbon economy is not only vital for consumers and the planet, but also for future-proofing growth," Lila Karbassi of the U.N. Global Compact said in a statement.

Today's announcement comes on the first day of Climate Week, a summit that will run through Sunday in New York City, where government and private-sector leaders will converge to talk about the warming planet and what to do about it. (218 words)

(Excerpted from *https://www.scientificamerican.com/article/major-companies-set-carbon-slashing-goals/*)

Reference Article 3: Scrutiny over Wood and Coal Fires in UK Homes
英国家庭取暖将受检查

素材简介： 政府就家庭取暖进行监控并提出倡议，以便可以很好地改善空气污染问题。

Ministers are calling for evidence to help improve air quality in cities. They want people to ensure that wood is dry before burning, and that solid fuels are as clean as possible. But the UK is being given a final warning by the European Commission today for breaching laws on NOx emissions. The government is being told it will face court action in Europe unless its planned Clean Air Strategy does what it's supposed to.

While environmentalists may wonder whether today's announcement on homes fires is a smokescreen, the government insists it's not. It says the domestic burning of house coal, smokeless solid fuels and wet wood is the single largest primary contributor of harmful sooty particles. Householders and businesses are being asked for their views on proposals to cut emissions.

The government says drying wood can reduce particles by half and produce more heat from less fuel. A spokesman said it is considering a range of options to tackle particle emissions, including:

1. Encouraging consumers to switch from house coal by only allowing the sale of low sulphur smokeless alternatives;

2. The introduction of sulphur limits for all smokeless solid fuels;

3. And new powers for local authorities to take action for persistent smoke offences where local air quality is harmed.

Environment Minister Thérèse Coffey said, "We all have a role to play in improving the air we breathe. Many of us enjoy a cosy fire, but burning dirtier fuel has a real impact on the quality of air for our family and friends. Pollution is about more than just transport. If we make the switch to burning cleaner domestic fuel, we can continue to enjoy burning wood and smokeless coal in stoves and fires in our homes."

She says they're not considering banning domestic burning.

Prof Frank Kelly from Kings College London told BBC News, "If the particulates data are correct then yes it's a good thing as it's important that all sources of pollution are tackled in order to improve air quality to reach WHO guideline values."

Some academics said the homes fires consultation was a diversion from other government failings on pollution.

Rosie Rogers from Greenpeace said: "It's not a good look when a government that promised environmental leadership has to be chivvied by Brussels into doing something about illegal air pollution."

"Michael Gove promised to make cleaning up our cities' air a top priority but has little to show for it as yet."

The government said it would solve air pollution overall in its Clean Air Strategy, expected after Easter.

The Mayor of London, Sadiq Khan, wants to ban wood burning in the capital—but there will no enforcement powers to enter homes to see whether people are burning wood or not.

Also today, it was revealed that the Brixton Road in London has already reached the NOx limit for the whole of 2018.

Jonathan Bartley, co-leader of the Green Party, said, "The fact we're not even out of January and London's filthy air has already hit the yearly pollution limit is damning. The Government's failure to tackle this public health emergency is just one of the cracks in its new green veneer."

"If the Government is serious about tackling this crisis it must bring forward the ban on petrol and diesel cars, introduce a proper scrap page scheme, invest in public transport and expand clean air zones across the country." (566 words)

(Excerpted from *http://www.bbc.com/news/science-environment-42873645*)

Reference Article 4: Warming Puts Squeeze on Ancient Trees
气候变化下的古树

素材简介： 气候变暖的一个后果是，树的栖息地高山区域正在升温，导致古树的成长产生了一系列其他影响。

One of the consequences of a warming world is that high mountain habitats, which used to be too chilly for trees, are heating up. "There is now newly available real estate above what we call tree line—the sort of literal line in the sand above which trees can't grow because it's too cold. But now it's not."

Brian Smithers is an ecologist at U.C. Davis. He compares this slow-moving migration to land-grabs back in pioneer times. "You know, they fired the guns and all the settlers made a mad dash to claim their stake. It's that, but if everybody were crawling on their bellies or something like that instead."

Smithers is studying this upslope race among bristlecone pines. These trees can live for more than 5,000 years—making them the oldest individual organisms on Earth. Many of them eke out

环保类素材 | **79**

a living in dry, rocky soils, on windblown ridgelines around 11,000 feet, in eastern California and Nevada. "They look like the worst bonsai tree imaginable. They just look gnarled and twisted, something that looks like it's taken a beating for 5,000 years and still living."

So, as tree line rises, these giant bonsais are following. But Smithers says the ancient trees now have a competitor—a species called limber pines. The limbers are passing the bristlecones at tree line, sprouting seedlings in that fresh real estate upslope more quickly. 'Quickly' being a relative term. "It's the tortoise and the slightly faster tortoise." Smithers documents the race in the journal *Global Change Biology*. [Brian V. Smithers et al., Leap-frog in slow-motion: divergent responses of tree species and life stages to climatic warming in Great Basin sub-alpine forests]

The leapfrogging limber pines could put bristlecones in a bind, hemmed in by competing seedlings upslope, and hotter temperatures downslope. And that, Smithers says, would have long-lasting consequences. "You know, we talk about the effects of climate change happening on scales of 100 years. What's going to happen by 2100. But in 5,000 years someone will be able to go to this stand and say, oh it looks like this because people made climate change happen 5,000 years ago. It just changes the scale, when we talk about the effects of climate change." Assuming, that is, we stick around long enough to notice. (387 words)

(Excerpted from *https://www.scientificamerican.com/podcast/episode/warming-puts-squeeze-on-ancient-trees/*)

Reference Article 5: China Honors Its Promise to Protect Nature
中国尊重保护自然的承诺

素材简介: 中国采取一系列措施保护自然区，采用了双管齐下的做法，比如当地政府派出巡逻队控制非法放牧、协调生态保护和社区发展、政府与非政府组织合作。

As a conservationist, 27-year-old Wang Chunli knows what a rewarding yet bumpy ride the country must take before reaching its "Beautiful China" destination by the middle of the century. For the past two years, she has been wrestling with the paradox between humanity and nature.

In December 2016, Wang paid her first visit to Xianghai National Nature Reserve in the northeastern province of Jilin. She was amazed by the rich landscapes, but shocked by the severe human disturbance in the reserve. "I didn't expect so many people to be living in a nature reserve. There were even residents among the habitat of red-crowned cranes and in the heartlands of rare plants," she said.

The reserve, built in 1981, is an important wetland for migratory birds to reproduce and refresh themselves during their journeys. It sprawls across more than 1,000 square kilometers and 12 villages in Jilin's Tongyu county. More than 15,000 people are still living in the reserve. Before 2015, 30 percent of the core zone, in which human activity is strictly prohibited, was farmland.

Zhang Xuejun, who was born and raised in Xianghai, has witnessed firsthand how humans have occupied the reserve. "When the wetland was first built, everyone appreciated the pleasant environment. But when they saw that putting sheep out to graze was lucrative, they all rushed to grab land in the core zone," the 56-year-old said.

Initially, the local government sent out patrol teams to control illegal grazing. But the move was only partially successful because grazing was not limited to a single location.

In recent years, the provincial government has attempted to solve the puzzle with a resettlement project. It demolished 248 houses and shacks, returned 6,711 hectares of farmland to grassland and every year the villagers are given 8,000 yuan ($1,260) as reimbursement for every hectare they have lost. However, driven by the profit motive, people still catch rare birds and poison fish in the core zone. "The biggest challenge is to coordinate ecological protection and community development, by which the government can cooperate with NGOs," said Wang, who has been running a pilot program since 2016.

Improving local lives

In December 2016, after two years of research and negotiations, the Paradise Foundation, an NGO in Beijing, signed a 30-year agreement with the reserve and the Jilin government to establish the Xianghai Ecological Protection Center. The center, which covers half the reserve's core zone, is directly managed by the foundation and supervised by the local government. When Wang was appointed as director of the center, the first thing she did was to visit a number of nearby villages to learn about the needs of local residents. "Wang and her team always come to talk about the importance of ecological protection, so I know that wetland acts as the Earth's kidneys. Now they are looking for good ideas to improve our lives," Zhang said.

The center adopted a two-pronged approach: first, local villagers were recruited to form patrols and crack down on poachers, which created jobs; second, environmentally friendly industries were established, such as growing organic grains and breeding chickens that are native to the area.

Despite Wang's efforts, most villagers still sit on the fence, apprehensive because of their inexperience and the bleak market prospects. Zhang was one of a small number of residents who agreed to breed the chickens. "I believe in the concept of ecological protection. For the sake of our descendants, we need to make changes," he said.

Ecological breeding demands zero use of chemicals and fertilizers. Zhang bought 500 chicks and raised them in a 6-hectare wooded area he owns. More than 100 died because of low temperatures, disease and predators, but after careful calculation of the costs, Zhang is still optimistic regarding profits. (668 words)

(Excerpted from *http://www.mwr.gov.cn/english/Medianews/201803/t20180306_1031947.html*)

素材简介: 埃克森美孚的研究证实了化石燃料几十年前在全球变暖中的作用,然而,在 80 年代末,埃克森公司减少了二氧化碳的研究,反而掩盖了碳排放对气候变化的影响。尽管遭到了科学家的怀疑,它还是把自己的力量投入到了导致全球变暖的具体原因调查中。它游说阻止联邦和国际行动来控制温室气体排放。它帮助建立了一个巨大的错误信息大厦,直到今天。

At a meeting in Exxon Corporation's headquarters, a senior company scientist named James F. Black addressed an audience of powerful oilmen. Speaking without a text as he flipped through detailed slides, Black delivered a sobering message: carbon dioxide from the world's use of fossil fuels would warm the planet and could eventually endanger humanity.

"In the first place, there is general scientific agreement that the most likely manner in which mankind is influencing the global climate is through carbon dioxide release from the burning of fossil fuels," Black told Exxon's Management Committee, according to a written version he recorded later.

It was July 1977 when Exxon's leaders received this blunt assessment, well before most of the world had heard of the looming climate crisis.

A year later, Black, a top technical expert in Exxon's Research & Engineering division, took an updated version of his presentation to a broader audience. He warned Exxon scientists and managers that independent researchers estimated a doubling of the carbon dioxide (CO_2) concentration in the atmosphere would increase average global temperatures by 2 to 3 degrees Celsius (4 to 5 degrees Fahrenheit), and as much as 10 degrees Celsius (18 degrees Fahrenheit) at the poles. Rainfall might get heavier in some regions, and other places might turn to desert.

"Some countries would benefit but others would have their agricultural output reduced or destroyed," Black said, in the written summary of his 1978 talk.

His presentations reflected uncertainty running through scientific circles about the details of climate change, such as the role the oceans played in absorbing emissions. Still, Black estimated quick action was needed. "Present thinking," he wrote in the 1978 summary, "holds that man has a time window of five to ten years before the need for hard decisions regarding changes in energy strategies might become critical."

Exxon responded swiftly. Within months the company launched its own extraordinary research into carbon dioxide from fossil fuels and its impact on the earth. Exxon's ambitious program included both empirical CO_2 sampling and rigorous climate modeling. It assembled a brain trust that would spend more than a decade deepening the company's understanding of an environmental problem that posed an existential threat to the oil business.

Then, toward the end of the 1980s, Exxon curtailed its carbon dioxide research. In the decades that followed, Exxon worked instead at the forefront of climate denial. It put its muscle behind efforts to manufacture doubt about the reality of global warming its own scientists had once confirmed. It lobbied to block federal and international action to control greenhouse gas emissions. It helped to erect a vast edifice of misinformation that stands to this day. (441 words)

(Excerpted from *http://insideclimatenews.org/news/15092015/Exxons-own-research-confirmed-fossil-fuels-role-in-global-warming*)

Reference Article 7: Climate Change Lies Are Exposed
气候变暖为谎言

素材简介：本文就气候调查的结果，有针对性地对全球变暖这一话题进行了阐述，认为气候变化为谎言。

A high-level inquiry into the Intergovernmental Panel on Climate Change found there was "little evidence" for its claims about global warming. It also said the panel had emphasized the negative impacts of climate change and made "substantive findings" based on little proof. The review by the Inter Academy Council (IAC) was launched after the IPCC's hugely embarrassing 2007 benchmark climate change report, which contained exaggerated and false claims that Himalayan glaciers could melt by 2035.
……

Among the blunders in the 2007 report were claims that 55 per cent of the Netherlands was below sea level when the figure is 26 per cent.

It also claimed that water supplies for between 75 million and 250 million people in Africa will be at risk by 2020 due to climate change, but the real range is between 90 and 220 million.

The claim that glaciers would melt by 2035 was also rejected.

Professor Julian Dowdeswell of Cambridge University said, "The average glacier is 1,000ft thick so to melt one at 15ft a year would take 60 years. That is faster than anything we are seeing now so the idea of losing it all by 2035 is unrealistic."(195 words)

(Excerpted from *https://www.express.co.uk/news/uk/196642/Climate-change-lies-are-exposed*)

Reference Article 8: Dockside Green
绿色运动

素材简介：绿色运动正在世界许多地方流行起来，建筑业尤其如此。健康投资是一个很好的投资。基于这一趋势，绿色倡议形成。有关设备的细致设计、规划、可循环利用等都需要在考虑范围之内。

The green movement is catching on in many pockets of the world. This is especially true in the construction industry. Today's buzz words, which include global warming and zero emissions, are causing everyday people (not just celebrities) to look for ways to reduce their carbon footprint. Purchasing an environmentally-friendly home is a good investment for those who are concerned about their own health and the well-being of our planet. Based on this trend, entire districts, known as eco-communities, are being designed with green initiatives in mind. One of these communities is Dockside Green in the Canadian province of British Columbia. Its goal is to become the world's first zero-emission neighborhood.

Dockside Green is a mostly self-sufficient community along the harbor front of Victoria, the capital city of British Columbia. The community is home to around 2,500 people and includes residential, office, and retail space. It includes a variety of environmental features, some of which are unprecedented.

The planners and builders of Dockside Green have the environment in mind with every choice they make. They ensure proper ventilation and guarantee residents clean air indoors. Interior and exterior building materials, such as paints and wood, are natural and non-toxic. One of these is bamboo which is used because it's very durable and can be grown without the use of dangerous pesticides.

Energy efficiency is one of the top priorities in eco-communities like Dockside Green. Not only do energy-efficient appliances and light fixtures reduce the environmental impact of heating, cooking and lighting, they also save residents money. Dockside Green claims that home owners use 55% less energy than the average Canadian. Though many residents are sharing space by investing in condo-style living, they have their own individual utility meters for electricity and gas. Studies show that people use around 20% less energy when they are billed for exactly what they use.

Eco-communities also take the future into account by recycling waste and reducing carbon emissions. At Dockside Green, waste water is treated and reused on-site for flushing toilets, and a biomass gas plant converts waste wood into a renewable form of gas for hot water systems, stoves and gas heaters. The community also reduces carbon emissions by using local suppliers for all their transport and maintenance needs, and residents are encouraged to use a mini transit system and join the community's car share program.

The first two stages of development at Dockside Green were completed in 2011, and additional plans to increase sustainability are in the works. Similar green communities are now found all over the world, especially smaller ones known as ecovillages or "intentional communities". Most have 50 to 150 residents, all of whom are trying to reduce their carbon footprints and create a model for sustainable living in the future. (470 words)

(Excerpted from *https://www.englishclub.com/reading/environment/eco-community.htm*)

Reference Article 9: Dogs Are Turning Blue in Mumbai Suburbs Due to Untreated Industrial Waster in River.

孟买郊区的狗因为未经处理的工业污水而变蓝

> **素材简介：** 流浪狗经常陷入对食物和水的需求。因此，文章就工业领域直接释放未经处理的污染物入河而对动物造成的伤害这一事实的描写，以此来唤醒人类对于动物的保护。

Dogs in the suburbs of India's financial capital Mumbai are reportedly turning blue due to untreated industrial wastes being released into a river. Stray dogs near Navi Mumbai's Taloja industrial area often wade into the Kasadi river for food and water.

The group filed a complaint with the Maharashtra Pollution Control Board (MPCB), saying the untreated waste that industries were releasing directly into the river was causing suffering to the animals.

Taloja is said to have nearly 1,000 pharmaceutical, food and engineering factories.

"It was shocking to see how the dog's white fur had turned completely blue," Arati Chauhan, resident of Navi Mumbai who runs the animal protection cell said. "We have spotted almost five such dogs here and have asked the pollution control board to act against such industries," she added.

MPCB officials said they had taken cognisance of the complaint. "Allowing the discharge of dye into any water body is illegal. We will take action against the polluters as they are destroying the environment," the board's regional officer Anil Mohekar said. "We have directed our sub-regional officer to investigate," he added.

Animal rights activists are wondering if the move has come a bit too late.

"We have only spotted blue dogs so far. We do not know if birds, reptiles and other creatures are affected or if they have even died owing to the dye discharged into the air," Chauhan said. (234 words).

(Excerpted from *http://www.ibtimes.co.uk/dogs-are-turning-blue-near-mumbai-suburbs-due-untreated-industrial-waste-river-1634620*)

Reference Article 10: Parakeet Invasion of Mexico Driven by Europe's Ban on Bird Imports

欧洲禁止进口禽类而导致鹦鹉入侵墨西哥

> **素材简介：** 小和尚鹦鹉（Myiopsitta monachus）入侵墨西哥。根据公布的一项调查，此次入侵对禽流感扩张的影响还是不可小觑的。因此这会促使欧洲禁止进口禽类，同时在其他国家也会有广泛的影响。

Small, emerald-coloured birds called monk parakeets (Myiopsitta monachus) invaded Mexico in the span of a decade because of trade policies thousands of kilometres away in Europe, according to a study released this month. The research highlights how fears over avian flu, which prompted a ban on bird imports in Europe, had wide ranging effects in other countries.

Monk parakeets, a type of parrot native to South America, popped up in countries such as the United States in the 1960s and have established themselves from Brooklyn to Brussels. There were only a handful of reported sightings of the bird in Mexico City in 2005. But by 2015, feral monk parakeets were documented in 97 cities throughout the country, say researchers in a study published on 19 September in *PLOS ONE*. Monk parakeets are considered agricultural pests, and their enormous communal nests can cause blackouts when built on electrical equipment. But they are popular as pets, and so have been part of the international parrot trade.

...Usually, it's hard to work out when a non-native species first appeared in an area, says Hobson. But the arrival of monk parakeets in Mexico has a sharply defined start and end point, thanks to shipping documentation and bird sightings recorded by citizen scientists using apps such as iNaturalist and eBird, Hobson says.

UNINTENDED CONSEQUENCES

She and her colleagues contend that two pieces of legislation shifted the global demand for monk parakeets from Europe to Mexico. In 2004, concerns about the spread of avian influenza in Europe led to an import ban on birds from southeast Asia. By 2007, the European Union had banned the importation of all wild-caught birds, regardless of their origin.

As EU demand for monk parakeets crashed, the international market for the birds shifted to Mexico, where regulatory changes in 2008 had made it illegal to purchase native Mexican parrots as pets, in an effort to preserve wild population numbers. The monk parakeet was one of the few options left for people who wanted to lawfully purchase a parrot.

More than half a million monk parakeets were imported into Mexico as part of the pet trade between 2000 and 2015. Hobson and her colleagues used international trade data to determine that 90% of those birds entered Mexico starting in 2008 and ending in 2014, mostly from Uruguay. The increase in wild monk-parakeet sightings throughout Mexico roughly coincided with the changes in regulations and commercial imports.

"This whole invasion seems like it was just a fascinating series of unforeseen consequences of regulation changes," says Hobson. It's important to think about how policy changes can both protect human populations and have unexpected negative results—such as the introduction of an invasive species, she says.

SETTING A BASELINE

Mexico stopped its commercial imports of monk parakeets in 2014 over concerns about the possible spread of avian influenza. The country declared the monk parakeet an invasive species in late 2016, and is required by law to devise a species management plan. This doesn't necessarily mean the invasion is over, Hobson says, because there are a lot of monk parakeets in Mexico that can escape their owners and reproduce in the wild. It's also still unclear what effect the animals are having on the country's native wildlife, urban infrastructure and local economy.

The study's findings punctuate the importance of banning the international trade in parrots, as well as the need for evaluating the unintended consequences of legislative and management action, says Michael Russello, an evolutionary biologist at the University of British Columbia in Kelowna, Canada.

The baseline data provided by the study "will be invaluable for tracking the spread and potential establishment of self-sustaining monk-parakeet populations in Mexico moving forward, and monitoring the performance of any management action", Russello says. (629 words)

(Excerpted from *https://www.scientificamerican.com/article/parakeet-invasion-of-mexico-driven-by-europe-rsquo-s-ban-on-bird-imports/*)

媒体类素材

Reference Article 1: Silicon Valley Will Lead Us to Our Doom
硅谷将毁灭人类

素材简介： 富兰克林·弗尔的新书 "World Without Mind" 指责硅谷的企业在宣扬推动世界发展的背后有意识形态层面的图谋。科技公司让用户上瘾，从中牟利、侵犯隐私并开展秘密的社会工程学实验。比如，Google 在抹杀个性和人的自主性，Facebook 在操控人们的行为。总之，这些硅谷的科技公司正在侵犯我们的隐私，扼杀我们的独立性、创造性和人性。

In Franklin Foer's new book, "World Without Mind," the veteran journalist lays out a more ominous view of where Big Tech would like to take us—in many ways, already has taken us. Silicon Valley, he argues, may say it wants to improve the world. But its true endgame is the advancement of an ideological agenda. And it's a terrifying one.

By introducing addictive new features, the book says, these companies have made us hopelessly dependent. Once hooked, consumers are robbed of choice, milked for profit, deprived of privacy and made the subjects of stealth social engineering experiments.

In some of the more surprising and futuristic sections, he argues that Google's expansions have less to do with new businesses than with a sweeping artificial intelligence-driven ideology meant to reduce human autonomy. (Anyone who has ever found their brains unable to process directions without the help of Google Maps has begun to get a small taste of what will be, in Foer's estimation, a much larger meal.)

The author saves some of his most provocative rhetoric for Facebook. Calling its M.O. a "paternalistic nudging," he describes a company that treats humans as a giant data set, noting how Facebook employees can run "experiments" on the service's tens of millions of users. The Mark Zuckerberg-led firm, he says, furnishes the illusion of free will and individual identity. But what really compels it is the achievement of certain social outcomes. By manipulating the news feeds of its massive user base, Facebook seeks to do everything from getting preferred political candidates elected (by subtly motivating the Americans who would vote for them) to controlling collective emotions (by adding or removing positive adjectives in feeds).

Foer could hardly be called a Luddite: He admits purchasing and owning myriad digital devices over the years and readily acknowledges the improvements they've afforded. But such conveniences mask a dirtier agenda, he argues.

"[It's] chilling to hear [co-founder Larry Page] contemplate how Google will someday employ more than one million people," Foer writes as he describes the company's effort to blend humans with machines and dilute the human will. "That's not just a boast about dominating an industry where he faces no true rivals; it's a boast about something far vaster, a statement of Google's intent to impose its values and theological convictions on the world."

But he mostly and persistently, with the zealotry of the companies he derides, builds a strong philosophical case. Like an occupying power dividing up territory, he asserts, Big Tech has imposed its will on the resident population with neither our input nor our permission. These firms have a program: to make the world less private, less individual, less creative, less human. (470 words)

(Excerpted from *https://www.stuff.co.nz/technology/97072097/author-silicon-valley-will-lead-us-to-our-doom*)

Reference Article 2: The Time to Regulate Online Advertising Is Now
是时候规范网络广告了

素材简介： 俄罗斯特工在 2016 年大选期间买通社交媒体上的广告，此次事件体现出 "personalization" 和 "microtargeting" 可以成为武器。广告向我们展示我们的个人数据是如何被使用或者滥用的。当今，已经没有中立的网络界面了，而界面背后是对其进行控制的科技公司。是时候规范这些界面了。

Washington and Silicon Valley have been shocked by each new discovery recently of how Russian operatives bought ads on Google, Facebook, Twitter and other social media networks during the 2016 campaign. Kremlin-linked troll farms bought cheap advertising with a very wide reach, possibly getting their messages in front of millions of American voters.

Such ads are our clearest example yet of the ways that personalization and microtargeting—basics in the business of data on the Internet—can be weaponized.

Ads are the best signal we have to show us how our personal data is being used. We've begun to see examples of how targeted advertising online has moved from the commercial into the political sphere. An Australian Facebook ad team presented leaked research suggesting how emotionally unstable teens might be targeted. The Trump campaign deployed "Super Predator" dark posts targeting black voters to suppress turnout just before the election. But Russia's digital tactics demonstrate just how far exploitative microtargeting can go.

Today there is no neutral interface, no unfiltered feed. From music recommendations to algorithmically generated news feeds, even search results and front pages of news sources, our digital lives are tailored to match our unique behavioral patterns. We can't toggle between a neutral experience and a personalized one.

It's hard to find the fuzzy line between appropriate uses and misuses of the technology. What's the difference between a retargeted ad selling shoes vs. one discussing protection of the Second Amendment?

This is about more than just annoying ads. It's about our agency to understand and control the interfaces with which we live every day.

Facebook has responded with an action plan to address election integrity issues. Ads targeted to various users will be available on one page for users to compare to what others are seeing. Facebook will also finally make political advertising disclosures more transparent, as regulation of TV and other media already requires. But these efforts do not address the wider influence of microtargeting and personalization on this and other platforms.

Interfaces dealing in user data need to be held accountable to their users. Beyond the ones Facebook has proposed, there are a number of solutions that platforms and regulators can pursue.

First, interfaces need to develop means of expressing the degree to which an experience is personalized to users. This allows platforms to explain the inputs that go into the personalized feed or recommendation, and also gives users a means of interacting with and responding to those inputs or algorithm weights.

Second, we need to apply some of the lessons from traditional advertising to the Wild West that is online advertising. We need to regulate appropriate and inappropriate uses of microtargeting, with consumer protection principles in mind.

Finally, we need to develop more data and better literacy of these practices to develop normative stances on what are acceptable and appropriate forms of targeting. (493 words)

(Excerpted from *The time to regulate online advertising is now*, by Sara M. Watson, October 12, 2017, *Washington Post*)

Reference Article 3: How to Keep Your Private Conversations Private for Real? 如何让你的私人谈话不被泄露

素材简介：网络改变了我们的通讯方式，互联网上的任何对话都会留下痕迹，这些痕迹会被大公司用于心理分析和心理操控。最近的一些新闻报道这些通讯记录被黑客攻击。有一些基本的方法可以让我们避免信息遭到泄露，但如果是非常秘密的对话最好还是当面交谈。

Before computers, what we said disappeared once we'd said it. Neither face-to-face conversations nor telephone conversations were routinely recorded. The Internet changed this. We now chat by text message and email, on Facebook and on Instagram. These conversations—with friends, lovers, colleagues, fellow employees—all leave electronic trails.

That our data is used by large companies for psychological manipulation—we call this advertising—is well-known. So is its use by governments for law enforcement and, depending on the country, social control. What made the news over the past year were demonstrations of how vulnerable all of this data is to hackers and the effects of having it hacked, copied and then published online. We call this doxing.

Doxing isn't new, but it has become more common. It's been perpetrated against corporations, law firms, individuals, the NSA and—just this week—the CIA. It's largely harassment and not whistleblowing, and it's not going to change anytime soon. The data in your computer and in the cloud are, and will continue to be, vulnerable to hacking and publishing online. Depending on your prominence and the details of this data, you may need some new strategies to secure your private life.

There are two basic ways hackers can get at your email and private documents. One way is to guess your password. That's how hackers got their hands on personal photos of celebrities from iCloud in 2014.

How to protect yourself from this attack is pretty obvious. First: Don't choose a guessable password. Second, turn on two-factor authentication where you can, like Google's 2-Step Verification. This adds another step besides just entering a password, such as having to type in a one-time code that's sent to your mobile phone. And third, don't reuse the same password on any sites you actually care about.

The other way hackers can get at your personal stuff is by breaking in to the computers the information is stored on. This is how the Russians got into the Democratic National Committee's network and how a lone hacker got into the Panamanian law firm Mossack Fonseca.

Protecting yourself is difficult, because it often doesn't matter what you do. If your email is stored with a service provider in the cloud, what matters is the security of that network and that provider. Most users have no control over that part of the system. The only way to truly protect yourself is to not keep your data in the cloud where someone could get to it.

None of this is perfect, of course. When secrecy is truly paramount, go back to communications systems that are still ephemeral: Pick up the telephone and talk. Meet face to face. (476 words)

(Excerpted from *https://www.washingtonpost.com/posteverything/wp/2017/03/08/conversations-online-are-forever-now-heres-how-to-keep-yours-private/?utm_term=.881e8a4c9619*)

Reference Article 4: Lawsuit Also Challenges Transit Agency's Rejection of Ads by PETA, Carafem, and Milo Yiannopoulos
交通局拒绝 PETA、Carafem 和 Milo Yiannopoulos 的广告的行为被提起诉讼

> **素材简介：**华盛顿都会区交通局拒绝了一些广告，包括 ACLU、Carafem、PETA 和 Yiannopoulo 的广告。ACLU 起诉了交通局的广告限制，宣称其违反了宪法第一修正案。此次事件凸显了政府试图压制所有关于公共交通内的争议性言论的后果。

The American Civil Liberties Union and its affiliates in the District of Columbia and Virginia today challenged the Washington area transit system's advertising restrictions as violations of the First Amendment. The free speech lawsuit follows the rejection of ads from four groups that hail from across the political spectrum, images of which are here.

The Washington Metropolitan Area Transit Authority rejected a series of ACLU ads displaying the text of the First Amendment in English, Spanish, and Arabic; a Carafem ad for medication abortions using what is described as the "10-Week-After Pill"; and several PETA ads suggesting that people "Go Vegan." Ads for Yiannopoulos' new book, "Dangerous," were first accepted by WMATA, then removed from the transit system after riders complained.

The lawsuit argues that parts of the agency's ad policies violate the First Amendment by discriminating against particular ads and advertisers deemed controversial by WMATA officials. The policies were adopted in 2015 following controversy surrounding a set of anti-Muslim advertisements. The current guidelines ban ads "intended to influence members of the public regarding an issue on which there are varying opinions," ads that "support or oppose an industry position or industry goal without any direct commercial benefit to the advertiser," and ads "intended to influence public policy," among others.

"This case highlights the consequences of the government's attempt to suppress all controversial speech on public transit property," said Arthur Spitzer, legal director of the ACLU-DC and lead counsel in the case. "The First Amendment protects the speech of everyone from discriminatory government censorship, whether you agree with the message or not."

One of the rejected PETA ads showed a pig with text below reading, "I'm ME, Not MEAT. See the Individual. Go Vegan." The ads were rejected for violating several of WMATA's guidelines.

Another of the rejected ads was from Carafem, a nonprofit health care network that specializes in providing women access to birth control and medication abortion. The submitted ad featured a large image of a white pill and below it, the text "10-Week-After Pill" and "For abortion up to 10 weeks. $450. Fast. Private. carafem.org."

"The four plaintiffs in this case perfectly illustrate the indivisibility of the First Amendment," said Lee Rowland. "In its zeal to avoid hosting offensive and hateful speech, the government has eliminated speech that makes us think, including the text of the First Amendment itself."

The lawsuit asks the court to order the agency to accept and run the ads in its trains and stations and in and on its buses. The lawsuit also asks the court to declare four sections of WMATA guidelines unconstitutional because they violate free speech rights, are arbitrarily enforced, and are unconstitutionally vague. (483 words)

(Excerpted from *https://www.aclu.org/news/aclu-sues-dc-metro-over-rejection-first-amendment-ad*)

Reference Article 5: Snapchat's New Snap Map Feature Raises Privacy Concerns
Snapchat 的地图功能引发了隐私问题

素材简介： Snapchat（照片分享平台色拉布）推出的 Snap Map 可以让用户和好友分享自己的具体位置，这种隐私泄露引起了家长和儿童安全倡导者的担忧。虽然 Snapchat 的发言人称，用户可以随时关掉位置分享或者选择向哪些好友分享位置，但是家长还是要提高警惕并且给予孩子必要的安全教育。

A new update to the popular social networking app Snapchat that allows certain users of the app to track down your exact location is raising privacy concerns for parents and child safety advocates.

The new Snapchat feature, called "Snap Map," lets you decide whether or not to share your location with your friends in the app, or stay in "ghost mode," the app's default setting. If you decide to share your location, then an emoji representing you will appear to pinpoint your exact location on a map to your friends within the Snapchat app. The emoji marking where someone is on the map will "only update when you open Snapchat," the tech company explained in a blog post.

But experts are concerned.

"It is very easy to accidentally share everything that you've got with more people than you need to, and that's the scariest portion," cyber security expert Charles Tendell told ABC News of the Snapchat update.

A spokesperson for Snapchat told ABC News in a statement that the "safety of our community is very important to us and we want to make sure that all Snapchatters, parents and educators have accurate information about how the Snap Map works."

"With Snap Map, location-sharing is off by default for all users and is completely optional. Snapchatters can choose exactly who they want to share their location with, if at all, and can change that setting at any time," the spokesperson said. "It's also not possible to share your location with someone who isn't already your friend on Snapchat, and the majority of interactions on Snapchat take place between close friends."

Experts recommend that parents stay aware of updates to apps like Snapchat. They also suggest parents make sure they know who their kids' friends are on Snapchat and also talk to their children about who they add on Snapchat.

Childnet International, a children's internet safety advocacy group, released tips for how to safely use the Snap Map feature, which includes to only share your location with people you know in person, and never with strangers. In addition, the group advises to not add contacts to Snapchat if you don't already know them in person.

The organization also advises that you can switch off the location-sharing feature at any time, and to put careful consideration into when you choose to share your location.

"Think about where you're sharing your location. Location services such as Snap Maps can lead people to your house," Childnet International said in a blog post. "Think about what times you're on the app and whether these are locations you want to share—if not, then turn this off within your settings." (448 words)

(Excerpted from *http://abcnews.go.com/Lifestyle/snapchats-snap-map-feature-raises-privacy-concerns/ story?id=48271889*)

Reference Article 6: WhatsApp Sharing Data with Facebook Raises Alarm for Privacy Advocates

WhatsApp 与 Facebook 共享数据引发了隐私维权人士的担忧

素材简介： WhatsApp 要与它的母公司 Facebook 共享用户数据，这引起了人们对于隐私问题的担忧。WhatsApp 称这样做可以更好地打击垃圾邮件，跟踪基本的使用数据，并向用户展示更多相关的广告和朋友建议。并且，跟 Facebook 共享数据是经过加密处理的，所以不会泄露用户隐私。但是，用户数据分享还是引起了很大争议。

Changes announced by WhatsApp have drawn the ire of privacy advocates, who say that the messaging service's plan to share user data with parent company Facebook is against the law and should be blocked.

The changes will allow the popular app—which says it has more than one billion users—to "coordinate more with Facebook" by sharing the user data, they said. The move prompted The Electronic Privacy Information Center (EPIC) and the Center for Digital Democracy to announce they would be filing a complaint with the Federal Trade Commission (FTC).

WhatsApp says it will allow the companies to better fight spam, track basic usage statistics and display more relevant advertisements and friend suggestions to users.

In other words, Facebook would be able to use phonebook data from WhatsApp to help users find friends who they chat with on WhatsApp, but who they have not "friended" on Facebook, a WhatsApp spokesperson told ABC News.

The messaging service insists that the contents of users' messages, "stay private and no one else can read them. Not WhatsApp, not Facebook, nor anyone else," when they're encrypted, and maintains that banner advertisements will continue to be barred within its app.

Users can decide to opt-out of the changes, though some time restrictions apply.

"WhatsApp complies with applicable laws. As always, we consider our obligations when designing updates like this," a WhatsApp spokesperson said. "We've made our terms and privacy policy easily accessible, provided an overview of the key updates, and empowered people to make decisions that are right for them, including offering a control for existing users over how their data can be used."

However, even the basic sharing of user data has generated controversy.

Facebook acquired the messaging service in 2014 for $22 billion, according to Bloomberg.

At the time the acquisition was announced, a blog post on the WhatsApp website told users, "Here's what will change for you, our users: nothing," and said "WhatsApp will remain autonomous and operate independently."

The blog post—from February, 2014—does not explicitly rule out data sharing with the parent company.

In a complaint filed with the FTC a few weeks after the acquisition was announced, EPIC said, "WhatsApp built a user base based on its commitment not to collect user data for advertising revenue," and noting that "Facebook routinely makes use of user information for advertising purposes," claimed that it intended to use WhatsApp user data for this purpose.

Facebook, like many free online services, uses user data to target advertising at users that is relevant to their interests.

Therefore, EPIC claimed, that the acquisition would "violate WhatsApp users' understanding of their exposure to online advertising and constitutes an unfair and deceptive trade practice," which it claimed would be in violation of FTC rules. (493 words)

(Excerpted from *http://abcnews.go.com/Business/Technology/whatsapp-sharing-data-facebook-raises-alarm-privacy-advocates/story?id=41717305*)

Reference Article 7: 5 Tips to Stay Safe on the Social Network
5 个在社交网络上保持安全的方法

素材简介： 在社交网络上保持安全的 5 个方法：1. 知道你在和谁分享；2. 通过隐私设置选择谁可以查看你的个人信息；3. 选择安全性高的密码，设置登录提示；4. 屏蔽那些你不愿意与之互动的人；5. 当心谣言。

It's "Data Privacy Day" and Facebook is celebrating by reminding its 1.35 billion monthly active users how to take control of their presence on the social network.

Facebook found in a survey that many people are likely to get privacy tips from their friends, Erin Egan, the social network's chief privacy officer, said in a blog post.

Break out the cake, champagne or treat of your choice to celebrate "Data Privacy Day" and run through these five quick tips from Facebook to make sure you're in control of your digital footprint.

Know Who You're Sharing With

Remember, you can tailor your audience for every post by clicking on the button next to the "post" button and choosing who can see it.

Take the Privacy Check-Up

An expanded privacy checkup tool featuring a friendly blue dinosaur is available by clicking on the padlock in the upper right corner of your Facebook page.

Once there, the dinosaur will guide you through steps to review who can see posts, which apps you use and who has access to your personal information, including your birthday and photos.

Security Features

A strong password and login, which will let you know if someone tries to log into your account from a new location, will help keep your data iron-clad.

To set up login alerts, go to "security settings," choose "login alerts" and check whether you'd like to be notified of activity via Facebook notifications, text or email. Save your changes and you're good to go.

Take Control

You have the power to untag yourself from a photo or story. Users can also block anyone who they'd rather not interact with on Facebook by going to the person's page, clicking the "..." and choosing "block." Make full use of these functions and take control.

Watch Out for Rumors

Earlier this month, a Facebook copyright hoax that gained steam in 2012 went viral again. The message claims to put copyright protections on a user's posts after they share the status update.

Her's the thing: Facebook doesn't own your posts. Under the social network's privacy policy, they have the right to distribute and share the things a user posts, subject to their privacy and application settings.

The bottom line: Be mindful of rumors. (400 words)

(Excerpted from *http://abcnews.go.com/Technology/facebook-tips-stay-safe-social-network/ story?id=28557036*)

Reference Article 8: The Good and Bad of Digital Media
数字媒体的优缺点

素材简介: 历史学家如何有效地利用互联网加强他们的研究？他们如何向更广泛的受众展示这项研究？针对这两个问题 Cohen（科恩）和 Rosenzweig（罗森茨维格）在他们的书里进行了回答。本书审视了数字媒体对历史学家带来的积极影响和消极影响。书中列出了 7 个积极影响，如数字媒体可以让历史学者和大众更方便地接触历史文献。其中也列出了 5 个消极影响，如数字媒体无法保证其历史信息是真实的。总体来说，还是好处大于坏处。

How can historians effectively use the Internet to enhance both their research and how they present that research to a wider audience? Daniel J. Cohen's and Roy Rosenzweig's, Digital History: A Guide to Gathering, Preserving, and Presenting the *Past on the Web* attempts to answer this question by examining the potential possibilities and pitfalls digital media presents to historians. Within their introduction, Cohen and Rosenzweig define the seven major positive aspects of digital media as:

Capacity: Digital media gives historians the ability to exponentially expand storage space for object or archival research. This expanded space also allows archives and museums share collections not on display in their institutions with the public.

Accessibility: By using formats such as online exhibits, web sites, and digitized archives historians can reach larger academic or non-academic audiences than ever before.

Flexibility: Digital media has allowed historians to move beyond the use of text sources to include other forms of media such as sound and moving images.

Diversity: The openness of the web has given beginning, amateur, or hobby historians that may not be able to publish in scholarly journals an outlet to present their work to a broader audience.

Manipulability: The use of search engines lets historians search across broad swaths of sources in a short period of time, this makes the research process much quicker than only using print sources and microfilm.

Interactivity: By creating online sources, historians can directly and conveniently interact with a larger audience.

Hypertextuality: The broad scope of the web provides an expanded ability to move from narrative to narrative quickly.

These seven aspects of digital media remain particularly useful for historians because they expand our research options, broaden our audiences, and give us the opportunity to engage in direct conversation with other academics and the general public. In contrast to these positive aspects of digital media, the authors also warn historians of the more negative aspects of digital history, including:

Quality: Because of the openness of the web anyone can publish low quality or historically inaccurate work.

Durability: As technology rapidly changes, archivists struggle to keep track of and preserve born digital material.

Readability: Online scholarship can reduce the readability of articles by overloading readers with images and sound clips in addition to an already dense argument.

Passivity: Many of the more interactive components in digital history have trouble using the computer to detect "gray" areas.

Inaccessibility: Many scholarly databases only allow access to institutions able to pay the subscription fees. Also, there is a substantial "digital divide" between those who can and cannot access the Internet.

Throughout the reading, I thought the authors most effectively demonstrated the positive side of digital media by noting the ability to increase public accessibility to history through the use of the Internet. By illustrating how online archives, exhibits, and articles, can provide both historians and the general public with access to historical materials that otherwise may have been unavailable to them, Cohen and Rosenzweig make a very persuasive argument encouraging the use of digital media. In regards to the darker side of digital media, the authors best argue that as corporations become more involved in history on the web, the accessibility praised above becomes limited. This seemed particularly relevant in regards to databases such as JSTOR or Project Muse that offer incredibly useful services, but only to those institutions that can afford to pay the hefty subscription fees. By illustrating both the pros and cons of digital media, and by providing a background of the digital history field, Cohen and Rosenzweig's work helps technologically inept historians ground themselves in the basics of digital media. (612 words)

(Excerpted from *http://www.dighist.org/2011/01/the-good-and-bad-of-digital-media/*)

Reference Article 9: How Much Screen Time Is Ok?
使用电子产品时间多久合适?

素材简介: 8 岁及以下儿童使用电子产品的占比由 2011 年的 52% 增长到 2013 年的 75%。教育软件可以提升学前儿童的认知能力和社交能力等。网络还可以使青少年得到更多的学习机会和社交机会。但使用电子产品最大的健康威胁是肥胖。此外，睡前限制使用电子产品很重要，因为电子产品还会影响睡眠时间和睡眠质量。

To provide some guidance to parents grappling with these vexing issues of kids using digital devices, the American Academy of Pediatrics has issued new guidelines for how children should spend time in front of all types of screens. Here's a look at some of the issues they considered as they formulated their advice.

How much media are most kids using each day?

Use of mobile devices like smartphones has risen dramatically in the last few years. When the Kaiser Family Foundation began surveying parents in 2011, they found that 52% of children ages 8 and under had access to a mobile device. By 2013, that figure had jumped to 75%. Other studies have shown that most babies start interacting with digital media at the tender age of 4 months, and that most 2-year-olds use a mobile device on a daily basis.

Some TV shows and apps can be educational, right?

That's true. Studies have shown that content from PBS programs like "Martha Speaks" and "Sesame Street" can improve cognitive, literacy and social outcomes for preschoolers. However, the authors wrote that most "educational" apps have not been tested, and are often made with little or no input from educators or developmental specialists.

What about older kids and adolescents? Should we try to keep them off screens too?

Actually, the authors note that there may be several benefits to media use in older children. Social networks and Internet access can expose kids to new ideas and immersive learning experiences, as well as make it easier for them to maintain friendships across distances. It also makes collaborating with classmates more convenient.

In addition, social media networks can provide safe communities for kids who may feel alienated or left out at school—for example, children with an illness or disability, or those who identify as lesbian, gay, bisexual or transgender.

Are there actual health risks associated with too much media use?

Yes. The big one is obesity. A recent study found that among 2-year-olds, every additional hour spent in front of a screen per week translated into a measurable increase in body mass index.

A large international study with nearly 300,000 children and adolescents found that those who watched between 1 and 3 hours of TV a day were 10% to 27% more likely to be obese than kids who watched less than 1 hour per day.

Why is it important to limit screen time before bedtime?

There is a growing body of evidence that media use has a detrimental effect on sleep for kids (and grown-ups) of all ages. For example, studies show that infants who are exposed to screens in the evening hours sleep for fewer hours at night than infants who had no evening screen exposure. Among preschoolers, having a TV, computer or mobile device in the bedroom was associated with fewer hours of sleep per night. (487 words)

(Excerpted from *http://www.latimes.com/science/sciencenow/la-sci-sn-screen-time-kids-pediatricians-20161020-snap-story.html*)

Reference Article 10: How Digital Media Affects Children?
数字媒体如何影响孩子？

素材简介： 现在的孩子对电子产品非常精通，那么，数字媒体对孩子的影响到底是好还是坏呢？答案是既好又不好。数字媒体可能降低孩子的认知能力和专注力，但是电子产品在学校教学中也起到了重要作用。我们需要做的是适度使用电子产品。

Remember when you were a kid—before Facebook, Twitter, high-speed Internet, smartphones, and online video? Times are different now and digital media is cultivating a new generation of kids.

You've seen it—the 2-years-olds who are master photographers with their parents' smartphone cameras and the 6-year-olds who can already type faster than most developers.

Kids these days have bedrooms jam-backed with TVs, video game consoles, and computers—they're spending less time outside exercising and more time hanging out on the couch playing Call of Duty. But is multimedia all bad? And how does it affect children?

The following infographic from Now Sourcing explores two important sides of this question. Is media bad or good for kids? Well, yes and no.

Is Media Making Kids Stagnate?

For good reason, 73% of parents like to limit their kids' TV time, and 66% talk to their kids about the dangers of social media sites. Surprisingly, only a small proportion of respondents actively monitor their kids' social presences and privacy settings—despite concerns.

Then there's the perspective that media harms intelligence—42% of Americans agree that in 2020, young technology users will have major cognitive problems including an inability to focus, lack of long-term foresight, and limited critical thinking ability. Ouch.

Is Media Making Kids Smarter?

In the classrooms, teachers perceive media and technology as invaluable teaching tools. Only a small proportion of respondents—26%—feel that incorporating tablets in the classroom would be a distraction to learning. The rest? Well, they think tablets are just what the classroom needs.

Where teachers agree with parents is in the areas of attention span—without checks and balances, online media can really hurt a kid's ability to focus.

As with all great things in life (junk food, play dates, and study-time), what kids need most is balance. Too much, too little—there is a fine line. To say that digital media's kids are going to grow into lackluster adults, however? That may be a stretch.

Hats off to today's brilliant, media-savvy kids who will inevitably pioneer tomorrow's technology. (368 words)

(Excerpted From *https://contently.com/strategist/2013/05/15/the-good-and-the-bad-of-how-digital-media-affects-children-infographic/*)

文娱艺术类素材

Reference Article 1: The Definition about the Modern Arts
当代艺术的定义

素材简介： 什么是当代艺术？艺术家、批评家、策展人、画廊、拍卖行、收藏家，还是公众？这些群体是如何形成今天的多方面的定义的？历史提供了最好的答案。

Who gets to say what counts as contemporary art? Artists, critics, curators, gallerists, auctioneers, collectors, or the public? Revealing how all of these groups have shaped today's multifaceted definition, Terry Smith brilliantly shows that an historical approach offers the best answer to the question: What is Contemporary Art?

Smith argues that the most recognizable kind is characterized by a return to mainstream modernism in the work of such artists as Richard Serra and Gerhard Richter, as well as the retro-sensationalism of figures like Damien Hirst and Takashi Murakami. At the same time, Smith reveals, postcolonial artists are engaged in a different kind of practice: one that builds on local concerns and tackles questions of identity, history, and globalization. A younger generation embodies yet a third approach to contemporaneity by investigating time, place, mediation, and ethics through small-scale, closely connective art making. Inviting readers into these diverse yet overlapping art worlds, Smith offers a behind-the-scenes introduction to the institutions, the personalities, the biennials, and of course the works that together are defining the contemporary. The resulting map of where art is now illuminates not only where it has been but also where it is going. (198 words)

(Excerpted from *https://search.credoreference.com/content/topic/johns_jasper_1930*)

Reference Article 2: Broad Sense of Art
广义上的艺术

素材简介： 广义上说，艺术是人类技术、想象力和发明的全部过程和产物。在当代的使用中，艺术的定义通常反映艺术理论，这个术语包括文学、音乐、戏剧、绘画和雕塑。通俗地说，这个词最常用来指视觉艺术。在西方文化中，古希腊人引入的艺术思想和理论仍然影响着我们对艺术的理解和判断。

In contemporary usage, definitions of art usually reflect art theory, and the term may encompass literature, music, drama, painting, and sculpture. Popularly, the term is most commonly used to refer to the visual arts. In Western culture, artistic thought and theories introduced by the ancient Greeks still influence our perceptions and judgements of art.

Representation and inspiration

Two currents of thought run through our ideas about art. In one, first considered by the Greek philosopher Aristotle (c. 384 BC), art is concerned with mimesis (imitation), the representation of appearances, and gives pleasure through the accuracy and skill with which it represents the real world. The other view, derived from the Greek philosopher Plato (c. 427 BC), holds that the artist is inspired by the Muses (or by God, or by the inner impulses, or by the collective unconscious) to express that which is beyond appearances–inner feelings, eternal truths, or the essence of the age.

Art forms

In the visual arts of Western civilizations, painting and sculpture have been the main art forms for many centuries. This has not always been the case in other cultures. Islamic art, for example, is one of ornament, for under the Muslim religion artists were forbidden to imitate the divine right of creation by portraying living creatures. In some cultures, masks, tattoos, pottery, and metalwork have been the main forms of visual art. Recent technology has made new art forms possible, such as photography and cinema, and today electronic media have led to entirely new ways of creating and presenting visual images. See also prehistoric art; the arts of ancient civilizations, for example Egyptian art; indigenous art traditions, for example Oceanic art; medieval art; the arts of individual countries, such as French art; individual movements, such as Romanticism, cubism, and Impressionism; and painting and sculpture. (301 words)

(Excerpted from *http://search.credoreference.com/content/topic/art*)

Reference Article 3: Art and Other Disciplines
艺术与其他学科

素材简介：视觉艺术通常与其他学科相关，一个明显的联系是使用一种视觉媒介，如绘画，来翻译与另一学科相关的信息，例如，达·芬奇的许多画作都是对土著植物的简单研究。艺术和其他学科之间的另一个共同的联系可以从精确的数学和科学理论中看到，或者观众在绘画中看到节奏，将音乐和艺术的语言和情感联系起来。虽然绘画、版画或雕塑可能只对美学起作用，对作品与其他题材的关系的理解将扩大和深化其传达的意义。

The visual arts are often interrelated with other disciplines, such as mathematics, music, or science. One obvious association is the use of a visual medium, such as painting, to translate information pertaining to another discipline—many of Leonardo da Vinci's paintings, for example, were simply studies of indigenous flora. Another common association between art and other disciplines can be seen in the precise mathematics and scientific theories used to create the flickering visual effects of op art, or when a viewer 'sees' rhythm in a painting, linking the language and emotion of music and art. Although paintings, prints, or sculptures may function on aesthetics alone, the understanding of a work's relationship with other subject matter will broaden and deepen its conveyed meaning.

Art and culture

Art reflects history and is an indispensable part of peoples' culture. Art and culture are intricately connected, so that the art of a given place reflects not only the historical context in which it was made, but also the conditions under which it was produced. For example, in some cultures decorative tiles will be elaborately painted and glazed and fired in an electric kiln, while in others tiles may only be adorned with simple incised designs and then left in the sun to bake—the elementary process of the latter reflecting the available materials and environmental conditions of the surrounding geographical area. At the same time, art and culture tend to affect each other; cultural issues often play a major role in an artist's work, while an artist's work may influence an entire generation. For example, while pop art was a comment on consumerism, particularly that of the USA and UK, op art influenced 'popular' culture, as its basic concepts were used in areas such as fashion and contemporary design.

Artists and society

Many artists use societal issues (events in a community) as their inspiration, content, and theme, either being motivated to address them or represent them. As a result, their work can sometimes cause a heightened awareness of political or social issues, or even a shift in contemporary attitudes. Artists often portray historical events by expressing their own feelings about them, and most social artists create works with the sole intention of demonstrating their concerns. As a consequence, an artist's record of a battle, atrocity, or social problem may be more subjective (influenced by personal opinion) than other media. Many artists, such as Goya, Käthe Kollwitz, and Honoré Daumier, have used their talents often in political contexts, to affect change, appeal for a cause, or create awareness. (423 words)

(Excerpted from *http://search.credoreference.com/content/topic/art*)

Reference Article 4: Art Education
艺术教育

素材简介：艺术教育与美国公立学校的其他教育趋势和运动一样，不可避免地受到历史事件和条件、社会需求和通识教育背景的交叉影响。艺术被认为是一种人性化的治疗努力，辅助身体、心理、情感的发展和培养创新能力。

Art education, like other educational trends and movements in American public schools, has been inexorably influenced by the intersection of historical events and conditions, perceived societal needs, and the context of general education. Since art education was introduced in American schools in the mid-19th century, three general movements within the art education field have been identified: art to support society, art to support the child's individual development, and art as a unique curricular discipline. Each of these functions in the justification and content of art education can be viewed as a manifestation of reform or of dissent, depending on the particular viewpoint taken.

During the 19th century, art was promoted to support the well-being of the social order and to develop a strong economically independent nation. Art, narrowly defined as mechanical drawing, was first introduced in 1847 at Boston English High School to train draftsmen for the Industrial Revolution. In 1870, Massachusetts passed the first law making drawing a required high school subject. The rationale for art was to develop skills in working with tools, materials, and techniques. Walter Smith's book *Teacher's Manual for Freehand Drawing and Designing* (1876) consisted of a series of paced exercises in which students were required to copy geometric patterns of lines and shapes. Smith viewed art education as a sequence of drawing lessons that were so clear and precise that non-art specialists could teach students to draw.

The child-centered approach to art education emerged in the 1920s as a reaction to the lack of concern for individual growth and development associated with the society-centered approach. For John Dewey and the Progressive movement, art served as a catalyst to the child-centered approach. The work of Viktor Lowenfeld, an Austrian art educator who, before the Holocaust, fled to the United States, provided the impetus. His *Creative and Mental Growth* (1947) reflects his postwar vision of art as a tool for enhancing individual creativity through freedom of expression. In contrast to the "art to support society" closed-ended instruction, teaching strategies associated with "art to enhance the child's development" were open-ended, relying on unguided discovery and embracing creative expression. Art was deemed a humanizing and therapeutic endeavor that aided the development of physical, mental, emotional, and creative capabilities. (378 words)

(Excerpted from *https://search.credoreference.com/content/topic/art_education*)

Reference Article 5: Art Practice
艺术实践

素材简介： 加州大学伯克利分校的艺术实践部门所提供的严谨务实、概念和关键的训练在世界著名的公立研究型大学都享有盛誉。加州大学伯克利分校采取多种形式和途径为社会积极准备当代艺术学生。它提供的创新性的具体媒体和跨学科课程的学士和硕士学位的课程，强调了专业技能在历史学科中的方法运用，结合了多种形式的社会实践。

UC Berkeley's Department of Art Practice provides rigorous practical, conceptual, and critical training within the context of a world-renowned public research university. The department's mission is to prepare students for professional lives within contemporary art, while acknowledging that these can take multiple forms and approaches. With MFA students, greater emphasis is placed on developing long-term artistic practices. Undergraduate students, particularly within a university, can expect a broader range of training and career possibilities. The department emphasizes an ethical, global scope, with a necessary encouragement of diversity of viewpoints and modes of practice. It offers innovative media-specific, and interdisciplinary courses leading to B.A. and MFA degrees. Studio and seminar courses provide essential skills within conceptual and critical frameworks. The faculty consists of national and internationally recognized artists working across a range of media including painting, drawing, photography, printmaking, ceramics, sculpture, installation, performance, video, animation, sound, and the newly emerged fields of programming, game design, and virtual and augmented reality. While strongly remaining a studio art program, the department embraces other disciplines, including design, with active collaborations with other departments to offer hybrid art courses as part of an expanded vocabulary of art making. The department emphasizes disciplinary skills within a historicized interdisciplinary approach, incorporating multi-form and social practices coupled with rigorous critical approaches. The department continues its commitment to educating students for the contemporary world by addressing ongoing global, sociopolitical and cultural shifts, as well as incorporating new technologies as tools for innovative art practices. (249 words)

(Excerpted from *http://art.berkeley.edu*)

Reference Article 6: Art Practice
艺术实践

> **素材简介：** 以手工制造为主的一般应用设计领域这个术语是由 19 世纪末的英国创造的。作为当时旨在复兴装饰艺术的运动的标签，它满足了把美与日常生活的美结合起来的道德需要。艺术和手工艺运动的美学和政治方面影响了现代主义的发展。艺术和手工艺运动也蔓延到欧洲大陆，在 19 世纪末和 20 世纪初颇具影响力。

Term for that general field of applied design in which hand fabrication is dominant. The term was coined in England in the late 19th cent. as a label for the then-current movement directed toward the revivifying of the decorative arts. The chief influence behind this movement was William Morris. By the mid-19th cent., factory processes had almost entirely driven artisans from their ancient trades and threatened to obliterate the techniques they used to produce beautiful objects of utility. The Gothic revival, however, had brought into existence a great body of knowledge concerning the arts of the Middle Ages, and Morris, together with the Pre-Raphaelite painters and a small group of architects and designers, returned to these arts as a rich source of inspiration.

The pupils and followers of Morris multiplied, and proficient artisans developed. Their methods aimed at a practical demonstration not only of Morris's aesthetic creed but also of his ideas concerning socialism and the moral need for integrating beauty with the accessories of daily life. The aesthetic and political aspects of the arts and crafts movement influenced the development of modernism, particularly as they were later reflected in the core philosophy of the Bauhaus. The revival of folk arts has continued to prosper in some quarters, especially in remote communities and among Native Americans of the Southwest and the Eskimos (see North American Native Art).

A less aestheticized version of the arts and crafts movement was important in the United States, where it spread from England and flourished from the late 19th cent. to about 1915. It was prominent in American architecture and design, notably in the buildings and interiors of Greene and Greene and in the "mission-style" oak furniture of Gustav Stickley (1858–1942) and his contemporaries. The movement's precepts were also applied to ceramics, glassware, utensils, and other objects of American daily life. The arts and crafts movement also spread to continental Europe, where it was quite influential during the late 19th and early 20th cent. (334 words)

(Excerpted from *https://search.credoreference.com/content/topic/arts_and_crafts*)

Reference Article 7: Origins of Modern Art
现代艺术的起源

素材简介： 在 19 世纪下半叶，画家们开始反对经典的构图规范、精心绘画、调和着色和英雄题材。教会和国家的资金赞助急剧下降，同时艺术家的观点变得更加独立和主观。

In the second half of the 19th cent., painters began to revolt against the classic codes of composition, careful execution, harmonious coloring, and heroic subject matter. Patronage by the church and state sharply declined at the same time that artists' views became more independent and subjective. Such artists as Courbet, Corot and others of the Barbizon School, Manet, Degas, and Toulouse-Lautrec chose to paint scenes of ordinary daily and nocturnal life that often offended the sense of decorum of their contemporaries.

Impressionism

Monet, Renoir, and Pissarro, the great masters of impressionism, painted café and city life, as well as landscapes, working most often directly from nature and using new modes of representation. While art had always been to a certain extent abstract in that formal considerations had frequently been of primary importance, painters, beginning with the impressionists in the 1870s, took new delight in freedom of brushwork. They made random spots of color and encrusted the canvas with strokes that did not always correspond to the object that they were depicting but that formed coherent internal relationships. Thus began a definite separation of the image and the subject. The impressionists exploited the range of the color spectrum, directly applying strokes of pure pigment to the canvas rather than mixing colors on the palette. In sculpture, dynamic forms and variations of impressionism were created by Rodin, Renoir, Degas, and the Italian Medardo Rosso.

Nineteenth-Century Painting after Impressionism

In the 1880s, Seurat and Signac developed the more detailed and systematic approach of neoimpressionism, while Van Gogh and Gauguin, using bold masses, gave to color an unprecedented excitement and emotional intensity (see postimpressionism). At the same time, Cézanne painted subtler nuances of tone and sought to achieve greater structural clarity. Flouting the laws of perspective, he extracted geometrical forms from nature and created radically new spatial patterns in his landscapes and still lifes. Other important innovations of the late 19th cent. can be seen in the starkly expressionistic paintings of the Norwegian Edvard Munch and the vivid fantasies of the Belgian James Ensor. In the 1890s the Nabis developed pictorial ideas from Gauguin, while sinuous linear decorations were produced throughout Europe by the designers of art nouveau. (364 words)

(Excerpted from *http://search.credoreference.com/content/topic/modern_art*)

Reference Article 8: The Isms of Early Twentieth-Century Art
二十世纪早期艺术

素材简介：从 20 世纪开始，颜色在绘画中占据了至高无上的地位。同时野兽派和表现主义等艺术形式的存在也为艺术的发展作出了杰出贡献。

From the early 20th cent. color reigned supreme and invaded the contours of recognizable objects with the brilliant patterns of fauvism (1905–8), dominated by Matisse and Rouault in France, the orphism of Robert Delaunay and Frank Kupka, and the explosive hues of the German group Die Brücke, which included such practitioners of expressionism as Kirchner and Nolde. Kandinsky transformed (c.1910) color into a completely abstract art absolutely divorced from subject matter. The fauvists and expressionists shared an appreciation of the pure and simplified shapes of various examples of primitive art, an enthusiasm that was generated by Gauguin and extended to Picasso, Brancusi, Modigliani, Derain, and others.

Cubism

About 1909 the implications of Cézanne's highly organized yet revolutionary spatial structures were expanded by Picasso and Braque, who invented an abstract art of still lifes converted into shifting volumes and planes. Cubism, developed by the artists of the school of Paris, went through several stages and had an enormous influence on European and American painting and sculpture. In sculpture its notable exponents included Picasso, Duchamp-Villon, Lipchitz, González, and Archipenko, who began to realize the possibilities of convex and concave volumes. Cubism was absorbed in Italy by the exponents of futurism (c.1909–c.1915) and in Germany by the Blaue Reiter group (1911–14); both these movements were cut short by the advent of World War I. Fauvism and cubism were introduced by members of the Eight to a generally shocked American audience in the Armory Show of 1913, and from then on Americans began to participate significantly in the development of modern art (see American art).

Geometric Abstraction

At roughly the same time as cubism was developing, Russia made extraordinary contributions to the current of nonfigurative art. The sculptors Naum Gabo and Antoine Pevsner joined the movement known as constructivism (c.1913–c.1921), and the painter Casimir Malevich founded suprematism (1913). In Holland members of the Stijl group (1917–31), including Mondrian and Theo van Doesburg, created a disciplined, nonobjective art. These Russian and Dutch developments in the second decade of the 20th cent. were applicable to many varieties of art and industrial design, and their principles converged in the teachings of the Bauhaus in the 1920s. Kandinsky, the highly imaginative Paul Klee, and the American Lyonel Feininger were among the celebrated exponents of the Bauhaus. (383 words)

(Excerpted from *http://search.credoreference.com/content/topic/modern_art*)

Reference Article 9: Arts in New Century
新世纪的艺术

素材简介： 20 世纪 70 年代多媒体实验的兴起，各种以技术为基础的媒体的广泛使用一直延续到新世纪的艺术中，通常包括电影、视频、声音、表演（见表演艺术）和建筑（主要是安装艺术）等元素。从 21 世纪开始，数字艺术家利用复杂的计算机、软件和视频设备创造出各种各样的作品。

Arising from the multimedia experiments of the 1970s, the widespread use of a variety of technology-based media has persisted into the art of the new century. Often included are elements of film, video, sound, performance (see performance art), and architecture (principally in installation art). Another trend that has widened the definition and scope of contemporary art has been the conceptually driven use of both photography and language as the substance of numerous works of art—in Kiefer's photographic collages, in Kruger's words and photographic images, in Bruce Nauman's neon phrases, in Lawrence Weiner's painted words, in Holzer's billboarded, carved, electronically reproduced, or otherwise created linguistic neotruisms, and in many other artists' works. Another contemporary art movement, digital art, was pioneered in the 1970s but did not become prevalent until the beginning of the 21st cent. Digital artists make use of sophisticated computers, software, and video equipment to create an extremely varied body of works.

Postmodern art has also blurred the distinctions between painting and sculpture (and sometimes architecture), with artists often including in their works a host of wildly nontraditional materials. Since the 1960s shaped paintings and painted sculpture have become commonplace, while the materials of art have ranged from Rauschenberg's stuffed goat to Joseph Beuys' globs of fat to the smeared body fluids of various contemporary artists. Moreover, a wide variety of spaces and places, both private and public, have become arenas for the frequently ephemeral work of many contemporary artists. (242 words)

(Excerpted from *http://search.credoreference.com/content/topic/contemporary_art*)

Reference Article 10: Jasper Johns
贾斯培·琼斯

素材简介： 贾斯培·琼斯是一名画家、雕塑家、"新达达运动"版画家和流行艺术先驱。他的作品探讨了真实物体与它们在绘画和雕塑中的表现的区别，以及他所描绘的图像和物体的基本事实和经验的区别。

Jasper Johns is a painter, sculptor, and printmaker of the neo-dada movement of the 1950s and early 1960s and an important precursor of pop art. He is best known for his paintings from the mid-1950s to the mid-1960s of flags, targets, maps, alphabet letters, and Roman numerals and his quasi-abstract paintings with fragmentary and enigmatic figurative imagery and attached objects.

His work explores the distinction between real objects and the representation of them in painting and sculpture and the essential facts and experiences of the images and objects he depicts. His works often question the distinction between the two-dimensional and the three-dimensional and epitomize the modernist pursuit of flatness and the revelation of the materials and techniques used to make art. In his work, marks and brushstrokes of paint are often important as individualized indicators of meaning and identifiers of things depicted and arranged in evenly dispersed, flat compositions. Johns' work is often seen as the fulfillment of some of the fundamental intentions and ideas of modernism that can be traced back to Gustave Courbet, Edouard Manet, impressionism, and cubism.

Johns was born on May 15, 1930, in Augusta, Georgia, and grew up in South Carolina. After serving in the Army during the Korean War, he moved to New York City to pursue his youthful interest in art and soon became friends with Robert Rauschenberg and John Cage. In 1954, he destroyed most of his early work when someone compared it to the dadaist Kurt Schwitters. His circle of friends in New York in the 1950s was part of neo-dada and was intrigued by the Zen-based theories of Cage. He has usually painted on canvas with oils and encaustic and often added everyday found objects to his paintings or attached and combined canvases to one another. He has created sculptures by covering ordinary objects with a thick, malleable, gray material he calls "Sculpt-Metal."

In the early 1960s, Johns's paintings became larger and more complex in their seemingly disconnected colors, shapes, textures, painting techniques, and subjects. Their exploration of the very meaning of art also became more complex, and their biographical implications became more important. Device (1961–1962) features two rulers, which are mounted to the canvas and were used to create circular striations in the paint. This seems to be a literal commentary on the techniques of the artist and the use of tools and implements to achieve a goal, demonstrating that the artist's brush or palette knife is a "device" of a highly mechanical, arbitrary nature. Diver (1962) features a spinning wheel produced by a rotating device and a gray scale on the left half, while the right has broad, brushy areas of bright reds, oranges, yellows, and blues with the names of the colors stenciled on then. In the middle there are handprints followed by long, armlike streaks and footprints, suggesting that the artist has taken a "dive" into the abstract tendencies of painting. It implies that an artist's involvement with his work is a total commitment and a bold immersion into the creative, technical processes. According to What? (1964) features large areas of loosely painted orange-red, blue, and yellow, a narrow band of gray-toned circles, and the circular patterns of wooden slats rotated as devices. At the bottom is a painting attached to the canvas and seen from the back. It is a portrait of Marcel Duchamp with the title of Johns's painting written on it. At the top is one side of a chair cut down its middle and the cast of the side of a person's leg and hip as he sits in the chair. The question that is the title seemingly refers to Johns's ongoing search for meaning in art. (637 words)

(Excerpted from *https://search.credoreference.com/content/topic/johns_jasper_1930*)

新东方ACT课程指定用书

ACT
写作教程

新东方教育科技集团国外考试推广管理中心　编著

海豚出版社
DOLPHIN BOOKS
CIPG　中国国际出版集团

感谢以下老师为本教材的编写付出辛苦努力

刘烁炀	宋鹏昊	姚宇西	陈慧琳
史新竹	刁　爽	邹小苑	吕倩倩
栗　欣	田　甜	杜　鹃	贾思婕
王　雪			

1872 年的夏天，中国留学史正式拉开序幕。"中国留学之父"容闳组织了第一批幼童赴美留学。此后至 1875 年，清政府每年遴选 30 名少年渡洋深造，四年共派出 120 名。遥想当年，没人愿意出国留学，尚未开眼看世界的中国人，认为西方人是茹毛饮血的"蛮人"。接踵而来的战争惊醒沉醉于"天朝上国"迷梦的国人，留学热潮高涨。19 世纪末的留英法德热潮，20 世纪初的留日热潮，五四运动后的留法热潮，许多热血学子远渡重洋，吸取西方先进的社科文化。季羡林先生曾说过："对中国近代化来说，留学生可以比作报春鸟，比作普罗米修斯，他们的功绩是永存的。"如今，随着国力的增强，中产阶级日益壮大，普通百姓有条件把孩子送出去，接受更加完整、有创造意义的高等教育。然而历经沧桑始终不变的是，这些留学生的发展牵系着祖国的腾飞。新东方在历史的浪潮里，承担着一种使命，兢兢业业地助力一批又一批学子更高更远地飞翔。

看 2017 年教育部公布的数字，我们有 60.84 万多学生出国深造，其中出国留学攻读本科学历的学生占到了三成多。中国的父母越来越具备国际眼光，愿意摆脱高考的独木桥，给孩子更多的选择，更广阔的发展空间。我很高兴看到我们有越来越多优秀的同学走出国门，去到国外更广阔的世界。我一直鼓励学生们要多读书、多旅行、多交往、多思考，而出国留学，正是很好的实现自我的方式。现在的孩子日益展现出独立思考和奋发追求自己人生目标的能力。我认为 90 后、00 后及未来的 10 后，都凸显了我们这些老一代人没有的能力。他们更加有自己的判断力，有明确且卓越的志向。此外，他们大多很独立，愿意把所有的事情放到桌面上来谈，更加愿意主张自己的权利，更加愿意自觉地完善自己。就像无数位通过自身努力获得 SAT、ACT 考试高分的学生那样，他们都还那么年轻，却已经是国内最优秀的中学生。他们通过自己的努力考取了世界上最知名的高校，但学习优异并不是他们的全部，他们首先是立体的、丰富的人。他们的思想，他们对于世界的看法，对于理想的追求和执着，这一切不仅体现了新一代生生不息的生命力，而且为他们的同龄人提供了榜样的力量，这也让我们更加放心地让他们独自去更远、更加充满挑战的地方书写自己的精彩。

新东方倡导"终身学习，全球视野，独立人格"，真正的学习生涯，并不只是求知甚至是求成功的华山一条路，更应该求真求实，培养理性精神和健全人格。在越来越多的年轻人选择的留学之路上，新东方希望能提供最大的辅助，使更多的年轻人可以海阔天空施展自己的才华，可以热情专注研究自己的爱好，可以拓展自己的思维，可以好好阅读、争论、探究，让自己"独立之精神、自由之思想"开花结果。

俞敏洪

新东方教育科技集团董事长

前言
PREFACE

如何写出一篇好的文章?

相信翻开这本书的同学都是带着这样的问题而来的。作为一名写作老师,曾经有无数的同学问过我这个问题。结果经常是几个小时之后,同学们虽然满意而归,但我还是在反问自己:到底怎么能让所有人写好一篇文章?

其实我认为在没有任何前提的情况下讨论这个问题本身就是错误的。

大学在辩论队的时候,我们每次拿到一个新的辩题都会对它进行解构,只有把一句话"大卸八块"之后才会开始实质性的讨论。

按照这一思想,我觉得讨论"如何写出一篇好的文章"之前,我们要明确的是如何定义"好"的概念。

回到本书的主题:ACT。在诸多的北美考试中,ACT 考试一直以来是我最爱的一门考试。整个考试的很多考点是对学生快速理解和快速应用的能力的考查,在我看来真的是帮助学生开始铺垫大学应有的一些技能。而在我第一次为新的 ACT 写作备课的时候,我有一种绝望感,因为这个考试从评分标准来看简直是要求太高,几乎难以完成。

问题的核心:对于 ACT 写作来说,"好"不只是要有好的语言基础(Language Use)、好的文章结构(Organization)、好的逻辑发展(Development and Support),还要在文章思想和分析(Ideas and Analysis)上有所建树。

这最后一点恰中中国学生的要害。

"天下文章一大抄",这便是我在上学的时候对于写作的看法。

从小学开始,语文老师们推崇的无非是"华丽的辞藻"和"优美的语言",作为一个"直男癌晚期患者",我对于这些内容一直是嗤之以鼻。在我实在忍不住老师和家长的唠叨,拿起几本流行杂志之后,我发现那些被老师们夸赞的文章大多都是在借鉴他人之作。

其实这也没什么,有些文豪也是模仿出身。

大学第一次写科学论文的时候,全班都在一种恐慌之中。没人知道怎么写,更没人知道怎么写是好的。

"多看几篇别人的文章就好了,模仿模仿也就会了。"

导师们纷纷下了相似的方子。而我们,按方拿药,药到病除。

在"一分千金"的中高考中,创新的风险太大。宁可守拙中庸,不愿求新弄险。问题是当我们在模仿的同时，脑袋是变聪明了还是变空白了？

在 ACT 写作的思想和分析（Ideas and Analysis）面前，我们纷纷露出了原形。

本篇并不是说模仿不好，也不是说不能参照前人之作。毕竟本书本身就是一个素材库，供同学们参考、练习。前言放在这里，希望的是把我的建议给同学们，让同学们能更加有效地利用这本书。

问题不在于是否应该模仿，而是应该怎么模仿。

本书在话题章节中反复强调的通过阅读提高写作（Improve writing by reading）正是如何模仿的核心。基于阅读和背诵，通过模仿，达到创造的目的，这便是"模仿"一篇文章应该有的样子。模仿是必需的，但模仿并非机械地背诵与抄写，亦非简单改一两个词便可收工。模仿的核心在于创造；模仿的核心在于信而不尽信，形似而神异。

布鲁姆的认知理论正是本书的理论基础。我们必须经过记忆和理解（阅读与背诵）才能最后走到创造的金字塔尖。要注意的是，两者之间还有着应用、分析和评价三层，这三层就是我们平时忽视而写好 ACT 作文最为重要的内容。

对于 ACT 这种需要体现自己观点的文章，甚至是同学们以后需要写的文书，一篇好的文章是要有"灵魂"的。"好"在于言之有物，而所有的论证和语言都是为了凸显这一目的。写文章切勿仅仅以"考试"或"练习"为目的，每一篇文章都有一个想法值得传播，每一个段落都有一个观点值得阐述。只有意识到了这一点，ACT 作文才有可能写得"好"，我们的讨论才有意义。

而本书的作用，除了为大家解构 ACT 写作之外，更重要的是提供给大家足够的话题和内容来着手模仿。一方面学习好的写作手法和写作技巧，另一方面质疑这些文章，让自己不但能理解文章的出发点和逻辑，而且能由此得到自己对于这一话题的观点，并在自己模仿的文章中去传播自己的想法。

其实，此中的道理 ACT 写作在其题目的要求上已经非常明确了：

Analyze and evaluate multiple perspectives on a complex issue——阅读本书文章；

State and develop your own perspective on the issue；
Explain and support your ideas with logical reasoning and detailed examples；　　质疑文章并找
Clearly and logically organize your ideas in an essay；　　到自己的观点；

Effectively communicate your ideas in standard written English——模仿本书文章写法。

在我看来，这就是怎么写好一篇文章。

姚宇西

国外考试推广管理中心北美产品经理

自 2015 年 9 月改革之后，ACT 写作难度大幅度提升，要求考生辩证地思考社会话题，精确地分析其内涵及其延伸问题，并使用适当的论证方式和文体结构去支持自己的观点，让观点的表达连贯而富有逻辑。

从写作改革之初至今，ACT 写作的要求和分数计算都发生了变化，给广大考生带来了一定的不确定性。为了给考生学习和备考提供更多的素材，给教师备课和教学提供更多的参考，新东方国外考试推广管理中心出版了《ACT 写作教程》。这本书集结了新东方一线优秀教师的多年授课研发经验，从研究考试题库范畴、分析写作思路到深度研发内容，这本教程历经两年时间才成型出炉。

一、本书章节设置介绍

本书有三个章节，第一章节概述 ACT 写作，让初识 ACT 写作的考生认识写作；第二章节介绍写作结构和论证逻辑；第三章节介绍八个常见社会话题，分别是教育、工作、社会进步、个人选择、科技创新、环保、媒体、文娱艺术，涵盖了 ACT 写作话题。同时，本书也参考了 SAT 写作、TOEFL 独立写作以及 GRE 写作常考话题，所以本书的话题涵盖度大于 ACT 写作已考试题范围。

二、本书设计逻辑介绍

考生在初识 ACT 写作时，首先提出的问题是：ACT 写作是什么？考查什么能力？写作结构和逻辑是怎么样的？所以，本书在第一章节介绍了 ACT 写作的基本信息和评分标准，第二章节梳理了写作的结构和论证逻辑。

作为学术类考试，ACT 写作题目注重考查考生的思维能力，那么遇到常见的社会话题，考生又该如何去判断和思考，精确地分析其内涵及其延伸问题？如何建立并支持自己的观点？所以，本书第三章节把常见话题分了八类，每类话题的设计逻辑根据考生学习新知识的思维顺序和学习习惯来进行步骤设计。八个话题的具体章节大致设置为：

- **Topic Analysis**
- **Topic Vocabulary**
- **Extended Reading - Reference Article 1**

  Analysis of Article（Main Points ／ Pros and Cons ／ Key Words ／ Vocabulary ／ Read-Recite-Imitate-Create）

- **Extended Reading - Reference Article 2**

  Analysis of Article（Main Points ／ Pros and Cons ／ Key Words ／ Vocabulary ／ Read-Recite-Imitate-Create）

- **Prompt 1**

  Prompt Analysis

  Model Essay 1

    - Words
    - Phrases
    - Sentences

- **Prompt 2**

  Prompt Analysis

  Model Essay 2

　　其中"Topic Analysis"（话题分析）包括：本话题与考试的相关性、话题延伸、话题难度分级和对应的备考建议。"Topic Vocabulary"（话题词汇）涵盖了精心筛选的相关话题高频写作词汇。"Extended Reading"（拓展阅读）侧重于"meaning focused input"（语境素材输入），为学生更好的语言输出做准备。素材的解构包括观点分析、观点提炼、词句分析、词句仿写。最后到输出环节，我们对模拟题目写作步骤做分步操作拆解，从题目和观点的分析、范文的原创到范文的分析。

　　其实考生如果仔细阅读，可以发现本书有两条线：主线和辅线。主线按照话题来分，辅线着重把评分标准的每个纬度贯穿在八个话题里，比如范文的分析结合了评分纬度的思想和分析（Ideas and Analysis）、展开和支持（Development and Support）、组织结构（Organization）、语言的使用（Language Use），力求更好地满足考生备考和教师备课的需求。我们在各个环节帮助考生深度分析话题，严谨使用论证方式和结构，连贯而富有逻辑地表达观点，通过仿写习得地道的语言。

三、练习及素材使用说明

为了更好地解决考生们在考试中最常见的表达不熟练、多样性受限的问题，本书配备的章节练习分为词汇练习、翻译句子练习、篇章练习三个部分，为考生提供更多的演练素材，确保考生们能够最大程度地延伸练习和思考，举一反三。

为了更好地解决考生们在写作考试中无话可说、素材缺乏的问题，本书每个话题匹配十个素材篇章，选自出版物、国外期刊和网站等原汁原味的素材，让考生阅读地道的英语语言表述的篇章，为考生提供更多的写作语料，帮助考生更加自如地发挥。

四、使用方法和建议

本书是新东方 ACT 写作课程指定教材，体系科学且完整，有系统的分析和讲解，考生可咨询所在地新东方了解和报名线下课程。

本书同样适合自学，每个章节的学习时间为两小时，自学时需要注意分析章节的素材，思考模拟题，并主动完成写作任务。每个章节学习完，也需要完成其作业以及素材的学习任务。

我们希望本书成为 ACT 写作备考攻略全集，帮助 ACT 备考人群和 ACT 教师实现从入门到冲刺的"一站式"参考。

⭐ **注意：**

查看 ACT 考试的最新信息请前往 ACT 官网：www.act.org。

陈慧琳

actwriting@xdf.cn

国外考试推广管理中心 SAT/ACT 产品主管

目录
CONTENTS

第一章
ACT 写作概述

ACT 考试（American College Testing）被称为"美国高考"，是对考生综合能力的测试，分为英语、数学、阅读、科学推理和写作五个部分。虽然写作部分为选考，考生具有自主选择考试的权利，但是书面表达作为优质高校看重的重要技能，对帮助大学了解考生书面英语表述及分析能力有至关重要的作用。因此 ACT 写作在申请时的重要程度绝对不容小觑，也成为广大考生不容忽视的考试项目。

2015 年，ACT 写作部分进行了改革，由原来的单一观点论述改变为基于多观点进行剖析的议论文，话题范围也由原来的教育类话题改变为灵活多变的广泛话题。这些改变都对考生的思辨能力、表达的熟练程度以及书写速度提出了更高的要求，考生必须进行针对性的准备才能够取得理想的成绩。

I 基本信息

ACT 写作考试时间 40 分钟，评估考生的写作技能，尤其是高中课堂和大学入门写作课程所强调的写作技能。考试题目中会引入一个社会热点话题，并提供三个不同角度的看法供考生参考和思考。这三个观点可能持肯定态度、否定态度或中立态度。考生需要阅读并深入思考这三个观点，清晰陈述自己的观点，论证时能够至少和一个既定观点产生联系，完成一篇限时作文。官方没有提出具体的字数要求，但是就考试经验而言，在内容有效的情况下，字数越多越好。

题目示例

Multilingual Education

According to a new study by the Council on Foreign Relations, some eight in 10 Americans speak only English, and the number of schools teaching a foreign language is in decline. However, the opposite is true among our economic competitors. Additional languages are studied in European primary and secondary schools and are taken up by European college students in much larger numbers than in the United States. Should we encourage our citizens to pick up a different language? Since our nation is largely monolingual but is entering an increasingly multilingual world, it is highly significant to examine multilingual education closely.

Read and carefully consider these perspectives. Each suggests a particular way of thinking about multilingual education.

Perspective One	Perspective Two	Perspective Three
The country will not be able to keep pace—much less lead—global economy unless it moves to equip citizens with multilingual languages. Multilingual language boosts the competency of the nation.	Multilingual learning takes time away from other subjects. It hinders students' academic development.	Multilingual should be a choice rather than a requirement. Students should have their rights to choose what they want to learn in school.

Essay Task

Write a unified, coherent essay in which you evaluate multiple perspectives on multilingual education. In your essay, be sure to:

- clearly state your own perspective on the issue and analyze the relationship between your perspective and at least one other perspective
- develop and support your ideas with reasoning and examples
- organize your ideas clearly and logically
- communicate your ideas effectively in standard written English

Your perspective may be in full agreement with any of those given, in partial agreement, or completely different.

II 评分标准

　　ACT 写作阅卷人员会从四个维度对考生作文的总体质量进行评估，分别是：思想和分析（ideas and analysis）、展开和支持（development and support）、组织结构（organization）和语言的使用（language use）。同一篇考生作文由两个老师从这四个维度分别进行评分，每个维度的分数范围是 1～6，最终的写作得分是两个老师的评分相加而得到的。

Scoring Rubric	评分标准
Ideas and Analysis: • The argument critically engages with multiple perspectives on the given issue. • The argument's thesis reflects nuance and precision in thought and purpose. • The argument establishes an insightful context for analysis of the issue and its perspectives. • The analysis examines implications, complexities and tensions, and/or unyielding values and assumptions.	**思想和分析：** • 文章能就话题从多个角度进行辩证分析。 • 主旨句的表述清晰准确。 • 文章提供了论点成立的条件或背景。 • 文章仔细分析了问题的复杂性和可能产生的后果。
Development and Support: • Development of ideas and support for claims deepen insight and broaden context. • An integrated line of skillful reasoning and illustration effectively conveys the significance of the argument. • Qualifications and complications enrich and bolster ideas and analysis.	**展开和支持：** • 正文的展开使观点更深刻。 • 说理和举例的逻辑完整、严谨。 • 清晰地给出观点成立的限定条件，并且合理地预测可能产生的后果。
Organization: • The response is unified by a controlling idea or purpose. • A logical progression of ideas increases the effectiveness of the writer's argument. • Transitions between and within paragraphs strengthen the relationships among ideas.	**组织结构：** • 文章有明确的统领全文的观点。 • 思路的发展逻辑性强。 • 段内和段间的过渡使逻辑清晰、严谨。
Language Use: • Word choice is skillful and precise. • Sentence structures are consistently varied and clear. • While a few minor errors in grammar, usage, and mechanics may be present, they do not impede understanding.	**语言的使用：** • 用词有技巧、准确。 • 句型多样，表达清晰。 • 虽然存在一些语法错误，但不影响理解。

（6分）

（续）

	Scoring Rubric	评分标准
5分	**Ideas and Analysis:** • The argument productively engages with multiple perspectives on the given issue. • The argument's thesis reflects precision in thought and purpose. • The argument establishes and employs a thoughtful context for analysis of the issue and its perspectives. • The analysis addresses implications, complexities and tensions, and/or underlying values and assumptions.	**思想和分析：** • 文章能就话题从多个角度进行合理的分析。 • 主旨句的表述准确。 • 文章提供了论点成立的条件或背景较为合理。 • 文章提出了问题的复杂性和可能产生的后果。
	Development and Support: • Development of ideas and support for claims deepen understanding. • A mostly integrated line of purposeful reasoning and illustration capably conveys the significance of the argument. • Qualifications and complications enrich ideas and analysis.	**展开和支持：** • 正文的展开能进一步挖掘观点。 • 说理和举例紧扣题目。 • 能够给出观点成立的限定条件，并且预测可能产生的后果，使观点更丰富。
	Organization: • The response is mostly unified by a controlling idea or purpose. • A logical sequencing of ideas contributes to the effectiveness of the argument. • Transitions between and within paragraphs consistently clarify the relationships among ideas.	**组织结构：** • 文章绝大部分围绕中心思想展开。 • 思路的发展比较有逻辑性。 • 段内和段间的逻辑关系清晰。
	Language Use: • Word choice is precise. • Sentence structures are clear and varied often. • While minor errors in grammar, usage, and mechanics may be present, they do not impede understanding.	**语言的使用：** • 用词准确。 • 句型有一定的变化，表达清晰。 • 虽然存在一些语法错误，但不影响理解。

	Scoring Rubric	评分标准
4分	**Ideas and Analysis:** • The argument engages with multiple perspectives on the given issue. • The argument's thesis reflects clarity in thought and purpose. • The argument establishes and employs a relevant context for analysis of the issue and its perspectives. • The analysis recognizes implications, complexities and tensions, and/or underlying values and assumptions.	**思想和分析：** • 文章能就话题从多个角度进行分析。 • 主旨句的表述清晰。 • 文章提供了论点成立的相关条件或背景。 • 文章认识到了问题的复杂性和可能产生的后果。
	Development and Support: • Development of ideas and support for claims clarify meaning and purpose. • Lines of clear reasoning and illustration adequately convey the significance of the argument. • Qualifications and complications extend ideas and analysis.	**展开和支持：** • 正文的展开使观点更明确。 • 说理和举例的思路清晰。 • 能给出观点成立的限定条件，并且预测可能产生的后果。
	Organization: • The overall shape of the response reflects an emergent controlling idea or purpose. • Ideas are logically grouped and sequenced. • Transitions between and within paragraphs clarify the relationships among ideas.	**组织结构：** • 文章大体围绕中心思想展开。 • 思路的发展有一定的条理。 • 段内和段间的逻辑关系比较清晰。
	Language Use: • Word choice is adequate and sometimes precise. • Sentence structures are clear and demonstrate some variety. • While errors in grammar, usage, and mechanics are present, they rarely impede understanding.	**语言的使用：** • 用词有时候是准确的。 • 句型有一定多样性，表达清晰。 • 虽然存在一些语法错误，但不影响整体的理解。

Scoring Rubric	评分标准
Ideas and Analysis: • The argument responds to multiple perspectives on the given issue. • The argument's thesis reflects some clarity in thought and purpose. • The argument establishes a limited or tangential context for analysis of the issue and its perspectives. • Analysis is simplistic or somewhat unclear.	**思想和分析：** • 文章能从多个角度讨论给出的话题。 • 主旨句的表述较为清晰。 • 论点成立的条件或背景不是很贴切。 • 对话题的分析过于简单、不明确。
Development and Support: • Development of ideas and support for claims are mostly relevant but are overly general or simplistic. • Reasoning and illustration largely clarify the argument but may be somewhat repetitious or imprecise.	**展开和支持：** • 正文的展开大多是相关的，但都太过于笼统和简单。 • 说理和举例能适当地解释观点，但是有重复、絮叨的话或者切题性不够。
Organization: • The response largely coheres, with most ideas logically grouped. • Transitions between and within paragraphs sometimes clarify the relationships among ideas.	**组织结构：** • 思路的发展比较连贯，有一定的逻辑性。 • 有些段内和段间的逻辑关系比较清晰。
Language Use: • Word choice is general and occasionally imprecise. • Sentence structures are usually clear but show little variety. • Distracting errors in grammar, usage, and mechanics may be present, but they generally do not impede understanding.	**语言的使用：** • 用词比较笼统、不准确。 • 句型表达清晰，但缺少多样性。 • 一些语法错误会阻碍理解，但不影响整体的阅读。

3 分

Scoring Rubric	评分标准
Ideas and Analysis: • The argument weakly responds to multiple perspectives on the given issue. • The argument's thesis, if evident, reflects little clarity in thought and purpose. • Attempts at analysis are incomplete, largely irrelevant, or consist primarily of restatement of this issue and its perspectives.	**思想和分析：** • 文章没能从多个角度对话题进行分析。 • 主旨句的表述不清晰。 • 分析不完整或跑题，或者只是对话题和题目中给出的分论点进行复述。
Development and Support: • Development of ideas and support for claims are weak, confused, or disjointed. • Reasoning and illustration are inadequate, illogical, or circular, and fail to fully clarify the argument.	**展开和支持：** • 正文没有围绕观点展开或者干脆跑题。 • 说理和举例太少且缺乏逻辑性，或者出现逻辑断层。
Organization: • Grouping of ideas is inconsistent and often unclear. • Transitions between and within paragraphs are misleading or poorly formed.	**组织结构：** • 思路发展不清晰。 • 段内和段间的逻辑关系不明确。
Language Use: • Word choice is rudimentary and frequently imprecise. • Sentence structures are sometimes unclear. • Distracting errors in grammar, usage, and mechanics are present, and they sometimes impede understanding.	**语言的使用：** • 只有基本的词汇量，而且大多时候用词不准确。 • 句子结构不清楚。 • 语法错误很明显，有时候会影响理解。
Ideas and Analysis: • The argument responds intelligibly to the task. • The writer's intentions are difficult to discern. • Attempts at analysis are unclear or irrelevant.	**思想和分析：** • 文章没有针对话题进行讨论。 • 主旨不明确。 • 分析不清楚或者跑题。

（表格左侧：上半部分为 "2分"，下半部分为 "1分"）

（续）

	Scoring Rubric	评分标准
1 分	**Development and Support:** • Ideas lack development, and claims lack support. • Reasoning and illustration are unclear, incoherent, or largely absent.	**展开和支持：** • 没有展开观点。 • 说理和举例不明确、跑题，或者根本没有进行说理或举例。
	Organization: • There is little grouping of ideas. • When present, transitional devices fail to connect ideas.	**组织结构：** • 思路没有组织在一起。 • 段内和段间缺乏逻辑关系。
	Language Use: • Word choice is imprecise and often difficult to comprehend. • Sentence structures are often unclear. • Errors in grammar, usage, and mechanics are pervasive and often impede understanding.	**语言的使用：** • 用词不准确，而且很难理解。 • 句子结构不清楚。 • 语法错误太多，影响理解。

III 篇章结构

常见的 ACT 考场作文是五段论，“开头段 + 三个主体段落 + 结尾段”，开头段清晰提出观点，主体段阐明至少和一个既定观点的联系，结尾段总结并重申观点。下面的这篇作文，是一篇较典型的考场作文。

Stepping into a worldwide economy, America has unavoidably become more of a melting pot where colors blend together. Languages start to show their significance as the passports on this international stage. Although conservatives still deem “American-centered world” patronizingly, more nations have put emphasis on multilingual education. In this aspect, Americans seem to be put at a disadvantage for inadequate investment in multilingual learning. As far as I am concerned, multilingual capability is highly indispensable for Americans to outcompete other nations, both on campus and for economy.

开头段：“社会背景＋反方观点＋作者观点”，这样的开篇方式非常容易模仿和展开思路。通过介绍现在美国社会发展的现状以及多语种在社会发展中的作用，引出一些持保守意见者的看法。突出多语言学习的重要性后，引出自己的观点。需要注意的是，任何

Some educators contend that it is students' right to choose what they should learn, including multilingual learning. Truly, American education does endow students with greater freedom of curriculum choices based on interests. However, immature students have no adequate insight to foresee the qualities needed after they enter the workforce and either awareness to well equip themselves with well-rounded abilities. Sometimes they shall shy away from challenging subjects like a second language and lean more on easier ones. It is educators' responsibility to guide students toward more socially-adaptive courses. Multilingual subjects are definitely one of those.

第一个主体段：针对 Perspective Three 进行具体论述。需要注意的是 Perspective Three 是个中立观点，文中可以支持也可以反对，关键是看这个分论点能够如何对文章的总观点做出贡献。显然，作者在这里进行了批判性思考，首先承认美国教育赋予学生的课程自由，但是从学生的特点出发，否认了对于学生主动迎难而上的美好期待。本段以议论为主，没有涉及例子，这样的论证方式没有问题。但是需要在其他段落中体现不同的论证方式，例证结合。最终文章的分数是建立在整篇的论证基础上。

The other heated controversy the public mainly focuses on is whether multilingual learning takes away time from other subjects, hindering students' academic development. It seems that students now face mountainous burdens in their daily life and one more additional subject would be the last straw. Nevertheless, never should people underestimate students' potential. With fully utilized schedule and proper guidance, students can better handle pressure between subjects. What's more, studies show that learning additional languages improves one's ability to focus, plan and solve problems. This means that such students are better able to move efficiently from one subject to another. A recent research by University of Georgia concluded that bilingual students perform better on SAT than their monolingual peers. These multilingual students outperformed their peers throughout their scholastic careers. Thus, why not encourage more students to involve in multilingual education?

第二个主体段：回应 Perspective Two，这是典型的驳论段落。驳论即引出反方观点，并予以针对性反驳，解决对方的疑问和质疑。本段首先从人们日常的错误假设出发，再引出多语种的学习对于学生学术表现的积极意义，并通过研究予以证明。我们通常并不能够在考场的有限时间内真正快速找到可以利用的学术研究，这就需要在日常练习的过程中，熟悉并模仿调查报告或研究（research/study）的写作方法，并能较完整且高效地在考场上完成调查报告或研究构建。

Moreover, multilingual learning yields benefits beyond the classroom. Our nation is largely monolingual but is entering an increasingly multilingual world. When students graduate, a lack of fluency in a second language dims their career prospects. They need to engage in intense communication with their economic competitors. Mastering a second language adds to their advantages and promotes them to be the most-sought-after-employees. Multilingual students will be more shinning among their counterparts and their performance will also contribute more to the thriving of America economy. The University of Florida study has revealed that in large cities such as Miami, the second-language ability brings in more than $7,000 of increased annual income. Access to a second language truly leads to access to more opportunities both for individual development and for local economy.

第三个主体段： 对 Perspective One 进行展开和支持。展开和支持（development and support）是评分标准中非常重要也是很多考生在写作中不好把握的一项。日常练习除了积累表达，还要重视思路的线性发展，能够较丰满、充实地完成推理和举例（reason and example）。本段论证为什么学习多语种能够对学生未来发展及美国社会经济发展产生直接关系，这对应了本文总观点中的 "indispensable both on campus and for economy"，并利用数据完成了对于分论点的支撑。

Despite of the increasing academic pressure and higher expectation on this generation, it is highly worthy for both the young and the elders to pick up one more language. As more foreign competitors crowd into American society and more Americans seek for abroad job opportunities, mastering more languages will definitely demonstrate striking advantages for people.

结尾段： "总结分论点 + 重申观点" 是非常推荐的收尾方式，按照这个思路可以对上文进行总结并有效呼应开头。日常练习注意开头和结尾的快速练习，争取考试的时候留更多时间给中间段落思考和展开。

第二章
ACT 写作
段落开展方法

　　开头段是彰显思路和实力的第一段，要求考生清晰地表明观点。大多数考生在开头段中经常遇到的问题是：（1）不知如何下笔，也不知道开头段写多长为宜。限时情况下，比较理想的状况是用4～5分钟迅速完成开头段写作，3～4句话为宜，这就要求考生在备考时掌握擅长使用的开头段方法。（2）观点表述不清晰。整篇文章都是观点的延伸，观点一定要清晰准确，能够呈现本篇文章议论的中心，且不引起歧义。

例1：Background + Opposite Views + Thesis Statement

Although human society has been advancing at a turbo-charged rate in science, technology, education, medicine and agriculture, poverty still scourges hundreds of millions of people on the earth. Some people argue that it is absolutely unrealistic for people to live in a world with no poverty, while others reason that it is one's own responsibility and diligence that keep him or her out of poverty. **However, I am firmly convinced that only when governments establish a fair social and political system can poverty be truly eliminated.**（选自第三章"社会进步类"话题 Model Essay 1，P86）

　　本段中，作者首先展示现在社会飞速发展的同时，贫穷依旧根深蒂固。然后展示反方的两个观点：（1）贫穷的绝对消失是不现实的；（2）人们有义务通过自我的努力脱贫。最后，作者阐释自己的观点：只有政府建立公正的社会和政治系统，贫穷才能真正消除。

例2：Background + Problems + Thesis Statement

The popularity of the technology has freed human from repetitive and boring tasks, as more tasks are completed by machines instead of humans. The awareness of the effects caused by the technology makes us focus on not only what we can do with machines, but also the negative influence caused by the popularity of technology, especially on the environment. **Although the usage of technology increases our standard of living to some extent, it detracts us from the value of environment.**（选自第三章"环保类"话题 Model Essay 1，P166）

　　本段中，作者首先展现科技的发展将人们从重复无聊的劳动中解脱出来的现实，接着提出问题，即人们开始思考科技的发展是否有消极后果。最后阐述观点：科技虽然提升生活品质，但是也给环境带来了负面影响。

II 主体段例证开展方法

主体段落的逻辑展开是考试时限时写作的难点，也是评分标准中展开和支持（development and support）的重点得分项。常见的主体段落议论开展方法有举例论证、因果论证、对比论证和驳论，考生们需要在考前较熟悉地掌握这些议论开展的方式，找到自己比较擅长的议论方法。

1. 例证 Exemplification

举例论证即用例子去支持观点（claim），常用结构：Topic Sentence（主题句）+ Explanation（解释）+ Example（举例）。例子可以选用来源于历史、时事、文学或生活中的人物和事件，例子的结构可以采取独立的一个例子、平行的两个或三个例子。

例 1：Topic Sentence + Explanation + Example

Since music can play individuals' sentiments in such a credible manner, it can also help create a social tendency when many individuals are subject to the same ideas embedded in music. Music can infiltrate people with some ideas or values to enhance or even create social tendencies. **A recent incident of Chinese community protesting against racial discrimination in YG's song serves as very potent evidence. YG disseminates in his song "Meet the Flockers", a very dangerous direction to rob the Chinese Americans. Surely, the song reflects crimes happening in Chinese community, but what's sinful about it is that the song turns what is a secret within some robbers into a public knowledge, which reinforces the stereotype about Chinese Americans and encourages people, especially immature underage boys, to emulate the shameful deed. It is reported that the song has actually created a crazy trend to break in Chinese shops and houses.** While this racial violence results from a series of factors, value-carrying music clearly plays a role in this trend.（选自第三章"文娱艺术类"话题 Model Essay 3，P261）

本段中，主题句（topic sentence）明确写出该段分论点，即音乐能够引导社会趋势。第二句话进行简单的解释。接下来用"a recent incident of...serves as very potent evidence"引出例子。最后一句话进行总结：音乐的确可以创造社会趋势。优秀例子的关键是让细节紧紧围绕关键词展开。本段的关键词是主题句（topic sentence）中的"music""create"和"social tendency"。该例子说明一首歌会影响人们的认知和行为，并且掀起一股流行趋势。

例2：Topic Sentence + Explanation + Parallel Examples

Thus, both being pragmatic and idealistic can help people succeed in different ways. It is no overstatement to say that almost all the successful people have idealistic vision and pragmatic behaviors. The combination of the two values complement each other and benefit people every time when they keep trying hard. **Nelson Mandela could not survive his 27 years in prison without the dream of eliminating racism; also, he focused on dismantling the legacy of apartheid by fostering racial reconciliation. Likewise, Elon Musk could be cast in the sea of commerce without the dream of changing the world and humanity; also, he worked intensely on numerous experiments on reducing global warming through sustainable energy production and consumption. Michael Jordan could not create a basketball legend without his goal to prove himself; also, he spent thousands of hours practicing on the playground to strive for prolific scoring.** （选自第三章"个人选择类"话题 Model Essay 1，P117）

本段中，作者使用了三个小例子的平行，呈现不同领域的成功人士都是既具备实用性又拥有理想主义的梦想。三个例子通过虚拟论证和对比，有效地引导读者得出结论，证明自己的分论点。这样的例证手法不仅可以对分论点形成依托，还能够增强文章的气势和文采，同时不会对例证细节要求过高，因此考生可以在考场上快速构思写出。这是很实用的例子写法，值得考生学习。

2. 因果论证 Cause-Effect

因果论证中，通过展示事情发生的因果关系，清晰地引出结论。常用结构：Topic Sentence（主题句）+ Cause-Effect（因果）。

例1：Topic Sentence + Cause-Effect

When it comes to academics, students who we would consider pragmatic tend not to pursue an education for its own sake. Instead, they tend to cut whatever corners are needed to optimize their grade average and survive the current academic term. But, is this approach the only way to succeed academically? Certainly not. **Students who earnestly pursue intellectual paths that truly interest them are more likely to come away with a meaningful and lasting education. In fact, a sense of mission about one's area of fascination is strong motivation to participate actively in class and to study earnestly, both of which contribute to better grades in that area. Thus, although the idealist-student might sacrifice a high overall grade average, the depth of knowledge,**

academic discipline, and sense of purpose the student gains will serve that student well later in life.

(Excerpted from *GRE CAT Answers to the Real Essay Questions, by Mark Alan Stewart, J.D., 2008*)

　　本段中，作者通过因果论证支持自己的分论点。作者论证了不是仅抱有实用主义态度的学生的学习态度。因为他们更加注重有意义的和持久的教育影响，他们拥有强烈的使命感和对学科的兴趣，所以参与度更高、学习更加积极。通过因果关系的建立和描述，作者得出结论，理想主义的学生可能暂时会牺牲一些目前的分数，但是他们的长期学术表现将更加出色。这样便有效地印证了作者的分论点：实用主义不是学术成功的唯一路径。

例2：Topic Sentence + Cause-Effect + Example

On the one hand, hobbies play an essential role in a person's career development because they are the intrinsic momentum that propels a person to strive for more accomplishments. **Further, owing to the inborn intuition for a certain scope, one is motivated to learn more, therefore contributing even further to the chances of success.** A great amount of evidence from daily life and, on a larger scale, human history supports that hobbies formed in early childhood dictate how a person develops in terms of the sphere of knowledge or technique related to the area of hobbies. Usually, one's passion for a certain field provides the most fruitful direction for his or her later career. For instance, Mozart, the musician started as a musical prodigy, after which he wound up a successful composer due to his passion for music and consistent training as well. This case lessons that the more you feel passionate for what you do, the more proficient and successful you will become. （选自第三章"工作类"话题 Model Essay 1，P61）

　　本段中，作者在议论部分使用了因果论证的方式，再用例子做了进一步的支撑。作者通过指出一个人内在动力对外在行为的驱动作用，支持分论点"爱好在人们的职业发展中起着重要的作用"。因果论证能够最直接地展现分论点中建立的因果联系，非常简洁。

3. 对比论证 Contrast

例1：Topic Sentence + Contrast + Example

Indeed, all work demands people's efforts, but never is there only one way that promises success. **When it comes to pragmatic people, they accept who they are and do things for their own sake. While idealistic people are unsatisfied with themselves and** try harder to reach a higher level. **For the former people, down-to-earth work ensures safety but cuts whatever corners, while for the latter people, they willingly embrace challenges thus have a higher likelihood of becoming the spark that ignites others.** Born with no legs and arms, the Australian motivational speaker Nick Vujicic dares to do all things that normal people do, surfing in the sea, riding an elephant, and even kicking the ball with professional football players. Not content with physical capability, he founded an international non-profit organization Life Without Limbs to help more people to regain tremendous confidence. Had he been a pragmatic person, he would have just lain in sofa and waited for help. Nevertheless, his idealistic dream to be a better man saved and reshaped him to be a role model who concerned with millions of physically disadvantaged people.（选自第三章"个人选择类"话题 Model Essay 1，P115）

本段中，作者采用对比论证来证明"不是仅有一种路径能够帮助人们取得成功"。作者先论证实用主义的人注重眼前利益，再论证理想主义的人不满足于自我，不断挑战更高的水平和难度，接着进一步分析实用主义的人这样做是走捷径来确保暂时的安逸，最后对比理想主义者会乐于拥抱挑战，然而更有机会取得成功。这样鲜明的论证角度能够帮助读者迅速通过对比得出结论，进而认同作者的观点。

例2: Topic Sentence + Contrast Examples + Conclusion

Apart from destroying people's academic life by baffling them, technological advance in communication encroaches on basic human interactions. **15 years ago, without high-tech products, my uncle Murphy, a senior engineer, would chat with his colleagues about current fairs like the skyrocketing price of 93# and 97# gas or soaring stock market during the noon break or after work. Moreover, they would exchange their ideas of educating the next generation and share the most exhilarating parts in their life like raising up a daughter. Obviously, because people back that time did not possess advanced products like iPhone and Microsoft Surface, not to mention the social networking applications like Line, an Asian counterpart of Facebook. The communication without the assistance of modern technology, actually, kept their lives simple and happy. On the contrary, 15 years later when my cousin Breton, who is an engineer in an international company, has lunch with his coworkers, they neither see each other's eyes nor communicate with each other. Instead, they just keep lowering heads, texting back and forth, and updating their Facebook and Twitter to find out how many "likes" they get from their last posting picture of the Beef Wellington. In** this sense, even though advanced products like iPhone could allow individuals to have a closer contact with people in the virtual world, they gradually deprive them of face-to-face communication. Accordingly, technologies designed for connecting friends, unfortunately, have weakened their relationships and have made their communication and interaction more superficial. （选自第三章"科技创新类"话题 Model Essay 1，P143）

本段中，作者通过对比 15 年前父亲日常沟通的情况和 15 年后科技发展对父亲生活的影响，自然地引出结论：科技已经影响了人们的日常交往，并极大地减少了人与人之间的交流机会。

4. 驳论 Counterargument

驳论中，先对相反的观点做一个让步，即引出对方观点并承认对方观点中看似合理的方面，然后再针对性反驳对方的观点。驳论展示作者对一个话题仔细和有逻辑的考量，能够展示作者的思辨，让作者观点更加公正地得到认同。

例 1：Concession + Rebuttal + Conclusion

As for Perspective Two, I concede that there are plenty of job opportunities, and in normal circumstances, those who are self-responsible and self-disciplined can work their way out of poverty if they are industrious. The supporters of this perspective claim that people are poor and jobless because of their own laziness or inadequacies. **They may sound right in their assertions, but they fail to reflect on how the external forces, such as discrimination in employment market, a lack of economic opportunity, and failed public education, adversely affect the socially and financially disadvantaged, thereby dampening their drive to seek better opportunities.** In the words of Dr. William Julius Wilson, a world-renowned professor in sociology at Harvard University, "policy makers indirectly contributed to concentrated poverty in inner-city neighborhoods with decisions that decreased the attractiveness of low-paying jobs and accelerated the relative decline in low-income workers' wages." Without access to good education or equal employment opportunities, how can the disadvantaged and marginalized work their way out of impoverishment? Thus, I disagree with Perspective Two for its subjectivity and one-sidedness. （选自第三章"社会进步类"话题 Model Essay 1，P87）

本段中，作者首先承认在正常情况下那些自我负责和自律的人通过勤奋工作可以摆脱贫穷，也把该观点的理由呈现出来，然后再去反驳。作者再次强调是外在的因素，比如职业市场的歧视、工作机会的匮乏、失败的美国公立学校的教育对本来就在社会和经济地位处于劣势的穷人带来负面的影响。作者用世界著名的哈佛大学的社会学教授威廉·朱利叶斯·威尔逊博士（Dr. William Julius Wilson）的一本书里的一句话来增加文章论点的说服力。最后在结尾句再次表明自己的立场，因为 Perspective Two 的主观性和片面性而不赞同它。

例2：Concession + Rebuttal + Example

People may claim that celebrities gain so much from the society and naturally should shoulder more stress from the society, including the risk of privacy exposure. This claim is not convincing. Truly, celebrities enjoy better lives and access to more resources than normal people. However, what people often ignore is their hard work behind screens. Celebrities win over support not because of their private life, but because of their ceaseless devotion to careers. Celebrities have to pay arduous efforts to secure their social status and reputation. Hence, overdue attention to celebrities' privacy will distract people from recognizing the valuable endeavors. When Michael Jackson was criticized of mistreating the little boy, nearly all the media denied Michael's previous efforts and treated him so meanly that it hardly tried to see the justice behind this made-up accuse. （选自第三章"媒体类"话题 Model Essay 2，P198）

本段中，作者先引出对方观点，即"celebrities gain so much from the society and naturally should shoulder more stress from the society, including the risk of privacy exposure（名人理应承担更大压力，包括公众对于他们隐私的过度关注，因为他们从社会中获取得太多了）"，接着开展有力的反驳：名人成功的背后付出了巨大的努力，不应被公众理所应当地消费，因此公众对名人隐私的过度关注会忽略名人的真正贡献，最后通过迈克尔·杰克逊的例子，呼吁人们理性对待名人隐私。

III 结尾段开展方法

作文进行到结尾段落，时间已经所剩不多了。建议考生在2～3分钟内迅速收尾，2～3句话为宜，完成作文的总结部分。

例：Conclusion + Restate Opinion

To conclude, although poverty is pervasive all over the world and it is one's own obligation to fight against poverty, only when governments establish social equality can the life of the less fortunate be truly transformed. **Therefore**, it is incumbent on the governments to build a fair social and political system to eradicate poverty.（选自第三章"社会进步类"话题 Model Essay 1，P89）

请阅读下面题目，并完成相关练习。

Multilingual Education

According to a new study by the Council on Foreign Relations, some eight in 10 Americans speak only English, and the number of schools teaching a foreign language is in decline. However, the opposite is true among our economic competitors. Additional languages are studied in European primary and secondary schools and are taken up by European college students in much larger numbers than in the United States. Should we encourage our citizens to pick up a different language? Since our nation is largely monolingual but is entering an increasingly multilingual world, it is highly significant to examine multilingual education closely.

Read and carefully consider these perspectives. Each suggests a particular way of thinking about multilingual education.

Perspective One	Perspective Two	Perspective Three
The country will not be able to keep pace—much less lead—global economy unless it moves to equip citizens with multilingual languages. Multilingual language boosts the competency of the nation.	Multilingual learning takes time away from other subjects. It hinders students' academic development.	Multilingual should be a choice rather than a requirement. Students should have their rights to choose what they want to learn in school.

Essay Task
Write a unified, coherent essay in which you evaluate multiple perspectives on multilingual education. In your essay, be sure to: • clearly state your own perspective on the issue and analyze the relationship between your perspective and at least one other perspective • develop and support your ideas with reasoning and examples • organize your ideas clearly and logically • communicate your ideas effectively in standard written English Your perspective may be in full agreement with any of those given, in partial agreement, or completely different.

根据你所学到的关于开头段、主体段和结尾段的开展方法，完成下面内容开展：

Introduction: _____

_____

_____

_____

Topic Sentence 1: _____

Support 1: _____

_____

_____

_____

_____

Topic Sentence 2: _____

Support 2: _____

_____

_____

_____

_____

Topic Sentence 3: _____

Support 3: _____

_____

_____

_____

_____

Ending: _____

_____

_____

_____

参考范文

Stepping into a worldwide economy, America has unavoidably become more of a melting pot where colors blend together. Languages start to show their significance as the passports on this international stage. Although conservatives still deem "American-centered world" patronizingly, more nations have put emphasis on multilingual education. In this aspect, Americans seem to be put at a disadvantage for inadequate investment in multilingual learning. As far as I am concerned, multilingual capability is highly indispensable for Americans to outcompete other nations, both on campus and for economy.

Some educators contend that it is students' right to choose what they should learn, including multilingual learning. Truly, American education does endow students with greater freedom of curriculum choices based on interests. However, immature students have no adequate insight to foresee the qualities needed after they enter the workforce and either awareness to well equip themselves with well-rounded abilities. Sometimes they shall shy away from challenging subjects like a second language and lean more on easier ones. It is educators' responsibility to guide students toward more socially-adaptive courses. Multilingual subjects are definitely one of those.

The other heated controversy the public mainly focuses on is whether multilingual learning takes away time from other subjects, hindering students' academic development. It seems that students now face mountainous burdens in their daily life and one more additional subject would be the last straw. Nevertheless, never should people underestimate students' potential. With fully utilized schedule and proper guidance, students can better handle pressure between subjects. What's more, studies show that learning additional languages improves one's ability to focus, plan and solve problems. This means that such students are better able to move efficiently from one subject to another. A recent research by University of Georgia concluded that bilingual students perform better on SAT than their monolingual peers. These multilingual students outperformed their peers throughout their scholastic careers. Thus, why not encourage more students to involve in multilingual education?

Moreover, multilingual learning yields benefits beyond the classroom. Our nation is largely monolingual but is entering an increasingly multilingual world. When students graduate, a lack of fluency in a second language dims their career prospects.

They need to engage in intense communication with their economic competitors. Mastering a second language adds to their advantages and promotes them to be the most-sought-after-employees. Multilingual students will be more shinning among their counterparts and their performance will also contribute more to the thriving of America's economy. The University of Florida study has revealed that in large cities such as Miami, the second-language ability brings in more than $7,000 of increased annual income. Access to a second language truly leads to access to more opportunities both for individual development and for local economy.

Despite of the increasing academic pressure and higher expectation on this generation, it is highly worthy for both the young and the elders to pick up one more language. As more foreign competitors crowd into American society and more Americans seek for abroad job opportunities, mastering more languages will definitely demonstrate striking advantages for people.

第三章
ACT 写作话题
分类

话题一　　教育类

Topic Analysis

　　教育类话题和考生们息息相关，一直是改革前的 ACT、改革后的 ACT 和改革后的 SAT 写作关注的热门考点。改革前的 ACT 写作题目大量围绕教育类话题开展；在改革后的 ACT 写作中，教育类话题依旧火热，考试出现过的话题分别为校园运动（athletics）、理工科教育（STEM education）和大小学校对比（larger schools）。这一类的话题考生们应该非常熟悉，难度不大，写起来不会无话可说。关键是要言之有物，联系自身学习和环境，关注热点的教育现象。考生们在准备教育类话题时，可以从校园学习生活、学生（或教师）行为和价值观及未来就业入手，多方面地进行话题讨论和思维拓展。

Topic Vocabulary

impart knowledge 传授知识

expand one's knowledge 扩大知识

extracurricular activities 课外活动

academic performance 学业表现

slack off 懈怠

a healthy/positive outlook on life 对生活的一种健康的、积极的人生观

academic attainment 学术造诣

elective courses and compulsory courses 选修课程和必修课程

promote the students' psychological well-being 促进学生心理健康

comprehensive coverage of sth. 全面覆盖

self-paced education 自学

well-adjusted adults 自我调节能力好的成人

fulfill one's responsibilities 履行自己的职责

study intensively 深入研究

repress individuality 压抑个性

rote memorization 死记硬背

use lateral thinking 运用横向思维

follow sth. indiscriminately 盲从

generalist 通才

versatile 全面的

lack self-discipline 缺乏自律

be proficient in 精通的

be well-acquainted with 熟悉的

stifle one's creativity 压抑创造力

sharpen one's intellect 发挥一个人的才智

develop expertise in 培养专业知识

a good conscience 良心

absorb the quintessence 吸收精髓

be emotionally detrimental 情感上受伤害的

cut-throat competition 恶性竞争

differentiate virtue from evil 明辨是非

disrespectful and undisciplined behavior 不敬和散漫的行为

juvenile delinquency 未成年人犯罪

live an indolent life 过着懒散的生活

maintain the continuity of learning 保持学习的连续性

mature and sustained commitment 成熟的和持续性的承诺

rebellious and aggressive action 叛逆和激进

Extended Reading

Reference Article 1: Repeal a Ban on Bilingual Education

1 The state Senate voted Tuesday to ask California voters to repeal a ban on bilingual education in the state, saying children in other countries are successfully learning multiple languages.

2 The senate voted to put a measure on the ballot in November 2016 that would repeal major parts of Proposition 227, the 1998 ballot measure approved by voters that requires schools to teach in English.

3 "Children who participate in multilingual programs not only outperform their peers, they also have higher earning potential when they enter the workforce," said Sen. Ricardo Lara (D-Bell Gardens), who authored SB 1174. The bill was approved 27 to 8 and next goes to the Assembly for consideration. He called the status quo "linguistic tyranny, where we [politicians] decide what language our kids are going to learn."

4 The bill divided Republicans, with Senate GOP leader Bob Huff of Diamond Bar supporting the measure for giving school districts local control "so innovation can take place." But eight other Republicans, including Sen. Jim Nielsen of Gerber, voted against the bill, saying it would worsen the state's high drop-out rate, which is partly caused by a large number of students being unable to read and understand English.

5 "You are putting children out who are functionally illiterate in two languages," Nielsen said of bilingual education. "English is the common language of this country. It is how we do business all over the world." Sen. Mark Wyland (R-Escondido) also voted against the bill. "I can't take the chance that a single child's life will be compromised in any way by a lack of fluency in English," he said. (271 words)

(Excerpted from *Senate supports asking voters to repeal ban on bilingual education, by Patrick McGreevy, May 27, 2014. Los Angeles Times.*)

Analysis of Article

Pros of Bilingual Education and Cons of English-only Education

Bilingual education will improve students' academic performance at school.

Bilingual education increases students' chance of earning more money in the workplace.

English-only education reflects linguistic tyranny, leaving students no right of deciding what language(s) they will study.

Cons of Bilingual Education

Dual-language education will generate more Limited English Proficient (LEP) students, and consequently increase the drop-out rate.

Key Word: "California Proposition 227 (1998)"

Proposition 227 was passed in 1998, and it changed the way that "Limited English Proficient" (LEP) students are taught in California. Specifically, it

---

- Requires California public schools to teach LEP students in special classes that are taught nearly all in English. This provision had the effect of eliminating "bilingual" classes in most cases.
- Shortens the time most LEP students stay in special classes.
- Proposition 227 eliminated most programs in the state that provided multi-year special classes to LEP students by requiring that (1) LEP students should move from special classes to regular classes when they have acquired a good working knowledge of English and (2) these special classes should not normally last longer than one year.
- Required the state government to provide $50 million every year for ten years for English classes for adults who promise to tutor LEP students.

The bill's intention was to educate Limited English proficiency students in a rapid, one-year program, but in the meantime, the methods of education enacted by the proposition reflect the electorate's support of assimilation over multiculturalism. It was repealed by Proposition 58 on November 8, 2016.

Vocabulary

bilingual *adj.* 双语的

multilingual *adj.* 多种语言的

outperform *v.* 做得比……好

illiterate *adj.* 文盲的，不识字的

have higher learning potential 有更高的学习潜力

enter the workforce 进入职场

linguistic tyranny 语言暴政

fluency *n.* 流利

Improve Writing by Reading

写作就像艺术创造一样，水平不好的作者只会简单直接地抄袭（copy）别人的作品，但是好的作家会善于发现别人作品的精华，善于借鉴和提取（steal）精华。伟大的作家就像伟大的艺术家一样可以把从别人作品中提取的精华融会贯通（shape）到自己的作品中。所以，必须要先成为一个好的阅读者，你才能成为一个好的作者。有充足的高质量阅读材料的输入，才能在写作中有出彩的输出。

在此，作者把如何通过阅读来提升写作归纳为四个步骤，Read（阅读）—Recite（背诵）—Imitate（模仿）—Create（创造），请参考以下对这四个步骤的定义及演示的例子。

1. Read：不仅读懂信息，更重要的是体会语言本身，体会英语作为母语的人如何用英文表达自己的思想，如何用词。

2. Recite：背诵用得出彩的词，尤其是动词、词组、句型和有深刻思想的句子。

3. Imitate：想象一个语境去模仿使用提取的词、词组、句型等，模仿一遍胜过死记硬背十遍。

4. Create：把从别人作品中提取的精华融会贯通到自己的写作中。

Read-Recite-Imitate-Create

Example one:

1. Read: Children who participate in multilingual programs not only outperform their peers, they also have higher earning potential when they enter the workforce.（从阅读文章中提取词组）

2. Recite: **enter the workforce**（背诵提取的词组）

3. Imitate: We cannot expect students readily adapt to the working environment when they **enter the workforce** without proper guidance on career preparation.（模仿使用提取的词组）

4. Create: However, immature students have no adequate insight to foresee the qualities needed after they **enter the workforce** and either awareness to well equip themselves with well-rounded abilities.（把所提取的词组应用在写作中 Model Essay 1）

Example two:

1. Read: I can't take the chance that a single child's life will be compromised in any way by a lack of fluency in English.

2. Recite: **a lack of fluency in**...

3. Imitate: We are surprised to find **a lack of fluency in** his native language after so many years since he left his homeland.

4. Create: When students graduate, **a lack of fluency in** a second language dims their career prospects.

Reference Article 2: Weigh Restoring Bilingual Education in Public Schools

1 Ricardo Lara was in college when California voters approved a law that required public school students to speak and learn only in English. It was a debate, the now-state-senator remembers, that was tainted with racial undertones. "There was a lot of shame cast on us," said Lara (D-Bell Gardens). "There was a clear sentiment that we were somehow different and un-American because we were Spanish speakers." For the children of Mexican immigrants such as him, who had gone through bilingual education programs and valued their immersion in two languages and cultures, Lara said it was upsetting.

2 Proposition 58 supporters remember what they called the racial undertones of the 1998 law. Proposition 227 came just four years after Proposition 187, which sought to prohibit immigrants who were illegally in the country from access to public benefits. (The measure passed but was ultimately deemed unconstitutional.) In between the two contentious campaigns was the 1996 passage of Proposition 209, which outlawed affirmative action programs.

3 Now on the Nov. 8 ballot, almost two decades later, is a measure that seeks to overhaul that law. Proposition 58, the product of 2014 legislation written by Lara, would repeal English-only instruction in public schools, giving local parents and teachers the control to develop their own multilingual programs.

4 Supporters argue the bureaucratic red tape on bilingual and multilingual education is harmful to students in a global economy, where the most-sought-after employees speak more than one language. "Prop. 58 is long overdue," said Eric Heins, president of the California Teachers Assn. "We are really a diverse state now, and we are participating in a worldwide economy. For our students to only know one language puts them at a disadvantage, and the research bears that out."

5 Researchers say interest in multilingual education is reemerging across the country. The issue is no longer as racially or politically charged,

they said, and among the upper middle class is a growing recognition that knowing multiple languages is an asset.

6 But in California, teachers and school officials said the development of new programs has been hampered by the 1998 edict, which requires all children to learn in English unless parents request otherwise. Less than 5% of California public schools now offer multilingual programs, even as there are now 1.4 million English learners—about 80% of whom speak only Spanish.

7 Research on whether the law (Proposition 227) worked and how success should be measured has been mixed. The proposition was lauded as successful after standardized test scores improved among students learning English months after the vote. But further studies have shown bilingual and multilingual programs also can achieve results with more and better trained teachers and accountability measures in place. And they help students not only learn English, educators said, but also retain their native language. Ilana Umansky, an assistant professor at the University of Oregon, found that while it takes most students slightly longer to reach English proficiency in multilingual programs, more students overall reach the goal. (508 words)

(Excerpted from *Bilingual education has been absent from California public schools for almost 20 years. But that may soon change, by Jazmine Ulloa, Oct. 12, 2016. Los Angeles Times*)

Analysis of Article

The Advantages of Bilingual Education

English-only education prevents students from immersing in two languages and cultures. It is tainted with racial undertones.

Monolingual system is harmful to students in global economy; after all, we are entering a multilingual era.

While it takes most students slightly longer to reach English proficiency in multilingual programs, more students overall reach the goal, and they get students to retain their native language.

Vocabulary

undertone *n.* 潜在的含义

sought-after *adj.* 广受欢迎的，吃香的

diverse *adj.* 变化多样的，多种多样的

asset *n.* 资产，有用的东西

immersion in two languages and cultures 沉浸在两种语言和文化中

put someone at a disadvantage 使某人处于不利地位

reach English proficiency 精通英语

Read-Recite-Imitate-Create

Example one:

1. Read: Supporters argue the bureaucratic red tape on bilingual and multilingual education is harmful to students in a global economy, where the most-sought-after employees speak more than one language.

2. Recite: **the most-sought-after employees**

3. Imitate: **The most-sought-after employees** are always equipped with the same characteristics.

4. Create: Mastering a second language adds to their advantages and promotes them to be **the most-sought-after-employees**.

Example two:

1. Read: We are really a diverse state now, and we are participating in a worldwide economy.

2. Recite: **a worldwide economy**

3. Imitate: This **worldwide economy** calls for more people with talents.

4. Create: Since stepping into **a worldwide economy**, America has unavoidably become more of a melting pot where colors blend into together.

Example three:

1. Read: For our students to only know one language puts them at a disadvantage.

2. Recite: **put...at a disadvantage**

3. Imitate: Your speech **put** us poor people **at a disadvantage**.

4. Create: In this aspect, Americans seem to **be put at a disadvantage for** inadequate investment in multilingual learning.

Prompt 1

Multilingual Education

According to a new study by the Council on Foreign Relations, some eight in 10 Americans speak only English, and the number of schools teaching a foreign language is in decline. However, the opposite is true among our economic competitors. Additional languages are studied in European primary and secondary schools and are taken up by European college students in much larger numbers than in the United States. Should we encourage our citizens to pick up a different language? Since our nation is largely monolingual but is entering an increasingly multilingual world, it is highly significant to examine multilingual education closely.

Read and carefully consider these perspectives. Each suggests a particular way of thinking about multilingual education.

Perspective One	Perspective Two	Perspective Three
The country will not be able to keep pace—much less lead—global economy unless it moves to equip citizens with multi-lingual languages. Multilingual language boosts the competency of the nation.	Multilingual learning takes time away from other subjects. It hinders students' academic development.	Multilingual should be a choice rather than a requirement. Students should have their rights to choose what they want to learn in school.

Essay Task

Write a unified, coherent essay in which you evaluate multiple perspectives on multilingual education. In your essay, be sure to:

- clearly state your own perspective on the issue and analyze the relationship between your perspective and at least one other perspective
- develop and support your ideas with reasoning and examples

- organize your ideas clearly and logically
- communicate your ideas effectively in standard written English

Your perspective may be in full agreement with any of those given, in partial agreement, or completely different.

Prompt Analysis

P1	✓ The development of American economy depends highly on multilingual talents. ✓ 美国经济的发展高度依赖于多语人才。 【Eg.】international corporation, transnational conference 跨国集团，跨国会议
	✗ Technology, not language, changes and leads the world. ✗ 科技，而非语言，改变和引领世界。 【Eg.】Apple company, intelligent machines, Google company 苹果公司，智能机器，谷歌公司
P2	✓ Multilingual learning stimulates potential of talents. ✓ 多语言学习有助于学生的学术表现。 【Eg.】study on multilingual learning 有关多语学习的研究数据
	✗ Currently required courses pose great pressure on students and those who seek domestic development need not study a second language. ✗ 学生们已经面临了很大的学业压力，那些在国内寻求发展的学生不必学习第二语言。 【Eg.】research on campus burden 针对校园压力的调查研究
P3	✓ Only subjects that interest student can explore their potential more fully. ✓ 学生们学习感兴趣的学科才能够充分发掘他们的潜能。 【Eg.】Steve Jobs (founder of Apple), Evan Williams (founder of Twitter) 苹果创始人史蒂夫·乔布斯，推特创始人埃文·威廉姆斯

> ✗ Students are not experienced enough to decide which subject is more beneficial for future.
>
> ✗ 学生们没有足够的经验来选择对他们未来发展有益的学科。
>
> 【Eg.】related research 相关研究

("P" is short for "Perspective", the same below)

Model Essay 1

Stepping into **a worldwide economy**, America has unavoidably become more of a melting pot where colors blend together. Languages start to show their significance as the passports on this international stage. Although conservatives still deem "American-centered world" patronizingly, more nations have put emphasis on multilingual education. In this aspect, Americans seem to be **put at a disadvantage** for inadequate investment in multilingual learning. As far as I am concerned, multilingual capability is highly indispensable for Americans to outcompete other nations, both on campus and for economy.

> 开头段："社会背景＋反方观点＋作者观点"，这样的开篇方式非常容易模仿和展开思路。通过介绍现在美国社会发展的现状以及多语种在社会发展中的作用，引出一些持保守意见者的看法。突出多语言学习的重要性后，引出自己的观点。需要注意的是，任何作文的观点都要准确和有针对性，即主体段落所阐释的内容必须对观点产生有效支撑。在这个开篇中，"both on campus and for economy" 确实在下面的发展中进行了有效阐述。

Some educators contend that it is students' right to choose what they should learn, including multilingual learning. Truly, American education does endow students with greater freedom of curriculum choices based on interests. However, immature students have no adequate insight to foresee the qualities needed after they **enter the workforce** and either awareness to well equip themselves with well-rounded abilities. Sometimes they shall shy away from challenging subjects like a second language and lean more on easier ones. It is educators' responsibility to guide students toward more socially-adaptive courses. Multilingual subjects are definitely one of those.

第一个主体段：针对 Perspective Three 进行具体论述。需要注意的是 Perspective Three 是个中立观点，文中可以支持也可以反对，关键是看这个分论点能够如何对文章的总观点做出贡献。显然，作者在这里进行了批判性思考，首先承认美国教育赋予学生的课程自由，但是从学生的特点出发，否认了对于学生主动迎难而上的美好期待。本段以议论为主，没有涉及例子，这样的论证方式没有问题。但是需要在其他段落中体现不同的论证方式，例证结合。最终文章的分数是建立在整篇的论证基础上。

The other heated controversy the public mainly focuses on is whether multilingual learning takes away time from other subjects, hindering students' academic development. It seems that students now face mountainous burdens in their daily life and one more additional subject would be the last straw. Nevertheless, never should people underestimate students' potential. With fully utilized schedule and proper guidance, students can better handle pressure between subjects. What's more, studies show that learning additional languages improves one's ability to focus, plan and solve problems. This means that such students are better able to move efficiently from one subject to another. A recent research by University of Georgia concluded that bilingual students perform better on SAT than their monolingual peers. These multilingual students outperformed their peers throughout their scholastic careers. Thus, why not encourage more students to involve in multilingual education?

第二个主体段：回应 Perspective Two，这是典型的驳论段落。驳论即引出反方观点，并予以针对性反驳，解决对方的疑问和质疑。本段首先从人们日常的错误假设出发，再引出多语种的学习对于学生学术表现的积极意义，并通过研究予以证明。我们通常并不能够在考场的有限时间内真正快速找到可以利用的学术研究，这就需要在日常练习的过程中，熟悉并模仿调查报告或研究（research/study）的写作方法，并能较完整且高效地在考场上完成调查报告或研究（research/study）构建。

Moreover, multilingual learning yields benefits beyond the classroom. Our nation is largely monolingual but is entering an increasingly multilingual world. When students graduate, **a lack of fluency in** a second language dims their career prospects. They need to engage in intense communication with their economic competitors. Mastering a second language adds to their advantages and promotes them to be **the most-sought-after-employees.** Multilingual students will be more shinning among their counterparts and their performance will also contribute more to the thriving of America economy. The University of Florida study has revealed that in large cities such as Miami, the second-language ability brings in more than $7,000 of increased annual income. Access to a second language truly leads to access to more opportunities both for individual development and for local economy.

> **第三个主体段:** 对 Perspective One 进行展开和支持。展开和支持（development and support）是评分标准中非常重要也是很多考生在写作中不太好把握的一项。日常练习除了积累表达，还要重视思路的线性发展，能够较丰满充实地完成推理和举例（reason and example）。本段论证为什么学习多语种能够对学生未来发展及美国社会经济发展产生直接关系，这对应了本文总观点中的"indispensable both on campus and for economy"，并利用数据完成了对于分论点的支撑。

Despite of the increasing academic pressure and higher expectation on this generation, it is highly worthy for both the young and the elders to pick up one more language. As more foreign competitors crowd into American society and more Americans seek for abroad job opportunities, mastering more languages will definitely demonstrate striking advantages for people.

> **结尾段:** "总结分论点 + 重申观点"是非常推荐的收尾方式，按照这个思路可以对上文进行总结并有效呼应开头。日常练习注意开头和结尾的快速练习，争取考试的时候留更多时间给中间段落思考和展开。

Words

unavoidably *adv.* 不可避免地

patronizingly *adv.* 自认为高人一等地

stark *adj.* 完全的

inadequate *adj.* 不充分的

outcompete *v.* 把……竞争出局

socially-adaptive *adj.* 适应社会的

outperform *v.* 胜出

Phrases

a melting pot 大熔炉

blend into 融入

put emphasis on 强调

be highly indispensable for... 对……非常不可或缺

endow...with... 赋予……以……

equip...with... 使……具备

shy away from... 回避，躲避

lean on 依赖，依靠

face mountainous burden 面临山一样的压力

the last straw 最后一根稻草

fully utilized schedule 充分利用时间

yield benefits 有益处

improve one's career prospect 提升职业前景

be highlighted by the fact that... 被事实证明……

crowd into 蜂拥而入

Sentences

Although conservatives still deem... 尽管保守派依然认为……

The other heated controversy the public mainly focus on is whether...
另一个公众关注的热点争议是……

Never should people do... 人们绝不应该做……

It is highly worthy for...to...……对于……是非常有价值的

Prompt 2

Career Preparation in High School

High schools are supposed to prepare students for future career paths.
There are students who intend to pursue college education while there are
others who do not. Some educators think that high schools have the duty to
provide career training for those who choose not to go to college. However,
others counter that vocational education is unnecessary and may even
distract students from academic study. Given the controversy over this
issue, it is worth considering whether high schools should invest time and
money to develop programs or courses that enhance career readiness.

Read and carefully consider these perspectives. Each suggests a particular way of thinking about the career preparation in high school.

Perspective One	Perspective Two	Perspective Three
High schools should help all students develop skills for future work. Even if some students go to college after high school, they still need those knowledge and relevant techniques in workplace sooner or later in their life.	Career preparation programs should be provided especially for those who do not want to pursue higher education. In particular, some students are at risk of failing their academic courses. With vocational education, they can still cater to social needs and find good jobs.	High schools should not provide career preparation programs for any group of students because all of them are encouraged to attend tertiary education which best prepares them for future workforce. Without a college education, it is very difficult for a student to thrive and live a good life.

Essay Task

Write a unified, coherent essay in which you evaluate multiple perspectives on career preparation in high school. In your essay, be sure to:
- clearly state your own perspective on the issue and analyze the relationship between your perspective and at least one other perspective
- develop and support your ideas with reasoning and examples
- organize your ideas clearly and logically
- communicate your ideas effectively in standard written English

Your perspective may be in full agreement with any of those given, in partial agreement, or completely different.

Prompt Analysis

P1	✓ The ultimate goal of education is to cultivate students to be individuals who are able to at least have a suitable job. ✓ 教育的目标是令受教育者起码能够找到一份合适的工作。 【Eg.】general examples 泛指例证

	✕ It is not necessarily the responsibility of high schools to prepare students for the workplace. Even if they will not attend colleges or universities, they can at least go to vocational schools to learn the required skills. ✕ 有些学生高中毕业后不继续读大学，他们可以去职业学校学习工作中需要的技能。 【Eg.】general examples 泛指例证
P2	✓ The diversity of intrinsic abilities determines the variety of the purposes. ✓ 人天生能力的不同决定了其目标的不同。 【Eg.】different inclinations 不同的才能
	✕ Vocational education may interfere with academic study, which is also significant to personal development. ✕ 职业教育可能干扰学术研究，而它对个人成长也是很重要的。 【Eg.】abilities, such as logical thinking and reasoning, that derives from academic study 各项从学术研究过程中获得的能力，如逻辑思维能力和推理能力
P3	✓ Tertiary education qualifications tend to be an integral part of today's recruitment criteria. ✓ 如今，高等教育文凭是招聘标准的重要组成部分。 【Eg.】general examples of specialists 一些具体行业的泛指例证
	✕ People are not born equally suitable for higher education, or they are restricted by circumstances. ✕ 不是每个人天生都适合学术，或者一些外在条件限制了他们。 【Eg.】certain circumstances such as poverty 外在特殊情况，如贫穷

Model Essay 2

In today's different education patterns, there emerge a variety of paths for personal development. Most students intend to pursue a college degree while others enter workforce immediately after graduating from high school. The question under heated discussion is whether schools have the obligation to provide alternative programs for students aiming at these two largely different purposes. Given that the most crucial concern of high schools is how to best serve all students, I hold the contention that two-fold curricula should be implemented to cater to the different needs of students.

开头段：背景介绍＋争议问题＋提出观点。作者首先在开头描述现在人们教育多元化发展的现状，展示不同的学生的不同教育追求。接着引出受争议的问题，即学校是否有义务为学生提供不同的教育选择。作者在段末提出主张：学校应该开设兼顾学业发展和职业发展且满足不同学生需求的课程。

It should first be made clear that the ultimate goal of education is to cultivate students to be individuals who are able to realize their value, and working is a fundamental, though not the only, way to achieve this. In other words, education should be comprised of both academic study and career training. It is true that in most cases, high schools focus on the academic abilities needed in college, yet these abilities still wage their power even in non-academic spheres. To be more precise, for students who are eager to work, things they learn in high school including communicative skills, techniques of operating office software, and the abilities to repair machineries, still play pivotal roles in work even if they do not go to college. Furthermore, with regards to the students who are prepared to go to college, they can by no means ignore these abilities for the simple reason that they have to, in turn, utilize them in their jobs after graduation from universities. Therefore, the established high school education already embraces the so-called career preparation since the aforementioned skills from high school study are universal and enduring. In this sense, I am in partial agreement with the first perspective on the ground that the meaning of skills for future career is diversified and encompassing.

第一个主体段：论证学术能力的重要性：作者首先从问题的本质出发寻找前提条件，即具备工作技能是提升学生的有效途径。作者接着用分类讨论的方法，从不同角度将问题具体化解决：针对那些高中毕业就去工作的学生，具备职业技能能够帮助他们顺利进入工作情景；针对那些高中毕业去大学进修的学生，早晚也需要具备工作技能。两方面论证帮助作者得出结论：高中教育应该不仅限于学术培养。

Based on the foundation of the ultimate goal of education and probing into a deeper level, another significant crux of the argument lies in equality between students. Apart from teaching basic learning skills, high schools are encouraged to provide certain job training to those who do not intend to go to college. It is essential to recognize that the academic capacity of students vary to a great extent, contingent on their inborn gifts, living environment and personal aspirations. If a student desires to pursue higher education, he or she will seek far more opportunities to acquire working skills from college and internships in due course. On the contrary, those who are less competent on studying, are, in all probability, susceptible to unemployment and poverty. Nevertheless, sufficient career training is highly likely to prevent that from happening. Moreover, students are more engaged and successful if they were able to attend courses that are programmed to fit their interest, goals, and needs. Thus, the possible solution is, as suggested in the second perspective, for the career-oriented students to take an adequate number of general education sessions and supplemented ones designed for job training. In this approach, equality could be elevated between students with differed purposes and expectations.

> **第二个主体段：** 论证工作能力的重要性：作者从平等的角度出发，讨论不同的学生具备不同的就业潜质，学校教育有义务考虑到这一点，让不同的学生都能有针对性地进行职业准备。对于那些先天及后天具备优势条件的学生，他们接受高等教育后，在职场上更有竞争力，而对于那些不具备优势的学生而言，他们亟需学校提供的职场准备，提升职业竞争力。

In contrast, the dichotomy between students who go to college and those who do not exerts a negative influence on both the individuals and the society. To deny the fact that not all students can and want to go to college is to deny the variety of the existing trends of personal development. The underlying mistake behind this notion is that it neglects the numerous factors that determine whether a student advances to tertiary education or not. For instance, some families can by no means afford the expensive tuition fees for college. Also, some students with low academic records are denied their access to universities. What's more, there are students who simply have no incentives, and rather, they are particularly talented at doing something not less meaningful and rewarding than going to college. Under these circumstances, if they are forced to go to universities, it would be a waste of talent and resources for both students and society. To be concise, university is not the only way for all students.

第三个主体段：驳论段：反方观点＋反方理由＋反驳＋具体化＋重申观点。作者从反方立场出发，并进行驳斥，即忽视并非所有学生都能够上大学的现实就是在否认个人发展的多元现状。决定人们是否继续追求高等教育的因素太多了。作者通过具体化的例子展现为什么有的学生身不由己不再选择进修。最后作者总结，大学并非所有人的唯一出路，社会应该尊重学生的自由选择。

To wrap up, high school education is vital to students, whether they are going to college or not. Those academic-bound students can never afford to neglect the curriculum laden with knowledge that offers a solid foundation for university studies. In addition, career-oriented students also absorb nutrition from high school studying experiences in a broad sense. Simultaneously, the latter are encouraged to receive an appropriate amount of job training to better equip themselves for the upcoming challenges.

结尾段：概述两方面的总体理由＋结论。作者通过两方面的概括总结，得出最终的结论，呼应开头段观点，完善收尾。

教育类作业

（一）完形填空练习：请在以下 20 个词组中找出合适的词组填入下面两段文字中

1. impart knowledge 传授知识

2. expand one's knowledge 扩大知识

3. extracurricular activities 课外活动

4. academic performance 学业表现

5. slack off 懈怠

6. a healthy/positive outlook on life 对生活的一种健康的、积极的人生观

7. academic attainment 学术造诣

8. elective courses and compulsory courses 选修课程和必修课程

9. promote the students' psychological well-being 促进学生心理健康

10. comprehensive coverage of sth. 全面覆盖

11. repress individuality 压抑个性

12. rote memorization 死记硬背

13. use lateral thinking 运用横向思维

14. follow sth. indiscriminately 盲从

15. lack self-discipline 缺乏自律

16. stifle one's creativity 压抑创造力

17. sharpen one's intellect 提高才智

18. develop expertise in 培养专长

19. disrespectful and undisciplined behavior 不敬和散漫的行为

20. live an indolent life 过着懒散的生活

完形填空一

The recent Harvard research demonstrates that （1） in extracurricular activities can not only （2） beyond class but also indirectly improve （3）. In terms of this aspect, schools should organize various activities on and off campus.

完形填空二

（1） is not a reliable way for students to learn, which greatly （2）; instead, teachers can encourage students in class to use （3） between subjects rather than （4） by turning the class into a teacher-centered one.

（二）汉译英练习

1. impart knowledge 传授知识

   教师的使命是传授知识和教育人。

2. expand one's knowledge 扩宽知识面

   听著名专家和学者的学术讲座可以扩宽你的视野和知识面。

3. extracurricular activities 课外活动

   他们通常在学校功课和课外活动方面都表现非常好。

4. academic performance 学业表现

   最近的一项研究表明睡觉对学习成绩的重要性。

5. slack off 懈怠

   如果你懈怠了，很可能就会落后于人。

6. a healthy/positive outlook on life 对生活的一种健康的、积极的人生观

   心怀乐观，人们就能克服任何困难。

7. academic attainment 学术造诣

   学术造诣反映一个人真实的知识水平和学习能力。

8. elective courses and compulsory courses 选修课程和必修课程

   如果必修课不及格，就不能被授予毕业证书。

9. promote the students' psychological well-being 促进学生心理健康

   学校可以通过组织多样的志愿活动促进学生的心理健康。

10. comprehensive coverage of sth. 全面覆盖

    这个贫困项目旨在全面覆盖中国所有的贫困乡村。

11. self-paced education 自学

    很多人现在通过自学提升自己的职业竞争力。

12. well-adjusted adults 自我调节能力好的成年人

    他们能够很好地适应新环境并准备好超越前辈。

13. fulfill one's responsibilities 履行自己的职责

    总统呼吁这个国家的所有人履行自己作为公民的职责。

14. study intensively 深入研究

    她集中注意力，投入到研究项目中，希望能够早日结束任务。

15. repress individuality 压抑个性

    要求学生上必修课压抑他们的个性。

16. rote memorization 死记硬背

    死记硬背不是高效学习的办法。

17. use lateral thinking 运用横向思维

    两党应运用横向思维来寻求更好的双赢方案。

18. follow sth. indiscriminately 盲从

因为老师在过去拥有不可挑战的权威，学生们会盲从老师教的任何内容。

19. generalist 通才

很难去抉择是选择做通才还是专才。

20. versatile 全面的

他是一位非常全面的演员，在很多领域都很有才能。

21. lack self-discipline 缺乏自律

缺乏自律的人一事无成。

22. be proficient in 精通的

这个工作岗位需要精通英语的人。

23.：be well-acquainted with 熟悉的

我们的导游非常熟悉这座城市，他带领我们去了很多有特色的地方。

24. stifle one's creativity 压抑创造力

一个只有老师发言的课堂肯定会压抑学生的创造力。

25. sharpen one's intellect 提高才智

这个新引进的机器人项目极大地提升了学生们的创造力。

26. develop expertise in 培养专长

成功的高中教育帮助年轻的学生培养解决问题的专长。

27. a good conscience 良心

高枕无忧。

28. absorb the quintessence 吸收精髓

太肤浅地学习帮助不了你什么，你应该吸收每门学科的精髓。

29. be emotionally detrimental 情感上受伤害的

当顾客指责说她欺骗时，这个心理学家感觉到内心受到了伤害。

30. cut-throat competition 恶性竞争

这个公司在市场上遭遇了恶性竞争，因此它必须确保产品的出色质量。

31. differentiate virtue from evil 明辨是非

父母应该教会孩子明辨是非，来保护自己不受伤害。

32. disrespectful and undisciplined behavior 不敬和散漫的行为

他不敬和散漫的行为让每个想帮助他的人都心灰意冷。

33. juvenile delinquency 未成年人犯罪

社会会把未成年人犯罪归罪于他们的父母。

34. live an indolent life 过着懒散的生活

懒散地生活永远不能确保你过上富裕的生活。

35. maintain the continuity of learning 保持学习的连续性

只有保持学习的持续性才能够让你更长时间地记住知识。

36. mature and sustained commitment 成熟的和持续性的承诺

作为一个成年人，你应该牢记你做出的成熟和持久的承诺。

37. rebellious and aggressive action 叛逆和激进的行为

青春期意味着诸多叛逆和激进的行为。

（三）写作实操

Prompt 3

The Purpose of Education

In the contemporary society, education has been paying an increasing attention to practicality. Students are encouraged to select majors that are closely tied with the job market, expecting an easier job-hunting in this gloomy economic atmosphere. However, does this mindset put the true value of education in the first place or merely focus on releasing tensions in the job market? What is the primary purpose of school education? Is preparing students for job market the mere obligation of schools? Given the increasing human-made disasters across the globe created by those with higher education, professional skills, expertise and a solid foundation of theoretical knowledge in any given area, it is worth rethinking about the essence and purpose of education.

Read and carefully consider these perspectives. Each suggests a particular way of thinking about the purpose of education.

Perspective One	Perspective Two	Perspective Three
The crux of the high unemployment rate is the incompatibility between jobs and skills. The employment rate will go up if schools equip graduates with job skills for job market.	School education should not focus merely on job-related skills or theoretical knowledge. The foremost purpose of education is to cultivate qualified global citizens.	In spite of the importance of training students with job-related skills, it is even more essential for school education to cultivate students with ethics. People with job skills but without ethics will only bring about destruction to human society.

Essay Task

Write a unified, coherent essay in which you evaluate multiple perspectives on the purpose of education. In your essay, be sure to:

- clearly state your own perspective on the issue and analyze the relationship between your perspective and at least one other perspective
- develop and support your ideas with reasoning and examples
- organize your ideas clearly and logically
- communicate your ideas effectively in standard written English

Your perspective may be in full agreement with any of those given, in partial agreement, or completely different.

Extended Reading

Reference Article: All Nations Should Help Support the Development of a Global University Designed to Engage Students in the Process of Solving the World's Most Persistent Social Problems

I agree that it would serve the interests of all nations to establish a global university for the purpose of solving the world's most persistent social problems. Nevertheless, such a university poses certain risks which all participating nations must be careful to minimize—or risk defeating the university's purpose.

One compelling argument in favor of a global university has to do with the fact that its faculty and students would bring diverse cultural and educational perspectives to the problems they seek to solve. It seems to me that nations can only benefit from a global university where students learn ways in which other nations address certain social problems—successfully or not.

It might be tempting to think that an overly diversified academic community would impede communication among students and faculty. However, in my view any such concerns are unwarranted, especially considering the growing awareness of other peoples and cultures which the mass media, and especially the Internet, have created. Moreover, many basic principles used to solve enduring social problems know no national boundaries; thus a useful insight or discovery can come from a researcher or student from any nation.

Another compelling argument for a global university involves the increasingly global nature of certain problems. Consider, for instance, the depletion of atmospheric ozone, which has wanted the Earth to the point that it threatens the very survival of the human species. Also, we are now learning that dear-cutting the world's rainforests can set into motion a chain of animal extinction that threatens the delicate balance upon which all animals—including humans—depend. Also consider that a financial crisis—or a political crisis or natural disaster in one country can spell trouble for foreign companies, many of which are now multinational in that they rely on the labor forces, equipment, and raw materials of other nations.

Environmental, economic, and political problems such as these all carry grave social consequences—increased crime, unemployment, insurrection, hunger, and so forth. Solving these problems requires global cooperation—which a global university can facilitate.

Notwithstanding the foregoing reasons why a global university would help solve many of our most pressing social problems, the establishment of such a university poses certain problems of its own which must be addressed in order that the university can achieve its objectives. First, participant nations would need to overcome a myriad of administrative and political impediments. All nations would need to agree on which problems demand the university's attention and resources, which areas of academic research are worthwhile, as well as agreeing on policies and procedures for making, enforcing, and amending these decisions. Query whether a functional global university is politically feasible, given that sovereign nations naturally wish to advance their own agendas.

A second problem inherent in establishing a global university involves the risk that certain intellectual and research avenues would become officially sanctioned while others of equal or greater potential value would be discouraged, or perhaps even proscribed. A telling example of the inherent danger of setting and enforcing official research priorities involves the Soviet government's attempts during the 1920s to not only control the direction and the goals of its scientists' research but also to distort the outcome of that research—ostensibly for the greatest good of the greatest number of people. Not surprisingly, during this time period no significant scientific advances occurred under the auspices of the Soviet government. The Soviet lesson provides an important caveat to administrators of a global university: Significant progress in solving pressing social problems requires an open mind to all sound ideas, approaches, and theories—respective of the ideologies of their proponents.

A final problem with a global university is that the world's preeminent intellectual talent might be drawn to the sorts of problems to which the university is charged with solving, while parochial social problem go unsolved. While this is not reason enough not to establish a global university, it nevertheless is a concern that university administrators and participant nations must be aware of in allocating resources and intellectual talent.

To sum up, given the increasingly global nature or the world's social problems, and the escalating costs of addressing these problems, a global university makes good sense. And, since all nations would have a common interest in seeing this endeavor succeed, my intuition is that participating nations would be able to overcome whatever procedural and political obstacles that might stand in the way of success. As long as each nation is careful not to neglect its own unique social problems, and as long as the university's administrators are careful to remain open-minded about the legitimacy and potential value of various avenues of intellectual inquiry and research, a global university might go along way toward solving many of the world's pressing social problems.

(Excerpted from *GRE CAT Answers to the Real Essay Questions, by Mark Alan Stewart, J.D., 2008*.)

话题二　　工作类

Topic Analysis

　　工作是现代社会的一大主题，也是每个正在接受中学教育的学生需要思考的人生问题。虽然改革后的 ACT 写作目前还未直接考过工作类话题，但是改革后的 SAT 写作中该话题已频繁出现，如针对工作强度（working long hours）、女性群体工作（women winning Nobel Prize）、学徒制度的建立（apprenticeship）等问题的讨论。鉴于 ACT 写作和 SAT 写作话题的重合率很高，所以该话题很可能会出现在未来的 ACT 写作中。工作这一话题所涉及的方面十分广泛，从工作的选择与规划，到工作前所接受的培训与教育、影响工作成败的因素、理想与现实的差距等，都有可能成为题目的出发点。考生在备考时，可以阅读 SAT 写作中近年出现的工作类篇章，扩展自己的思路。

Topic Vocabulary

make a much greater contribution to 作出更大的贡献

reach success 取得成功

exploitation 剥削

brain drain 人才外流

mobility of labor 劳工流动性

definite objectives 明确的目标

career goals 职业目标

dedication 全身心投入

a sense of fulfillment 成就感，充实感

personal growth 个人成长

balance work and life 平衡工作和生活

workaholic 工作狂

seek personal development 追求个人发展

cultivate one's independence and toughness 培养自己的独立性和坚韧性

creative work 创造性工作

promotion opportunity 晋升机会

a sense of accomplishment 成就感

climb the social ladder 突破社会阶层

work overtime 加班

bright prospect 光明的前景

be closely bound up with... 与……息息相关

expand one's view 开阔视野

a well-paying job 高收入工作

enrich one's social experience 丰富一个人的社会阅历

accumulate experience 积累经验

improve one's capabilities 提高某人的能力

ideal workplace 理想的工作场所

meet the challenge 迎接挑战

material gains 物质利益

Extended Reading

Reference Article 1: Six Tips for Turning Your Hobby into Your Job

1 How did you choose your profession? Did you pick a job that you thought would be easy? Or lucrative? Or glamorous? Or, did you pursue a career related to your interests and hobbies? Chances are, you didn't base your decision on the latter—but you probably should have.

2 Why? Hobbies are the things you choose to do; activities that you're probably good at and enjoy doing, and these personal expressions "will give us unedited clues as to our real desires and interests," says Joyce K. Reynolds, an expert business coach.

3 She says looking for career clues in one's choice of hobbies, interests and vocational activities will provide the most fruitful direction for highly successful career choices. "In fact, the earlier we are able to observe our personal tastes as they show up in hobbies and outside activities, the more powerful a lead these things will provide in steering us to meaningful professional and career choices."

4 Career coach Phyllis Mufson agrees. "A hobby you really enjoy can be an important part of choosing a career because your hobby is a window into what you love and value and do most naturally, which are all important components of a career where you'll flourish." (220 words)

(Excerpted from *https://www.forbes.com/sites/jacquelynsmith/2013/10/07/six-tips-for-turning-your-hobby-into-your-job/#2b6a534e3248*)

Analysis of Article

Main Points

Hobbies are the things you choose to do, and activities that you're probably good at and enjoy doing.

Looking for career clues in one's choice of hobbies, interests and vocational activities will provide the most fruitful direction for highly successful career choices.

Vocabulary

lucrative *adj.* 利润丰厚的

glamorous *adj.* 璀璨的

fruitful *adj.* 有成果的

flourish *v.* 繁荣

Read-Recite-Imitate-Create

Example one:

1. Read: Chances are, you didn't base your decision on the latter—but you probably should have.

2. Recite: **Chances are**...

3. Imitate: **Chances are** that people switch their jobs when they are lack of sense of belonging.

4. Create: **Chances are** that if a person could not support himself, hardly would he have the possibility to live a decent life, let alone succeed in any way.

Example two:

1. Read: Looking for career clues in one's choice of hobbies, interests and vocational activities will provide the most fruitful direction for highly successful career choices.

2. Recite: ...**provide the most fruitful direction for**...

3. Imitate: Reasonable financial incentives will **provide the most fruitful direction for** the advancement of the employees' work performance.

4. Create: Usually, one's passion for a certain field **provides the most fruitful direction for** his or her later career.

Reference Article 2: In Pictures: Jobs and Careers Related to 10 Popular Hobbies

1 While there can be tremendous joy in earning income from doing something that you might happily do for free, there are also practical benefits. "It can be easier to segue into a hobby-related career since you may already have many of the skills, experiences and personal connections needed for success," says Nancy Collamer, a career coach at MyLifestyleCareer.com. But you need to spend time seriously evaluating whether turning your hobby into your work is a good idea, she adds. "Sometimes it's best to leave the two as separate and distinct parts of your life."

2 Here are a few ways to monetize a hobby:

3 Teach others to do what you love. Teach piano lessons, offer cooking classes, or teach another language, if those are your passions. You can do this by teaching through a college or continuing education program, by creating your own classes, or by creating your own webinars or tele-seminar series online, Collamer says.

4 Sell/import/invent/craft a product or accessory for enthusiasts in your hobby. For example, if you are a wine enthusiast, you might import hand-blown wine glasses from a different country, or invent a unique wine refrigeration device, or develop a line of fun wine-themed T-shirts. "Hobbyists tend to be very enthusiastic, passionate and willing to spend money on items related to their hobby," Collamer says. "Just think of what baseball enthusiasts are willing to pay for World Series tickets."

5 Teach the business of the hobby. "I actually talk about this in my book (*Second-Act Careers: 50+ Ways to Profit From Your Passions During Semi-Retirement*), using an example of a man who used to work for Microsoft in marketing, but his hobby was magic, and now he teaches marketing to magicians," Collamer says. So let's say your background is in publishing, but you love cooking, you could specialize in teaching people in the food industry how to get their cookbooks published. "I have another example in my book of a woman who teaches people

how to make a living importing goods from Ecuador, for people who love to travel and/or shop."

6 Speak or write about your hobby. Hobby related how-to topics, historical perspectives, and compelling stories, are all of interest to enthusiasts, Collamer says. And you could get paid to do it.

7 Create a tour or performance series around what you love. "The other day I met a woman who bills herself as a 'Founding Fathers Fanatic' and she performs at schools, in character, to teach students about the Founding Fathers," Collamer says. "Another example of this is Tony Mula, who turned his love of pizza and Brooklyn into the highly successful 'A Slice of Brooklyn' pizza tours," she adds. "I also know of a bike enthusiast who runs bike tours in California."

8 Appraise, repair or fix items related to what you love. Most hobbies have "stuff" connected to them, and sometimes, that stuff needs to be fixed by a skilled and knowledgeable person. "You could fix computers, appraise collectibles, repair bicycles, source missing parts for highly unusual items, and so on," Collamer says.

9 "The next time you find yourself confused as to how to generate income from your hobbies, search out the most successful entrepreneurs in your area of interest and study their business models and revenue streams," Collamer suggests. "Ask yourself: Is their income coming from consulting services, videos, accessories, events, classes or product sales? What is their mix of products and services? What is their pricing strategy?" In doing this, you'll discover proven models for monetizing your hobbies, as well as helpful information about how to price your own services and products.

10 Mufson, who has interests outside of career coaching, says she managed to turn a hobby into a lucrative part-time gig. "I personally turned my hobby of creating gemstone jewelry into a side-line business," she explains. "Jewelry making is an expensive hobby and early on I decided to make it pay for itself. Since then I have developed two online stores and a relationship with a jewelry gallery that sells most of my work."

11 Not everyone is going to wind up a star by following a well-loved hobby into a professional setting, Reynolds says. "We can't all be Olympic skaters, NBA top scorers or real estate moguls. However, it can be taken as a promise that, if we follow the lines and design of our natural interests and loves, we will give ourselves the very best chance to grow into the most successful human beings we can be. It will also ensure that we have more days we love because we're doing the things that most interest us, nourish us, and give us expression," she concludes. (827 words)

(Excerpted from *https://www.forbes.com/sites/jacquelynsmith/2013/10/07/six-tips-for-turning-your-hobby-into-your-job/#338d3a113248*)

Analysis of Article

Main Points of the Synthesis of Career and Hobbies

1. Teach others to do what you love.
2. Sell/import/invent/craft a product or accessory for enthusiasts in your hobby.
3. Teach the business of the hobby.
4. Speak or write about your hobby.
5. Create a tour or performance series around what you love.
6. Appraise, repair or fix items related to what you love.

Vocabulary

appraise *n.* 评定

nourish *v.* 滋养

monetize *v.* 变现

Read-Recite-Imitate-Create

Example one:

1. Read: In fact, the earlier we are able to observe our personal tastes as they show up in hobbies and outside activities, the more powerful a lead these things will provide in steering us to meaningful professional and career choices.
2. Recite: **The + 比较级，the + 比较级**
3. Imitate: **The longer** a person works in a certain field, **the more** experienced and professional he becomes.

4. Create: This case lessons that **the more** you feel passionate for what you do, **the more** proficient and successful you will become.

Example two:

1. Read: Not everyone is going to wind up a star by following a well-loved hobby into a professional setting, Reynolds says.

2. Recite: **wind up**

3. Imitate: Not everyone is going to **wind up** a caliber after years of arduous work and practice.

4. Create: Without the former, one could **wind up** being crippled by the listlessness and boredom while without the latter, one is prone to be poverty-stricken.

Example three:

1. Read: However, it can be taken as a promise that, if we follow the lines and design of our natural interests and loves, we will give ourselves the very best chance to grow into the most successful human beings we can be.

2. Recite: **It can be taken as a promise that**...

3. Imitate: **It can be taken as a promise that** whether one can give full play to his talents depends on mostly on whether he has definite goals.

4. Create: **It can be taken as a premise that** the notion of being realistic should not be ignored.

Prompt 1

Personal Interest and Career Development

The specialization and diversity of today's jobs have become increasingly evident and young people are facing a wider range of choices when planning their career path. From a traditional perspective, a number of factors should be taken into account for making decisions in career planning. However, it is also suggested that only by truly enjoying the job can a person achieve more. Also, today's society even embraces people who start their business purely based on their hobbies, such as those who open their own handcrafts shops. The question concerning the balance of personal interest and career development is gaining attention. Can personal hobbies be regarded as the standard for young people to select an occupation?

Read and carefully consider these perspectives. Each suggests a particular way of thinking about personal interest and career development.

Perspective One	Perspective Two	Perspective Three
Young people are free to do whatever they want because interest serves as the most inspiring element in doing a job well.	Before undertaking a particular career path, young people should be realistic and think about money, security, etc. Otherwise, they would regret.	Sometimes interest enables the young people to perform better in their work, but not everyone can find a job related to their interest.

Essay Task

Write a unified, coherent essay in which you evaluate multiple perspectives on personal interest and career development. In your essay, be sure to:

- clearly state your own perspective on the issue and analyze the relationship between your perspective and at least one other perspective
- develop and support your ideas with reasoning and examples
- organize your ideas clearly and logically
- communicate your ideas effectively in standard written English

Your perspective may be in full agreement with any of those given, in partial agreement, or completely different.

Prompt Analysis

P1	√ Interest makes it possible for young people to remain passionate about what they are doing, thus elevating their eager to pursue more. √ 兴趣的确可以令人保持激情，而激情使人努力奋发向上。 【Eg.】Mozart 莫扎特，Einstein 爱因斯坦

	✗ Interest doesn't necessarily play a positive role if certain skills are absent. ✗ 光有兴趣但没有天分或者技能也是不行的。 【Eg.】Audrey Hepburn 奥黛丽·赫本
P2	✓ The reality leaves no room for people who are not capable of making a living from their job even if they love it. ✓ 光有热情但是不能获得基本的物质回报是无法在现实中生存下去的。 【Eg.】Van Gogh 梵高
	✗ Taking into consideration the pragmatic factors might, in some way, restrict a person's choices. ✗ 考虑太多现实问题往往会限制一个人的选择甚至才华的施展。 【Eg.】Van Gogh 梵高
P3	✓ A great many people have achieved success in fields they were not meant to be in as true abilities are commonly needed in all sorts of occupations. ✓ 有些人不是在最初所在的领域成功，而是在别的领域，因为能力是相通的。 【Eg.】Ma Yun 马云
	✗ Doing a job well requires efforts only. ✗ 做好一份工作只需要努力。 【Eg.】general examples 泛指例证

Model Essay 1

Central to the issue of career planning of today's young people is the conflict between personal inclination and realistic concerns. It is many people's contention that successful job development resides in passion and enthusiasm while many others emphasize money and material gains over enjoyment. I think these two ideas are not mutually exclusive. People can have job security while doing what they like.

开头段：背景介绍，设定讨论范畴，并指出问题的核心，即爱好与现实之间的矛盾对立，然后指出两种观点，即一种人认为热情和兴趣是第一位的，而另一种人认为现实因素更重要。最后提出本文的观点，即爱好和工作保障是可以两全的。

On the one hand, hobbies play an essential role in a person's career development because they are the intrinsic momentum that propels a person to strive for more accomplishments. Further, owing to the inborn intuition for a certain scope, one is motivated to learn more, therefore contributing even further to the chances of success. A great amount of evidence from daily life and, on a larger scale, human history supports that hobbies formed in early childhood dictate how a person develops in terms of the sphere of knowledge or technique related to the area of hobbies. Usually, one's passion for a certain field **provides the most fruitful direction for** his or her later career. For instance, Mozart, the musician started as a musical prodigy, after which he wound up a successful composer due to his passion for music and consistent training as well. This case lessons that **the more you feel passionate for what you do, the more proficient and successful you will become.**

第一个主体段： 论证兴趣对职业发展的重要性，主要利用了因果论证法和例证法的组合。兴趣能够推动人们不断地朝着目标努力，从而增加成功的几率。然后，作者列举了莫扎特的例子，说明兴趣在他的音乐事业中扮演的重要角色。

On the other hand, a utilitarian attitude that focuses on material levels towards the choice of occupation is reasonable as the pragmatic aspects such as money, promotion opportunities stability, and stability allow for the satisfaction of basic living standards, thus leading to a long-term development. **Chances are** that if a person could not support himself, hardly would he have the possibility to live a decent life, let alone succeed in any way. Take the British writer, W. S. Maugham as an example. In the search of career, he went to Paris and studied painting, which he was slightly talented and interested in. After one-year practice, he realized that his limited talent in painting could at best make him a court painter but never a master artist. On account of that, he made a decisive cease and started to write and later on gave the world his masterpiece *The Moon and Sixpence*. Therefore, **it can be taken as a**

premise that the notion of being realistic should not be ignored.

On balance, the dichotomy between pursuing a field of career that one is interested in and one that yields concrete results seems to be insensible. As to the question of hobby versus money, they are not mutually exclusive. A fulfilling working life consists of both the echo of personal inclination to the work and the tangible profits. Without the former, one could **wind up** being crippled by the listlessness and boredom while without the latter, one is prone to be poverty-stricken.

In conclusion, personal interest and career planning are not dichotomous. A person is encouraged to take up an arduous journey towards the union of personal preferences and the capacity of creating value in the jobs.

Words

intrinsic *adj.* 固有的，本质的

momentum *n.* 动力

strive for... *v.* 为……而努力

dictate *v.* 决定，影响

utilitarian *adj.* 功利的

occupation *n.* 职业

pragmatic *adj.* 实用的

premise *n.* 前提

dichotomy *n.* 对立，截然相反

tangible *adj.* 有形的

cripple *v.* 使跛，使残废

listlessness *n.* 无精打采

boredom *n.* 厌倦

poverty-stricken *adj.* 为贫穷所困扰的

Phrases

emphasize...over... 强调……

in terms of... 就……而言

a decent life 体面的生活

mutually exclusive 相互排斥

consist of... 由……组成

be prone to... 易于……，有……的倾向

Sentences

A great amount of evidence from...supports that... 很多证据可以支持……

Somebody could not do..., let alone do... 某人不能做某事，更不用说做另外一件事

Prompt 2

Payment and Contribution

As the monopolization of international corporations expands, the polarization of income between the high-paying and low-paying jobs has become intensified than ever before. Contrary to what most people believe, those who have the most lucrative jobs are actually destroyers rather than contributors to the society. On the contrary, those who make great contributions to human society do not have decent salaries. What causes this unfair and whimsical phenomenon? Why those who make the greatest contributions do not have decent salaries? It is worth considering whether one's payment should be based on his or her contributions.

Read and carefully consider these perspectives. Each suggests a particular way of thinking about payment and contribution.

Perspective One

The reason why some people have high-paying jobs is that they make great contributions to the world. The more contributions one makes, the more money he or she makes.

Perspective Two

A high-paying job cannot give people a sense of fulfillment. It is the contribution to human society that makes people feel fulfilled.

Perspective Three

A high-paying job has nothing to do with contributions to the world. Those who have made the greatest contributions to the world are not paid decently.

Essay Task

Write a unified, coherent essay in which you evaluate multiple perspectives on payment and contribution. In your essay, be sure to:

• clearly state your own perspective on the issue and analyze the relationship between your perspective and at least one other perspective
• develop and support your ideas with reasoning and examples
• organize your ideas clearly and logically
• communicate your ideas effectively in standard written English

Your perspective may be in full agreement with any of those given, in partial agreement, or completely different.

Prompt Analysis

P1	✓ Financial incentives can motivate people to work harder. ✓ 经济上的奖励机制可以激发人们工作更努力。 【Eg.】scientists, doctors and engineers in the developed countries 发达国家的科学家、医生和工程师们
	✗ High salaries are not based on contributions to society. ✗ 高收入不取决于对社会的贡献。 【Eg.】bankers, CEOs and financial engineers of Wall Street 银行家、华尔街的 CEO 和金融工程师们

P2	✓ Most people intrinsically want to make contributions to their communities. ✓ 大多数人本质上想要为自己的群体做贡献。 【Eg.】Helen Keller, Mother Teresa, Nicolas Tesla, Joseph E. Stiglitz 海伦·凯勒，特蕾莎修女，尼古拉斯·特斯拉，约瑟夫·斯蒂格利茨
	✗ People's values are so different, and some people live for money。 ✗ 人们的价值观非常不一样，有的人为钱而活。 【Eg.】bankers, CEOs and financial engineers of Wall Street 华尔街的银行家、CEO 和金融工程师们
P3	✓ Social and economic system determines unfair income distribution。 ✓ 社会和经济体制决定收入分配的不公。 【Eg.】Teachers, firefighters and policemen in most countries are not paid decently. 很多国家的老师、消防员和警察没有获得应有的收入。
	✗ One's extraordinary talent is the determinant factor in a high salary. ✗ 一个人卓越的才华是高收入的决定性因素。 【Eg.】inventors, Elon Musk, Steve Jobs 发明家，伊朗·马斯克，史蒂夫·乔布斯

Model Essay 2

Objectively speaking, most people's salaries are not proportional to their contributions to human society. Some people wrongly assume that those who have high-paying jobs are the greater contributors to the world, so the more contributions they make, the higher salaries they should receive. However, the truth is that those who make the greatest contributions to human society are not paid as much as they deserve and a high-paying job has nothing to do with how much one contributes. Although a high salary can somehow give people a sense of achievement, it is the contribution to the world rather than a high-paying job that makes people feel fulfilled.

开头段： 第一句引出话题，大部分人的收入和贡献不成正比；第二句转述不赞成的观点；第三句和第四句表述自己赞成的观点。整篇文章的立场是反对 Perspective One，赞同 Perspective Two 和 Perspective Three。

The proponents of Perspective One argue that a high salary can be justified because the more contributions people make, the higher salaries they should have. Is it really the case? According to the research of Joseph E. Stiglitz, a Nobel Prize laureate in economics, "By 2007, the year before the crisis, the top 0.1 percent of America's households had an income that was 220 times larger than the average of the bottom 90 percent. Wealth was even more unequally distributed than income, with the wealthiest 1 percent owning more than a third of the nation's wealth." Isn't the polarization of income startling? Have the wealthiest 1 percent earned their incomes by making great contributions to the society? As Joseph E. Stiglitz points out, "the 1 percent are by and large not those who earned their incomes by great contributions—they are not the great thinkers who have transformed our understanding of the world or the great innovators who have transformed our economy." Likewise, some colonizers legalized the pirates to rob the foreign cargoes and split the robbed wealth with them. Later, they legalized the pirates to be navy to sail out farther to rob, kill and colonize for them. It is obvious that those colonizers did not earn their incomes by making any contributions to the world. On the contrary, they accumulated their wealth by robbery and slaughter, which has caused devastating disasters, sufferings and tribulations to people all over the world. Therefore, I absolutely disagree with Perspective One.

第一个主体段： 主题句是那些支持 Perspective One 的人的理由。然后作者引用诺贝尔经济学奖得主的研究数据来反驳 Perspective One 的不合理性。同样作者举例论证，有的殖民者把海盗合法化去抢劫外国商船来获得财富，后来把海盗变成海军去全世界抢夺财富，从而反驳 Perspective One，因为他们都不是通过对社会的贡献取得巨额收入的，而是通过掠夺获得财富。结尾句表述自己的立场，不赞同 Perspective One。整个段落使用了举例论证来支持作者的观点。

I unhesitatingly agree with Perspective Two that a high-paying job does not necessarily give people a sense of fulfillment but it is their contributions to human society that make them feel fulfilled. Throughout history, there are numerous number of people who have been working for the greater good and the betterment of human society. Whether or not you are a theist, you would applaud for the good work of Mother Teresa who loved, clothed, fed, took care of and healed the emotional and physical wounds of the poorest of the poor. It is the amazingly loving woman who brought the fragrance of heaven to the earth, and her love warmed the broken hearts and kindled the hope for humanity. Undoubtedly, Mother Teresa modeled a life of compassion, kindness, disinterestedness, philanthropic love and personal fulfillment. Personally, I am so grateful for the doctors, teachers, engineers and peace keepers without boarders who work for the greater good and the well-being of our human society. Although they do not have high-paying jobs, they live a fulfilled life by making this world a better place for human kind.

第二个主体段：主题句作者表明立场，赞同 Perspective Two。通过用名人特罗莎修女的实例来增强自己的论证，同时也用那些跨国界的医生、老师、工程师等实例来支持自己的观点。结尾强调那些人虽然没有高薪酬，但是他们通过让世界变得更好而过着一种非常充实的人生。主体段结构是总分总，首尾呼应，平行结构。

As for the most lucrative jobs, ironically, they belong to the private bankers—Rothschilds, Rockefellers, Morgans who issue the US dollars in the name of Federal Reserve that is their privately owned agency. In the words of Alan Greenspan, the former chairman of Federal Reserve, in an interview with Jim Lehrer at PBS NewsHour Weekend, "Federal reserve is an independent agency that means basically there is no other agency of government which can overrule the actions we take." Undoubtedly, those who work for the bankers such as CEOs and executives of financial industry on the Wall Street also receive outsize bonuses. As quoted from Joseph E. Stiglitz, "the huge gap between CEO payment and that of the typical worker—more than 200 times greater—a number markedly higher than in other countries." Isn't it evident that their excessive incomes are not related to their contributions to the world? By a sharp contrast, those who have the most important jobs such as teachers, engineers, doctors, construction workers and firefighters...are often not paid decently in many countries. Thus, I am in agreement with the Perspective Three.

第三个主体段：主题句作者表明立场，那些最赚钱的工作是属于那些控制美元发行的私人银行家们和那些金融行业的 CEO 们和金融工程师们。作者再次引用诺贝尔经济奖得主的研究数据来支持自己的论证。结尾再次表明自己的立场，赞同 Perspective Three。

In conclusion, there is no link between one's contributions to the society and his or her income. While unfair income distribution is universal, one must fully consider the detrimental impact of the increasing income inequality caused by unfair social and economic system. Idealistically, people's incomes should be based on their contributions, which is the hallmark of a democratic and civilized society.

结尾段：虽然不公平的收入分配制度是普遍的现象，但是必须要考虑由于不公正的社会和经济制度带来的收入不公平所造成的社会隐患。并提出自己的展望，一个民主和文明社会的标志是应该让人们的贡献来决定收入。

工作类作业

（一）完形填空练习：请在以下 20 个词组中找出合适的词组填入下面两段文字中

1. make a much greater contribution to 作出更大的贡献

2. reach success 取得成功

3. exploitation 剥削

4. brain drain 人才外流

5. mobility of labor 劳工流动性

6. definite objectives 明确的目标

7. career goals 职业目标

8. dedication 全身心投入

9. a sense of fulfillment 成就感，充实感

10. personal growth 个人成长

11. balance work and life 平衡工作和生活

12. workaholic 工作狂

13. seek personal development 追求个人发展

14. cultivate one's independence and toughness 培养自己的独立性和坚韧性

15. creative work 创造性工作

16. promotion opportunity 晋升机会

17. a sense of accomplishment 成就感

18. climb the social ladder 突破社会阶层

19. work overtime 加班

20. bright prospect 光明的前景

完形填空一

（1）involves a great amount of imagination, and once completed, gives people （2）. Meanwhile, it is usually finished independently, so it tends to （3）. On the other hand, it sometimes requires prolonged hours of designing and drafting, so people might find it difficult to （4）.

完形填空二

（1）are those who spend excessive time on working. By （2）, they sacrifice personal life for the purpose of （3）at work. Sometimes, it is merely a behavior directed at gaining more （4）.

（二）汉译英练习

1. make a much greater contribution to 作出更大的贡献

   遗憾的是，其他领域的专业人士对人类社会作出了更大的贡献，得到的报酬却少得多。

2. reach success 取得成功

   参赛者对奖金的期望值与他们取得成功所克服的竞争有很大的联系。

3. exploitation 剥削

   不幸的是，很多雇主愿意雇用童工就是为了比雇用成年员工省钱，这种剥削的方式应该受到抵制。

4. brain drain 人才外流

   如今，人才外流问题日趋严重。

5. mobility of labor 劳工流动性

   不同地区房价的差异阻碍了劳动力的流动。

6. definite objectives 明确的目标

   能否充分发挥才干，关键在于是否有明确的目标。

7. career goals 职业目标

   跳槽的原因可以归结为人们为了追求自己的职业目标。

8. dedication 全身心投入

   薪酬是对一个人成功的技能和奉献的认可。

9. a sense of fulfillment 成就感，充实感

   如果自己的工作对社会和经济的发展颇具意义，随之觉得这份工作的价值所在，那么一种成就感就会油然而生。

10. personal growth 个人成长

    个人发展和归属感这类因素对激励员工有重要作用。

11. balance work and life 平衡工作和生活

    当代女性既要照顾家庭又要工作，所以她们必须学会如何平衡工作和生活。

12. workaholic 工作狂

    当今，很多人迫于生活的压力终日辛苦工作，俨然成了工作狂。

13. seek personal development 追求个人发展

    找工作时，求职者不仅看中工资待遇，而且越来越重视追求个人发展。

14. cultivate one's independence and toughness 培养自己的独立性和坚韧性

    经历挫折未必是一件坏事，人们可以从中培养自己的独立性和坚韧性。

15. creative work 创造性工作

    为了取得更大的发展，我们不能墨守成规，而应该积极进行创造性工作。

16. promotion opportunity 晋升机会

    除了提高工资待遇之外，晋升机会也是激励员工的一种有效机制。

17. a sense of accomplishment 成就感

不断挑战自己、突破极限能够给人带来很大的成就感，从而让我们觉得人生是有意义的。

18. climb the social ladder 突破社会阶层

人们所处的社会阶层是比较固定的。如果想突破社会阶层，接受教育往往是一种有效的方式。

19. work overtime 加班

由于工作任务太多，员工往往被迫加班，他们的睡眠和生活都会受到一定程度的负面影响。

20. bright prospect 光明的前景

未来经济的光明前景给社会带来了希望。

21. be closely bound up with... 与……息息相关

现代社会，电子产品与我们的生活和工作息息相关。

22. expand one's view 开阔视野

多出国走走可以帮助我们开阔视野，给予我们不同的角度去认识世界。

23. the from-nine-to-five 朝九晚五一族

朝九晚五一族虽然有固定的生活节奏，但是往往会感到单调和乏味。

24. a well-paying job 高收入工作

不可否认，很多人之所以上大学就是想在毕业时找到一份高薪的工作。

25. enrich one's social experience 丰富一个人的社会阅历

参加社会实践活动对个人成长非常有益，它可以丰富一个人的社会阅历。

26. accumulate experience 积累经验

我们要勇于尝试，并从中吸取教训、积累经验。

27. improve one's capabilities 提高某人的能力

学无止境，我们要不断进取，提高自身的能力。

28. ideal workplace 理想的工作场所

很多未入职场的人都会幻想一个理想的工作场所，在那里人际关系单纯。但是进入职场后就会发现现实与理想的差距。

29. meet the challenge 迎接挑战

我们不能满足现状，要不断迎接新的挑战，寻求更大的突破。

30. material gains 物质利益

在规划地区发展时，政策决策者不能只考虑眼前的物质利益，更主要的是构建一个可持续发展的蓝图。

Prompt 3

Apprenticeship

Employment is one of the most concerned topics among the public. Preparing the potential job seekers for the workforce takes the efforts of not only the government and schools but also businesses. However, the status quo is that most businesses are unwilling to assume this responsibility even though they often complain that there are far less eligible workers than they need. Some advocate that businesses should help train students so that their resume is qualified in applying an actual job. Given the increasing advocate for apprenticeship and companies' resistance to the trend, it is worth considering whether businesses should take the responsibility to adopt apprentice programs.

Read and carefully consider these perspectives. Each suggests a particular way of thinking about apprenticeship.

Perspective One	Perspective Two	Perspective Three
It is not fair or reasonable for schools or government to take full responsibility of cultivating the youth for future career. If businesses do not help train them, there will always be a gap between vacant occupations and job seekers.	Adopting apprentice programs would impose additional pressure on companies. Experienced workers are distracted to train apprentices, who are very likely to work for the competitive companies after graduation.	It is quite unfair for students, who work diligently in studying and in applying for a job but still cannot reach the standard of employers. Therefore, businesses either adopt apprenticeship or hire job seekers with no work experience.

Essay Task

Write a unified, coherent essay in which you evaluate multiple perspectives on apprenticeship. In your essay, be sure to:

- clearly state your own perspective on the issue and analyze the relationship between your perspective and at least one other perspective
- develop and support your ideas with reasoning and examples

- organize your ideas clearly and logically
- communicate your ideas effectively in standard written English

Your perspective may be in full agreement with any of those given, in partial agreement, or completely different.

Reference Article: CU Apprentice Program Builds Workforce, Community

1 ATLANTA—Last month, Gary Fisher, senior recruiter at the Atlanta-based Delta Community CU, was joking about a student from Delta's apprentice program one day becoming president/CEO.

2 But Fisher quickly stopped himself because, really, is it all that far-fetched, considering where the program has already taken many of its participants?

3 For nearly a decade, Delta Community has taken students from Atlanta metro high schools, plugged them into part-time teller roles at the credit union, and watched them blossom into either full-time employees, college students, or both.

4 After launching the program in 2006—with two students—the Delta Community High School Apprentice Program has continued to expand, growing to 18 participants this year. Each student works as a teller at branches near their high schools under the guidance of branch management.

5 "Because of our great trainers and the great people we have at Delta Community, we turn someone with no work experience into someone who is a very qualified teller in 30 days," Fisher told News Now.

6 In addition to picking up valuable professional experience and skills, the work bolsters the apprentices' resumes for both college and professionally, and provides the students with competitive salaries.

7 The students also receive quality financial education during orientation, as the corporate trainers teach the students—as they gear up for their teller positions—about credit unions and the services they provide.

8 "I learned about the financial services industry, and also about customer service and teamwork," Shelby Montpas, now a full-time electronic funds specialist at the credit

union, said recently. "My apprenticeship in 2011 brought focus to my career goals and has made me a better student as I work toward my college degree."

9 While the program creates numerous opportunities for the students, it also benefits Delta Community.

10 Last year, 13 of the 16 participants returned as full-time employees of the credit union, meaning Delta Community was able to bring on 13 employees who were already trained for the job, even as some pursued their college education.

11 Further, of the 72 students who have gone through the program since 2006, 47 continue to work for the credit union, including 12 in full-time positions and 35 in part-time positions.

12 "(It's) a win-win," Fisher said. "The students get a paycheck and valuable job skills. The credit union gains these wonderful young members, plus helpful support for its front-line employees. Most importantly, our members receive better service because we have extra help—especially on busy afternoons and Saturdays."

13 Though all apprentices start in part-time teller roles, many of the students have been promoted to a number of different departments, such as corporate training, member services, retirement investment services and e-commerce.

14 "We're almost to the point now where folks who started as apprentices years ago are ready to move up to leadership roles," Fisher said.

15 Hence, why one day an apprentice may become CEO. No joke.

16 "We're seeding the company with talent," Fisher said. "And I just see this thing continuing to grow. More and more students, (who also) become members for life, will be the future of the company."

(Excerpted from *CU apprentice program builds workforce, community, by Tom Sakash, August 5, 2015, CUNA News*)

话题三　　社会进步类

Topic Analysis

　　自从 ACT 写作改革以来，社会进步类话题成为考试的热点，引导学生思考社会热点现象以及个人与社会的关系，如针对公共健康和个人自由（public health & individual freedom）、法律（bad laws）、个人成功与群体价值（personal success & common good）、成人和玩具（adults playing toys）等的讨论。高中生的阅读中有很多有关社会进步类话题的文章，如有很多文章谴责战争的不公平和不道德来唤起人们对战争的思考，针对贫富差距大的讨论等，这些都可以成为展开论证的素材。只有当更多人有意识地去监督政府的职责、关注社会进步类话题、思考社会的进步，社会才有可能变得更加民主和繁荣。作为 ACT 的考生有必要去思考社会进步类话题，思考如何推进社会的进步。

Topic Vocabulary

vested interest 既得利益

at the expense of 以……为代价

civil disobedience 非暴力反抗

comply with 遵守

appalling silence 令人震惊的沉默

social turmoil 社会动乱

be fueled by 被激化

bestial behaviors 卑劣的动物般的行为

nonviolent civil resistance 非暴力的文明抵抗

be stripped of one's dignity and identity 某人被剥夺尊严和身份

the valley of despair 绝望的山谷

hamper one's development 阻碍某人的发展

a penetrating analysis 有洞察力的分析

be inextricably tied to 密不可分

be substantiated by 被证实

shoulder one's responsibility 肩负某人的责任

condemn rather than condone sth. 谴责而不是纵容某事

as evidenced by the fact that 正如被这个事实证实的那样

It is incumbent on sb. to do sth. 做某事是某人的责任

endanger social stability and safety 威胁社会稳定和安全

moral dilemma 道德困境

be prioritized over 优先于

thwart terrorist attacks 打击恐怖袭击

national security 国家安全

intrude on personal privacy 侵犯个人隐私

government surveillance 政府监控

the hallmark of 标志

a civilized and democratic society 文明和民主的社会

eliminate poverty 消除贫穷

financial burden 财政负担

polarization of the rich and the poor 富人和穷人的极化

foster a climate of peace and prosperity 培养一个和平与繁荣的氛围

get rid of poverty and backwardness 摆脱贫穷落后

enhance comprehensive national strength 增强综合国力

harmonious world 和谐世界

boost the local tertiary industry 促进当地第三产业的发展

strengthen the enforcement of laws 加强执法

rely on science and technology to rejuvenate the nation 依靠科技兴国

optimize the distribution of resources 优化资源配置

revival of customs and traditions 风俗传统的复兴

preserve historical and cultural heritages 保护历史文化遗产

Extended Reading

Reference Article 1: Are We Helping the Poor? Welfare Saves Millions from Poverty, but It Would Be Better If It Didn't Have to

1 Opponents of America's welfare state tend to make two kinds of arguments. The first, that of philosophical libertarians, regards food stamps, housing supports and unemployment payments as unjust transfers from some citizens to others. The second, less doctrinaire and more in vogue, holds that welfare programs do not benefit their intended recipients.

2 A new study led by Christopher Wimer and Liana Fox, researchers at Columbia University, calls the second claim into question. The safety net, they say, has saved millions of Americans from falling into poverty over the past four decades. Why are we just learning about this now? Well, it turns out we've been using bad statistics.

3 Poverty rates would have actually increased slightly over the time period, from 27% to nearly 29%. But after accounting for taxes and transfers, poverty falls by approximately 40%, from 26% to 16%. The figure also shows the growing anti-poverty role of taxes and transfers in reducing poverty, from only about 1 percentage point in 1967 to nearly 13 percentage points in 2012.

4 Bringing down poverty by 40% is a big deal, and as Kevin Drum notes, the fact that poverty only ticked up slightly since the economy tanked in 2008 shows that the safety net has "significantly ameliorated a human catastrophe over the past five years." According to the Columbia study, welfare programs have also **made a significant dent in** child poverty and in "deep poverty", the percentage of the population earning under 50% of the poverty line.

5 Those impressive figures, Mr. Drum argues, should not obscure a less sunny result: the stubbornly high proportion of working-age poor people in America. While poverty among the elderly has fallen impressively since 1967 (around the time Medicare was introduced), the percentage of poor Americans aged 18-64 hasn't budged much. The figure dipped from 1967 to 1979, but today is right back where it was 35 years ago, at 15%.

6 Arnold Ahlert jumps on that piece of Mr. Drum's analysis to argue that social welfare programs disincentivize work and entrench, rather than alleviate, poverty. The figures "paint a damning picture of leftist re-distribution schemes", he writes: The largest decrease in the percentage of poor Americans occurred before LBJ's War on Poverty began. From 1950 to the late 1960s, Census Bureau data show the poverty rate in a dramatic decline. Immediately after LBJ's "Great Society" programs **kicked into gear**, the poverty rate began to stagnate. And it has more

or less stagnated ever since, despite trillions of dollars of government spending on means-tested programs.

7 The study is flawed: many of the welfare benefits Messrs Tanner and Hughes criticize are also available to the working poor, undercutting the claim that the safety net entangles people in perpetual joblessness. And few families receive all of the benefits laid out in the study. recipients' drive to seek employment, whether they are technically impoverished or not. But real-world reporting bears out what common sense suggests: welfare benefits will **dampen some recipients' drive to seek** employment, whether they are technically impoverished or not. (508 words)

(Excerpted from *The Economist, by S.M./NEW YORK, Dec. 18th 2013.*)

Analysis of Article

Pros of Government's Poverty Alleviation

The safety net has saved millions of Americans from falling into poverty over the past four decades.

Welfare programs have also made a significant dent in child poverty and in deep poverty.

Cons of Government's Poverty Alleviation

Philosophical libertarians, regards food stamps, housing supports and unemployment payments as unjust transfers from some citizens to others.

Less doctrinaire and more in vogue, holds that welfare programs do not benefit their intended recipients.

Key Words

safety net

deep poverty

unemployment payments

welfare programs

Vocabulary

libertarian *n./adj.* 自由意志者/自由意志的

doctrinaire *adj./n.* 教条主义的/空论家

---

in vogue 正在流行

ameliorate *v.* 改善，减轻

catastrophe *n.* 大灾难

disincentivize *v.* 抑制

entrench *v.* 牢固

alleviate *v.* 减轻，缓和

redistribution *n.* 重新分配

budge *v.* 移动，使让步

entangle *v.* 卷入，使纠缠

perpetual *adj.* 永久的

impoverished *adj.* 贫困的

Read-Recite-Imitate-Create

Example one:

1. Read: According to the Columbia study, welfare programs have also made a significant dent in child poverty and in "deep poverty", the percentage of the population earning under 50% of the poverty line.

2. Recite: **make a significant dent in**

3. Imitate: Poverty relief program has **made a significant dent in** poverty.

4. Create: As evidenced by the fact that most of the European countries have successfully **made a significant dent in** poverty by building a fair social system to provide every member of the society with equal opportunities.

Example two:

1. Read: Immediately after LBJ's "Great Society" programs kicked into gear, the poverty rate began to stagnate.

2. Recite: **kick into gear**

3. Imitate: European welfare system has **kicked into gear** and has eventually eradicated poverty completely.

4. Create: Because as soon as a fair social system **kicks into gear**, poverty will be eliminated effectively.

> Example three:
>
> 1. Read: But real-world reporting bears out what common sense suggests: welfare benefits will dampen *some* recipients' drive to seek employment, whether they are technically impoverished or not.
> 2. Recite: **dampen one's drive to do sth.**
> 3. Imitate: Unfair social and economic system **dampens workers' drive to** work hard.
> 4. Create: They fail to reflect on how the external forces, such as discrimination in employment market, a lack of economic opportunity, and failed public education, adversely affect the socially and financially disadvantaged, thereby **dampening their drive to seek** better opportunities.

Reference Article 2: The Government's Role in Ending Poverty and Homelessness

Over the last few weeks I've been highlighting the extent of poverty and homelessness in British Columbia and, in particular, Greater Victoria. It's clear that significant work still needs to be done to address these issues. But it's also important to recognize the good work that has and is taking place. Through new subsidized housing units, the provision of rent supplements and other programs, local groups, in partnership with the Province, have provided housing and prevented homelessness for many vulnerable people in Greater Victoria. Despite these efforts, combating poverty and homelessness remains a struggle, not only in British Columbia, but also throughout Canada. We cannot solely rely on the work of non-profit organizations and charitable groups to resolve these issues—they need government leadership and help from all of us. And all levels of government must step up and provide the resources and support so desperately needed.

1. How did we get here?

In the 1960s and 1970s, amendments to the National Housing Act (NHA) launched a number of public housing and support programs that led to the creation of around 200,000 social housing units over a 10-year span. However, these programs were short-lived due to cutbacks in social

Словарь

housing and related programs beginning in the mid 1980s. Today, annual national investment in housing has decreased by over 46% and current federal operating agreements are set to expire over the next 20 years, putting an additional 365,000 Canadian households at risk.

2. Federal Role

In April 2014, the Canadian Government announced plans to renew the Homelessness Partnering Strategy (HPS), an approach to addressing homelessness by working in partnership with communities, provinces and territories, other federal departments and the private and not-for-profit sectors. With a commitment of nearly $600 million over five years and a new focus on using a Housing First approach, this is certainly a step in the right direction.

3. Provincial Role

In response to BC's homelessness crisis, the provincial government **launched its Homelessness Prevention Program.** This program expands rent supplements to four at-risk groups, helping individuals facing homelessness access rental housing in the private market. However, it does nothing to provide more affordable housing. Instead, many argue that it is time for BC to adopt **a comprehensive poverty reduction plan—** one that would significantly reduce poverty and homelessness through legislated targets and timelines.

4. Community Role

While effective action is still needed at the federal and provincial level, a number of communities across Canada have been **making significant strides towards ending homelessness** in their cities. Through the implementation of community plans, cities such as Lethbridge and Medicine Hat are well on target to end homelessness in their communities. One of the champions of the recent community success has been the Canadian Alliance to End Homelessness. (457 words)

(Excerpted from *http://www.andrewweavermla.ca/*, by *Teresa Hartrick, January 6, 2015.*)

Analysis of Article

Pros of Government's Poverty Alleviation

Subsidized housing units, the provision of rent supplements and other programs, have provided housing and prevented homelessness for many vulnerable people.

All levels of government must step up and provide the resources and support so desperately needed.

Homeless Partnering Strategy addresses homelessness by working in partnership with communities, provinces and territories.

Vocabulary

subsidize *v.* 资助

supplement *v./n.* 补充/增补

vulnerable *adj.* 易受伤的

amendment *n.* 修正案

desperately *adv.* 绝望的

comprehensive *adj.* 综合的，广泛的

legislate *v.* 立法

ingredient *n.* 要素

Read-Recite-Imitate-Create

Example one:

1. Read: Instead, many argue that it is time for BC to adopt a comprehensive poverty reduction plan—one that would significantly reduce poverty and homelessness through legislated targets and timelines.

2. Recite: **a comprehensive poverty reduction plan**

3. Imitate: Only by adopting **a comprehensive poverty reduction plan** can poverty be eliminated completely.

4. Create: It is self-evident that it is within the ability of most governments to end poverty by adopting **a comprehensive poverty reduction plan**.

Example two:

1. Read: While effective action is still needed at the federal and provincial level, a number of communities across Canada have been making significant strides towards ending homelessness in their cities.

2. Recite: **make significant strides towards ending homelessness/ eradicating poverty**.

3. Imitate: Many advanced countries have **made significant strides towards eradicating poverty**.

4. Create: By establishing a fair social system, those governments **have made significant strides towards eradicating poverty** completely and have helped individuals to reach the full potential of their talents.

Example three:

1. Read: In response to BC's homelessness crisis, the provincial government recently launched its Homelessness Prevention Program.

2. Recite: **launch homelessness prevention program**

3. Imitate: Any democratic government should **launch homelessness prevention program** to provide a shelter for the homeless.

4. Create: German government **launches homelessness prevention program** to eradicate deep poverty.

Prompt 1

Government's Obligation to Eliminate Poverty

In spite of the extraordinary progress made in human society, poverty still likes a plague devastating the life of hundreds of millions of people across the globe. Even in the developed country like the US, millions of people face stark poverty and cannot afford the necessities of life. Rich as it is, the social inequality in the US is higher than any other developed country. The poverty statistics are so shocking that worry the public especially the academic world. Even those with jobs are struggling to make ends meet, and more than one fifth of American people cannot afford higher education. Will such a divided society have a future in the competitive world? Given the repercussions of increasing social inequality in the US, it is urgent than ever before for the government to eliminate poverty.

Read and carefully consider these perspectives. Each suggests a particular way of thinking about government's obligation to eliminate poverty.

Perspective One	Perspective Two	Perspective Three
Poverty has been existing since the beginning of the human history and its existence is inevitable in the human society no matter how much advancement humans have accomplished. It is extremely idealistic and impractical to dream of a world with no poverty.	In the contemporary society, there are plenty of employment opportunities. As long as people are hardworking, they will receive a decent salary, and most importantly it is one's own obligation to work his/her way out of poverty.	The social inequality is a decisive factor in depriving people of their wealth and causing poverty. Only when governments establish a fair social system can poverty be eradicated completely.

Essay Task
Write a unified, coherent essay in which you evaluate multiple perspectives on government's obligation to eliminate poverty. In your essay, be sure to: • clearly state your own perspective on the issue and analyze the relationship between your perspective and at least one other perspective • develop and support your ideas with reasoning and examples • organize your ideas clearly and logically • communicate your ideas effectively in standard written English Your perspective may be in full agreement with any of those given, in partial agreement, or completely different.

Prompt Analysis

P1	√ Poverty is inevitable in human society. √ 贫困在人类社会是无法避免的。 【Eg.】Greed and dishonesty of corporations and corrupt governments 集团的贪婪和不诚信及腐败的政府
	✗ It is feasible to eliminate poverty completely. ✗ 完全消除贫困是可行的。 【Eg.】the wellbeing of many European nations, the choice of governments 北欧政府的福利安乐，政府选择
P2	√ Individuals can end poverty themselves if they are industrious. √ 如果个体勤奋的话可以终结贫困。 【Eg.】Abraham Lincoln, Jack London 亚伯拉罕·林肯，杰克·伦敦
	✗ It is impossible for the impoverished to work their way out of poverty without economical and educational opportunities. ✗ 没有经济和教育的机会，穷人不可能摆脱贫困。 【Eg.】*The Price of Inequality* and *The Great Divide* by Joseph E. Stiglitz 约瑟夫·斯蒂格利茨的著作《不平等的代价》和《主要分水岭》
P3	√ Poverty is inextricably tied to the social, political and economic inequality. √ 贫困和社会、政治以及经济的不平等密不可分。 【Eg.】"the challenges of growing inequality" by John F. Kennedy Jr. Forum, Oscar-winning documentary "Inside Job" 哈佛大学肯尼迪论坛"日益增长的不公带来的隐患"，奥斯卡金奖纪录片《监守自盗》
	✗ survivor of fittest ✗ 适者生存 【Eg.】evolution theory, Grandma Moses 进化论，摩西老祖母

Model Essay 1

Although human society has been advancing at a turbo-charged rate in science, technology, education, medicine and agriculture, poverty still scourges hundreds of millions of people on the earth. Some people argue that it is absolutely unrealistic for people to live in a world with no poverty, while others reason that it is one's own responsibility and diligence that keep him or her out of poverty. However, I am firmly convinced that only when governments establish a fair social and political system can poverty be truly eliminated.

> **开头段**：三句式首段法。第一句：引出作文题目的话题，比如说这篇文章是关于"poverty"的，作者就把"poverty"这个关键词作为开头段的背景句。第二句：转述作者不赞同的两个观点。第三句：陈述作者自己的立场。

It is true that human society has been accompanied by poverty ever since the beginning of human history, but it is still realistic to eliminate poverty completely from the earth. As evidenced by the fact that most of the European countries have successfully **made a significant dent in** poverty by building a fair social system to provide every member of the society with equal opportunities. As for the homeless, German government **launches homelessness prevention program** to eradicate deep poverty; as for those who have disability and cannot work, German government provides two incomes for one family member to stay at home to take care of the disabled. What is more, all the Germans are entitled to have free education from kindergarten to Ph.D education, plus free medicare. Likewise, Norwegian government establishes the system of equal income distribution to pay the trash men the same as university professors. By establishing a fair social system, those governments **have made significant strides towards eradicating poverty** completely and have helped individuals to reach the full potential of their talents. As quoted from the book entitled "The Price of Inequality" by Joseph E. Stiglitz, a Nobel laureate in economics, "We have the wealth and resources to eliminate poverty: Social Security and Medicare have almost eliminated poverty among the elderly. And other countries, not as rich as the United States, have done a better job of reducing poverty and inequality." It is self-evident that it is within the ability of most governments to end poverty by **adopting a comprehensive poverty reduction plan**. Therefore, I unhesitatingly oppose the second claim of perspective one.

> **第一个主体段：** 第一句的前半句中，作者做出让步，承认贫穷确实是从古至今都存在于人类历史中，然后马上反驳提出自己的立场，贫穷是可以被消灭的。然后作者通过举例论证来支持自己的立场，用了德国和罗威政府的实例来证明贫穷是可以被消除的。接下来作者又引用了诺贝尔经济奖得主约瑟夫·斯蒂格利茨的一本书《不平等的代价》，来进一步支持文章的论点。题目的指令中要求使用例子和推理去支持自己的论点，使用权威的人物引言和现代的真实事例可以让作者的观点更具有说服力。结尾句和首句之间首尾呼应，再次重申作者不同意 Perspective One 的第二部分，用总分总的段落结构来写主体段，逻辑会更清晰。

As for Perspective Two, I concede that there are plenty of job opportunities, and in normal circumstances, those who are self-responsible and self-disciplined can work their way out of poverty if they are industrious. The supporters of this perspective claim that people are poor and jobless because of their own laziness or inadequacies. They may sound right in their assertions, but they fail to reflect on how the external forces, such as discrimination in employment market, a lack of economic opportunity, and failed public education, adversely affect the socially and financially disadvantaged, thereby **dampening their drive to seek** better opportunities. In the words of Dr. William Julius Wilson, a world-renowned professor in sociology at Harvard University, "policy makers indirectly contributed to concentrated poverty in inner-city neighborhoods with decisions that decreased the attractiveness of low-paying jobs and accelerated the relative decline in low-income workers' wages." Without access to good education or equal employment opportunities, how can the disadvantaged and marginalized work their way out of impoverishment? Thus, I disagree with perspective two for its subjectivity and one-sidedness.

> **第二个主体段：** 对于 Perspective Two，作者也在段首做出让步，承认在正常情况下那些自我负责和自律的人通过勤奋可以摆脱贫穷，也把那

些持有这个观点的人的理由呈现出来，然后再去反驳。作者再次强调外在的因素，比如职业市场的歧视、缺乏的工作机会、失败的美国公立学校的教育给本来就在社会和经济地位处于劣势的穷人带来负面的影响。作者用世界著名的哈佛大学的社会学教授威廉·朱利叶斯·威尔逊博士一本书里的一句话来增加文章的论点的说服力。最后在结尾句再次表明自己的立场，即并不赞同 Perspective Two 的主观性和片面性。

I unhesitatingly agree with Perspective Three, because as soon as a fair social system **kicks into gear**, poverty will be eliminated effectively. It accords with common sense that poverty is inextricably tied to the social, political and economic inequality. To illustrate this point, I can think of no better example than five Harvard professors who attended John F. Kennedy Jr. Forum and presented a penetrating analysis on "the challenges of growing inequality". Their insights are further substantiated by the Oscar-winning documentary "Inside Job" directed by Charles Ferguson. The documentary provides undeniable facts on how the financial industry launder money, defraud customers, cook the books and plunge millions of people back into poverty. As Joseph E. Stiglitz put, "government policies have been central to the creation of inequality in the United States. If we are to reverse these trends in inequality, we will have to reverse some of the policies that have helped make America the most economically divided developed country and, beyond that, to take further actions to lessen the inequalities that arise on their own from market forces." Obviously, as long as inequality and exploitation are embedded in economic, social and political system, poverty will continue to impoverish the underprivileged. Therefore, only when governments shoulder their responsibilities to establish a fair social and political system can poverty be truly eliminated.

第三个主体段： 这个段落是对作者支持的 Perspective Three 进行论证，因为是作者赞同的观点，为了让文章的论点更有说服力，作者引证了三个权威资源来支持自己的论点。首先，指出贫穷和社会、经济、政治的不公平是密不可分的一个常识；然后，用哈佛大学公开课肯尼迪政治论坛关于"日益增长的不公带来的隐患"的讨论来支持自己的论点；接着用获得奥斯卡金奖的纪录片《监守自盗》，一部记录和分析华尔街和华尔街政府如何洗劫老百姓财富的纪实作品来加强文章的论点；最后，再次用诺贝尔经济学奖得主的话来总结文章的论点。结尾部分再次重申自己的立场，首尾呼应，完成总分总的主体段落结构。

To conclude, although poverty is pervasive all over the world and it is one's own obligation to fight against poverty, only when governments establish social equality can the life of the less fortunate be truly transformed. Therefore, it is incumbent on the governments to build a fair social and political system to eradicate poverty.

结尾段： 对不赞同的两个观点让步后，重申自己的立场和原因。

Words

concede *v.* 承认，退让

industrious *adj.* 勤勉的

scourge *v.* 痛斥，蹂躏

diligence *n.* 勤奋

eliminate *v.* 消除，排除

unhesitatingly *adv.* 毫不犹豫地

accelerate *v.* 加速，促进

Phrases

at a turbo-charged rate 以惊人的速度

a Nobel laureate in 在某个领域的诺贝尔奖得主

long-lasting consequences 深远的影响

fail to do 没有能够

world-renowned 世界著名的

the socially and financially disadvantaged 社会上和经济上处于劣势的人群

reach the full potential of one's talents 实现某人的最大潜力

the underprivileged 社会地位低下的人

a penetrating analysis 有洞察力的分析

be inextricably tied to 密不可分

be substantiated by 被证实

shoulder one's responsibility 肩负某人的责任

Sentences

Young as he is, he is very knowledgable. adj + as + subject + verb（让步状语从句）

I am firmly convinced that... 我坚信……

As evidenced by the fact that... 正如这个事实证实的那样……

To illustrate this point, I can think of no better example than... 没有比这个更好的例子去阐明这个论点……

They may sound right in their assertions, but they fail to do sth. 他们的断言听起来好像是对的，但是他们没有去……

It is incumbent on sb. to do sth. 做某事是某人的责任

Even more shocking is the fact that... 更让人惊讶的事实是……

Science and technology constitute a primary productive force 科学技术是第一生产力

Prompt 2

Defy or Obey Unjust Laws

Throughout the history, unjust laws have existed in the legal system of every government. They only serve the ruling party and those with vested interests at the expense of the majority. The very existence of unjust laws in any society is anti-democratic. By the contrast, just laws are the hallmark of a truly civilized and democratic society. Thanks to those courageous souls with integrity and a sense of justice, human society has made an extraordinary progress in terms of social and racial equality. As citizens, how should we approach unjust laws? What is the best way to act in order to ensure that the threats of unjust laws are eliminated and that they will be eventually repealed without causing social turmoil? These are questions worth examining in modern times because of the increasing social inequality caused by unjust laws.

Read and carefully consider these perspectives. Each suggests a particular way of thinking about the attitude towards unjust laws.

Perspective One	Perspective Two	Perspective Three
Even if the laws are unjust, people should abide by them and use peaceful ways to change them. To disobey the laws would endanger social stability and safety.	Breaking laws is unacceptable even if the laws are unfair. People should be patient because it takes time to rectify the defects of every law.	People should defy the laws that are unjust or immoral. Those who fight for the justice are the major contributors to building a democratic society.

Essay Task

Write a unified, coherent essay in which you evaluate multiple perspectives on the attitude towards unjust laws. In your essay, be sure to:

- clearly state your own perspective on the issue and analyze the relationship between your perspective and at least one other perspective
- develop and support your ideas with reasoning and examples
- organize your ideas clearly and logically
- communicate your ideas effectively in standard written English

Your perspective may be in full agreement with any of those given, in partial agreement, or completely different.

Prompt Analysis

P1	√ Fighting against unjust laws leads to social turmoil. √ 抗议不公正的法律会导致社会动乱。 【Eg.】French Revolution, British Revolution 法国革命，英国革命
	× Nonviolent social movement only brings social progress. × 非暴力的社会运动只会带来社会进步。 【Eg.】Mahatma Gandhi, Nelson Mandela, Martin Luther King 圣雄甘地，纳尔逊·曼德拉，马丁·路德·金

P2	✓ It takes time to perfect laws. ✓ 完善法律需要时间。 【Eg.】*The Emancipation Proclamation*《解放黑人奴隶宣言》
	✗ Abolishment of unjust laws is propelled by the courageous souls who fight against unjust laws. ✗ 不公正法律的废除取决于那些勇敢反抗它们的人。 【Eg.】Copernicus, William Wilberforce 哥白尼，威廉姆．韦伯福斯
P3	✓ Civil rights movement ✓ 民权运动 【Eg.】Martin Luther King 马丁·路德·金
	✗ People should obey laws even if they are unjust. ✗ 就算法律不公正，人们应该遵守它们。 【Eg.】colonial system 殖民体系

Model Essay 2

In the words of George Bernard Shaw, a world-renowned Nobel winner in literature, "The reasonable man adapts himself to the world; the unreasonable one persists in trying to adapt the world to himself. Therefore, all progress depends on the unreasonable man." Those who argue that people should comply with unjust laws believe that defying them would endanger social stability and safety; likewise, some people reason that it takes time to rectify the defects of every law and it is unacceptable to break unjust laws. However, from my perspective, it is those who defy unjust laws and fight for justice transform human society.

开头段：三句式首段法。第一句：用名人名言引出作文题目的话题。第二句：转述作者不赞同的两个观点。第三句：陈述作者自己的立场。

I concede that defying the laws may endanger social stability and safety when the protesters are fueled by anger and resentment, but history proves that nonviolent revolutions against unjust laws only bring forth positive social changes. To illustrate this point, I can think of no better example than Mahatma Gandhi whose campaign of nonviolent civil resistance to British colonization and the unjust laws imposed upon Indians led to India's independence in 1947. Gandhi effectively fought against unjust laws enacted by British Empire with his principles of truth, nonviolence, and courage. Inspired by the civil disobedience to unjust laws proposed by Gandhi, Nelson Mandela led nonviolent movement in South Africa and Martin Luther King led civil rights movement in the US. All those nonviolent social movements defied unjust laws openly but only brought forth social progress, never endangering social stability nor safety. By contrast, those who comply with unjust laws inevitably make themselves accomplices of genocides, wars, dictatorships, social and racial injustice. Based on the nonfiction written by Viktor E. Frankl, *Man's Search for Meaning*, some Jewish people competed for being camp wardens to kill their own people in gas chambers and crematoriums in exchange for food and clothing. As quoted from Frankl, "in the bitter fight for self-preservation he may forget his human dignity and become no more than an animal." Reflecting on history, when people comply with unjust laws, their appalling silence encourages bestial behaviors of humans. Therefore, I disagree with Perspective One completely.

第一个主体段：第一句的前半句中，作者做出让步，承认当抗议不公正的法律的人充满愤恨时会威胁社会安全，然后马上反驳并提出自己的立场，非暴力的抗争不但不会威胁社会安全，反而会带来积极的社会变革。作者通过举例论证支持自己的立场，比如说甘地、马丁·路德·金、曼德拉的非暴力地去抗争不公的法律带来的社会进步；接下来做了一个对比，引用了维克多·埃米尔·弗兰克尔的纪实作品来进一步支持文章的论点。题目的指令中要求使用例子和推理去支持自己的论点，使用权威的人物和现代的真实事例可以让作者的观点更具有说服力。结尾句和首句之间首尾呼应，再次重申作者不同意 Perspective One，用总分总的段落结构来写主体段逻辑会更好。

Admittedly, history has amassed ample objective proof to show that it takes time to rectify the defects of every law. However, the rectification or abolishment of unjust laws is propelled by the courageous souls who fight against unjust laws rather than just be patient. In the sixteenth century, a great debate arose when Copernicus vehemently challenged a long-held belief that the earth was the center of the solar system. Consequently, he was persecuted and paid a price both socially and politically for this remonstration. However, Copernicus remained his loyalty to guarding scientific truth and his heliocentric theory. Eventually, it is the courage and persistence of Copernicus that disabused geocentric theory. Most importantly, he fought against unjust laws regardless of the pressure from the government ruled by Catholic Church. Thanks to Copernicus' sterling rectitude and his fight for truth, humankind eventually gained a new understanding of astronomy. It is people like Copernicus who bravely fought against unjust laws that brought social progress to human society. From a historical perspective, only by defying unjust laws can they be rectified and repealed.

> **第二个主体段：** 对于 Perspective Two 作者也在段首做出让步，承认每一种不公正的法律的完善都需要时间，然后马上强调不公正的法律的废除都归功于那些勇敢对抗它们的人。作者用哥白尼的例子增加文章论点的说服力。最后在结尾句再次表明自己的立场。

I unhesitatingly agree with Perspective Three that those who defy unjust laws are great contributors to bringing social progress to establish a democratic society. Prior to 1960s in the United States of America, 100 years after *The Emancipation Proclamation* that abolished slavery, African Americans were still crippled by the chains of discrimination and manacles of segregation. Inspired by the courage of Rosa Parks, Martin Luther King led the civil rights movement to fight for their unalienable rights of life, liberty and the pursuit of happiness guaranteed by the American Constitution and *Declaration of Independence*. Despite the bleak circumstances, Dr. King was so optimistic that he gave an unforgettable speech entitled "I have a dream" to defy the unjust laws inflicted on African Americans and strive for their citizenship rights. As what Dr. King said in his speech, "And there will be neither rest nor tranquility in America until the African Americans are granted with their citizenship rights. The whirlwinds of revolt will continue to shake the foundations of our nation until the bright day of justice emerges." It is no overstatement to say that it is these devotees' courageous fight against social and racial injustice that led to the enactment of *Civil Rights Act* in 1964. Without their civil disobedience towards unjust laws, African Americans may still wallow in the valley of despair and they may still be stripped of their dignity and identity. Undoubtedly, those who fight for justice are definitely great contributors to building a democratic society.

> **第三个主体段：** 这个段落是对作者支持的 Perspective Three 进行论证，因为是作者赞同的观点，为了让文章的论点更有说服力，作者引用民权运动来加强文章的论点。结尾部分再次重申自己的立场，首尾呼应，使用总分总的主体段落结构。

To sum up, only by defying unjust laws can they be rectified or even abolished. Those who fight for justice and fight against unjust laws are true social reformers transforming the human society.

> **结尾段：** 重申自己的立场和原因。

社会进步类作业

（一）完形填空练习：请在以下 20 个词组中找出合适的词组填入下面两段文字中

1. at a turbo-charged rate 以惊人的速度

2. a Nobel laureate in... 在某个领域的诺贝尔奖得主

3. long-lasting consequences 深远的影响

4. fail to do 没有能够做什么

5. world-renowned 世界著名的

6. the socially and financially disadvantaged 社会上和经济上处于劣势的人群

7. reach the full potential of one's talents 实现某人的最大潜力

8. the underprivileged 社会地位低下的人

9. be inextricably tied to 被密不可分地捆绑在一起

10. condemn rather than condone sth. 谴责而不是纵容某事

11. as evidenced by the fact that 正如这个事实证实的那样

12. it is incumbent on sb. to do sth. 做某事是某人的责任

13. the hallmark of 标志

14. a civilized and democratic society 文明和民主的社会

15. eliminate poverty 消除贫穷

16. polarization of the rich and the poor 富人和穷人的极化

17. enhance comprehensive national strength 增强综合国力

18. harmonious world 和谐世界

19. boost the local tertiary industry 促进当地第三产业的发展

20. optimize the distribution of resources 优化资源配置

完形填空一

With the development of globalization, the fate of human beings （1） each other. Although technology, education, medicine and agriculture are advancing （2）, the （3） is more intensified than ever before.

完形填空二

（1） any democratic and civilized society is to take care of （2）. Therefore, （3） the government to （4） in order to build up a （5）.

（二）汉译英练习

1. vested interest 既得利益

   私人银行家和那些在金融业工作的人为了他们的既得利益垄断金融市场。

2. at the expense of... 以……为代价

   那些自私自利和腐败的政治家牺牲大众来取悦银行家们。

3. civil disobedience 非暴力反抗

   这个地区通过非暴力反抗脱离殖民统治而获得独立。

4. comply with 遵守

   只有当所有居民都遵守法律时，一个社会才有秩序和稳定。

5. appalling silence 令人震惊的沉默

   这个世界不会被恶人的邪恶毁灭，它只会被好人的令人震惊的沉默毁灭。

6. social turmoil 社会动乱

   不断加大的财富差距无法避免地会导致社会动乱。

7. be fueled by... 被……推动

   科技的进步是被创新推动的。

8. bestial behaviors 残暴的行为

   那些沉溺于残暴行为的人最终会失去人性。

9. nonviolent civil resistance 非暴力的文明抵抗

   人们通过非暴力的文明抵抗赢得了他们的居民权利。

10. be stripped of one's dignity and identity 某人被剥夺尊严和身份

    社会最底层的人被有歧视的社会制度剥夺了尊严和身份。

11. the valley of despair 绝望的山谷

    乐观者在面对让人畏缩的困难时从来不会在绝望的山谷中自暴自弃。

12. hamper one's development 阻碍某人的发展

    自大会阻碍一个人的发展。

13. at a turbo-charged rate 以惊人的速度

    知识正在以惊人的速度增长。

14. a Nobel laureate in 在某个领域获得诺贝尔奖的得主

    约瑟夫·斯蒂格利茨是一个在经济学上获得了诺贝尔奖的得主。

15. long-lasting consequences 深远的影响

    环境污染对人类社会有深远的影响。

16. fail to do 没能做什么

    如果科技无法平衡经济和环境，就会出现一系列的灾难。

17. world-renowned 世界著名的

有越来越多的世界著名的学者们为了人类社会的改良努力奋斗。

18. the socially and financially disadvantaged 社会上和经济上处于劣势的人群

海伦·凯勒把自己投身于帮助社会上和经济上处于劣势的人群。

19. reach the full potential of one's talents 实现某人的最大潜力

毅力和勤奋可以帮助人们实现他们最大的潜力。

20. the underprivileged 社会地位低下的人

特蕾莎修女关爱印度社会地位低下的人，为他们提供食物和衣物。

21. a penetrating analysis 有洞察力的分析

约瑟夫·斯蒂格利茨和其他哈佛大学的教授对导致美国社会问题的原因提供了一个有洞察力的分析——私人银行家发行美元和挟持政府。

22. be inextricably tied to 被密不可分地捆绑在一起

随着全球化的快速步伐，人类的命运被密不可分地捆绑在一起。

23. be substantiated by 被证实

有远见的经济学家们对经济坍塌的担忧被 2008 年的经济危机所证实。

24. shoulder one's responsibility 肩负某人的责任

有专业知识和洞察力的学者们应该肩负起他们的责任去服务于国家而不是金钱。

25. condemn rather than condone sth. 谴责而不是纵容某事

老师们应该谴责而不应该纵容学校欺凌。

26. as evidenced by the fact that 正如事实证实的那样

正如事实证实的那样，社会不公会阻碍经济的发展。

27. it is incumbent on sb. to do sth. 做某事是某人的责任

给学生灌输公正、诚实、同理心和同情心等高尚的价值观是教育者们的责任。

28. endanger social stability and safety 威胁社会稳定和安全

腐败的政府和为自我服务的政治家们会威胁社会稳定和安全。

29. moral dilemma 道德困境

医生发现疯牛病会导致老年痴呆时，他们面临着道德困境。

30. be prioritized over 优先于

社会公正应该优先于经济的发展。

31. thwart terrorist attacks 打击恐怖袭击

在当今世界，很多国家不得不打击恐怖袭击来保护他们的居民。

32. national security 国家安全

只有尊重其他国家和人民，一个国家才会真正地拥有国家安全。

33. intrude on personal privacy 侵犯个人隐私

一个诚实正直的政府从不会侵犯公民的个人隐私。

34. government surveillance 政府监控

政府监控必须受到严格的法律法规的限制。

35. the hallmark of 标志

照顾社会上和经济上处于劣势的人群是一个文明和民主的社会的标志。

36. a civilized and democratic society 文明和民主的社会

建立一个文明和民主的社会需要全体居民的最大努力。

37. eliminate poverty 消除贫穷

各国政府应该肩负起职责去消除国内和国外的贫穷。

38. financial burden 财政负担

全民免费医疗给政府造成很大的财政负担。

39. polarization of the rich and the poor 富人和穷人的极化

社会和经济的不公导致富人和穷人的极化。

40. foster a climate of peace and prosperity 营造一个和平与繁荣的氛围

全世界的学者们应该为人类营造一个和平与繁荣的氛围。

41. get rid of poverty and backwardness 摆脱贫穷落后

建立一个公平的社会和经济制度可以帮助一个国家摆脱贫穷和落后。

42. enhance comprehensive national strength 增强综合国力

经济发展和科技进步能够增强一个国家的综合国力。

43. harmonious world 和谐的世界

国家之间的和平共存一定能带来一个和谐的世界。

44. boost the local tertiary industry 促进当地第三产业的发展

旅游业的发展可以促进当地第三产业的发展。

45. strengthen the enforcement of laws 加强执法

政府需要加强执法来惩治腐败。

46. rely on science and technology to rejuvenate the nation 依靠科技兴国

依靠科技兴国是通向繁荣的最可靠的途径。

47. optimize the distribution of resources 优化资源配置

优化资源配置可以避免不必要的浪费。

48. revival of customs and traditions 风俗传统的复兴

一个国家风俗传统的复兴可以吸引更多的外国游客。

49. science and technology constitutes a primary productive force 科学技术是第一生产力

对于任何国家而言科学技术是第一生产力。

50. preserve historic and cultural heritages 保护历史文化遗产

在一个全球化的时代，对于所有国家来说保护历史文化遗产是非常重要的。

Prompt 3

Safety vs. Privacy

With the advent of digital technology, people's privacy is compromised when some ill-willed people peer into our lives. Even many governments start surveillance capturing citizens' phone calls, emails and text messages in order to thwart terrorist attacks or prevent crimes from endangering the society. Security cameras are everywhere to deter crimes but also intrude on people's privacy. The conflict between citizens' right to privacy and the need for safety has been intensified. Is government surveillance illegitimate and ethical? Should people sacrifice their privacy in exchange for safety? Given the moral dilemma between privacy and national security, it is worth considering whether one should be prioritized over the other. Read and consider these perspectives. Each suggests a particular way of thinking about the conflict between safety and privacy.

Read and carefully consider these perspectives. Each suggests a particular way of thinking about the safety and privacy.

Perspective One	Perspective Two	Perspective Three
Government surveillance intrudes on citizens' privacy in the name of national security. It is absolutely immoral for government to violate personal privacy for any reason.	Privacy must be given up so that government can prevent crimes from endangering the society. Government surveillance is understandable given the national threats from the evil conspiracy of some foreign governments.	Government surveillance should be conducted by strict laws. It should be only restricted to matters of national security and it should never intrude on personal privacy.

Essay Task

Write a unified, coherent essay in which you evaluate multiple perspectives on the safety and privacy. In your essay, be sure to:

- clearly state your own perspective on the issue and analyze the relationship between your perspective and at least one other perspective
- develop and support your ideas with reasoning and examples
- organize your ideas clearly and logically
- communicate your ideas effectively in standard written English

Your perspective may be in full agreement with any of those given, in partial agreement, or completely different.

Extended reading

Reference Article: United Nations: Rein in Mass Surveillance

(New York) – Governments around the world should heed the findings of the UN's human rights commissioner on mass surveillance, Human Rights Watch said today. Governments should rein in mass surveillance and respect the privacy of all Internet users, no matter where they are located.

United Nations High Commissioner for Human Rights Navi Pillay released a far-reaching report on July 16, 2014 warning that, globally, "mass surveillance [is] emerging as a dangerous habit rather than an exceptional measure" and reaffirming that state surveillance may only be conducted if it is necessary and proportionate to a legitimate goal. The report criticizes many common practices and justifications offered by the US, UK, and other governments in support of mass surveillance.

"The High Commissioner's report is a critical step that puts the right to privacy on firm legal foundation for the digital age," said Cynthia Wong, senior Internet researcher at Human Rights Watch. "With this report, all governments should immediately start to review their digital surveillance practices and bring them in line with international rights standards."

The report lays out states' obligations to safeguard the right to privacy in the digital age and identifies gaps in how that right is being protected with respect to countries' digital surveillance practices. As an immediate measure, the report called on governments to review their national laws, policies, and practices to ensure full conformity with international human rights law.

Human Rights Watch said that the UN report makes clear that the US and UK in particular need to reform their surveillance laws and practices. The US has taken almost no steps to curtail the scale and scope of data and communications that intelligence agencies can acquire on persons located outside US borders. The UK government had been largely silent on the issue until this week, when it rushed through a law to maintain the UK's ability to require Internet and telecom companies to retain certain metadata about all users in the UK, regardless of whether they are under suspicion of wrongdoing.

The UN General Assembly requested the report from the High Commissioner in a December 2013 resolution, co-sponsored by 57 member countries, to submit views and recommendations to the General Assembly and UN Human Rights Council on "the right to privacy in the context of domestic and extraterritorial surveillance," including on a "mass scale." The resolution was a response to ongoing revelations by the former US National Security Agency contractor Edward Snowden regarding mass surveillance by the US and UK.

In the report, Pillay reaffirmed that government surveillance must respect the right to privacy and clarifies how these obligations apply to current practices. The report made several crucial points:

- Surveillance must be necessary and proportionate: The onus is on governments to demonstrate that their surveillance practices are not arbitrary or unlawful. That means governments must show that surveillance is both proportionate and necessary to a legitimate aim.

- Countries have extraterritorial duties: Governments must respect the rights of individuals, regardless of their nationality or location, given that the Internet's infrastructure enables far-reaching extraterritorial surveillance. This was a key point of contention because some governments, like the US, did not accept responsibility for the right to privacy of individuals or non-nationals abroad when conducting surveillance.

- Metadata merits stronger protections: Metadata, or data about communications, can reveal highly sensitive information, especially when collected at large scale, and merits stronger safeguards than some national laws currently provide.

- Mere collection impacts privacy: The report states that the mere collection of communications or metadata can interfere with privacy, regardless of whether the information is viewed or used.

- Transparency and accountability: The High Commissioner cited a "disturbing lack of governmental transparency associated with surveillance policies, laws, and practices, which hinders any effort to assess their coherence with international human rights law and to ensure accountability." The report called for much greater transparency and emphasized that surveillance cannot be justified on secret law or regulations that grant too much discretion to authorities.

- Responsibilities of technology companies: The report stated that in any case, if technology companies comply with government requests for surveillance assistance without adequate safeguards, they risk complicity in any resulting human rights abuses

(Excerpted from *Human Right Watch, Alice Oshima,* https://www.hrw.org/news/2014/07/17/united-nations-rein-mass-surveillance)

Topic Analysis

　　个人选择是一个相对比较宽泛的话题，引导考生对人生观、价值观及生活方式进行思考，深度思考不同人身上所折射出的性格特点、生活习惯、所做选择及其人生影响。在改革后的 ACT 作文考试中，话题涉及应对挑战（challenges）、掌握技能（master skills）、与他人对比（compare oneself with others）、应对未来不确定性（planning and uncertainty）、名气（fame）、明智和决断（being wise and determining）、欲望（desire，whether wanting more is a good thing）、坏习惯（bad habits）、同情心（compassion）等，题目难度属于中等。由于和个人相关，这类题目大多需要考生结合人物事例进行论证，需要提前积累较丰富的名人素材，能够较熟练地展开细节写作。备考时，老师和考生可以从诚实、忠诚、自私、进取心、适应环境、从众、成功与失败的过程、方式和结果、生活方式选择等角度进行深入探讨和练习。

Topic Vocabulary

intention 意图

target 目标

ambition 抱负

ambitious 野心勃勃的

enthusiastic 有热情的

zealous 热情的，积极的

aggressive 积极进取的

nonconformist 不从众者

stick to 坚持

encounter resistance 遭遇阻力

abandon one's dream 放弃梦想

come to nothing 一事无成

come true（梦想等）实现

be compatible with 适合，一致

owe...to... 把……归因于……

attribute...to... 把……归因于……

struggle for... 为……而斗争

take pains to do sth. 努力做某事

succeed in doing sth. 成功做某事

make one's way 克服困难前进

strike to overcome difficulties 努力克服困难

steadfast adherence to... 坚守……

commit oneself to doing sth. 致力于某事

life schedule 生活计划

prioritized task 优先任务

abide by... 忠于……；遵守……

be engrossed in... 埋头于……

on no account 绝不要

under no condition 决不

be accustomed to... 习惯于……

adapt oneself to... 使自己适应……

have an advantage over... 胜过……

be anxious about... 为……焦虑不安

be ashamed of... 为……羞耻

be capable of... 能够做……

beyond dispute 无可争议

be eager for 渴望；期盼

economize on 节省

be born with 天生具有

break through 突破，冲破（障碍、困难）

cater to 迎合

turn the corner 开始好转

at the expense of... 以……为代价

make history 名垂千史

hold back 踌躇，犹豫

for the sake of... 为了……的利益

in light of... 考虑到……

look down on sb. 蔑视某人

get nowhere 一无所获

at the sacrifice of... 以……为代价

Extended Reading

Reference Article 1: Rosa Parks

1 Rosa Parks is a famous African-American woman who is often called "the mother of the civil rights movement." When she was born into a poor but hardworking African-American family in Alabama, no one suspected that she would become the spark that ignited the civil rights movement in the United States. This movement changed U.S. society forever by helping African-American people attain equal rights under the law.

2 Parks became famous quite by accident. One day in 1955, on her way home from her job in a Montgomery, Alabama, department store, she boarded a city bus with three other African-Americans. They sat in the fifth row, which was the first row African-Americans were allowed to sit in. A few stops later, the front four rows filled up, and a white man was left standing.

3 According to the laws of that time, African-Americans had to give up their seats to whites, so the bus driver asked Parks and the three other African-Americans to get up and move. Although the others complied, Parks refused. She later said she was not tired from work, but tired of being treated like a second-class citizen. The bus driver called the police, who arrested Parks and took her away in handcuffs.

4 Over the weekend, a protest was organized, and on the following Monday, African-American people in Montgomery began a boycott of the public buses. The boycott was tremendously successful, lasting for more than a year. The Supreme Court of the United States finally ruled that segregation on public transportation was unconstitutional. Because they had won a huge victory, African-Americans realized their power to change the system. (272 words)

(Excerpted from *Writing Academic English (Fourth Edition)*, by Alice Oshima, Ann Hogue, 2006.)

Analysis of Article

Main Points of Rosa Parks

This famous African-American woman ignited the civil rights movement.

She refused to give up her seat to the white and was arrested by police in handcuffs.

After her arrest, African-American people in Montgomery began a boycott of the public buses that lasted for more than one year.

The Supreme Court of the United States finally ruled the segregation on public transportation was unjust.

Vocabulary

suspect *n./v.* 怀疑

spark *n./v.* 火花；星火

ignite *v.* 点燃

comply *v.* 遵从，顺从

boycott *n./v.* 抵制

segregation *n.* 隔离

unconstitutional *adj.* 违反宪法的；不合章程的

Read-Recite-Imitate-Create

Example one:

1. Read: When she was born into a poor but hardworking African-American family in Alabama, no one suspected that she would become the spark that ignited the civil rights movement in the United States.

2. Recite: ...**become the spark that ignites**...

3. Imitate: Lincoln **became the spark that ignites** the civil war.

4. Create: For the former people, down-to-earth work ensures safety but cuts whatever corners, while for the latter people, they willingly embrace challenges thus have a higher likelihood of **becoming the spark that ignites** others.

Example two:

1. Read: She later said she was not tired from work, but tired of being treated like a second-class citizen.
2. Recite: **be tired of doing sth.**
3. Imitate: Lisa **is** so **tired of doing** endless chores at home.
4. Create: As for those idealistic fighters, they **are tired of satisfying with** temporary life.

Example three:

1. Read: The boycott was tremendously successful, lasting for more than a year.
2. Recite: **tremendously**
3. Imitate: Our life quality has improved **tremendously** after 1990s.
4. Create: Not content with physical capability, he founded an international non-profit organization Life Without Limbs to help more people to regain **tremendous** confidence.

Reference Article 2: Pragmatic vs. Idealistic Behavior

1 I agree with the speaker insofar as that a practical, pragmatic approach toward our endeavors can help us survive in the short term. However, idealism is just as crucial—if not more so—for long-term success in any endeavor, whether it be in academics, business, or political and social reform.

2 When it comes to academics, students who we would consider pragmatic tend not to pursue an education for its own sake. Instead, they tend to cut whatever corners are needed to optimize their grade average and survive the current academic term. But, is this approach the only way to succeed academically? Certainly not. Students who earnestly pursue intellectual paths that truly interest then are more likely to come away with a meaningful and lasting education. In fact, a sense of mission about one's area of fascination is strong motivation to participate actively in class and to study earnestly, both of which contribute to better grades in that area. Thus, although the idealist-student might sacrifice a high overall grade average, the depth of knowledge, academic discipline, and sense of purpose the student

gains will serve that student well later in life.

3 In considering the business world it might be more tempting to agree with the speaker; after all, isn't business fundamentally about pragmatism—that is, "getting the job done" and paying attention to the "bottom line"? Emphatically, no. Admittedly, the everyday machinations of business are very much about meeting mundane short-term goals: deadlines for production, sales quotas, profit margins, and so forth. Yet underpinning these activities is the vision of the company's chief executive—a vision that might extend far beyond mere profit maximization to the ways in which the firm can make a lasting and meaningful contribution to the community, to the broader economy, and to the society as a whole. Without a dream or vision— that is, without strong idealist leadership—a firm can easily be cast in the sea of commerce without clear direction, threatening not only the firm's bottom line but also its very survival.

4 Finally, when it comes to the political arena, again at first blush it might appear that pragmatism is the best, if not the only, way to succeed. Most politicians seem driven by their interest in being elected and reelected—that is, in surviving—rather than by any sense of mission, or even obligation to their constituency or country. Diplomatic and legal maneuverings and negotiations often appear intended to meet the practical needs of the parties involved—minimizing costs, preserving options, and so forth. But, it is idealists—not pragmatists—who sway the masses, incite revolutions, and make political ideology reality. Consider idealists such as America's founders, Mahatma Gandhi, or Martine Luther King. Had these idealists concerned themselves with short-term survival and immediate needs rather than with their notions of an ideal society, the United States and India might still be Britain colonies, and African Americans might still be relegated to the backs of buses.

5 In short, the statement fails to recognize that idealism—keeping one's eye on an ultimate prize—is the surest path to long-term success in any endeavor. Meeting one's immediate needs, while arguably necessary

for short-term survival, accomplishes little without a sense of mission, a vision, or dream for the long term. (548 words)

(Excerpted from *GRE CAT Answers to the Real Essay Questions, by Mark Alan Stewart, J.D., 2008.*)

Analysis of Article

Pros of Idealism

Academics: Students who earnestly pursue intellectual paths that truly interest them are more likely to come away with a meaningful and lasting education.

Business world: Leaders might extend far beyond mere profit maximization to the ways in which the firm can make a lasting and meaningful contribution to the community, to the broader economy, and to the society as a whole.

Political area: it is idealists—not pragmatists—who sway the masses, incite revolutions, and make political ideology reality.

Cons of Pragmatism

Academics: students tend to cut whatever corners are needed to optimize their grade average and survive the current academic term.

Business world: leaders may just pay attention to getting the job done and paying attention to the "bottom line".

Political area: Most politicians are only driven by their interest in being elected and reelected—that is, in surviving.

Vocabulary

endeavor *n.* 努力

optimize *v.* 优化，充分利用

earnestly *adv.* 认真地，诚挚地

emphatically *adv.* 强调地，有力地

underpin *v.* 加固（建筑或其他）地下基础

maneuver *v.* 演习，调遣

sway *n./v.* 摇摆，摆动

incite *v.* 鼓励，鼓动

insofar as... 在……限制内，在……范围内

for its own sake 为自身的原因

When it comes to... 当谈及⋯⋯

Read-Recite-Imitate-Create

Example one:

1. Read: When it comes to academics, students who we would consider pragmatic tend not to pursue an education for its own sake.

2. Recite: **When it comes to**...

3. Imitate: **When it comes to** duty, these people tend to shy away from it.

4. Create: **When it comes to** pragmatic people, they accept who they are and do things for their own sake.

Example two:

1. Read: When it comes to academics, students who we would consider pragmatic tend not to pursue an education for its own sake.

2. Recite: **for its own sake**

3. Imitate: **For your own sake**, you should take the test immediately.

4. Create: When it comes to pragmatic people, they accept who they are and do things **for their own sake**.

Example three:

1. Read: Instead, they tend to cut whatever corners are needed to optimize their grade average and survive the current academic term.

2. Recite: **cut whatever corners**...

3. Imitate: As a responsible businessman, you can never **cut whatever corners** to seek profits.

4. Create: For the former people, down-to-earth work ensures safety but **cuts whatever corners** to ensure ease, while for the latter people, they willingly embrace challenges thus have a larger chance to become the spark that ignites others.

Example four:

1. Read: Without a dream or vision—that is, without strong idealist leadership—a firm can easily be cast in the sea of commerce without clear direction, threatening not only the firm's bottom line but also its very survival.

2. Recite: **be cast in the sea of**...**without clear direction**

3. Imitate: She is like a helpless fish **cast in the sea without clear direction**.

4. Create: Elon Musk could be **cast in the sea of** commerce **without** the dream of changing the world and humanity.

Example five:

1. Read: But, it is idealists—not pragmatists—who sway the masses, incite revolutions, and make political ideology reality.

2. Recite: **make...reality**

3. Imitate: Only with great efforts can you **make** your dream **reality**.

4. Create: Dreams endow them with courage and motivation, which help them encounter difficulties and **make** dreams **reality**.

Example six:

1. Read: Had these idealists concerned themselves with short-term survival and immediate needs rather than with their notions of an ideal society, the United States and India might still be Britain colonies, and African Americans might still be relegated to the backs of buses.

2. Recite: **Had...did..., ... might still be...**

3. Imitate: **Had** the girl **refused** to offer help, this man **might still be** a beggar on the road.

4. Create: **Had** he **been** a pragmatic person, he **would have just lain** in sofa and waited for help.

Example seven:

1. Read: Had these idealists concerned themselves with short-term survival and immediate needs rather than with their notions of an ideal society, the United States and India might still be Britain colonies, and African Americans might still be relegated to the backs of buses.

2. Recite: **concern with**...

3. Imitate: Young people should **concern with** the future of the nation.

4. Create: Nevertheless, his idealistic dream to be a better man saved and reshaped him to be a role model who **concern with** millions disadvantaged people.

Prompt 1

Pragmatic Approach vs. Idealistic Approach

In any realm of life, whether academic, social, business, or political, people prefer pragmatic ways or points of view to idealistic ones. It is commonly thought that idealism easily breeds pride and prejudice that may cloud people's judgments. However, throughout the world, a large group of successful people seem to be more idealistic than pragmatic. They dream big to see larger pictures in life and their courage often yields more. Is pragmatism the only way to guarantee success and can people achieve success in a different way? Given ample examples of successful people with different approaches, it is thus necessary to consider whether people should be pragmatic or idealistic.

Read and carefully consider these perspectives. Each suggests a particular way of thinking about pragmatic or idealistic approach.

Perspective One	Perspective Two	Perspective Three
Only down to earth people can have the chance to succeed. All work needs people's ceaseless efforts.	It's hard for people to be both pragmatic and idealistic for the two characteristics conflict with each other. People should choose one approach and stick to it.	Idealistic people always have ambition that provides them with greater motivation. Satisfaction easily breeds ease and laziness.

Essay Task

Write a unified, coherent essay in which you evaluate multiple perspectives on pragmatic or idealistic approach. In your essay, be sure to:

- clearly state your own perspective on the issue and analyze the relationship between your perspective and at least one other perspective
- develop and support your ideas with reasoning and examples
- organize your ideas clearly and logically
- communicate your ideas effectively in standard written English

Your perspective may be in full agreement with any of those given, in partial agreement, or completely different.

Prompt Analysis

P1	✓ Although idealistic people can succeed, but only a small portion of people succeed in this way. Success is more reliably based on real actions. ✓ 虽然理想主义者确实成功了，但是这样成功的人毕竟是少数，不可借鉴。人们还是要踏踏实实才能成功，所有的成功都是建立在实际行动之上的。 【Eg.】inventor Nikola Tesla, writer J.K. Rowling 发明家尼古拉·特斯拉，作家 J.K. 罗琳
	✗ History has witnessed numerous success of idealistic people. ✗ 并非只有实用主义可以成功，历史上理想主义者成功的例子也屡见不鲜。 【Eg.】founder of Apple Steve Jobs, founder of Alibaba Ma Yun, basketball player Jeremy Lin 苹果创始人史蒂夫·乔布斯，阿里巴巴创始人马云，篮球明星林书豪
P2	✓ Pragmatism and idealism require different qualities and it's hard for people to be equipped with such qualities at the same time. ✓ 实用主义和理想主义对人的要求非常不一样，人们很难同时具备这样的品质。 【Eg.】general examples 泛例
	✗ These two values complement each other and can yield a better result. ✗ 这两种品质互补，最终可以产生更好的结果。 【Eg.】Martin Luther King Jr., Oprah Winfrey 民权运动领袖马丁·路德·金，脱口秀主持人奥普拉·温弗瑞

	✓ People shall pay greater efforts to realize their dreams.
	✓ 理想可以让人们愿意付出更多的努力。
P3	【Eg.】American President: Abraham Lincoln, founder of Microsoft: Bill Gates, Nobel Winner: Marie Curie 美国总统亚伯拉罕·林肯，微软创始人比尔·盖茨，诺贝尔奖得主居里夫人
	✗ Too unrealistic dreams lead to the wrong direction.
	✗ 过于理想主义很容易使人不切实际，走弯路。
	【Eg.】Gatsby in *The Great Gatsby*, "Corn Campaign" launched by leader of Soviet Union Khrushchev《了不起的盖茨比》中的主角盖茨比，前苏联总理赫鲁晓夫的"玉米运动"

Model Essay 1

People adore pragmatism and tend to attribute progress to those who tackle problems and offer solutions. In comparison, anyone, wandering and dreaming, is easily labeled as a daydreamer and criticized as a "difference". Truly, it seems that all people enjoy ready-to-come yields because idealistic goals provide no guarantee for outcomes. However, throughout history, it is not hard to spot people with big dreams accomplishing amazing achievements. From my perspective, thus, pragmatism and idealism complement each other and all pave way for success.

开头段：开篇让步结构"反方观点 + 反方假设的合理性 + 针对性反驳 + 提出观点"，让步思路提前，能够较好地展现作者的思辨，也能够较迅速地形成思路，丰富细节。这里的让步信息是泛泛地论述，和文中更具有针对性的驳论不同，注意信息量不要重合。另外，开头段写作注意观点的合理性，文中的论述要对观点形成紧密有效的支撑，不要想当然或者故意为了写观点而写观点，观点一定要建立在后文之上。

Indeed, all work demands people's efforts, but never is there only one way that promises success. **When it comes to** pragmatic people, they accept who they are and do things **for their own sake.** While idealistic people are unsatisfied with themselves and try harder to reach a higher level. For the former people, down-to-earth work ensures safety but **cuts** whatever corners, while for the latter people, they willingly embrace challenges thus have a higher likelihood of becoming the spark that ignites others. Born with no legs and arms, the Australian motivational speaker Nick Vujicic dares to do all things that normal people do, surfing in the sea, riding an elephant, and even kicking the ball with professional football players. Not content with physical capability, he founded an international non-profit organization Life Without Limbs to help more people to regain **tremendous** confidence. **Had** he **been** a pragmatic person, he **would have just lain** in sofa and waited for help. Nevertheless, his idealistic dream to be a better man saved and reshaped him to be a role model who **concerned with** millions of physically disadvantaged people.

> **第一个主体段**：本段针对 Perspective One 进行论述。Perspective One 是个典型的 "1+1" 模式的分论点，即 1 句话错误假设 +1 句话正确假设。这样的情况我们没有必要完全同意或者完全反驳，结合自己的观点进行针对性评价和展开即可。本段中，作者先承认了 "all work demands people's efforts（所有工作都需要付出努力）"，接着反驳 Perspective One 中的前一句话，即 "Only down to earth people can have the chance to succeed.（只有脚踏实地的人才能成功）"，通过取得成功的不同方式反驳 Perspective One。例证部分选取了名人事例，结合本段中心充分论证了并非只有脚踏实地的人才能够取得成就。

As for those idealistic fighters, they **are tired of satisfying with** temporary life. They dream big and take actions. Dreams endow them with courage and motivation, which help them overcome difficulties and make dreams reality. Such spiritual power is hardly seen on pragmatic doers, for they are confined and satisfied with what they have done and have little desire to jump out of their comfort zones. In the latest classic Indian film *Dangal*, the father dreamed to change India's international athletic status by unprecedentedly training his daughters to wrestle in public. He faced huge pressure and blame from everyone around him but faithfully believed in his dream. Paying unbelievable efforts, he did successfully train his two daughters to become Olympic wrestlers. His idealism empowered him to pursue his dreams firmly and reach far, and he fulfilled a common belief that where there is a will, there is a way.

第二个主体段：本段对第二段形成了深度的递进，支持 Perspective Three，论证理想化梦想的积极作用。作者通过对比实用主义者和理想主义者在动机上的不同，展示理想对人的有效激励。这一段中，作者使用了热门电影作为支撑，较高效地用四句话构建例子，讲述摔跤爸爸心怀理想勇于逐梦的故事。

Thus, both being pragmatic and idealistic can help people succeed in different ways. It is no overstatement to say that almost all the successful people have idealistic vision and pragmatic behaviors. The combination of the two values complement each other and benefit people every time when they keep trying hard. Nelson Mandela could not survive his 27 years in prison without the dream of eliminating racism; also, he focused on dismantling the legacy of apartheid by fostering racial reconciliation. Likewise, Elon Musk could **be cast in the sea of** commerce **without** the dream of changing the world and humanity; also, he worked intensely on numerous experiments on reducing global warming through sustainable energy production and consumption. Michael Jordan could not create a basketball legend without his goal to prove himself; also, he spent thousands of hours practicing on the playground to strive for prolific scoring.

第三个主体段：本段结合实用主义和理想主义，较理智地论证合理把握度的重要性，对应论述 Perspective Two。本段较出彩的地方是例子部分，作者使用了三个小例子的平行，呈现不同领域的成功人士都是既具备实用性又拥有理想主义的梦想。这样的例证手法不仅可以对分论点形成依托，还能够增强文章的气势和文采，同时不会对例证细节的要求过高，是很实用的例子写法，值得考生学习。

To conclude, no success is easily gained, which demands both efforts and ambition. People should consider what they lack and improve themselves accordingly. Only in this way can they perfect themselves and approach dreams more easily.

结尾段：重申自己的立场和原因。

Words

adore *v.* 崇拜

spot *v.* 发现，注意到

confine *v.* 限制

unprecedentedly *adv.* 前所未有地

sustainable *adj.* 可持续的

prolific *adj.* 多产的，丰富的

Phrases

attribute...to... 把……归因于……

be labeled as... 被贴标签为……

ready-to-come 即将到来的

provide guarantee for... 为……提供保障

pave way for... 为……奠定基础/通向……

according to the capability 依据能力

embrace challenge 面对挑战

capture a better view 看得更远/收获更好的未来

be content with 满足于……

sense of mission 使命感

be deprive of 被剥夺

jump out of comfort 跳出舒适区

make it through 度过

eliminate racism 消除种族主义

dismantle the legacy of 打破……的神话

racial reconciliation 种族和解

work intensely on... 致力于……工作

create a legend 创造传奇

Sentences

Truly, ... 确实是这样，……

It is not...that matters... 不是……起关键作用

If...had done..., ...would have done...如果之前……做了……，……就会……

Prompt 2

Prepare for the Rainy Days vs. Live for the Moment

No one knows how his or her future and fate would exactly turn out. In the face of this uncertainty, some people choose to live as though the only things that matter is to live for the moment and enjoy the present. Instead of planning for unclear future, they invest their energy on enjoying holidays, spending time with their families and friends or indulging themselves in other plugged-in pursuits. Likewise, people rely on what is currently working for them and seldom bother themselves with some adjustments or flexibility. In most cases, however, success is the result of careful planning, preparation, hard work, and reducing risks. Given the significance of planning ahead, it is time for people to reconsider about whether they should make a plan for life.

Read and carefully consider these perspectives. Each suggests a particular way of thinking about making a plan for life.

Perspective One	Perspective Two	Perspective Three
When people do not know what opportunities will occur to them, they cannot prepare for the unknown future. People should stay focused on the present and what is at stake.	By preparing for the future, people lay the groundwork that enables action and agility in dealing with complex tasks. Preparation also greatly reduces the possible risks in uncertainties.	Planning structures people's lives. Too much planning, however, results in tried-and-true practice and doing things the same way they were done before.

Essay Task

Write a unified, coherent essay in which you evaluate multiple perspectives on making a plan for life. In your essay, be sure to:

- clearly state your own perspective on the issue and analyze the relationship between your perspective and at least one other perspective
- develop and support your ideas with reasoning and examples
- organize your ideas clearly and logically
- communicate your ideas effectively in standard written English

Your perspective may be in full agreement with any of those given, in partial agreement, or completely different.

Prompt Analysis

P1	✓ People cannot prepare for the unknown future. Rather than wasting time on the unknown things, people should focus on what is at stake. ✓ 人们无法为未知的未来做准备。与其浪费时间在准备未知的事情上，人们应该只专注于目前确定的和紧迫的事情。 【Eg.】businesses under transformation 一些正在转型的企业的故事
	✗ People should be prepared for future uncertainties by keeping alert to upheavals. ✗ 人们应该警觉，为不确定性做准备。 【Eg.】Kodak company 柯达公司
P2	✓ With preparation, people have the agility to deal with complex situations. Preparation reduces the possible risks of uncertainties. ✓ 通过准备，人们灵活地来处理复杂任务。做准备也能够很大程度上减少不确定性可能带来的危机。 【Eg.】Xiaomi company 小米公司
	✗ When people are not sure about tomorrow, preparation might impede people from flexibly dealing with challenges. They should enjoy the present rather than bother themselves with unnecessary preparation. ✗ 当人们对未来不确定的时候，人们所做的准备会妨碍他们灵活地处理挑战。他们应该享受现在，而不要被不必要的准备所困扰。 【Eg.】daily examples 日常例子

P3	× Planning may afford people with a sense of control and it regulates people's lives. However, too much planning results in overreliance of the so-called experience. × 计划固然给人一种掌握人生的感觉，也让人们生活有规律。然而，过多的计划会让人们过度依赖曾经的经验。 √【Eg.】Kodak company 柯达公司
	× Careful planning can help people deal with uncertainties with ease. × 完善的计划可以帮助人们轻松处理不确定的事情。 【Eg.】Sony company, Panasonic company 索尼公司，松下公司

Model Essay 2

In a society characterized by Big Bang Disruption in which ideas and products are exponentially replaced by turbo-charged innovation, no one seems to know how the future will turn out. Faced with this uncertainty, some people choose to live for the present as though the only thing that matters is today. Instead of planning for the future, they have their minds fixed on enjoying every moment of the present, leaving no room for any necessary preparation for tomorrow. In fact, this lifestyle is misguided. Planning and preparing for uncertainties guarantees success because it can help startups find their own way and keep people from complacency.

开头段：先背景引入，说明 "no one seems to know how the future will turn out（未来谁也无法预料）"，然后提出对立观点，很多人愿意 "choose to live for the present（活在当下不去想未来）"（这反驳了 Perspective One 以及 Perspective Three 和 Perspective Two 是契合的），然后在段末话锋一转，直接提出自己的观点：有备而来才能成功。这种 "逆向开头法" 不同于一般的 "背景引入" 法，因为第一句中的 "seems to" 和第二句中的 "some people choose to" 已经隐隐透出对 "活在当下" 态度的不屑。倒数第二句中的 "in fact" 观点呼之欲出，最后一句中的 "planning" 和 "preparing" 剧透了后文的走向。其中 "Big Ban Disruption" 指科技日新月异。

Preparation and careful planning for uncertainties can help new companies find their way when they face fierce competition. The rise of Xiaomi, a technological company manufacturing smartphones, is a good case in point illustrating how preparation for uncertainties helps a startup turn uncertainties to its own advantage in the smartphone market. Founded in 2009, Xiaomi encountered strong overseas rivals in a chaotic time, without knowing what consumers needed as customers' preference changed from time to time. Faced with the uncertain future, Lei Jun, the co-founder of Xiaomi, decided not to indulge himself in the seemingly satisfying market share. Recognizing that only careful planning and preparation could reach consumers, Lei Jun thereafter conducted many investigations into people's cell-phone choices varied by gender, age, and income. Also, determined to further prepare for the fierce competition, Lei Jun required all his product managers to browse the user forum online collecting users' comments about the features of Xiaomi. Within a few minutes, remarks like "the disgusting sound of photo-shoot" would be gathered and sent to engineers' desks. It is precisely the preparation for making Xiaomi smartphones cater to costumers' needs that helped Xiaomi outsell its rivals in times of uncertainties. Had Xiaomi simply enjoyed its present, it would have lost its consumers. Had not Xiaomi done preparations when faced with uncertainty, it would have never succeeded at times of uncertainties.

> **第一个主体段：**本段针对 Perspective Two 展开论述。Perspective One 的第一句先介绍背景，第二句引出例子回应题目。这样的情况我们结合 Perspective Two 中给出的背景和观点进行拓展即可。本段中，作者用名人事迹举例，结合本段中心充分论证了计划（planning）可以帮助刚刚起步的公司在一众竞争中脱颖而出。

Aside from helping startups find their ways, careful preparation and planning can save people from complacency. Xiaomi' rise signifies the importance of preparation in the face of uncertainty, while Kodak's bankruptcy is a negative version telling people that in the face of uncertainty, simply ignoring possible risks and enjoying the present may spell catastrophic disasters. Kodak was once the front runner of its day by selling roll-films and marketing its printing service. Starting from 2009, however, the social networks like Twitter and Instagram that enabled online photo-sharing came into scene. People soon noted that posting pictures online and waiting for other people's comments and "likes" were more appealing than rushing to a Kodak Express to print the pictures. Kodak's approach to uncertainty, however, was to simply neglect the possible risks and reproduce its present glories in film and printing business. In contrast, Sony, Kodak's strongest competitor, started producing digital cameras to make its photos shareable and more compatible with social networks. However, Kodak launched two photo-sharing websites Ofoto and EasyShare encouraging photo-taking and photo-printing. This move, undoubtedly, means putting aside necessary preparation for the upcoming challenge. After discovering the two websites were merely for photo printing service, consumers lost interest in Kodak. Ultimately, the underprepared Kodak was outcompeted when tsunami of digital photos came. Admittedly, Kodak once succeeded. The obsession with the seemingly satisfactory present and reluctance to combat uncertainties, however, blinded and defeated it. Had Kodak prepared some alternative solutions, it would never have lost consumers.

第二个主体段： 本段对第二段形成了深度的递进，支持 Perspective Two，论证计划（planning）可以帮助商业巨头避免自鸣得意。作者通过著名事件进行例证，柯达（Kodak）作为读者心中曾经耳熟能详的品牌，到现在陨落，充分证明了观点，如果不计划（planning），就会陷入故步自封的旋涡。

To sum up, there are times when people need to take a realistic view and prepare for the future. Only by careful planning and proactive preparing can people reduce the risks of uncertainties that undermine their future life and achievements.

结尾段： 再次点题。并且在点题时，提到了"reduce risks"，这与 Perspective Two 是一致的。考生可以按照这个思路可以对上文进行总结并有效呼应开头。

（一）完形填空练习：请在以下 20 个词组中找出合适的词组填入下面两段文字中

1. ambition 抱负

2. stick to 坚持

3. encounter resistance 遭遇阻力

4. abandon one's dream 放弃梦想

5. come to nothing 一事无成

6. come true（梦想等）实现

7. attribute...to... 把……归因于……

8. steadfast adherence to... 坚守……

9. be engrossed in 埋头于

10. be capable of 能够做……

11. beyond dispute 无可争议

12. be eager for 渴望，期盼

13. break through 突破，冲破（障碍、困难）

14. cater to 迎合

15. at the expense of 以……为代价

16. make history 名垂千史

17. hold back 踌躇，犹豫

18. for the sake of 为了……的利益

19. in light of 考虑到

20. at the sacrifice of 以……为代价

完形填空一

All successful people have strong willpower, confidence, and optimism towards life. Take Walt Disney as an example. Initially, nobody liked his idea, but he did believe in himself and had the （1） to go to Hollywood. He continued improving and working on his idea. By （2） his firm belief, Walt Disney made his dream （3） and became one of the greatest masters in cartoon makers in the world.

完形填空二

（1） those trembling disadvantaged people under the unjust laws, the government should not （2） the rich, but should invest more on the poverty program. It is （3） that America cannot realize sustained domestic development （4） the interests of those poor.

（二）汉译英练习

1. intention 意图，计划

   这位总统最近宣布自己争取再度竞选的计划。

2. target 目标

   这个美国保险公司将成年人作为其主要顾客。

3. ambition 远大抱负

   乔治的父亲早在他童年时就灌输给他接受教育的志向。

4. ambitious 野心勃勃的

   他是一个精力非凡、具有政治远见以及抱负远大的人。

5. enthusiastic 热情的

   热烈的掌声给这次志愿者活动添加了几分隆重的色彩。

6. zealous 热情的，积极的

   她对慈善事业充满热忱。

7. aggressive 积极进取的

   这位主管是一位锐意进取、竞争意识很强的领导者，颇受大家尊重。

8. nonconformist 不从众的，不墨守成规的

   那个大学辍学者过着不墨守成规的生活，引起了很多关注。

9. stick to 坚持

   我们应该就事论事，不把问题个人化。

10. encounter resistance 遭遇阻力

    开发组遭遇到了来自领导的很大的阻力。

11. abandon one's dream 放弃梦想

    人们不应该轻易放弃梦想，而要克服困难，挑战自我。

12. come to nothing 一事无成

    希望多半落空，盖茨比也非例外。

13. come true（梦想等）实现

    她想做一个医生的愿望终于实现了。

14. be compatible with 适合，一致

    你的建议必须适合他的个性和作风。

15. owe...to... 把……归因于……

    父母经常向孩子灌输他们对子女恩重如山的想法。

16. attribute...to... 把……归因于……

    不要总是认为你的失败仅是外部因素造成的。

17. struggle for... 为……而斗争

    永不气馁地追求自由是非常值得的。

18. take pains to do sth. 努力做某事

成功的人都是那些肯努力实现梦想的人。

19. succeed in doing sth. 成功做某事

我相信在这次改革中你会成功的。

20. make one's way 克服困难前进

我们的前辈为争取自由，在困难中砥砺前行。

21. steadfast adherence to... 坚守……

这家公司要求所有的工人严格坚守一种标准。

22. commit oneself to doing sth. 致力于某事

他以专心从事慈善事业而出名。

23. life schedule 生活计划

吉米总是认为自己的生活和工作很辛苦。

24. prioritized task 优先级任务

每个优先级任务应该仔细记录并教授给员工。

25. abide by 忠于（诺言、原则等）；承担（后果等）

尽管你不愿面对现实，你不得不承担后果。

26. be engrossed in 埋头于

她埋头读书，没有听到人们在她周围的争吵。

27. on no account 绝不要

当被问及对目前工作的看法时，绝不要表现得消极。

28. under no condition 决不

任何情况下我们都不能首先使用核武器。

29. be accustomed to 习惯于

你不必花很长的时间就能习惯我们做事的方法。

30. adapt oneself to... 使自己适应……

大学的准备工作可以帮助大学毕业生快速地适应新的工作环境。

31. have an advantage over... 胜过……

我堂兄的竞争对手在产品质量上有明显的优势。

32. be anxious about... 为……焦虑不安

不要过度为未来担忧，你现在需要做的就是过好当下。

33. be ashamed of... 为……羞耻

这个男人为他背叛国家而羞耻，他曾把军事机密泄露给敌人。

34. be capable of... 能够做……

该公司不能够处理那种大订单。

35. beyond dispute 无可争议

那个男人应该支付老人每个月的赔偿金，这是无可争议的事实。

36. be eager for 渴望，期盼

对于那些期望别人听到自己言论的人，这无疑是令人沮丧的。

37. economize on 节省

因为经费有限，我们团队应该节省开支。

38. be born with 天生具有

爱丽丝生来就有音乐天分，她非常热衷于跳舞。

39. break through 突破，冲破（障碍、困难）

人们应该勇于打破风俗的限制，追求人生的自由。

40. cater to 迎合

不要急于迎合别人，人们应该先思后行。

41. turn the corner 开始好转

随着事情开始好转，我父母感觉欣慰多了。

42. at the expense of... 以……为代价

这个国家的解放是以无数士兵的牺牲为代价的。

43. make history 名垂千史

一个人不能够名垂千史，除非她/他为世界作出巨大贡献。

44. hold back 踌躇，犹豫

商业的停滞阻碍着这个国家的经济复苏。

45. for the sake of... 为了……的利益

为了这些年轻的学生，政府应该投资更多在当地教育上。

46. in light of... 考虑到……

我们必须根据不同情况判定责任。

47. look down on sb. 蔑视某人

大众都看不起那个年轻女人，因为她是个不婚主义者。

48. get nowhere 一无所获

如果方向不明确，努力就会付诸东流。

49. at the sacrifice of... 以……为代价

他以健康为代价取得了实验的成功。

The Right Direction of Charity

Charity value has an undeniable influence on the society. Charity reflects the noble quality of helping others, the spirit of caring for others, the courage to undertake social responsibility and selfless dedication to society. However, charitable organizations which are not perfect would have some negative consequences, as some people might become complacent, and even some could use the loopholes of this system for personal profit. Considering potential problems of charity mechanism, it is worth reflecting on the views about charity.

Read and carefully consider these perspectives. Each suggests a particular way of thinking about the charity.

Perspective One	Perspective Two	Perspective Three
The more money people have, the more they need to give to charity, as the profits they get are from the society. They need to take the social responsibility to reward the society.	Charity will not be the best way to bridge the gap between the rich and the poor. Giving money to these people may enhance their sense of dependence, which easily causes them to form a habit of being lazy.	Sometimes, the direct influence may not be the best one, while some other methods would help the ones who need help. To be specific, the jobs or the economic profits which have been created under the consideration of the government economic department would diminish the poverty to some extent.

Essay Task

Write a unified, coherent essay in which you evaluate multiple perspectives on the charity. In your essay, be sure to:

- clearly state your own perspective on the issue and analyze the relationship between your perspective and at least one other perspective
- develop and support your ideas with reasoning and examples
- organize your ideas clearly and logically
- communicate your ideas effectively in standard written English

Your perspective may be in full agreement with any of those given, in partial agreement, or completely different.

Reference Article: Donating to Charity: Are We Getting as Good as We Give?

Thirty new charities are set up every day, on average, in England and Wales. Most of them begin around a family kitchen table. There are, today, 164,108 charities in this country. Almost half of them raise less than £10,000 a year. Three-quarters have an annual income of below £100,000. Only 1 per cent handle more than £5m annually.

Small charities are, according to the chair of the Charity Commissioners, William Shawcross, "the lifeblood" of a sector of the economy with a total annual income of £64bn. "Rather more than the defence budget," he wryly adds.

......

Yet the charity world is not without its problems, and is changing in ways which worry many. Money is not the issue. UK giving increased by £1.1bn in 2012-13. The average amount donated is up by £2 to £29 a month, virtually back to pre-recession levels. Medical research overtook the 31,000 religious charities as our favourite cause. After them came hospitals and hospices, and children and young people. Aid agencies got twice as much from the public as animal charities. More than half the giving is in cash, with 31 per cent by direct debit.

Women give more than men and, intriguingly, the poor are more generous than the rich. The bottom fifth of society give 3 per cent of their income whereas the top fifth give just 1 per cent. That, apparently, is not new. The historian of philanthropy Frank Prochaska cites a London cleric who, around 100 years ago, said that "it is largely this kindness of the poor to the poor which stands between our present civilization and revolution".

The nation is big-hearted with its time as well as its cash. A million of us are unpaid charity trustees. More than three million are registered volunteers. In 2012, volunteers gave £24bn-worth of time—the equivalent of 1.5 per cent of GDP. But volunteering is driven by tastes rather than need.... So only 10 per cent of us give to charities for people with disabilities and only 6 per cent to old people. Animal charities get twice as many donations as those for the homeless.

While most American charitable giving is planned, British donors are largely reactive, giving only when asked, Breeze says. Some are even more random. One donor told her that he always gave to charities on his birthday. Britons also find it hard to get their heads round the fact that some charity is now big business. That was demonstrated by the ambiguities thrown up last year when a right-wing newspaper launched a thinly-disguised attack on overseas aid by highlighting the salaries of 14 aid agency chief executives.

......

Charities are changing in other ways, too. One trend is for charities to lose their individualism in their anxiety to attract wider support. The Royal Society for the Protection of Birds has morphed into a general environmental charity. Amnesty International has expanded from its particular focus on prisoners of conscience to human rights more generally and now campaigns on abortion in a way that has alienated some former supporters. The chair of the Charity Commission raised concerns about such dilution last year in a speech to the Lord Mayor's Charity Leadership Programme. "We must not sacrifice charities' distinctiveness at the altar of their continued success," Shawcross said.

There has been another big shift. The money that charities get from the state has grown massively in recent years. Many big charities have become fingers on the Government's hand. Charities working with the elderly, for example, are delivering services extremely efficiently on behalf of local government.

......

The danger is that the independence of charities will be compromised as they increasingly become government sub-contractors. Top charity figures, working as the panel on the Independence of the Voluntary Sector, recently warned of the risks of blurring these boundaries. Not least of the worries are the gagging clauses that require charities not to do anything that will "damage the reputation" of government or "attract adverse publicity". The charities' ability to speak out on behalf of the disadvantaged could be silenced by self-censorship.

Worse still, Government ministers have begun to make dangerous noises about the need to restrict the campaigning activities of charities where they get "too political". David Cameron's new minister for Civil Society, Brooks Newmark, raised hackles last week by saying that charities should keep out of politics and "stick to their knitting".

As the state withdraws from public service the potential for conflicts of interest can only grow. New developments in the charity world could exacerbate that. In another Lord Mayor's lecture this year, the venture capitalist Sir Ronald Cohen spoke about pioneering a kind of "social impact investment" to attract venture capital to philanthropic causes. There are both opportunities and dangers inherent in that idea.

The public will probably like Sir Ronald's idea that charities should stop focusing on the act of giving and focus instead on outcomes. But we are still so wedded to romantic notions about "the soul of charity" that a survey last revealed a third of people think charity chief executives should not be paid at all.

Yet even the media's fondness for stories about charity scandals do not dent the public's generous impulses. Shawcross is tightening up operations at the Charity Commission after politicians' suggestions that it was regulating charities poorly. And Comic Relief, after an outcry on Panorama, has instructed its investment managers to avoid firms majoring in arms, tobacco and alcohol. But issues that excite metropolitan insiders do not seem to dent public confidence. Sport Relief had its best year ever, despite the controversy, and the commercial sector is already getting behind next year's Red Nose Day.

......

The rise of social media has only boosted that, enabling ordinary people to bypass the political and media elite. Charities have learnt how to turn likes and retweets on Facebook and Twitter into income. The speed with which the ice-bucket challenge went viral last month shows the potential this route may offer.

The emergence of new charitable initiatives such as food banks has harnessed all this in a common-sense response by ordinary people to the problems caused by their political masters. Charities have a unique talent for responding to social need with initiative and creativity. They are a part of the instinctive genius of British political character that needs to be treasured.

(Excerpted from *http://www.independent.co.uk/life-style/health-and-families/features/giving-to-charity-are-we-getting-as-good-as-we-give-9722299.html*)

话题五　科技创新类

Topic Analysis

　　二十一世纪科学技术日新月异，由此产生的利弊备受热议。因此，包括 ACT、SAT 和 TOEFL 在内的很多标准化考试频繁考查该话题。改革后的 ACT 写作中，科技创新类话题出现了多次，如智能技术对社会的影响（intelligent machines）、创造力（creativity）、数码技术对人们的影响（tech-free time）、过度求新（latest and greatest）等。在经历了托福备考后，考生们对科技创新类话题并不陌生，基本能够从三个视角展开讨论，但是在备考 ACT 写作时仍然不能放松对该话题的练习。ACT 写作会从更深刻和独到的角度进行考查，如科技对人性的影响、科技对人类认识自己和世界的意义、科技对传统和文化的冲击等，这些是很多考生在托福备考阶段没有接触到的。

Topic Vocabulary

tablet 平板电脑

technological advance 科技的进步

technological innovation 科技创新

scientific and technological developments 科学和技术的发展

modern advancement 现代进步

enhancements in technology 科技的加强、进步

wonders of modern technology 科技创造的奇迹

accessible 可接近的

overloaded 过载的

attention span 注意力的持续时间

informed 有见识的、消息灵通的，有依据的

Big Bang Disruption 科技飞速发展的时代，新产品迭代特别快的时代

social media platform 社交媒体平台

social media page 社交网络的网页

plugged-in pursuit 让人上瘾的追求

overdependence on electronic devices 对电子设备的过度依赖

"tech-free time" 远离电子产品的时间

technological gadget 有科技含量的小装置

social media site 社交网站

cellphone and media usage 手机和社交媒体的使用

fruitful 富有成效的

game-changer 改变世界的人或者物

virtual world 虚拟世界

real life communication 现实生活中的交流

alternate 交替的

multiple 多种的、多样的、多重的

texting back and forth 来来回回发消息

disconnect someone from the world around them 使人与世隔绝

ear-splitting 震耳欲聋

grin 露齿笑

recurring 循环的，再发的

prune 修剪，删减

rampant 猖獗的，蔓延的

face-to-face interaction 面对面的互动

stay focused on 关注

respond to a text 回复消息

technological detachment 科技所造成的疏离

intangible 无形的，触摸不到的，难以理解的

supportive connections 支持性的关系

someone's posts get a ton of feedback 某人的"朋友圈"和"微博"得到非常多的点赞和评论

imminent sense of isolation 逼近的"被孤立"感，孤独感

important sense of well-being 重要的幸福感

Extended Reading

Reference Article 1: Is Technology Really Making Us Less Social?

1 We've all heard our parents say it; "Look up from your phone every once in a while", "Hey, talk to me don't text", "why are you being so anti-social on your phone?" Not only our cellphones, but also our laptops, televisions, creations like Facebook and other social media platforms. Are all of these inventions and enhancements in technology making us less social?

2 Some would say yes. People who lived before the day and age of technology would say people communicated more without these inventions. They ARE partially right. The only difference is their communication was face-to-face, ours is over the Internet or some other form of technology. When teens are looking at their phones instead of talking to their parents, usually they are talking to friends, or on social media sites such as Twitter, Facebook, and Instagram. All these are alternate forms of being social, just not face-to-face.

3 Keith N. Hampton, a Professor at Rutgers University of Communication and Information says technology is enriching our social relationships. Professor Hampton teaches "Yes, some things have changed—but maybe not as much as you might think. Consider 'what a strange practice it is...that a man should sit down to his breakfast table and, instead of conversing with his wife, and children, hold before his face a sort of screen on which is inscribed a world-wide gossip.' These words ring as true today as when they were written, in 1909. They were the observations of one of America's first and most renowned sociologists, Charles Cooley, about how morning delivery of the newspaper was undermining the American family. Thank goodness the scourge of the newsman is in decline."(Hampton). He has studied his students and colleagues and found the students have many more close relationships because of their cellphones and media usage than the older colleagues (Hampton).

4 In contrast, Professor Larry Rosen, a Psychologist from the University of California State, Dominguez Hills says the opposite. He holds that the multiple relationships we make online are not very fruitful, they aren't really close friends. He believes that technology has forced us to pay less attention to our real world communication and more to online communication. Professor Rosen says, "As a research psychologist, I have studied the impact of technology for 30 years among 50,000 children, teens and adults in the U.S. and 24 other countries. In that time, three major game-changers have entered our world: portable computers, social communication and smartphones. The total effect has been to allow us to connect more with the people in our virtual world—

but communicate less with those who are in our real world." (Rosen). Rosen believes we need to put the phones down and technology away and stay focused on our real life communication, even if that means less communication altogether. What do you think? Is technology making us less social? (450 words)

(Excerpted from *https://sites.psu.edu/siowfa15/2015/09/16/is-technology-really-making-us-less-social/*)

Analysis of Article

The disadvantage of using technology

The total effect has allowed us to connect more with the people in our virtual world—but communicate less with those who are in our real world.

The multiple relationships we make online are not very fruitful, since they aren't really close friends. Technology has forced us to pay less attention to our real-world communication and more to online communication.

Vocabulary

alternate *adj.* 交替的

fruitful *adj.* 有成效的

multiple *adj.* 多种的、多样的、多重的

virtual *adj.* 虚拟的

game-changers *n.* 改变世界者

Read-Recite-Imitate-Create

Example one:

1. Read: Are all of these **inventions and enhancements in technology** making us less social?
2. Recite: **inventions and enhancements in technology**
3. Imitate: Today we live with an abundance of **inventions and enhancements in technology**.
4. Create: In fact, **inventions and enhancements in technology** designed to make our lives easier, virtually, make our lives more complicated.

Reference Article 2: Technology Is Destroying the Quality of Human Interaction

1 I had a terrible nightmare the other night. Instead of meeting for a quick cup of coffee, my friend and I spent 30 minutes texting back and forth about our day. After that, instead of going in to talk to my professor during his office hours, I emailed him from home with my question. Because of this, he never got to know who I was, even though he would have been a great source for a letter of recommendation if he had. I ignored a cute guy at the bus stop asking me the time because I was busy responding to a text. And I spent far too much time on Facebook trying to catch up with my 1000+ "friends," most of whom I rarely see, and whose meaning sadly seems to dispel even more as the sheer number of "connections" I've made grows.

2 Oh wait, that wasn't a dream. This technological detachment is becoming today's reality.

3 Little by little, Internet and mobile technology seems to be subtly destroying the meaningfulness of interactions we have with others, disconnecting us from the world around us, and leading to an imminent sense of isolation in today's society. Instead of spending time in person with friends, we just call, text or instant message them. It may seem simpler, but we ultimately end up seeing our friends face to face a lot less. Ten texts can't even begin to equal an hour spent chatting with a friend over lunch. And a smiley-face emoticon is cute, but it could never replace the ear-splitting grin and smiling eyes of one of your best friends. Face time is important, and people need to see each other.

4 This doesn't just apply to our friends; it applies to the world around us. It should come as no surprise that face-to-face interaction is proven by studies to comfort us and provide us with some important sense of well-being, whether it's with friends or friendly cashiers in the checkout line of Albertson's. That's actually the motivation behind Albertson's decision last year to take all of the self-checkout lanes out of its stores: an eerie lack of human contact.

5 There's something intangibly real and valuable about talking with someone face to face. This is significant for friends, partners, potential employers, and other recurring people that make up your everyday world. That person becomes an important existing human connection, not just someone whose disembodied text voice pops up on your cell phone, iPad or computer screen.

6 It seems we have more extended connections than ever in this digital world, which can be great for networking, if it's used right. The sad fact of the matter is that most of us don't. It's too hard to keep up with 1,000 friends, let alone 200. At that point, do we even remember their names? We need to start prizing the meaning of quality in our connections, not sheer quantity.

7 One of my best friends from my hometown has 2,241 Facebook friends. Sure, her posts get a ton of feedback, but when I asked her about the quality of those relationships, she said to me that she really has few friends that she can trust and spend time with happily. Using a strange conundrum like this as a constructive example, we should consider pruning our rampant online connections at the very least.

8 Past evolutionary psychology research by British anthropologist and psychologist Robin Dunbar has revealed that people are actually limited to a certain number of stable, supportive connections with others in their social network: roughly 150. Furthermore, recent follow-up research by Cornell University's Bruno Goncalves used Twitter data to show that despite the current ability to connect with vast amounts of people via the Internet, a person can still only truly maintain a friendship with a maximum of 100 to 200 real friends in their social network.

9 While technology has allowed us some means of social connection that would have never been possible before, and has allowed us to maintain long-distance friendships that would have otherwise probably fallen by the wayside, the fact remains that it is causing ourselves to spread ourselves too thin, as well as slowly ruining the quality of social interaction that we all need as human beings.

10 If you are planning on buying or want to learn about Phentermine from UK have a look at this Phentermine website to buy Phentermine online or offline from United Kingdom.

11 So what are we doing with 3,000 friends on the Internet? Why are we texting all the time? Seems like a big waste of time to me. Let's spend more time together with our friends. Let's make the relationships that count last, and not rely on technology to do the job for us. (450 words)

(Excerpted from *https://thebottomline.as.ucsb.edu/2012/01/technology-is-destroying-the-quality-of-human-interaction by Melissa Nilles Arts & Entertainment Editor*)

Analysis of Article

The disadvantages of social networking sites

the Internet and mobile technology subtly destroy the interaction, disconnecting us from the world, and leading us to a sense of isolation.

Instead of spending time in person with friends, we send messages and we miss the chance to see our friends face to face.

Face-to-face interaction is important, because friends need to see each other.

While technology has allowed us to use some means of social connection and maintain long-distance friendships, it causes us to spread ourselves too thin, as well as slowly ruin the quality of social interaction that we all need as human beings.

Vocabulary

subtly *adv.* 微妙地

disconnect *v.* 使失去联系

ear-splitting *adj.* 震耳欲聋的

grin *v.* 露齿笑

recurring *adj.* 反复出现的

prune *v.* 删减，修剪

rampant *adj.* 猖獗的，蔓延的

Read-Recite-Imitate-Create

Example one:

1. Read: I had a terrible nightmare the other night. Instead of meeting for a quick cup of coffee, my friend and I spent 30 minutes **texting back and forth** about our day.

2. Recite: **text back and forth**

3. Imitate: When we have dinner, he always **texts back and forth**.

4. Create: Instead, they keep lowering heads, **texting back and forth**, and updating their Facebook and Twitter to find out how many "likes" they get from their last posting picture of the Beef Wellington.

Example two:

1. Read: It may seem simpler, but we ultimately **end up seeing** our friends face to face a lot less.

2. Recite: **end up doing something**

3. Imitate: Because of the bankruptcy of her company, she **ended up losing** all her money.

4. Create: Hopelessly, students find themselves **ending up wasting time** to identify which way is simpler and more effective.

Prompt 1

Modern Technology

People measure progress by technological advances which have freed them from labor, such as folding laundry, hauling heavy loads, and walking a long distance. However, do the benefits of scientific developments come at the cost of undesirable changes to people's lives? In such a society that judges itself on the development of new technology, people seem to be obsessed with high-tech products, which makes information more readily accessible to greater numbers of people than ever before. Having more accessible and better technology, however, has not made people wiser or informed. On the contrary, people are so overloaded with information today that they have become less, rather than more, able to make sense of the world. With the benefits and drawbacks of technology, it is worth considering whether technologies truly make people's lives better.

Read and carefully consider these perspectives. Each suggests a particular way of thinking about modern technology.

Perspective One	Perspective Two	Perspective Three
It is our nature to save ourselves from laborious tasks by making the full use wonders of modern technology. Few people can resist the conveniences made possible by technological advancements.	Technology has dramatically increased the speed with which we can communicate and share information. In the same time, however, using technology may distract people from focusing at length on anything, shortening their attention spans, and preventing them from truly learning about people around them.	Technologies afford people with increased access to information. Today's abundance of information, however, only makes it more difficult for people to distinguish the substantiated and informed opinions from the less informed ones and thus impede them from understanding the world.

Essay Task

Write a unified, coherent essay in which you evaluate multiple perspectives on modern technology. In your essay, be sure to:
- clearly state your own perspective on the issue and analyze the relationship between your perspective and at least one other perspective
- develop and support your ideas with reasoning and examples
- organize your ideas clearly and logically
- communicate your ideas effectively in standard written English

Your perspective may be in full agreement with any of those given, in partial agreement, or completely different.

Prompt Analysis

P1	✓ It is our nature to make the use of modern technology. Few people can resist the conveniences of technological advancements. ✓ 使用现代科技是我们的天性使然，大家难以抵挡高科技带来的便利。 【Eg.】vacuum cleaners, washing machine, bicycle sharing, Paypal 吸尘器，洗衣机，共享单车，贝宝
	✕ The so-called technologies, actually, make people's lives more complicated. ✕ 所谓的高科技，实际上让人们的生活更复杂了。 【Eg.】daily examples 日常例子
P2	✓ Technology helps people communicate and share information. Meanwhile, however, it distracts people from focusing at length on anything, shortening their attention spans, and preventing them from truly learning about people around them. ✓ 科技帮助人们交流和分享信息。但是与此同时，科技很难使人对一个话题保持持久的兴趣，也阻碍了他们深度了解周围的人。 【Eg.】daily examples 日常例子
	✕ Technologies afford users with access to connect their friends and strengthen their relationships. ✕ 科技能够让朋友之间的关系更紧密。 【Eg.】Facebook, smartphone "脸书"，智能手机

P3	✓ Technologies provide people with increased access to information. Too much information, however, only makes it difficult for people to distinguish the substantiated and informed comments from the less informed ones and thus impede people from understanding the world. ✓ 科技给人们提供了大量信息。但是信息过载，人们很难区分信息的真伪，阻碍人们了解世界。 【Eg.】daily examples 日常例子
	✗ With modern technologies, people can easily find answers to puzzles within split seconds. ✗ 有了现代科技，人们可以轻松解决困扰自己已久的问题。 【Eg.】Quora 一个问答网站（美国版知乎）

Model Essay 1

In a time characterized by Big Bang Disruption in which products and ideas are exponentially replaced by newer and advanced counterparts, people evolve new strategies to acquire knowledge, probe the unknown world, and connect each other. Traditional teaching happening in classroom and face-to-face communication, the time-honored ways for studying and socializing, however, are gradually shoved into oblivion. In fact, **inventions and enhancements in technology** designed to make our lives easier, virtually, make them more complicated. Far from being the so-called modern people, humans become victims of overloaded information and low-quality communication.

> 开头段：背景引入 + "剧透" 作者对于现代科技（modern technologies）的态度 + 亮出作者观点 + 开头段 "剧透" 出后文两个主体段。其实这样的一个主旨，是结合 Perspective Two（科技让人与人的交流变得不够真诚）和 Perspective Three（科技带来信息过载，人们很难区分信息的真伪）得出的。另外，开头段写作注意观点的合理性，文中的论述要对观点形成紧密有效的支撑，不要想当然或者故意为了写观点而写观点，观点一定要建立在后文之上。

Technologies originally designed to make people's lives easier, actually, overwhelm people with an immense sea of information and strip them of the chance to distinguish the truly informed comments from less substantiated ones. A good case in point is that 37 years ago, without any high technology products, my father, a high school student, listened to his teachers carefully in each class. In math classes, for instance, the teacher just gave one or two simplest and straightforward ways to solve a geometrical question so that students like my father could easily grasp. In this way, he acquainted himself with mathematic knowledge. Undoubtedly, the absence of advanced technologies, made students' lives quite simple and easy. It is another story 37 years later, however, when my brother began his schooling with the advent of high-tech products. Advanced applications like Yuantiku, a real-time application, affords users with thousands of answers when they upload pictures or input the questions. That is why my brother usually feels lost and confused whenever he uses the application. In this way, the abundance of information including the seemingly infallible answers or the so-called shortcuts to the simplest tasks like adding auxiliary lines in geometry makes the task itself more laborious, rather than easy, for people who crave for study like my brother. Hopelessly, students find themselves **ending up wasting time** to identify which way is simpler and more effective. As a result, technologies ruin students' learning skill and make their study complicated.

第一个主体段：本段针对 Perspective Three 进行论述。Perspective Three 的第一句话给出背景，第二句话点明观点。这样的情况，我们可以顺着 Perspective Three 给出的思路，描述现在我们所处的背景，即信息化时代，然后展开论述，确实信息过载让我们对信息真假难辨。例证部分结合身边人的故事，在控制变量的情况下进行了一个今昔对比论证，充分论证了现代高科技使人们对信息的鉴别能力下降。

Apart from destroying people's academic life by baffling them, technological advance in communication encroaches on basic human interactions. 15 years ago, without high-tech products, my uncle Murphy, a senior engineer, would chat with his colleagues about current fairs like the skyrocketing price of 93# and 97# gas or soaring stock market during the noon break or after work. Moreover, they would exchange their ideas of educating the next generation and share the most exhilarating parts in their life like raising up a daughter. Obviously, because people back that time did not possess advanced products like iPhone and Microsoft Surface, not to mention the social networking applications like Line, an Asian counterpart of Facebook. The communication without the assistance of modern technology, actually, kept their lives simple and happy. On the contrary, 15 years later when my cousin Breton, who is an engineer in an international company, has lunch with his coworkers, they neither see each other's eyes nor communicate with each other. Instead, they just keep lowering heads, **texting back and forth**, and updating their Facebook and Twitter to find out how many "likes" they get from their last posting picture of the Beef Wellington. In this sense, even though advanced products like iPhone could allow individuals to have a closer contact with people in the virtual world, they gradually deprive them of face-to-face communication. Accordingly, technologies designed for connecting friends, unfortunately, have weakened their relationships and have made their communication and interaction more superficial.

> **第二个主体段：** 本段对第一个主体段形成了深度的递进，进一步支持 Perspective Three，论证科技给人们交际方面带来的坏处。作者通过个人事例，对比过去和现在的不同，展示科技让人们之间的交往变得不再像过去一样真实，不再是面对面地进行情感层面的交流。

Despite the benefits brought by using modern technologies, those advancements designed to make people's lives easier and simpler, in fact, make them less informed and interactive.

> **结尾段：** "总结分论点＋重申观点"是非常推荐的收尾方式，按照这个思路可以对上文进行总结并有效呼应开头。日常练习注意开头和结尾的快速练习，争取考试的时候留更多时间给中间段落思考和展开。

Words

Big Bang Disruption *n.* 科技飞速发展的时代，新产品迭代特别快的时代
exponentially *adv.* 呈几何级数地
probe *v.* 探究
time-honored *adj.* 经过时间沉淀而越发正确的
socialize *v.* 交际、交往

shove *v.* 挤，强使

oblivion *n.* 被遗忘

overwhelm *v.* 淹没、吞没

straightforward *adj.* 简单的

grasp *v.* 抓住、理解

encroach on *v.* 干涉、侵犯

upload *v.* 上传

seemingly *adv.* 表面上的

infallible *adj.* 永远正确的

skyrocketing *adj.* 火箭般速度

baffling *adj.* 让人困惑的

exhilarating *adj.* 使人兴奋的

update *v.* 更新

interaction *n.* 互动、联系

Phrases

inventions and enhancements in technology 科技的进步

overloaded information 过载的信息

low-quality communication 低质量的交流

strip somebody of something 剥夺某人的……

acquaint somebody with 使某人对某事熟悉

feel lost and confused 感觉茫然

technological advance 科技进步

text back and forth 来来回回发消息

wonders of modern technology 现代科技所创造的奇迹

virtual world 虚拟世界

deprive somebody of 剥夺某人的……

in return 反过来

Sentences

In a time characterized by Big Bang Disruption in which... 在一个被称作"Big Bang Disruption"的年代

...are gradually shoved into oblivion ……已经被人遗忘

Prompt 2

Technological Advances

Modern Technology is power. In agriculture, medicine, and industry, for example, modern advancements have liberated us from hunger, disease, and tedious labor. Technological innovations and inventions intended to serve basic human needs or desires, however, have become so powerful that they are beyond humans' control. Given both the benefits and drawbacks of technologies, it is worth considering whether they help people or make people's lives more difficult.

Read and carefully consider these perspectives. Each suggests a particular way of thinking about technological advances.

Perspective One	Perspective Two	Perspective Three
The rapid pace of technological innovation has made modern people feel rushed. They adopt the relentless pace of the very machines designed to simplify their lives, but only to find their lives, whether at work or play, having not changed for the better.	No legitimate branch of science enables people to predict what the future would exactly turn out to be. Yet the degree of change in the world is so overpowering that the future, most people believe, is far brighter than any of their ancestor has ever contemplated before.	Sometimes, there are benefits of scientific and technological developments coming at the cost of undesirable changes to people's lives. Today, the purpose of modern technological advancements is to solve the unintended problems accompanying modern technology.

Essay Task

Write a unified, coherent essay in which you evaluate multiple perspectives on technological advances. In your essay, be sure to:

- clearly state your own perspective on the issue and analyze the relationship between your perspective and at least one other perspective
- develop and support your ideas with reasoning and examples

- organize your ideas clearly and logically
- communicate your ideas effectively in standard written English

Your perspective may be in full agreement with any of those given, in partial agreement, or completely different.

Prompt Analysis

P1	√ The rapid technological innovation makes modern people feel rushed. They adopt the relentless pace of the very machines designed to simplify their lives, but only to find their lives, having not changed for the better.
	√ 科技日新月异的节奏让现代人的生活节奏加快。他们接受机器带来的无情的节奏，本以为可以简化自己的生活，却发现自己的生活，无论是工作还是玩耍，都没有变得更好。
	【Eg.】daily examples 日常例子
	× Technology structures people's lives and make them much more regular. It is not a bad thing.
	× 科技让人们的生活变得有规律，这个不是什么坏事。
	【Eg.】daily examples 日常例子
P2	√ People cannot predict what the future would turn out to be. But most people believe that the future is far brighter than any of their ancestor has ever contemplated before.
	√ 没有人能够预测未来到底如何。但是大部分人相信，未来会越来越好。
	【Eg.】daily examples 日常例子
	× Far from continuingly benefiting people, modern technology may ruin people's lives.
	× 现代科技可能让人们的生活毁灭，而不会持续造福人类。
	【Eg.】smartphones, video games 智能手机，视频游戏

✓ Some scientific and technological developments come at the cost of undesirable changes to people's lives. People today should think more about solve the unintended problems accompanying modern advancements.

✓ 有时科技的发展是以给人们的生活带来了不好的改变为代价。现在，人们应该关注去解决科技产生的副作用。

【Eg.】light pollution 光污染

P3

× Technology today can solve some problems that our ancestors have never thought of before.

× 科技可以解决很多我们祖先解决不了的问题。

【Eg.】space technology 太空技术

Model Essay 2

Entering the 21st century, wonders of modern technology seem to be the real culprit of something disrupting people's lives. Modern technology designed to make people' lives simpler and better, however, spell troubles like light pollution, water pollution, and air pollution. Worse still, people today are too obsessed with electronic devices to a degree that they sometimes become the slaves of smart phones, tablets, and laptops. Despite bringing all the negative impacts, technologies are, actually, making our planet a better place. Those enhancements in science and technology change people's daily lives and help them better understand the world.

开头段：先陈述对立观点 + 话锋一转提出作者观点 + 开头段预设出后文两个主体段。其实这样的一个主旨符合 Perspective Two，科技进步让人们的生活变得更好了。这种方式比较容易上手，在陈述对立观点时也把这个话题的背景一并给出了，比较容易模仿。

Science and technology could change people's day-to-day experiences. With spacecraft, astronauts can probe the outer space. Thanks to super computers, IT engineers can process more information and analyze big data. Due to the enhancements in both ground and air transportation, ardent lovers of traveling can successfully reduce the time for their cross-continent trips. With improved biomedical applications like advanced medical imaging, retirees feel at ease to have a thorough physical examination. With ready-to-use infant formula, mothers can easily provide their newborn babies with nutritious food. In this way, scientific and technological developments can benefit human-beings in different aspects.

第一个主体段：本段针对 Perspective Two 进行论述。科技进步让生活的方方面面进步，然后再通过例证（exemplification）方式展开。本段在展开论述时，不是常规的名人事例详解，而是并列了不同领域的事例。这种排比举例的方法，短小精悍，很好操作也很好模仿。

Apart from making people's daily lives easier, technological advances afford people with a textured understanding of the world. In the past, with limited access, people could hardly obtain first-hand information. It is another story, however, in today's society marked by Information Era. Specifically, National Geographic website updates videos every day, enabling animal lovers to know predatory behaviors like how a Mongoose reacts to a cobra's attack and how a jaguar kills a crocodile in just one bite. Women who are fond of making up can easily view hundreds of pictures from fashion magazines or watch YouTube videos teaching them how to imitate Taylor Swift step by step. An iPhone application called "Quora" allowing for online inquires and different users' answers helps people easily find clues to any unsolved puzzles. Big fans of gourmet food can see home-made yoghurt waffles or sushi in Michelin-star restaurant on Instagram. In short, today's abundance of information made possible by technological attainments solves human beings' difficulties in exploring all corners of the world and overcoming their limitations to experience diverse landscapes, customs, languages, and foods as well. Modern technologies, especially cellphone application and websites with user-generated contents, undoubtedly, equip people with knowledge about different aspects of life and therefore shape their views about things and events of the world.

第二个主体段：本段对第一个主体段进行了深度的递进，并且在段首用"Apart from..."这个句型"承上启下"，再提出自己的观点。同样，例证运用排比来列举生活中的例子，短小精悍，方法和上一段统一。通过排比举例充分论证其观点：科技进步除了给人们带来各个领域的便捷，也让人们在知识层面上得到提升。

In short, technological developments make people's daily lives convenient and deepen people's understanding of the world.

结尾段："总结分论点 + 重申观点"是非常推荐的收尾方式，按照这个思路可以对上文进行总结并有效呼应开头。日常练习注意开头和结尾的快速练习，争取考试的时候留更多时间给中间段落思考和展开。

科技创新类作业

（一）完形填空练习：请在以下 20 个词组中找出合适的词组填入下面两段文字中

1. attention span 注意力持久度

2. overdependence on electronic device 对电子产品的过分依赖

3. social media platforms 社交平台

4. text back and forth 来来回回发消息

5. plugged-in pursuits 令人上瘾的追求

6. social media site 社交网站

7. virtual world 虚拟的世界

8. social media page 社交媒体网页

9. respond to a text 回复消息

10. stay focus on 关注

11. social connection 社交联系

12. social interaction 社交互动

13. maintain a friendship 维护一段友谊

14. connect with a great number of people 和很多人产生关联

15. real-life communication 现实生活中的交流

16. online communication 在线交流

17. wonders of modern technology 现代科技带来的奇迹

18. scientific and technological developments 科学和技术的发展

19. close relationship 亲密的关系

20. enrich social relationship 丰富社会关系

完形填空一

In a society where smartphones, tablets, and laptops are everywhere, people can hardly free themselves from high-tech products. However, people gradually have the habit of （1）. They constantly check their phones, （2）, update their social media pages, and engage in countless other （3）.

完形填空二

Starting from the last half of the 20th century, the society has morphed into a new phase in which high technology products are exponentially taking the place of their outdated counterparts. These （1） change people's lives. In spite of their benefits, there are some drawbacks accompanying the （2）. Technology has forced us to pay less attention to our （3） and more to （4）.

（二）汉译英练习

1. tablets 平板电脑

   我们生活在一个科技极大进步的年代，平板电脑的诞生就是科技进步的体现。

2. technological advance 科技的进步

   我们生活在一个以科技的进步为特征的时代。

3. technological innovation 科技创新

   没有科技创新，社会不会进步。

4. scientific and technological developments 科学和技术的发展

   科学和技术的发展也带来了自己的问题。

5. modern advancement 现代进步

   随着现代进步，我们可以做到很多过去我们祖先所不能做到的事情。

6. enhancement in technology 科技的加强、进步

   这些科技发明和进步真的会让我们更加缺乏交流吗？

7. wonders of modern technology 现代科技所创造的奇迹

   感谢科学带来的奇迹，现在的人们比过去的人们更容易接受医疗了。

8. accessible 可接近的

   因特网让一切变得更易于接近。

9. overloaded 过载的

   信息过载，让人们深感被淹没。

10. attention span 注意力的持续时间

    网络使得我们对特定事情的注意力的持续时间缩短。

11. informed 有见识的，消息灵通的，有依据的

    在一个以信息时代为特征的社会，人们现在比以前更加消息灵通。

12. Big Bang Disruption 科技飞速发展的时代，新产品迭代特别快的时代

    在一个科技大爆炸的年代，产品和想法都会迅速被更新、更先进的产品取代，人们似乎已经有心得方法去学习、探索未知世界，以及和周围的人交流。

13. social media platforms 社交媒体平台

    不仅仅是手机，我们的笔记本电脑、电视、Facebook 和其他社交媒体平台的运用改变了人们的生活。

14. social media page 社交媒体网页

    人们不停地看手机、发信息和照片，关注自己的社交媒体网页。

15. plugged-in pursuits 让人全情投入地追求

人们看视频、玩在线游戏，全情投入于各种具有吸引力的事务中。

16. overdependence on electronic devices 对电子设备的过度依赖

对电子设备的过度依赖成了一种新的瘾。

17. "tech-free time" 远离手机或电子产品的时间

在现代社会，我们需要一定的远离手机或电子产品的时间。

18. technological gadget 有科技含量的小装置

现在，科技含量的小装置使人入迷。

19. social media sites 社交网络

年轻人都热衷于玩社交网络。

20. cellphone and media usage 手机和社交媒体的使用

渐渐地，手机和社交媒体的使用悄然毁坏了人与人交流的意义，让人们和这个世界脱节，导致一种在社会上巨大的孤独感。

21. fruitful 富有成效的

网络似乎使人们的交流变得富有成效。

22. game-changer 改变世界的人或者物

网络似乎是当今社会最大的改变世界的事物。

23. virtual world 虚拟世界

最后的结果就是，人们可以在虚拟世界与人畅谈无阻，但是和现实世界中的人交流变少。

24. real life communication 现实生活中的交流

科技让我们的生活看起来更简单了，但我们在现实生活中的交流越来越少。

25. alternate 交替的

有很多种交替形式的社交化，并不是面对面交流。

26. multiple 多种的、多样的、多重的

我们有多种多样的交流方式。

27. text back and forth 来来回回发消息

吃午饭的时候，他来来回回地发消息。

28. disconnect someone from the world around them 使人与世隔绝

一些刻意的"远离手机"的时间似乎让很多人与世隔绝。

29. ear-splitting 震耳欲聋

我们怀念曾经面对面互动时震耳欲聋的笑声。

30. grin 露齿而笑

我怀念我们当时笑得合不拢嘴的时光。

31. recurring 循环的，再发的

网络上循环再发的谣言让受害者难受不已。

32. prune 修剪，删减

我们需要删减不必要的支出。

33. rampant 猖獗的，蔓延的

网络谣言非常猖獗。

34. face to face interaction 面对面的互动

更多时候，比起网络上的交流，我们更喜欢面对面的交流。

35. stay focused on 保持专注

有时人们应该关注现实世界里面的交流。

36. respond to a text 回复消息

有时候我们花费太多时间去回复一条消息。

37. technological detachment 科技所造成的疏离

这种由科技造成的疏离感已经成为现如今社会的事实。

38. intangible 无形的，触摸不到的，难以理解的

网络似乎是无形的。

39. supportive connections 支持性的关系

我们很在乎在社交网络中得到支持性的关系。

40. someone's posts get a ton of feedback 某人的"朋友圈"和"微博"得到非常多的点赞和评论

当一个人在朋友圈和微博得到了非常多的点赞和评论，这个人往往会很开心。

41. imminent sense of isolation 逼近的"被孤立"感，孤独感

网络常常给人带来逼近的"被孤立"感。

42. important sense of well-being 重要的幸福感

由于沉迷网络，现代人常常被剥夺了重要的幸福感。

（三）写作实操

Prompt 3

New and Improved

Given the importance of creativity and novelty, people naturally assume innovation as a high priority. Newness, modern people's obsession, is more enchanting to people than "tried and true" practice. Too often it seems that people are impressed by anything new and trendy—the latest television show, or music band, or technological gadget. No one wants to be called old-fashioned. In this way, people discard what is currently useful and prefer the most recent model, be it the latest version, the newest and most improved formula. They are not suspicious of any new ideas or products but accept them simply because they are new. Given both the benefits and drawbacks of new things, should people always embrace new ideas or new things?

Read and carefully consider these perspectives. Each suggests a particular way of thinking about the new ideas or new things.

Perspective One	Perspective Two	Perspective Three
People place too much value on newness. People seldom question and doubt the so-called novelty without closely examining the values of new things.	People cannot make strides by looking backward to old customs and tried-and-true practice. There can be no innovation or enhancement unless people look forward in pursuit of the new and untried territories.	People value novelty and hope to be different, but it seems that no matter how hard they try, they are surrounded by ideas and things that are done before. In fact, new ideas are not truly original but are based on things that already exist.

Essay Task

Write a unified, coherent essay in which you evaluate multiple perspectives on new ideas or new things. In your essay, be sure to:

- clearly state your own perspective on the issue and analyze the relationship between your perspective and at least one other perspective
- develop and support your ideas with reasoning and examples
- organize your ideas clearly and logically
- communicate your ideas effectively in standard written English

Your perspective may be in full agreement with any of those given, in partial agreement, or completely different.

Extended Reading

Reference Article: The American Obsession with Newness Is Suffocating Us

We are taught that if it were not broken, buy a new one anyway, and if it is broken, definitely throw it out.

I have this beautiful hand-me-down jacket from the early eighties that my mother got when she went to Argentina to cover a story for NBC. It's an incredible soft brown suede jacket like none I've ever seen, but the zipper is broken and one of the sleeves is ripped along the seam. It's been broken and ripped for five years now and I haven't gotten it fixed. I certainly don't know how to fix it myself. Honestly, I've considered just giving it away instead of going through the hassle of schleping it to a tailor and having it repaired.

What an awful instinct. I would rather throw away a gorgeous one-of-a-kind jacket that fits me perfectly, because it's in bad shape, than take it to get repaired.

But this reaction to a defective item is all too common today. And, as a child of modern American culture, it's not surprising that I would rather just chuck and replace than take the time to care for a possession.

We, in America, have created and bought into a throw-away culture. Instead of problem-shooting or repairing long-lasting items, we discard them and purchase new ones. This generation, as hard-working, flexible, and adaptive as we have become, has a very different relationship with things than our parents and grandparents did.

I grew up with antiques in my home and the expectation that each generation would also pass on their favored and prized possessions on to their own children and grandchildren. Things were acquired with thought and care, for the most part. When appliances broke or clothes tore or became stained, they were repaired and cleaned, not thrown away and replaced. My grandmother's silk dresses that she gave to me for fancy occasions still hold together, but that dress I bought for $30 recently is already unraveling in two places and is out of fashion, pushed to the back of the closet with other things I bought out of boredom or vague intrigue. Marketing is now an enormous industry that tells us we need to spend our money as frequently as possible on affordable things with very short shelf lives.

Looking around my house, I started to ask myself, "Have I purchased anything yet in my home that I would want my child to have or my nieces or nephews to inherit?" I'm in my late twenties and the answer is a resounding no. I have some lovely furniture from my parents and in-laws, and my husband refinished some second-hand furniture, but I'm not sure I have actually bought anything I would be proud to pass on to another and be confident that the value was more than purely sentimental.

I regret this truth. Our fast fashion world and our culture of rapidly cycling trends makes it easy and desirable to rid our homes of the old and bring in the new. We are called consumers now, because that's what we do continually: consume. We chew things up and spit them out, because we can. And because we're told to.

Not only are we told to buy more and more often, we are also more able to today than ever before. Or at least we are told that we are. I can't tell you how many letters I've gotten from banks offering me a credit card, and my credit score is far from perfect. If I hadn't been cautioned about the dangers of credit lines, I would be in some major debt right now. But many Americans fall into the trap of trying to keep up with the trends and continually purchase, throwing away the old and buying new things that will quickly lose their value, both to us and to the economy.

What if you committed to avoiding the fast fashion industry? What if you refrained from impulse, trend-based purchases and decided to only buy quality products every now and then? How about learning to fix something instead of chucking it, or at least taking it to a professional who can?

I've made a commitment to do exactly this, and I'm already finding myself creating a personal style that is far more reflective of my priorities than what I was finding at fast fashion outlets. By choosing to care for the quality items I already own and refraining from buying the cute and trendy things that will look out of style in a few months, I will not only invest in more timeless items, but can also do my wallet a big favor. I think of it as asset investment. By reflecting on the art, accessories, and furniture from my grandmothers and how much I still value them today, I can gauge how much I will value that table or that bracelet in twenty or forty years. Yes, I have to take the time to bring that jacket to the tailor and yes, I have to buy some silver polish and other product care items, but I am choosing not to conform to the hottest fleeting style, no matter how much it's being pitched to me left and right. Plus, you can learn to improve or fix anything on YouTube these days, right?

(Excerpted from *https://thetempest.co/2017/03/31/culture-taste/american-obsession-newness-suffocating/*)

话题六　　　　环保类

Topic Analysis

　　随着社会的进步和生活水平的提高，人们开始越来越关注环保。毕竟，作为整个生态环境的一环，人类的生存和发展离不开周围的自然环境。虽然改革后的 ACT 写作目前还未直接考过环保类话题，但是改革后的 SAT 写作中该话题已频繁出现，如光污染（Let There be Dark）、海洋保护（Arctic National Wildlife Refuge）、鸟类保护（Bad for the Birds, Bad for All of Us）、野生生态保护（A New Wave of National Parks）等。鉴于 ACT 写作和 SAT 写作话题的重合率很高，所以该话题很可能会出现在未来的 ACT 写作中。考生们在准备环保类话题时，一定要多从题目提供的角度进行思考，从日常生活习惯、市民行为和价值观、政府改革、政策导向等方面入手，多角度地进行话题讨论和思维拓展。

Topic Vocabulary

endangered species 濒危物种

adverse effect 不良效应

reusable material 可回收材料

ecological degradation 生态系统的退化

be permanently damaged 永久性损坏

desertification 荒漠化

non-renewable resources 非可再生资源

fertile land 肥沃的土地

boost crop yield 提高农作物产量

toxic chemical 有毒化学品

waste disposal 废物处置

water body pollution 水体污染

vegetation destruction 植被破坏

the overexploitation of resources 资源的过度开发

enhance environmental awareness 提高环保意识

advocate green activities 倡导绿色活动

redress the ecological balance 保持生态平衡

wreak havoc on natural resources 对自然资源的破坏

environmental deterioration 环境恶化

human intrusion into animals' habitat 人类对动物栖息地的入侵

municipal refuse 城市垃圾

domestic sewage 生活污水

suspended particles 悬浮颗粒

raise people's consciousness about environmental protection 提高人们的环境保护意识

state intervention 国家干预

reinforce the conservation of water and soil 加强水土保持

rare and endangered species breeding center 珍稀濒危物种繁育中心

exceed the carrying capacity of environment 超过环境承载能力

comply with environmental 遵守环境法规

exacerbate environmental problems 加剧环境问题

disposable packaging 一次性包装

Extended Reading

Reference Article 1: Hong Kong Bans Ivory Trade in 'Historic' Vote

1   A similar ban was brought in across mainland China earlier this year. Ivory sales will be phased out gradually in Hong Kong, stopping completely in 2021. Prior to the vote, demonstrators gathered outside Hong Kong's legislature with signs reading: "Do you really need ivory chopsticks?" "Shutting down this massive ivory market has thrown a lifeline to elephants," said Bert Wander of the global advocacy group Avaaz.

2   Ivory from animal tusks—mostly those of elephants—has been traded in Hong Kong for more than 150 years. It is considered the world's largest ivory market. Wild Aid Hong Kong, a conservation group, says the former British colony had a 670-tonne stockpile in 1989, when the global trade was banned. Only ivory dating from before that period is meant to be sold there, but campaigners say the legal trade is often a cover for illegal activities. In July 2017, authorities in Hong Kong said they had seized the world's biggest ever haul of ivory tusks—some 7.2 tonnes.

3 But what does a gradual ban mean? The trade in Hong Kong will cease in three stages. First, there will be a ban on hunting trophies and ivory from after 1975, when the Convention on International Trade in Endangered Species of Wild Fauna and Flora (CITES) took effect. Later, ivory obtained before 1975 will also be included. And finally, traders will be obliged to dispose of their stock by 2021.

4 The penalties for ivory smuggling will also increase considerably. Under the new law, offenders could be fined HK$10m ($1.3m; £1m), double the present amount, or imprisoned for 10 years instead of the current two.

5 Some activists feel the timeframe is unnecessarily long, however. They point out that African elephants are still being killed for their tusks in huge numbers. Poaching has seen the population fall by 110,000 over the past decade to just 415,000 animals, according to the International Union for Conservation of Nature. (327 words)

(Excerpted from *http://www.bbc.com/news/world-asia-china-42891204*)

Analysis of Article

Main Points of Environment

Hong Kong has voted to ban the trade in ivory.

analysis about Hong Kong's ivory market

the gradual ban meaning

the facts and figures behind China's ivory trade

Vocabulary

advocacy *n.* 辩护，支持

stockpile *v.* 储备

haul *v.* 拖，拉

hitherto *adv.* 迄今为止

trophies *n.* 奖杯

smuggling *v. & n.* 走私，偷运

hail *v.* 致敬

Read-Recite-Imitate-Create

Example one:

1. Read: It is considered the world's largest ivory market.

2. Recite: **It is considered**...

3. Imitate: **It is considered** that we need to have the comprehensive analysis about the importance of the environment.

4. Create: **It is considered** that a more rational perspective would help to see importance of the environment.

Example two:

1. Read: traders will be obliged to dispose of their stock by 2021.

2. Recite: ...**be obliged to**...

3. Imitate: We **are obliged to** analyze the negative side of technological advance.

4. Create: We **are obliged to** emphasize the negative impacts of technological activities.

Reference Article 2: Climate Skeptics Want More CO_2

1 A key argument used by climate skeptics to downplay the consequences of anthropogenic climate change is resurfacing: the idea that carbon dioxide emissions are a net positive for the planet's vegetation.

2 The line of reasoning is being used to push back on the underlying science of global warming. The Heartland Institute, which has sought to place climate contrarians on science advisory councils at U.S. EPA, even suggested that it might sue companies for not emitting more CO_2.

3 The idea that carbon has benefits has been used before. As the argument goes, plants rely on carbon dioxide to survive, and if the atmosphere contains more of the gas it could stimulate plant growth. That's a good thing for humans, who rely on them for oxygen and food, they say.

4 Researchers are still trying to fully understand the effects of rising CO_2 levels on plants around the world. But while CO_2 may indeed be a boon for vegetation in some ways, climate scientists have repeatedly pointed out that other effects of climate change may outweigh these benefits.

AN OLD ARGUMENT RESURFACED

5 Focusing on the benefits of increased atmospheric CO_2 has long been a talking point among those who question the mainstream science of climate change. The Heartland plan, in particular, calls for funding to be directed to Craig Idso, who heads the Center for Carbon Dioxide and Global Change. He has long promoted the benefits of carbon dioxide. Idso's work has been supported by Heartland as well as energy companies.

6 Idso, who was a featured speaker at this year's Heartland conference in Washington, regularly calls CO_2 the "elixir of life" and claims that the planet is headed toward explosive growth in plant life. His work frequently downplays the effect of carbon dioxide on the planet. He has claimed that increased crop yields sparked by rising CO_2 levels could create an economic boost of $10 trillion by 2050.

7 Idso did not return a request for comment.

8 Those talking points can also be found in Congress. Rep. Lamar Smith, the Texas Republican who chairs the House Science, Space and Technology Committee, argued in an essay for the Heritage Foundation that people should focus more on the benefits of rising temperatures. His piece, published in July, was named "Don't Believe the Hysteria Over Carbon Dioxide."

9 "While crops typically suffer from high heat and lack of rainfall, carbon enrichment helps produce more resilient food crops, such as maize, soybeans, wheat, and rice," Smith wrote. "In fact, atmospheric carbon dioxide is so important for plant health that greenhouses often use a carbon dioxide generator to increase production." (439 words)

(Excerpted from *https://www.scientificamerican.com/article/climate-skeptics-want-more-co2/*)

Analysis of Article

Main Points of Carbon Dioxide

Carbon dioxide emissions are a net positive for the planet's vegetation.

Climate scientists have repeatedly pointed out that other effects of climate change may outweigh these benefits.

Atmospheric carbon dioxide is so important for plant health that greenhouses often use a carbon dioxide generator to increase production.

Vocabulary

anthropogenic *adj.* 人类起源的

contrarian *n.* 采取相反态度

advisory *adj.* 劝告的，忠告的

resilient *adj.* 能复原的

maize *n.* 玉米

Read-Recite-Imitate-Create

Example one:

1. Read: The line of reasoning is being used to push back on the underlying science of global warming.

2. Recite: ...**be used to**...

3. Imitate: Ecosystem protection action would **be used to** help keep biodiversity.

4. Create: Environmental protection and virtuous circle to maintain redress the ecological balance would **be used to** find its apt position in individual's life or study.

Example two:

1. Read: The Heartland plan, in particular, calls for funding to be directed to Craig Idso.

2. Recite: **in particular**...

3. Imitate: The government, **in particular**, calls for placing efforts on the action to protection of environment.

4. Create: The society, **in particular**, calls for placing efforts on the economic and industrial development under the help of technology.

Prompt 1

Environmental Problems

We are facing the environmental problems which result from the use of technology. Meanwhile, society could depend upon technology to seek for solutions to these problems. Depending upon technology to tackle environmental problems is an important but not sufficient solution. Given the development of technology, which has the undeniable influence in promoting human development from all aspects, it is worth examining the negative consequence caused by technology during humanization.

Read and carefully consider these perspectives. Each suggests a particular way of thinking about consequence caused by technology during humanization.

Perspective One	Perspective Two	Perspective Three
Technology acts as the driving force of the development of economy. The use of technology shoulders the great responsibility for the environmental problems. The greedy demand of the economic benefits has crushingly devastated on the environment.	History has demonstrated that technology will be a help to assist people to solve many environmental problems. To be specific, the advanced technological innovation has provided a new access to diminishing these problems.	However, if human beings do not change their attitude toward the relationship between human and nature, technology alone will not be able to save people.

Essay Task

Write a unified, coherent essay in which you evaluate multiple perspectives on consequence caused by technology during humanization. In your essay, be sure to:

- clearly state your own perspective on the issue and analyze the relationship between your perspective and at least one other perspective
- develop and support your ideas with reasoning and examples
- organize your ideas clearly and logically
- communicate your ideas effectively in standard written English

Your perspective may be in full agreement with any of those given, in partial agreement, or completely different.

Prompt Analysis

P1	√ The popularity of technology has led to the environment problems. The greedy demand of the economic profits spoils the environment. √ 科技的普及应该对环境问题负很大的责任。人们对于经济贪婪的需求才会导致环境的破坏。 【Eg.】land reclamation, deforestation, gas emissions from automobiles 填海造田，砍伐树木，汽车尾气
	× Economic development is the foundation of all human activities. × 经济发展是人类一切活动的根本。 【Eg.】the early development of human beings, environmental destruction, deforestation 人类早期发展，环境破坏，过度砍伐
P2	√ Technology can help to address the environment problems, and the technology could have the innovation to reckon with the issues raised by technology. √ 科技可以帮助解决环境问题，科技也可以找出创新方法来应对由于科技所产生的新问题。 【Eg.】the exploitation of new energy, seeking for substitute of environmentally polluted energy 新能源的开发，寻找污染性能源的替代能源

	✗ The development of technology could have negative effects on the environment. ✗ 科技的发展会对环境造成负面影响。 【Eg.】The development of new energy, however, might inevitably trigger environmentally detrimental problems. 新能源的研发过程也会产生破坏环境的问题。
P3	✓ We hold positive attitude about the relation between the technology and environment. ✓ 我们积极对待环境和科技发展之间的关系。 【Eg.】the power of technology in agriculture and industry 科技在农业和工业方面的力量
	✗ Technology could have the undeniable negative consequence on the environment. ✗ 科技的存在会对环境产生不可否认的破坏。 【Eg.】unavoidable short-term demolition in forest, ocean 对森林和海洋有不可避免的短期影响

Model Essay 1

The popularity of technology has freed human from repetitive and boring tasks, as more tasks are completed by machines instead of humans. The awareness of the effects caused by the technology makes us focus on not only what we can do with machines, but also the negative influence caused by the popularity of technology, especially on the environment. Although the usage of technology increases our standard of living to some extent, it detracts us from the value of environment.

开头段：作者首先在文章一开始就对社会背景展开了描述，先肯定了科技对于人类所作出的贡献，之后就科技的发展提出问题，引导到本文的主旨环保问题，在问题提出后，作者提出了自己的观点。这样的开篇方式非常容易模仿和展开思路。引出环境的重要性后，引出自己的观点。

When pursuing the maximum profits has dominated value of this contemporary society, government could put the priority on funding technology to meet the social economic development with the sacrifice of environment. This statement is in agreement with Perspective One. The society, in particular, calls for placing efforts on the economic and industrial development under the help of technology. However, especially in these industrialized nations, environmental destruction might take place with the economic booming under the popularity of technology. The destruction of the Huanghe River in Asia, for instance, is of vital concern to the humans, especially for these local people, as the effective development to explore the nation for benefits by technology has spoiled the origination of environment.

第一个主体段：针对 Perspective One 进行具体论述。需要注意的是 Perspective One 首先肯定了科技对于经济发展的重要性，但随后指出来其对环境会造成负面的影响。文中给出一个具体的例子——黄河，极大地对此观点进行了肯定。

Access to government protection for the environment via the technology could carry several significant benefits, especially for the wilderness which has the uniqueness and value. It is considered that a more rational perspective would help to see relationship between the environment and the ecosystem. Every species has its specific function in the ecosystem. It fits into the balance of nature and lives within its environment. Technology would help the ecosystem to keep its circle of the nature. The solution to the world's growing environmental problems may also turn to the technology. We are obliged to emphasize the negative impacts of technological activities. Fortunately, technology would play its role in tackling the consequence caused by itself. It is possible to use the technological innovation to cope with the pollution of water, to avoid the deforestation, to use the technological innovation to address the transportation pollution on the air. This is in agreement with Perspective Two.

第二个主体段：回应 Perspective Two。本段首先提出自己的主观点，即用科技解决科技产生的问题，同时强调了环境的重要性，用来引起读者的思考。文章后面用了三个细节，通过三个细节做出归纳，用来证明用科技解决科技产生的问题的可行性，也再一次论证了此段的观点。我们通常并不能够在考场的有限时间内真正快速找到可以利用的例子，因此，举出三个方向的细节，再进行归纳，是考生可以在考场上完整且高效地完成文章的一种方法。

Nevertheless, in the first place, developing economy is not only one of the essential functions of the government, but also a common goal of most citizens. Being a species with great intelligence, humans have the right to exploit nature reasonably. For example, protection of wilderness areas is also advantageous for developing economy on account of that plenty of by-products cannot be neglected. To be specific, the protection system of wetlands and zoos under the modern technological devices has been established. The ticket for visiting could increase the income, stimulating the commerce. Even the construction of research center by the progressive technological innovation would bring numerous economic gains. Many environmental regulations would be promulgated by the government with a much more accurate attitude towards the global issue. Tackling the pollution caused by the manufactures will continue to be taken into consideration of the sustainable development. This is in agreement with Perspective Three.

第三个主体段：对 Perspective Three 进行展开和支持。先提出分论点，证明发展经济不仅仅是政府的功能之一，也是全市民的共同目标，人类有权利去合理开发自然资源。之后给出具体的细节论证，经过归纳总结出科技可以帮助解决问题。展开和支持（development and support）是评分标准中非常重要，也是很多考生在写作中不易把握的一项。日常练习除了积累表达，还要重视思路的线性发展，能够较丰满充实地完成推理和举例（reason and example）。

When we are facing up to so many challenges, we need to have the critical judgement about the advantages and the downsides of technology hidden insides. When we welcome the progress of the technology, we could also try to diminish the negative parts on the environment. We have put its muscle behind efforts to protect the environment. Environmental protection and virtuous circle to maintain redress the ecological balance would be used to find its apt position in individual's life or study, assisting humans to be on the right path to purchase their civilization.

结尾段："总结分论点 + 重申观点 + 对未来的畅想"是非常推荐的收尾方式，按照这个思路可以对上文进行总结并有效呼应开头。日常练习注意开头和结尾的快速练习，争取考试的时候留更多时间给中间段落思考和展开。

Words

detract *v.* 减损，贬低

dominated *adj.* 主控的

destruction *n.* 摧毁，破坏

spoil *v.* 破坏

rational *adj.* 理性的，理智的

apt *adj.* 恰当的，合适的

Phrases

give the priority of 给予优先权

under the popularity of... 在……的普及下

cope with 处理，应对

be in coherence 一致

face up 勇敢地面对

welcome the progress 迎接进步

Sentences

...in particular, calls for ... ……特别号召呼吁……

It is considered that……被认为……

...are obliged to... ……不得不……

Prompt 2

The Protection of Wilderness Areas

To keep the balance between the economic development and the natural development has become one of the most emergent issues for both developing countries and developed countries nowadays. Some countries start to attract more tourists to these areas. They hope to either stimulate local tourism or protect wilderness areas by arousing widespread attention. However, experiments of this idea in recent years seem to add more troubles to both wildlife and wildness areas. Should we reconsider the relationship between human beings and wildness areas? Given the popularity of wildness areas among humans, it is worth examining the implications of more human presence in these areas.

Read and carefully consider these perspectives. Each suggests a particular way of thinking about the protection of wilderness areas.

Perspective One	Perspective Two	Perspective Three
Wilderness areas are highly sensitive. Tourists swarming to visit these environmentally sensitive projects may pose irreversible threat to the wilderness areas.	Nature has its own of self-healing ability. The most practical and effective way to protect wilderness areas is to leave those places to take care of themselves.	It is a wise choice for government to develop tourism. Tourists can have positive effects on generating profit, which can be invested in environmental protection.

Essay Task

Write a unified, coherent essay in which you evaluate multiple perspectives on the protection of wilderness areas. In your essay, be sure to:
- clearly state your own perspective on the issue and analyze the relationship between your perspective and at least one other perspective
- develop and support your ideas with reasoning and examples
- organize your ideas clearly and logically
- communicate your ideas effectively in standard written English

Your perspective may be in full agreement with any of those given, in partial agreement, or completely different.

Prompt Analysis

P1	✓ Frequent visit will pose great threat to the highly sensitive wilderness areas. ✓ 频繁的人类活动会对敏感的野生区自然产生极大的威胁。 【Eg.】national parks, related research 国家公园，相关研究

	×	The tourists can help the public have an accurate attitude about the wilderness, which is beneficial for the future protection of wilderness areas.
	×	游客的到来可以提高人们对野生区的了解和认知，进而更有利于人们保护野生区。
		【Eg.】news report, tourism industry of South Africa 新闻报道，南非旅游业的发展
P2	✓	Wilderness areas can well adapt themselves to the nature and do not often need human involvement.
	✓	野生区有自适应自然的能力，不需要人们过多地干预。
		【Eg.】theory of evolution 进化论
	×	Wilderness needs human protection, and especially the technology support.
	×	野生区需要人们的保护，尤其是科研支持。
		【Eg.】endangered animals, such as golden monkey, panda 濒危动物，如金丝猴、大熊猫
P3	✓	Developing local tourism can yield profits and feedback the development of wilderness areas.
	✓	政府发展野生区旅游业可以增加财政收入，反哺野生区。
		【Eg.】related research, general example 相关研究，泛例
	×	Wilderness areas in the world mostly exist in these undeveloped areas, where the local government would be busy with other issues and ignore wilderness development.
	×	野生区大多在贫困地区，当地政府自顾不暇，会忽视野生区发展。
		【Eg.】Nepal wilderness 尼泊尔野生区

Model Essay 2

The relationship between humans and nature has always been a hotly debated controversy. Since tourism in wilderness areas requires little investment but yields great, countries worldwide are actively developing their wilderness regions to attract high-spending tourists, sometimes in the name of protecting these regions. The market for tourism in these areas is booming more rapidly than ever. However, these areas are indeed highly vulnerable to abnormal pressures and the presence of human beings is posing more stress to these regions ecologically. From my perspective, humans should leave nature develop by itself and only needed human involvement is encouraged.

> **开头段**：首先说明人与自然的关系，并展现很多国家热衷开发野生地区的社会背景。接着作者进行转折，指出这些做法的不足，并提出自己鲜明的观点。

To start off, although it sounds noble that government will use the money gained from tourism in wilderness areas to develop and protect these regions, it is more likely that government will be more attracted to short-term interests rather than long-term effects. Truly, the wild, remote, and untrammeled natural areas attract passionate hikers, photographers, and stargazers. It will help stimulate development of local areas and generate profits, especially those poor areas that highly rely on natural resources. However, these regions always face more severe problems in economy and heavily need the new income to solve other emergent issues. Thus depending on these profits to feedback wilderness areas is not reliable. Besides, investing in nature often pays off slowly which is not favorable to short-sighted government officials. Thus, saving the money for preservation of wilderness areas will be the last choice for government.

> **第一个主体段**：回应 Perspective Three，作者利用驳论，首先承认开发野生区确实带来收益，证明政府开发野生区的动机，接着指出 Perspective Three 中的漏洞，即繁忙且贫困的政府无暇且没有动力去回馈野生区发展，大规模的野生区开发并不会反哺自然环境。

What's more, frequent human appearance in sensitive wilderness areas often leads to more problems both economically and physically. Governments in these isolated areas welcome the new breed of "adventure tourist" and applaud for the currency it brings. They will encourage local community to emphasize more on tourism development and thus traditional farming work will gradually be abandoned, which has a profound effect on future economy. Hill-farmers in Nepal may give up their work for they can make more money as porters for foreign travelers. Also, these regions have marked seasonality and tourism is limited to quite clearly defined parts of the years. Tourism produces environmental impacts, adds to the depletion of resources as well as provokes changes in ecosystems, and heavily-visited protected areas will suffer from loss in conservation values. Yellowstone National Park has been a wonderland for tourists but as the crowd soar, wildlife suffers from disruption of living, traffic jam has become a common issue, and the park face great pressure in dealing with human traces.

第二个主体段： 回应 Perspective One，直接证明人对自然会产生不可逆转的影响。作者通过两个角度进行论证：（1）野生区旅游业的发展会使得本来依靠传统农作方式的农民放弃本行，对经济产生长远的不利影响；（2）固定时节的旅游业会带来大量的旅游压力，破坏野生区的环境。作者分别列举了尼泊尔农民和黄石国家公园的例子，简短有力地证明了分论点，即旅游业并不是发展野生区的理想选择。

Since so many problems arise, these issues have been brought to the attention of the public in order to save and maintain these areas from further harm. The best solution can be leaving the nature develop as its own and decrease as much human interference as possible. Evolution has witnessed nature's great power to adapt itself and its capability of self-healing after damages. Humans can offer help when it is needed, in the areas of endangered wildlife protection, preservation of wildlife biodiversity, or governance of pollutants. Appropriate support of research in these fragile areas can have positive effects. The renowned biologist and professor Pen Wenshi in Peking University has been devoting himself to the study and protection of endangered species such as the giant panda and the Chinese white dolphin. Different from other human activities, efforts like his work contributed a lot to ecological civilization and explore answers to the complex relationship between land, population, and wildlife.

第三个主体段： 回应 Perspective Two，首先证明大自然有自适应能力，不需要人类的过度干预，接着作者发展出自己的深入看法，即野生动物保护等有利于大自然的人类活动会产生积极的效果。作者用北大教授的例子证明科学地研究会对自然产生真正的保护，证明了总观点的后半部分。

In a word, tourism is not an ideal option for government to protect wilderness areas, but may incur potential problems on these regions and bring heavier economic and ecological burdens. Countries should allow wilderness areas to develop on their own track and support more beneficial research to guarantee sustainable development of wilderness regions.

结尾段： 重申观点并做出呼吁，简明扼要，凸显重心。

环保类作业

（一）完形填空练习：请在以下 20 个词组中找出合适的词组填入下面两段文字中

1. sustainable development 可持续发展

2. vegetation destruction 植被破坏

3. fertile land 肥沃的土地

4. waste disposal 废物处置

5. exacerbate environmental problems 加剧了环境问题

6. suspended particles 悬浮颗粒

7. endangered species 濒危物种

8. toxic chemical 有毒化学品

9. wreak havoc on natural resources 对自然资源的破坏

10. the overexploitation of resources 资源过度开发

11. enhance environmental awareness 提高环保意识

12. human intrusion into animals' habitat 人类对动物栖息地的入侵

13. advocate green activities 倡导绿色活动

14. disposable items 一次性物品

15. municipal refuse 城市垃圾

16. reusable material 可回收材料

17. ecological degradation 生态系统的退化

18. virtuous circle 良性循环

19. waste disposal 废物处置

20. water and soil erosion 水土流失

完形填空一

The increasingly serious desertification problem threatens （1）, increases the extinction rate of （2）, and causes （3）. Therefore, it is urgent to （4）.

完形填空二

We need to （1） activities, refuse to use （2）, use （3）, establish （4）, and maintain ecological balance.

（二）汉译英练习

1. endangered species 濒危物种

   熊猫是一种濒危物种，因此，中国政府已经将注意力放在保护它们上。

2. adverse effect 不良效应

   排放过量的二氧化碳或许会对全球环境造成不良影响。

3. reusable material 可回收材料

   科学家们最近发现了一种新的可回收材料，它或许可以运用到服装制造业上。

4. ecological degradation 生态系统的退化

   毫无疑问，从某种程度上说，生态系统的退化是人们面临的最严重的问题之一。

5. be permanently damaged 永久性损坏

   他的运动神经在车祸中遭受了永久性损坏，这意味着他再也不能站起来了。

6. desertification 荒漠化

   多亏了每个人的牺牲和坚持，我国在治理荒漠化上已经取得了重大成就。

7. non-renewable resources 非可再生资源

   煤炭，一种非可再生资源，数百年来被广泛地用于获取热量和电力。

8. fertile land 肥沃的土地

   我的家乡是一个有着清澈的溪水和肥沃的土地的祥和村庄。

9. boost crop yield 提高农作物产量

   袁教授因他在提高农作物产量方面无与伦比的贡献而被全世界尊敬和赞扬。

10. toxic chemical 有毒化学品

    根据报道，这个工厂排放出来的废水中含有多种有毒化学品，它们会污染河水甚至毒害居民。

11. waste disposal 废物处置

    中国在废物处置上还有很长一段路需要走，第一步就是普及垃圾分类的知识。

12. vegetation destruction 植被破坏

    当地的植被破坏太严重了，以至于政府不得不派出一个特别小队去处理它。

13. the overexploitation of resources 资源的过度开发

    第一次工业革命加速了社会的发展，但同时也导致了资源的过度开发。

14. enhance environmental awareness 提高环保意识

    提高环保意识并鼓励周围的人加入是我们学生的责任。

15. advocate green activities 倡导绿色活动

    令人欣慰的是越来越多的团队和组织倡导绿色活动，比如不开私家车而选择公共交通。

16. redress the ecological balance 保持生态平衡

    不只是政府，普通群众也应为保持生态平衡尽一份力。

17. wreak havoc on natural resources 对自然资源的破坏

    我们应当为对自然资源的破坏感到羞愧，对自然的不敬最终会毁掉我们自己。

18. environmental deterioration 环境恶化

    全国上下都在沉迷于经济的快速发展，却忽视了与此同时的环境恶化。

19. human intrusion into animals' habitat 人类对动物栖息地的入侵

人口数量的增加导致了人类对动物栖息地的入侵，这或许会导致物种灭绝。

20. municipal refuse 城市垃圾

有了新的全自动系统，城市垃圾的处理变得简单了许多。

21. domestic sewage 生活污水

如果我们能充分利用生活污水，水资源短缺就不再是一个严峻的问题。

22. suspended particles 悬浮颗粒

这个实验的其中一步是将水面上的悬浮颗粒过滤掉。

23. raise people's consciousness about environmental protection 提高人们的环境保护意识

为提高人们的环境保护意识，政府在电视和网上发布了公益广告。

24. state intervention 国家干预

既然很多企业不遵循自然规律，国家干预环境问题就是必要的。

25. reinforce the conservation of water and soil 加强水土保持

植树能够帮助加强水土保持，特别是在一些像中国陕西这样的区域。

26. rare and endangered species breeding center 珍稀濒危物种繁育中心

为保护熊猫，中国政府在成都设立了珍稀濒危物种繁育中心，在那里数千只熊猫过着舒适的生活。

27. exceed the carrying capacity of environment 超过环境承载能力

中国一直控制着经济发展的速度，以防超过环境承载能力。

28. comply with environmental regulations 遵守环境法规

他和他的企业被赞扬的原因是在生产过程中始终记得遵守环境法规。

29. exacerbate environmental problems 加剧环境问题

新的造纸厂毁坏了森林，污染了临近的河流，这加剧了当地的环境问题。

30. disposable packaging 一次性包装

众所周知，一次性包装使用得越少，我们的环境就会越好。

（三）写作实操

Prompt 3

Global Warming

Ever since the industrial revolution, the globe has been heated up. The main contributor of today's global warming is the combustion of fossil fuels. Combined with other industrial activities, the emission of carbon dioxide to the atmosphere is increasing at an alarming rate. Besides the greenhouse gas emissions from industrial production, deforestation is also a large contributor to excessive carbon dioxide in the atmosphere. To put it simply, anthropogenic source of carbon dioxide affects climate change by melting ice, by causing weather extremes such as hurricanes, typhoons and snowstorms, by drying out arid areas, and by disrupting the delicate balance of the oceans. Given the repercussions of global warming, what can we do to forestall global warming before it is out of our control?

Read and carefully consider these perspectives. Each suggests a particular way of thinking about global warming.

Perspective One	Perspective Two	Perspective Three
The threat of global warming can be eliminated by reducing energy consumption. People should choose green living lifestyle in order to save the earth.	If global warming is left unchecked, it will endanger humans' existence. It is urgent than ever before for both governments and citizens to tackle global warming.	The side effects of global warming are unknown. It is unnecessary for people to sacrifice their conveniences for the unknown future.

Essay Task
Write a unified, coherent essay in which you evaluate multiple perspectives on global warming. In your essay, be sure to: • clearly state your own perspective on the issue and analyze the relationship between your perspective and at least one other perspective • develop and support your ideas with reasoning and examples • organize your ideas clearly and logically • communicate your ideas effectively in standard written English Your perspective may be in full agreement with any of those given, in partial agreement, or completely different.

Extended Reading

Reference Article: What Is Global Warming?

A long series of scientific research and international studies has shown, with more than 90% certainty, that this increase in overall temperatures is due to the greenhouse gases produced by humans. Activities such as deforestation and the burning of fossil fuels are the main sources of these emissions. These findings are recognized by the national science academies of all the major industrialized countries.

Global warming is affecting many places around the world. It is accelerating the melting of ice sheets, permafrost and glaciers which is causing average sea levels to rise. It is also changing precipitation and weather patterns in many different places, making some places dryer, with more intense periods of drought and at the same time making other places wetter, with stronger storms and increased flooding. These changes have affected both nature as well as human society and will continue to have increasingly worse effects if greenhouse gas emissions continue to grow at the same pace as today.

The cause of global warming is the increasing quantity of greenhouse gases in the atmosphere produced by human activities, like the burning of fossil fuels or deforestation. These activities produce large amounts of greenhouse gas emissions which is causing global warming. Greenhouse gases trap heat in the Earth's atmosphere to keep the planet warm enough to sustain life, this process is called the greenhouse effect. It is a natural process and without these gases, the Earth would be too cold for humans, plants and other creatures to live.

The natural greenhouse effect exists due to the balance of the major types of greenhouse gases. However, when abnormally high levels of these gases accumulate in the air, more heat starts getting trapped and leads to the enhancement of the greenhouse effect. Human-caused emissions have been increasing greenhouse levels which is raising worldwide temperatures and driving global warming.

Greenhouse gases are produced both naturally and through human activities. Unfortunately, greenhouse gases generated by human activities are being added to the atmosphere at a much faster rate than any natural process can remove them.

Global levels of greenhouse gases have increased dramatically since the dawn of the Industrial Revolution in the 1750s. Only a small group of human activities are causing the concentration of the main greenhouse gases (carbon dioxide, methane, nitrous oxide and fluorinated gases) to rise:
- The majority of man-made carbon dioxide emissions is from the burning of fossil fuels such as coal and oil so that humans can power various vehicles, machinery, keep warm and create electricity. Other important sources come from land-use changes (ex: deforestation) and industry (ex: cement production).

- Methane is created by humans during fossil fuel production and use, livestock and rice farming, as well as landfills.
- Nitrous oxide emissions are mainly caused by the use of synthetic fertilizers for agriculture, fossil fuel combustion and livestock manure management.
- Fluorinated gases are used mainly in refrigeration, cooling and manufacturing applications.

Deforestation has become a massive undertaking by humans and transforming forests into farms has a significant number of impacts as far as greenhouse gas emissions are concerned. For centuries, people have burned and cut down forests to clear land for agriculture. This has a double effect on the atmosphere both emitting carbon dioxide into the atmosphere and simultaneously reducing the number of trees that can remove carbon dioxide from the air.

When forested land is cleared, soil disturbance and increased rates of decomposition in converted soils both create carbon dioxide emissions. This also increases soil erosion and nutrient leaching which can further reduces the area's ability to act as a carbon sink. (599 words)

(Excerpted from *https://whatsyourimpact.org/global-warming*)

话题七　　媒体类

Topic Analysis

在互联网飞速发展的今天，媒体成为人们竞相讨论的话题。该话题在改革后的 ACT 写作中也备受青睐。其涉及的内容比较宽泛，包括广告（advertisements）、名人隐私（celebrity's privacy）、信息失真（photo manipulation）等。很多考生对该话题深有感触，能够结合个人生活体验进行思考并陈述见解。但是，贴近生活的话题分析起来未必容易，考生们往往被思维定式束缚了手脚。以"photo manipulation"为例，不少考生只能想到朋友圈的修图，而忽略了杂志图片、广告宣传中的信息操控。建议考生们培养发散性思维，学会从不同的角度思考问题。

Topic Vocabulary

advertiser 登广告的人

endorse 赞助

digital media 数字媒体

old media 旧媒体（如报纸、书籍、电视、广播、电影等）

commercial advertisement 商业广告

manipulate 操纵

subliminal 潜意识；潜在意识的

inculcate 谆谆教导，反复灌输

impart to 传授

mislead 误导

exaggerate 夸张

divergent 分歧的

distorted information 扭曲的信息，信息失真

suppression of speech 抑制言论自由

freedom of speech 言论自由

diversity of thoughts and expressions 思想和表达的多样性

individualism 个人主义

conflict of opinions 观点冲突

identical captives without opinions 没有思想的俘虏

politically correct 政治正确

vulnerable group 脆弱群体

mutual respect 相互尊重

provocative 刺激的，挑拨的

sensitive 敏感的

insulting 侮辱的

selectively 选择性地

pulverize privacy 粉碎隐私

infringe on 侵犯

vexing issue 棘手的问题，令人烦恼的问题

disseminate 宣传，散播

Extended Reading

Reference Article 1: Instead of Cleaning up Their Act, American Fast-food Companies Are Finding New Targets Abroad

1 Over 20 years ago, American tobacco companies faced a major problem. A series of developments—smoking bans, the specter of higher cigarette taxes and anti-smoking public health campaigns—had seriously damaged domestic sales and had the potential to snuff them out in the future. Tobacco companies needed new markets, and fast. They found them in Asia, a region they had been eyeing since the early 1980s.

2 Today, growing health concerns about fast food and sugary beverages are forcing companies that sell processed food, fast food and beverages to confront a similar problem in the United States. In response, they've relying on Big Tobacco's look-abroad strategy from the 1990s. The Swiss food giant Nestle is making an incursion into rural Brazilian communities, KFC is setting up shop in parts of Ghana, and PepsiCo and Coca-Cola are relying on consumers in emerging economies for a growing share of their profits.

3 Beginning in the late 1960s and early 1970s, McDonald's and other fast-food chains saw markets in suburbs and along highways become increasingly saturated. They responded by aggressively expanding into urban, predominantly African American areas and launching

advertising campaigns targeting black consumers.

4 While this strategy allowed fast-food chains to continue growing domestically for several more decades, it also contributed to the transformation of African American diets in ways that played a role in disproportionately high rates of obesity among African American women and children today.

5 Market-segmented advertising campaigns accompanied fast food's expansion into minority communities. In 1971, McDonald's became the first of the major chains to hire a black ad agency to help them reach African American consumers, and other chains soon followed. McDonald's and its rivals would subsequently barrage African American consumers with ads in black magazines and on radio and television programs.

6 By 1990, McDonald's, Burger King and Wendy's dedicated one-fifth of their advertising dollars to African American consumers. This investment paid off. According to one report in 1998, McDonald's and Burger Kind derived 25 and 30 percent of their domestic profits respectively from minority customers.

7 More recently, a number of studies have revealed that fast-food companies direct considerably more advertising to African American children and adolescents than to their white counterparts. Combined with the easy availability of fast food in many urban minority neighborhoods, this targeted marketing helped to reshape African American diets in ways that have been implicated in the contemporary obesity epidemic.

8 In the years immediately before fast-food chains entered black communities, African American diets, which included staples such as legumes, root vegetables and greens, were generally healthier than white Americans' diets. Dietary surveys revealed that in 1965, African Americans satisfied dietary recommendations for fat, fiber, fruits and vegetables at a rage twice that of whites.

9 But over the next three decades, coinciding with the rise of fast food in

their neighborhoods, a transformation took place. By the 1990s, studies found that African Americans were now more likely to consume unhealthy diets than whites. After two decades of fast food's expansion into inner cities, urban minority neighborhoods were developing not into food deserts but "fast swamps," where fast food and bodegas proliferated, but supermarkets offering affordable healthy foods were scarce. This food environment helped to facilitate diets that traded in fresh fruits and vegetables for processed items higher in fat, sugar and salt. This dietary shift has contributed to high rates of obesity among African Americans.

10 These patterns linking obesity and proximity to fast food are likely to be replicated in the emerging markets where fast-food chains are now multiplying. Just as heavy advertising informed urban African American consumers' "choice" to consume fast food, food and beverage companies' marketing efforts are already prompting Brazilians and Ghanaians to abandon their healthier, traditional diets for Western foods advertised as modern and high-status. So while emerging markets help keep multinational food and beverage companies thriving today, their strategy, like Big Tobacco's decades ago, will exact a potentially devastating cost in the future. (683 words)

(Excerpted from *Instead of cleaning up their act, American fast-food companies are finding new targets abroad*, by Chin Jou, October 13, 2017. Washington Post.)

Analysis of Article

Main Points

Fast-food companies, such as KFC, McDonald's, PepsiCo, and Coca-Cola, are expanding markets in rural areas or emerging economies such as Brazil and Ghana after domestic markets are restricted.

Since 1960, McDonald's expanded into African American areas, launching advertising campaigns targeting black consumers. It hired a black ad agency and barraged African American consumers with ads in black magazines and on radio and television programs. Besides, McDonald's and other companies dedicated a large proportion of advertising money to African American consumers. As a result of the market expansion, it reshaped African American diets and therefore led to high rates of obesity.

These patterns linking obesity and proximity to fast food are likely to be replicated in the emerging markets where fast-food chains are now multiplying.

Vocabulary

domestic *adj.* 国内的，本国的

snuff out *v.* 扼杀，消灭

processed food *n.* 加工食品

emerging economy *n.* 新兴经济

fast-food chain *n.* 快餐连锁

saturate *v.* 使充满，使充斥

predominantly *adv.* 主要地，绝大多数

derive *v.* 得到，获得

staple *n.* 主食

replicate *v.* 复制

Read-Recite-Imitate-Create

Example one:

1. Read: While this strategy allowed fast-food chains to continue growing domestically for several more decades, it also **contributed to** the transformation of African American diets.

2. Recite: **contribute to**

3. Imitate: His hard work **contributed a lot to** the group success in this competition.

4. Create: Not only does our excessive reliance on advertisements **contribute to** irrational purchase, but it also hinders healthy economic growth and promotes dangerous cultural value.

Example two:

1. Read: In 1971, McDonald's became the first of the major chains to hire a black ad agency to help them reach African American consumers, and other chains soon followed.

2. Recite: **reach sb.**

3. Imitate: The Chinese singer held a concert in New York to **reach the overseas fans**.

4. Create: To get accepted by the black communities, they even hired a black advertisement agency to help them **reach African American consumers**.

Example three:

1. Read: Combined with the easy availability of fast food in many urban minority neighborhoods, this targeted marketing helped to reshape African American diets in ways that have been implicated in the contemporary obesity epidemic.

2. Recite: **reshape sth.**

3. Imitate: The volunteer service **reshaped his character**, making him a caring person.

4. Create: Surely, fast food is not a healthy and recommendable choice, but commercial ads induced the target consumers to start eating them and **reshape diets, consequently, increasing obesity among African Americans**.

Reference Article 2: Dove Apologizes for 'Racially Insensitive' Ad That Showed a Black Woman Turning into a White Woman

1 Dove has apologized and pulled down a Facebook advertisement that showed a black woman taking off her top to show a white woman in a lighter-colored top.

2 Critics condemned the advertisement for racism and in its inability to represent race accurately. *The Washington Post* reported.

3 Dove tweeted out its apology Saturday. "An image we recently posted on Facebook missed the mark in representing women of color thoughtfully. We deeply regret the offense it caused." Dove also released a statement with an apology, according to CNN. "This did not represent the diversity of real beauty which is something Dove is passionate about and is core to our beliefs, and it should not have happened." the company said in a statement Sunday. "We apologize deeply and sincerely for the offense that it has caused and do not condone any activity or imagery that insults any audience."

4 The company received heavy criticism for being "racially insensitive," according to "Good Morning America."

5 Makeup artist Naomi Black, also known as Naythemua, said the ad is "tone deaf." "We've putting out these ads with these subliminal messages that are telling young ladies that your darker skin is not beautiful enough, you need to purify and clean yourself," she said in a now-viral video.

6 "How can you see a body wash ad like this and not realize? It rubbed me and many people the wrong way," Blake told CNNMoney. "What are you telling the little black girls who watch this?"

7 Dove has previously been celebrated for its diversity, specially with the "My Beauty My Say," "Real Beauty," and "#BeautyBias" campaigns that promoted positive body images and confidence. But the company has faced racist accusations before. In 2011, Dove released an ad that lined women up based on their skin tone with "before" and "after" above each person. The company was also condemned for an advertisement in which it said "beauty comes in all shapes and sizes," which critics said indicated women are judged by their bodies, according to CNN. (364 words)

(Excerpted from *Dove apologizes for 'racially insensitive' ad that showed a black woman turning into a white woman*, by Herb Scribner, October 9, 2017. *Deseret News Entertainment*)

Analysis of Article

Main Points

Dove's ad with racial undertones received heavy criticism recently. In the ad a black woman turns into a white. This ad was condemned to be racially offensive and misleading black girls' cognition on beauty. Dove apologized for this, saying, "this did not represent the diversity of real beauty which is something Dove is passionate about and is core to our beliefs, and it should not have happened."

Vocabulary

thoughtfully *adv.* 周密地，体贴地

condone *v.* 宽恕，原谅

viral（*a.* 在网络上或用手机）广为传播的

racist accusation *n.* 种族歧视的指控

Read-Recite-Imitate-Create

Example one:

1. Read: The company received heavy criticism for being "racially insensitive," according to "Good Morning America."

2. Recite: **receive heavy criticism for**

3. Imitate: He **received heavy criticism for** losing all the passports of the tourists.

4. Create: Some brands **receive heavy criticism for** luring consumers to buy luxuries.

Example two:

1. Read: We've putting out these ads with these subliminal messages that are telling young ladies that your darker skin is not beautiful enough, you need to purify and clean yourself.

2. Recite: **subliminal messages**

3. Imitate: His words are full of **subliminal messages** that he is in love with her.

4. Create: Advertisers, though claiming to provide consumers with clear information to make efficient and wise purchase decisions, are actually manipulating consumers through **subliminal messages** to buy what they intend to sell.

Example three:

1. Read: The company was also condemned for an advertisement in which it said "beauty comes in all shapes and sizes."

2. Recite: **be condemned for**

3. Imitate: Adolf Hitler **is condemned for** many crimes, such as slaughtering the Jews.

4. Create: Thus, commercials are to **be condemned for** today's rampant materialism.

Prompt 1

Effects of Advertisements

Advertisements are everywhere! They are on TV, on the Internet, on billboards, on radio, on the wall of bathrooms, etc. On one hand, as an effective means of promoting products and services, they provide purchasing information for potential consumers and help companies make profits. On the other hand, they keep bothering us and make us annoyed. Commercials even put consumers under their tyranny: they control shopping behaviors and even our thoughts. Given the increasing dominance of advertisements in our lives, it is worth considering the implications and meaning of commercial advertisements in our lives.

Read and carefully consider these perspectives. Each suggests a particular way of thinking about commercial advertisements in our lives.

Perspective One	Perspective Two	Perspective Three
Advertisements are a helper for consumers in making purchasing decisions. They offer direct information for us to choose what best suits our needs.	Advertisements are becoming a powerful driving force of economic growth, because they help increase consumer spending and boost competition between companies.	Advertisements convey poisonous values. They amplify the enjoyment from possessing material things and thus feed materialism.

Essay Task

Write a unified, coherent essay in which you evaluate multiple perspectives on commercial advertisements in our lives. In your essay, be sure to:

- clearly state your own perspective on the issue and analyze the relationship between your perspective and at least one other perspective
- develop and support your ideas with reasoning and examples
- organize your ideas clearly and logically
- communicate your ideas effectively in standard written English

Your perspective may be in full agreement with any of those given, in partial agreement, or completely different.

Prompt Analysis

P1	✓ Advertisements can help consumers make informed purchasing decisions by providing them with relevant information.
	✓ 广告能给消费者提供有用的产品信息，帮助其做出正确的消费决策。
	【Eg.】mobile advertising 手机广告
	✗ Advertisements sometimes give out exaggerated information, which increases consumers' expectation for products. And the result is often disappointing.
	✗ 广告是厂商推销商品的一种手段，有些广告甚至会夸大产品功效，提高消费者预期，但产品最后往往令人失望。
	【Eg.】fast-food advertising for expanding overseas markets 快餐企业拓展海外市场的广告营销
P2	✓ Advertisements can increase consumer spending, and therefore propel businesses to expand production. Besides, they also help accelerate innovation. Thus, the economy gets boosted.
	✓ 广告通过拉动消费带动企业扩大生产。此外，广告也加速了同类企业的创新和研发。这些都有利于经济的发展。
	【Eg.】economics 经济学原理
	✗ Businesses dedicate too much budget to advertising, and overlook product quality.
	✗ 广告成本在企业成本的占比过多，所以很多企业把过多的经费放在广告上，但忽略了产品质量。
	【Eg.】Sanlu milk formula 三鹿奶粉

	✓ It is human nature to accumulate material things; we should not blame advertisements for materialism.
P3	✓ 物质主义是人类与生俱来的本能，广告只是利用了人们的本能进行产品推销，它并没有产生物质主义。
	【Eg.】those who store food for rainy days survived 人类进化时形成了储藏食物的习惯
	✗ Advertisements inculcate to consumers that it is enjoyable to possess materials, such as luxury purses. And that promotes materialism.
	✗ 广告反复向消费者灌输物质能给人带来快乐，从而使人们不断趋于物质主义，忽略了精神上的满足。
	【Eg.】Apple advertising 苹果广告

Model Essay 1

With the abundance and diversity of commodities, advertisements, as an efficient means of promotion, pervade every corner of our lives. Some brands **receive heavy criticism for** luring consumers to buy luxuries. Advertisements are so ubiquitous and manipulative that it is time for us to have a serious consideration on the consequence they have. The bombard of commercials, actually, brings about more harm than good.

开头段： 开头段采用传统的"背景 + 对立观点 + 主旨"模式展开。最后一句话明确提出广告的坏处大于益处。开头段最主要的部分是主旨句，主旨句既要做到观点明确、清晰，最好还能展现出思考的严谨性。这里的主旨句中"bombard of commercials"能够明确传递两个信息：首先，这里的广告特指商业广告；其次，是广告的"狂轰滥炸"（即过多的广告）带来的负面后果。

Advertisers, though claiming to provide consumers with clear information to make efficient and wise purchasing decisions, are actually manipulating consumers through **subliminal messages** to buy what they intend to sell. Advertisements used to inform consumers of the functions and advantages of certain products or services, but since there are few differences between various brands, advertisers start to play tricks to lure the audience. For example, when fast-food companies, such as KFC and McDonald's, were forced out from the domestic market due to health concerns, they relied on advertisements to expand markets in black communities and developing countries. To get accepted by the black communities, they even hired a black advertisement agency to help them **reach African American consumers**. Surely, fast food is not a healthy and recommendable choice, but commercial advertisements induced the target consumers to start eating them and **reshaped diets**, consequently, increasing obesity among African Americans. In this case, advertisements have become a strategy for mercenary companies to sell products but not a reliable source for consumers to get informed for making purchasing decisions.

> **第一个主体段：** 本段针对 Perspective One 进行论述。解释广告对于消费者决策的影响。第一句话是本段的主题句（topic sentence），简明介绍本段的核心观点，即虽然广告有时候能为消费者提供一些有用信息，但却日益误导消费者。然后通过 "for example" 引出麦当劳通过广告拓展市场而导致不健康饮食习惯的例子。最后一句话进行高度概括和总结，指出广告是唯利是图的企业营销商品的手段。

In a large sense, the over dependence on advertisements can take a toll on the economy. While advertisements, through increasing consumer spending, promote economic growth to some degree, their dominance in today's product promotion is creating monopoly, which is definitely an obstacle to free market. Companies with enough capital would make compelling advertisements and easily get products and services known among consumers, making it difficult for entrants with limited financial resources to compete against these brands. As a result, consumers also become a victim of the monopoly or oligopoly because it enables these dominant brands to raise prices and makes consumers less price sensitive. In the long run, the order of free market will collapse if the over reliance on advertisements does not get regulated.

> **第二个主体段：** 本段针对 Perspective Two 进行论述。该段以说理展开为主，从经济方面说明广告的消极影响。第一句话是主题句（topic sentence），提出广告会对经济产生不利影响。接下来做了简单的让步，然后进行反驳，即广告会产生垄断经济。紧接着使用因果论证方法解释

垄断如何阻碍经济发展：资金雄厚的大企业会占领行业市场，使新兴的企业很难与其竞争，并且消费者也会成为垄断经济的受害者。最后是可能的后果（implication），即长期发展下去会扰乱自由市场经济的秩序。

A more disconcerting consequence of advertisements is that it promotes a dangerous cultural value, materialism. Some people may argue that it is our intrinsic desire to possess material things, and we should not blame advertisements as a criminal. It is true that humanity needs basic materials, such as food, clothes, and shelters, to survive, but advertisements help push this kind of need to an extreme and uncontrollable level. Many luxury brands, in order to enhance brand loyalty and expand customer base, hire superstars to endorse products, delivering a message that the products are the symbol of wealth, status, and class. This leads to consumers buying brands that are way beyond their purchasing power just to show off in front of others, but they are probably unable to make ends meet. The distorted psychology is harmful for individuals to make purchase decisions and even misleads their attitude toward life. Thus, commercials are to **be condemned for** today's rampant materialism.

第三个主体段：本段针对 Perspective Three 进行论述。该段的第一句话明确了分论点，即广告的另一个危害是促使人们追求物质主义。然后提出了对立观点并进行反驳。接着，用奢侈品品牌进行举例，解释广告如何扭曲人们的心理，让人们盲目追求物质。最后总结说明广告应该为泛滥的物质主义承担责任。需要注意的是，ACT 写作不一定要有让步段，在段落内部使用让步句也同样能使逻辑严谨。

Commercial advertisements are supposed to help potential consumers make informed purchase decisions, but instead, they generate more damage than benefits. Not only does our excessive reliance on advertisements **contribute to** irrational purchase, but it also hinders healthy economic growth and promotes dangerous cultural value.

结尾段：重申观点和理由。

Words

pervade v. 遍及，蔓延
lure v. 诱惑，引诱

ubiquitous *adj.* 无所不在的

manipulate *v.* 操纵

bombard *n.* 轰炸

induce *v.* 引诱

mercenary *adj.* 唯利是图的

disconcerting *adj.* 令人不安的

endorse *v.* 赞助

irrational *adj.* 不理性的

hinder *v.* 阻碍

Phrases

take a toll on 产生不好的影响

make consumers less price sensitive 降低消费者对价格的敏感度

enhance brand loyalty 提高产品忠诚度

expand customer base 扩大顾客群

make ends meet 收支平衡

Sentences

so...that... 如此……以至于……

It is time for sb. to do... 是时候让某人做……

do-ing 作结果状语

Prompt 2

Celebrities and Their Privacy

For scores of celebrities, fame more often than not comes at a price—the loss of privacy. Living their day-to-day life under the spotlight, many celebrities find gossip columnists follow them into workplaces, to their children's schools, on vacations, and even into their own residential neighborhoods. The private lives of the rich and famous are routinely invaded and displayed for the public in the form of entertainment news, shows, and magazine headlines. Should celebrities be public servants to meet public's demand? Given the widespread concerns of celebrities' privacy, it is worth examining whether the public's involvement in celebrities' personal life is a good thing.

Read and carefully consider these perspectives. Each suggests a particular way of thinking about celebrities and their privacy.

Perspective One	Perspective Two	Perspective Three
Digital technology is very convenient in these days. Privacy exposure online can rapidly promote the celebrity's popularity.	Celebrities have their right to protect privacy. Too much invasion to their life will create unbearable burdens.	Celebrities have gained so much from society. Thus, they should shoulder more social stress, including public consumption of their privacy.

Essay Task

Write a unified, coherent essay in which you evaluate multiple perspectives on celebrities and their privacy. In your essay, be sure to:

• clearly state your own perspective on the issue and analyze the relationship between your perspective and at least one other perspective

• develop and support your ideas with reasoning and examples

• organize your ideas clearly and logically

• communicate your ideas effectively in standard written English

Your perspective may be in full agreement with any of those given, in partial agreement, or completely different.

Prompt Analysis

P1	√ Digital technologies are made use of for celebrities to become popular. √ 科技使隐私暴露成为名人增加知名度的有力武器。 【Eg.】Weibo, WeChat, Twitter 微博、微信、推特等社交媒体的信息传播
	× Too much privacy exposure bothers celebrities a lot. × 过度的隐私暴露会给名人带来烦恼。 【Eg.】Wikileaks 维基解密

P2	✓ Celebrities have the basic right of privacy. Overly exposing privacy imposes tremendous pressure on them. ✓ 名人也有保护隐私的基本权利。过度侵犯隐私会给他们带来巨大的压力。 【Eg.】famous actors like Jackie Chan 著名演员成龙
	✗ Celebrities inevitably live under pressure. Pressure equals to public attention. ✗ 名人无法避免生活在压力下，越大的压力代表越多的社会关注，他们应该承担。 【Eg.】Oprah Winfrey 奥普拉·温弗瑞甚至主动向媒体吐露隐私，也获得了巨大的成功
P3	✓ Celebrities derive much profit from being famous, so they should not complain for privacy exposure. ✓ 名人获得的好处太多了，他们不应该抱怨公众消费他们的隐私。 【Eg.】online stars 网红
	✗ People gain fame through hard work. Too much focus on their privacy will cover up their efforts and the value of their work. ✗ 名人是通过努力取得成功的，人们对隐私的过度关注会掩盖名人的努力和他们作品的价值。 【Eg.】famous actors like Leslie Cheung 著名演员张国荣患抑郁症

Model Essay 2

All human beings have a strong sense of curiosity, from the ancient time when primitive people explored the uncultivated land to the contemporary eras when modern people see through their telescopes. People's curious appetites are constantly growing. Especially when celebrities become the center of gossip after 1900s, the public's desire to access their privacy has exploded sharply. However, public figures call for more protection of their privacy and rational passion towards their work and life because they become fed up with seeing their privacy intruded on. From my perspective, celebrities have the right to guard their private information and the public should be rational on celebrities.

开头段：作者从人的好奇心共性入手，展示人的好奇心逐渐膨胀的事实，接着将人们的好奇心和名人联系到一起，引出观点。

In this information age, private information diffuses so rapidly that arouses public attention. A piece of news will be transferred on social media among millions of people in one second, which is an efficient way for celebrities to increase their fame. Moreover, people are eager to share what they know with others, for gossiping about celebrities helps people win over intimacy and recognition from others. This really helps celebrities to attract attention. Nevertheless, it's considerably risky for them to attract eyeballs in this way. Once the public's desire cannot be satisfied, they want to peek through the celebrities' life more deeply. Curiosity will be converted into more problems to celebrities' life.

第一个主体段：作者联系 Perspective One，证明隐私暴露在这个信息年代确实能够吸引人们的注意，回应 Perspective One 中对隐私暴露的支持。但是，作者进而进行反驳，证明过多的隐私暴露在这个年代实际上会产生更大的麻烦，和第二个主体段落进行衔接。

Zealous pursuit of celebrities' privacy always creates too much burden and sometimes even brings tragedies. Distorted passion of the public always goes beyond control and reach far into their private lives. Paparazzi with high-tech cameras tries every means to take a photo of celebrities' affairs. Crazy fans follow their idols everywhere they go. Critics invest too much energy discussing about the recent divorce of the famous couple. All these actions and opinions trap celebrities in the tent of pressure and their only space of freedom, home, is even intruded helplessly. Some of them suffer from severe depression; some are forced to quit the career; some even commit suicide because of offensive public opinions. Under severe depression, the famous Chinese actor Leslie Cheung chose to end his life at a young age largely because of the public rumors of his privacy.

第二个主体段：回应 Perspective Two，首先论证对于名人隐私的过度追求会对他们的私生活产生极大的消极影响。作者罗列了三个小事实，通过平行举例的手法，揭露了过度暴露隐私产生的危害。作者接着展示了名人所受到的具体影响，也通过平行举例的手法，让本段显得生动具体。

People may claim that celebrities gain so much from the society and naturally should shoulder more stress from the society, including the risk of privacy exposure. This claim is not convincing. Truly, celebrities enjoy better lives and access to more resources than normal people. However, what people often ignore is their hard work behind screens. Celebrities win over support not because of their private life, but because of their ceaseless devotion to careers. Celebrities have to pay arduous efforts to secure their social status and reputation. Hence, overdue attention to celebrities' privacy will distract people from recognizing the valuable endeavors. When Michael Jackson was criticized of mistreating the little boy, nearly all the media denied Michael's previous efforts and treated him so meanly that it hardly tried to see the justice behind this made-up accuse.

第三个主体段：回应 Perspective Three，证明名人的成功背后付出了巨大的努力，隐私不应被公众理所应当地消费，因此公众对名人隐私的过度关注会忽略名人的真正贡献。作者通过迈克尔·杰克逊被诬告虐童时，媒体无一例外地对他进行负面报道，而没有公正地对待他，呼吁人们理性对待名人隐私，不要忽略他们所做的努力。

All in all, while privacy exposure increases popularity, it will cause long-term negative effects towards both the celebrities and the society. We should leave more space for celebrities to have peaceful moments in life because they have their own rights to deal with their own business.

结尾段：本段按照"重申观点＋建议"的方法结束全文。

媒体类作业

（一）完形填空练习：请在以下 **20** 个词组中找出合适的词组填入下面两段文字中

1. advertiser 登广告的人

2. digital media 数字媒体

3. old media 旧媒体（如报纸、书籍、电视、广播、电影等）

4. commercial advertisement 商业广告

5. manipulate 操纵

6. subliminal 潜意识；潜在意识的

7. inculcate 谆谆教导，反复灌输

8. impart to 传授

9. mislead 误导

10. freedom of speech 言论自由

11. illusion of free will and independence 自由意志和独立的错觉

12. individualism 个人主义

13. conflict of opinions 观点冲突

14. politically correct 政治正确

15. vulnerable group 脆弱群体

16. sensitive 敏感的

17. insulting 侮辱的

18. pulverize privacy 粉碎隐私

19. infringe on 侵犯

20. disseminate 宣传，散播

完形填空一

Once we rest our vigilance, （1） and the Internet would take clandestine control of our lives and even our thoughts. You may get the （2） but you have already been （3） . For example, when you make a so-called satisfactory purchase, you even have no idea about details of the product. When you firmly believe that genetically modified organism (GMO) is detrimental to health, you do not even know a bit of the pertinent science. When you think you've voted for the president in your own interest, you do not even have a thorough understanding of his policies.

完形填空二

Censorship, though intending to protect ＿(1)＿ from ＿(2)＿ or dangerous information, sometimes violates individuals' ＿(3)＿. Everyone has the right to share his/her thoughts, and there is no excuse to severely restrict how people think and what people believe. A society of diversity and democracy should embrace ＿(4)＿.

（二）汉译英练习

1. advertiser 登广告的人

   我正在网上浏览租赁信息，结果发现我丈夫是其中一个登广告的人，他想把我们的公寓卖了。

2. endorse 赞助

   吸引人的广告比产品质量更重要，这已是公开的秘密。所以很多品牌企业花费大量资金聘请明星代言它们的产品。

3. digital media 数字媒体

   现代人习惯了使用数字媒体获取或传播信息，而不是用纸媒。

4. old media 旧媒体（如报纸、书籍、电视、广播、电影等）

   现代人不再仅仅局限于旧媒体（如报纸、书籍和电视）来获取信息。数字媒体成为人们获取信息和表达观点的更有效的途径。

5. commercial advertisement 商业广告

   公益广告和商业广告不同。前者的目的是教育大众，而后者的终极目标是推广产品和服务，赚取利润。

6. manipulate 操纵

   青少年智力发展还未成熟，对复杂的事件没有清晰的判断，所以他们很容易被别有用心的人操控。

7. subliminal 潜意识；潜在意识的

   有些消费者认为他们不会受到广告的影响，但事实上广告不断地向他们传递潜意识的信息，以此来控制他们喜欢什么和购买什么。

8. inculcate 谆谆教导，反复灌输

   现在读书的人越来越少了，所以政府采取了一系列措施向市民灌输读书的价值。

9. impart to 传授

   学校不仅仅要向学生传授知识，还应该帮助他们树立正确的观念、培养良好的品格。

10. mislead 误导

    我们必须对这件事进行全面调查，否则可能会被一些似是而非的信息误导。

11. exaggerate 夸张

这个男孩很淘气，喜欢对他的日常经历夸大其词。

12. divergent 分歧的

一个自由的社会愿意接受不同的观点并鼓励人们表达自己的想法。

13. distorted information 扭曲的信息，信息失真

尽管社交媒体使我们能够获取更多信息，但同时也使我们很难从众多失真信息中辨别出哪些是真实的。

14. suppression of speech 抑制言论自由

审查制度有时候会成为抑制言论自由的合法借口。

15. freedom of speech 言论自由

在一个民主社会中，言论自由应该受到尊重和保护。

16. diversity of thoughts and expression 思想和表达的多样性

言论自由是宪法赋予人们的基本权利，它让我们能够充分表达自己，使社会有多元化的思想和表达。

17. individualism 个人主义

媒体上的主流思想会扼杀个人主义：向人们施加统一的思想和价值，不鼓励独特性。

18. conflict of opinions 观点冲突

观点冲突在头脑风暴的过程中很普遍也很有益。它鼓励人们打破固化思维和成见，激发更好的想法。

19. identical captives without opinions 没有思想的俘虏

当今，年轻人习惯在网上搜索信息却不加以思考，导致他们正逐渐沦为没有思想的俘虏。

20. politically correct 政治正确

我们在公共场合表达观点时，需要做到政治正确。我们不应该视其为一种限制，而是一种表示尊重的方式。

21. vulnerable group 脆弱群体

空调对于病人或者老人等脆弱群体非常重要。

22. mutual respect 相互尊重

虽然网民可以匿名发表观点，但是我们还是应该注意言行，抱以互相尊重的心态。

23. provocative 刺激的，挑拨的

香水广告的内容可能极具挑逗性，画面往往是一个穿着性感的女性在引诱一位帅气的男性。

24. sensitive 敏感的

女性比男性更敏感。她们容易因美丽的故事感动，也容易因悲惨的事件伤心。

25. insulting 侮辱的

朝人脸上砸钱是非常侮辱性的行为，男人就算再穷也很难承受这样的侮辱。

26. selectively 选择性地

网上充满了各种信息，有真有假。所以，我们要有怀疑精神，有选择性地相信。

27. pulverize privacy 粉碎隐私

互联网在为我们带来便捷的同时也粉碎了我们的隐私。

28. infringe on 侵犯

有些人抱怨审查制度侵犯了公民自由表达的权利。

29. vexing issue 棘手的问题，令人烦恼的问题

工业的迅速发展使环境保护成了一个棘手的问题。

30. disseminate 宣传，散播

一些激进分子利用社交媒体传播扭曲的危险信息，以制造恐慌。

（三）写作实操

Prompt 3

Scandals

The popularity of the media, such as Twitter or Facebook, has exposed mass of information to the public. New types of media try to absorb the attention of the public, and as a result, many scandals concerning some personal information have been exposed to an increasing number of people. Individuals, who have the curiosity, would like to focus their attention to these scandals, causing some negative influence on the society. While, some think that scandals are useful because they interest the audience in some social problems in some way, but the fact is that many people only focus on the negative effects of scandals. Thus, it is worth considering the meaning and consequences of scandals.

Read and carefully consider these perspectives. Each suggests a particular way of thinking about the scandals.

Perspective One	Perspective Two	Perspective Three
Scandals, especially the ones concerning celebrities, can help the public to focus on some existing but ignored social issues, which could act as the driving force in promoting the pro-social behaviors.	The curiosity of the public would turn the public figures into the victims, as the public might dig out more information related to their personal life, or about their relatives or friends. As a result, it could make something gone amiss the original purpose of the publish of scandals.	The purpose of the media which report the negative news, needs to be reconsidered, as some media would like to absorb as much as attention from the public without considering about these negative effects. The incorrect values they are disseminating may misguide the public, especially some teenagers.

Essay Task

Write a unified, coherent essay in which you evaluate multiple perspectives on scandals. In your essay, be sure to:

- clearly state your own perspective on the issue and analyze the relationship between your perspective and at least one other perspective
- develop and support your ideas with reasoning and examples
- organize your ideas clearly and logically
- communicate your ideas effectively in standard written English

Your perspective may be in full agreement with any of those given, in partial agreement, or completely different.

Extended Reading

Reference Article: Scandal

A scandal can be broadly defined as an accusation or accusations that receive wide exposure. Generally there is a negative effect on the credibility of the person or organization involved. Society is scandalized when it is made aware of blatant breaches of moral norms or legal requirements. In contemporary times, exposure is often made by mass media. Such breaches have typically erupted from greed, lust or the abuse of power. Scandals may be regarded as political, sexual, moral, literary or artistic but often spread from one realm into another. The basis of a scandal may be factual or false, or a combination of both.

Contemporary media has the capacity to spread knowledge of a scandal further than in previous centuries and public interest has encouraged many cases of confected scandals relating to well-known people as well as genuine scandals relating to politics and business. Some scandals are revealed by whistleblowers who discover wrongdoing within organizations or groups, such as Deep Throat (William Mark Felt) during the Watergate scandal in the 1970s in the United States. Whistleblowers may be protected by laws which are used to obtain information of misdeeds and acts detrimental to their establishments. However, the possibility of scandal has always created a tension between society's efforts to reveal wrongdoing and its desire to cover them up.

A political scandal occurs when political corruption or other misbehavior is exposed. Politicians or government officials are accused of engaging in illegal, corrupt, or unethical practices. A political scandal can involve the breaking of the nation's laws or moral codes and may involve other types of scandal.

In 2012, Michael Woodford who successfully steered Olympus, a Japanese company to fame, turned a whistleblower when even as a CEO of the firm, exposed the financial scandal worth $1.7 billion fled Japan fearing for his life. Though persecuted his revelations proved to be true resulting in booking the culprits. Portraying a damaging status of corporate Japan, Woodford, in his memoirs has said: "I thought I was going to run a health-care and consumer electronics company, but found I had walked into a John Grisham novel."

Since the development of printing, the media has had greater power to expose scandals and since the advent of mass media, this power has increased. The media also has the capacity to support and/or oppose organizations and destabilize them thereby becoming involved in scandals themselves as well as reporting them.

Following the Watergate scandal in the United States, other English-speaking countries have borrowed the suffix "gate" and added it to scandals of their own.

Journalistic scandals relate to high-profile incidents or acts, whether done purposefully or by accident. It could be in violation of normally in vogue ethics and standards of journalism. It could also be in violation of the 'ideal' mission of journalism: to publish "news events and issues accurately and fairly."

The American quiz show of the 1950s generated "hypnotic intensity" among viewers and contestants. The CBS Television show *The $64,000 Question* which started on 7 June

1955 and such other shows as *The Big Surprise*, *Dotto*, *Tic Tac Dough*, and *Twenty One* became the most publicized quiz shows, but soon generated scandals after a series of revelations that contestants of several popular television quiz shows conspired with the show's producers to rig the outcome. The quiz show scandals were driven by a drive for financial gain, a willingness of contestants to "play along" with the assistance, and the lack of regulation prohibiting the rigging of game shows. In October 1958, a New York grand jury was instituted by prosecutor Joseph Stone and the matter was examined with recording of closed-door testimony. Following this, the US Congress ruled rigging a quiz show a federal crime.

The TV soap opera titled "Scandal" a popular show on the American Television ABC channel has been dubbed a "self-absorbed, overblown, overacted, pretentious, soliloquy-laden car-wreck-of-a-series."

(Excerpted from *https://en.wikipedia.org/wiki/Scandal*)

话题八   文娱艺术类

Topic Analysis

随着物质水平的提高，人们对于艺术的追求也越来越高，我们的日常生活中已经渗透了很多艺术气息。ACT写作也热衷于考查文娱艺术类话题，题目会涉及音乐的影响（power of music）、音乐的普及对其价值的影响（free music）、艺术复制品的影响（copies of art pieces）等。艺术离日常生活比较远，而且比较抽象，所以该话题的难度系数很高。考生们在准备文娱艺术类话题时，可以搜罗一些有代表性的音乐、绘画、摄影、影视作品，并分析作品中蕴含的意义，以便在考场上灵活发挥。

Topic Vocabulary

artistic value 艺术价值

the inherent advantages of...……的潜在好处

cultural diversity 文化多元化

cross-cultural communication 跨文化交流

achievements of art 艺术成就

visual enjoyment 视觉享受

cradle of culture 文化摇篮

mainstream culture 主流文化

national pride 民族自豪

local customs and practices 风土人情

attract people's eyes 吸引人们的眼球

artistic taste 艺术品位

adhere to the tradition 坚持传统

architectural vandalism 破坏建筑行为

carry forward... 弘扬……

cultural needs 文化需求

artistic reflection 艺术反映

cause irreversible damage 造成不可逆转的损失

national identity and value 民族特性和价值观

remove prejudice and misunderstanding 消除偏见和误解

artistic standards 艺术水准

enjoy great popularity 广受欢迎

cultural devolution 文化退化

cultural insights 文化视角

lasting artistic works 永恒的艺术作品

break with old customs 抛弃传统

carry down from generation to generation 代代相传

echo 共识

attach more importance to... 更重视……

spiritual enhancement 精神升华

eclipse 使……相形见绌

pastimes 消遣方式

meditation 沉思

an essence of immortality 永恒的精髓

instructive 有启发性的

edification 熏陶

cultural differences 文化差异性

Time is fleeting and art is longlasting 时光飞逝，艺术永恒

Extended Reading

Reference Article 1: Cultural Heritage

1 Any cultural or cultural tradition that inherits from cultural heritage requires a certain entity and some other forms, which includes works of art, written records and so on, and the most important of them are rituals and ceremonies. First, they show the spirit of a culture that cannot be shown by other entities. In addition, ritual or form is not just about cultural inheritance and other related issues, but there are much reflection about daily life. All the spiritual connotation is reflected in the expression, and some are gradually developed in the expression.

2 Learning popular culture can further strengthen our social values, as a result, we could have the communication with contemporary society; secondly, lacking the understanding about the culture will not help us to be able to keep up with the times and be isolated. But pop culture contains some unhealthy ingredients such as violence, pornography,

etc. But the critical judgement would assist us to find the essence of it, making the popular culture become classics in the history.

3 It is certainly understandable that government should start looking at ways of improving their public facilities to a sustainable development. Government have to make a real innovation in keeping the stability of the society, which means that people should get good service from their government. There was a statement said that government should utilize the money for public importance, and do not use this money for other things like arts (music and theatre). Personally, I disagree with that statement. In the following paragraphs, I will give my reasons to support my opinion.

4 Nowadays, to face the period of development, as a country they have to compete with other countries. Arts can offer a positive contribution to the development of the quality of life as a country. I believe that each country has their ability then they can compete with the others. For example, recently there are some world competitions related to 'singing' such as World Choir Competition, ASIAN Idol, etc. Every country sends their best participants to follow the competition. Two years ago, Indonesian delegate taking part in World Choir Competition held on 15–17 March 2013 at Belgium. They have to compete with 57 countries, and finally, they got gold medals for several categories.

5 In addition, I think that if a government invests some money to arts sector, it will create many advantages for the country itself. For instance, Indonesia has talented people in painting field, which means that they can make a beautiful creation to sale. One of popular paintings is 'Monalisa' drawing. The painting already became everlasting painting because it was drawn by the talented person, which the painter already created many advantages for himself and his country. Another essential thing is people have to make a good teamwork with the government to produce huge advantages related to arts creations.

6 In conclusion, the government should invest some money to improve arts creation because it has a big opportunity to make a country more successful. (503 words)

(Excerpted from https://www.ielts-mentor.com/writing-sample/writing-task-2/1155-ielts-writing-task-2-sample-240-government-investment-in-the-arts-such-as-music-and-theatre)

Analysis of Article

Main Points of Cultural Heritage

Any cultural or cultural tradition that inherits from cultural heritage requires a certain entity and some other forms.

Learning popular culture can further strengthen our social values.

Vocabulary

inherit *v.* 继承

entity *n.* 实质，本质

inheritance *n.* 继承，遗产

pornography *n.* 色情描写

Read-Recite-Imitate-Create

Example one:

1. Read: Any cultural or cultural tradition that inherits from cultural heritage requires a certain entity and some other forms, which includes works of art, written records and so on,

2. Recite：...**inherits from**...

3. Imitate: Any understanding about arts that **inherits from** social value requires certain personal perceptions, which includes education level, social experience and so on.

4. Create: Any understanding about culture that **inherits from** social understanding requires a certain unique aspect, which includes education background, social experience and so on.

Example two:

1. Read: lacking the understanding about the culture will not help us to be able to keep up with the times and be isolated.

2. Recite: **(not)doing sth. will not help us to be able to do sth.**

3. Imitate: **lacking** the awareness about environment protection **will not help us to be able to** catch up with the trend of sustainable development.

第三章 ACT 写作话题分类 | **209**

4. Create: **lacking** the awareness about heritage protection **will not help us to be able to** have the comprehensive understanding about the culture.

Reference Article 2: Arts Function

1 Art is used to express the artist's creativity, to attract the audience's sense of beauty, or to guide the audience to think about something better. Art, if it is used in other purposes, such as commerce, is called applied art. The purpose of non-motive art is to express people's instinctive appreciation of harmony and beauty; to experience mystery; to express imagination; to communicate with the world; to perform ritual and symbolic functions. The artistic purpose of motivation is communication, entertainment, political purpose, treatment, reflection of social conditions, publicity.

2 Works of art are often not able to give those artists, especially those young artists, enough income; at the same time, many artists do not want to use their works as the tool for money, and thus their economic status was very embarrassed. The museum of art works is a window for the public, it allows the public to have the opportunity to understand art, to understand the social problems reflected by art and historical things reflected by art. Many painters or sculptors use a perceptual way to create many works that reflect the social corruption, which makes the public aware of the phenomenon of corruption.

3 As the most of the countries' revenue is collected from the public through the taxation system, it is imperative that governments spend the available fund for the most effective public services of the nation which is beneficial to society at large. Some people believe that governments should allocate sufficient fund for promoting music and arts as these kinds of entertainment activities help adults as well as children to get much relaxation, reduce their tensions and stresses in their busy day to day life. However, from my point of view, countries should employ most of their funds in important public services such as education, health and transport systems rather spending money on entertainment activities as this sector is less beneficial to the public

than that of the importance of the three sectors mentioned above.

4 The most important sector of the economy is the education as the development of this sector is one of the crucial requirements for a sustainable growth of a country in a long run. The governments all over the world have the responsibility to ensure that every citizen of the country is educated, at least to read and write. The investment in this sector will be in the form of establishing more schools, universities and vocational training centres for the school drop-outs and also providing scholarships for continuing higher education.

5 The next essential sector of the economy is the health. It is vital that everyone in the society has the means to get the basic health benefits. Governments can invest in the health sector in many ways. The medical practitioners should be taken care by providing them with the sufficient remuneration and benefits so that the important skill migration in the medical field of the country could be avoided. Also, the authorities can educate the general public and implement many vaccination programs across the countries to eradicate many diseases such as polio, chicken pox and malaria.

6 The last but not the least significant sector of the country is the public transportation system. States' funds should be deployed in putting up proper transport network systems such as the building of metro-train facility around the city. More lanes on the highway roads can be built to facilitate the car-pooling for the commuters. This facility will reduce the carbon fuel emission and helps to reduce the global warming.

7 In conclusion, governments should spend a major portion of their funds on highly demanding public-service sectors such as health, education and public transportation rather than spending a huge money on the entertainment sectors such as theatres and music. (631 words)

(Excerpted from *https://www.ielts-mentor.com/writing-sample/writing-task-2/1155-ielts-writing-task-2-sample-240-government-investment-in-the-arts-such-as-music-and-theatre*)

NOTES

第三章 ACT 写作话题分类 | **211**

Analysis of Article

Main Points of Arts Function

Art is used to express the artist's creativity.

Art is used to attract the audience's sense of beauty.

Art is used to guide the audience to think about something better.

Art is used to express people's instinctive appreciation of harmony and beauty.

Art is used to experience mystery.

Art is used to express imagination.

Art is used to communicate with the world.

Art is used to perform ritual and symbolic functions.

Many artists do not want to use their works as the tool for money, and thus their economic status was very embarrassed.

Vocabulary

instinctive *adj.* 天生的

publicity *n.* 公众信息

embarrass *n.* 尴尬

perceptual *adj.* 感知的

Read-Recite-Imitate-Create

Example one:

1. Read: Art is used to express the artist's creativity, to attract the audience's sense of beauty, or to guide the audience to think about something better.

2. Recite：**is used to do sth., to do sth., or to do sth.**

3. Imitate: Music **is used to express the artist's idea, to attract the listener's sense of rhythm, or to guide the public to think about art better**.

4. Create: literature **is used to express the author's idea, to attract the reader's sense of thinking, or to guide the public to think about literature better**.

Example two:

1. Read: It is imperative that governments spend the available fund for the most effective public services of the nation which is beneficial to society at large.

2. Recite: **It is imperative that sb. spend sth. for sth.**

3. Imitate: **It is imperative that government spend** the available **fund for** the environment protection.

4. Create: **It is imperative that government spend** the available **fund for** the culture heritage.

Prompt 1

The Investment on the Art by the Government

Arts could improve quality of life. Arts could improve a person's connotation. Arts could make people know how to find the beauty in life. Arts, the discovery and the understanding of the beauty, would even change person's character. Therefore, it is worthy for government to spend some investment on the promotion of arts, such as building some art gallery, constructing of theater, etc. When the government invests on the arts, it would select the most representative ones to do the promotion; as a result, the integrity of the arts could be spoiled, and even it would accelerate the decline of some minority arts forms. Given the complexity that the investment on the arts needs not only the public but also the government, it is necessary to have the comprehensive thinking about the investment.

Read and carefully consider these perspectives. Each suggests a particular way of thinking about the investment on the art by the government.

Perspective One

Art education is the main motivation of personal aesthetic appreciation development, and it acts as an important way to improve individuals' quality of life and ability. The influence of arts on the teenagers could not be denied; as a result, government needs to invest on the arts.

Perspective Two

As we all know, arts might be dedicated to the main social value. Government funding might directly or indirectly influence artists' decision and choices, leading the booming of one specific culture. As a result, it could threaten the integrity of the arts.

Perspective Three

Arts could be the best representative of the culture to help us to find our connections between the past and future from the historical aspect. Respecting the art indicates that we need to follow the trend of arts. Sometimes, arts education about the importance of culture influence is necessary.

Essay Task

Write a unified, coherent essay in which you evaluate multiple perspectives on the investment on the art by the government. In your essay, be sure to:

- clearly state your own perspective on the issue and analyze the relationship between your perspective and at least one other perspective
- develop and support your ideas with reasoning and examples
- organize your ideas clearly and logically
- communicate your ideas effectively in standard written English

Your perspective may be in full agreement with any of those given, in partial agreement, or completely different.

Prompt Analysis

P1	√ Art is the representative of the social value. The investment on the arts is necessary, because arts could enhance the life standard. √ 艺术是社会价值的代表，投资艺术很有必要性，因为艺术可以提高人们的生活质量。 【Eg.】the investment in the art gallery and theatre 艺术画廊、剧院等的投资

	× People might have different aesthetic appreciation ability; even some people might only focus on the life standard enhancement.
	× 不是人人都具有鉴赏艺术的能力，更多的人仅需要物质生活质量的提高。
	【Eg.】construction of the infrastructure 基础设施的建设
P2	✓ Government would have their own favor to invest, which might lead the artists development trend, spoiling the integrity of the arts.
	✓ 政府投资艺术会有倾向性，会引导艺术家的发展方向，因此会破坏艺术的整一性。
	【Eg.】the investment on the most typical ones, such as literature in the west 对最具有代表性的进行投资，如西方对文学的投资
	× The ones who are selected as the representative might only be the indicators of this temporary trend, thus we need to do the right selections.
	× 被挑选出来的具有代表性的艺术可能只是现阶段艺术发展方向的代表，因此我们需要做出正确的选择。
	【Eg.】investment on the Peking Opera 对中国京剧的投资
P3	✓ Arts have different functions in different time periods.
	✓ 艺术在不同的时间段有其存在的不同意义。
	【Eg.】The popularity of literature has been placed by drama, then by TV or movie 艺术形式先是文学，再是话剧，再是电视剧或是电影
	× Arts might only have their merit when most of the people could understand them.
	× 艺术只有被大多数人理解了才有意义。
	【Eg.】inscriptions on bones or tortoise shells of the Shang Dynasty 商朝的甲骨文

Model Essay 1

With the considerable achievements in economy and the improvements of people's living quality, the government has paid more attention to updating public cultural services, including establishing and funding art museums, galleries and theaters. Any understanding about culture that inherits from social understanding requires a certain unique aspect, which includes education background, social experience and so on. As a result, there comes with a heated controversy about the necessity of the investment on the art by the government, and whether government preference will impair the integrity of the arts. In this aspect, the government funds might lead to the prosperity of one specific form of arts and spoil the others. As far as I am concerned, the role of arts should not be neglected, as the benefits of investment on arts may be less visible, but they are essential to the sound development of the society in the long term.

> **开头段：** "社会背景 + 双方观点 + 作者观点" 是比较常见的开头方式，这样的开篇方式非常容易模仿和展开思路。通过介绍现阶段政府投资艺术的背景引出不同的看法，之后表达出自己的观点。

It is imperative that government should spend the available fund for the culture heritage. Some people emphasize that education about the importance of art culture is indispensable, which is in agreement with Perspective One. Truly, arts are the link between the past and the future, which could help people discover and understand beauty. Lacking the awareness about heritage protection will not help us to be able to have the comprehensive understanding about the culture. Establishing and supporting great art facilities, like the British Museum, will not only bring honor and knowledge to the local community, but also become well-known scenic spots for tourists from all over the world. The investment on the art by the government has set a great model to us about how to protect the culture heritage in an appropriate way, as the culture preserve institution has showed the public the specific method to preserve the arts, and the culture academy has devoted the energy to explore the essence of these heritage. All the efforts could not only show individuals various forms of beauty but also build a more pluralistic society, which will improve the diversity of the arts from the heritage.

> **第一个主体段：** 针对 Perspective One 进行具体论述。作者在这里肯定了政府投资艺术的重要性，先是对艺术的存在意义进行了思考，之后以大英博物馆为例，证明了投资艺术所带来的好处。ACT 作文对于例子的具体选择也可以体现出考生的知识体系。

As Perspective Two mentions, the other heated controversy the public mainly concern is whether leading the booming of one specific culture by the government threatens the integrity of the arts. It seems that government funding has an invisible impact on artists' decisions and choices, so that it will bring negative influence on the freedom of creation. To be specific, literature is used to express the author's idea, to attract the reader's sense of thinking, or to guide the public to think about literature better. Nevertheless, there are various kinds of folk arts going to disappearing without enough funds and support, such as the New Year picture and the shadow puppet show of China, which is a serious threat to the integrity of the arts. Government funding as the solution could find and record the dying folk art, attract more public attention, and help artists combine the traditional craft art with the today's new life. Public cultural policies also give a demonstration to private investors, so that the whole society will pay more consideration to developing cultural industry, which benefits different kinds of subcultures. Thus, the investment on the art by the government actually enhances the integrity of the arts.

> **第二个主体段：** 回应 Perspective Two，作者首先就第二个观点进行了解释，之后进一步解释了 Perspective Two 错误的来源，这是典型的驳论段落。驳论即引出反方观点，并予以针对性反驳，解决对方的疑问和质疑。本段首先从人们日常的错误假设出发，再引出投资艺术对于艺术发展整一性的积极意义，并且辅以细节证明。

Besides, government investment plays an important role beyond protection, which is a right attitude mentioned by Perspective Three. The investment on art education could strengthen its function of improving individuals' quality and ability. Human, the only species who have the ability to recall the past and anticipate the future, would have the better understanding about the culture from all aspects. As a result, citizens, especially teenagers, will not only touch and understand the traditional culture from the past, but also improve their connotation and creativity in the future. Therefore, government needs to invest the arts to train more inventive and talented people.

第三个主体段： 对 Perspective Three 进行展开和支持。本段论证政府投资艺术的好处以及具体的投资发展方向，这对应了本文总观点中的 "The investment on art education could strengthen its function of improving individuals quality and ability"。

The investment on the art by the government could help minority culture enter the stage before the public, save dying folk art, and develop culture industry. The art education will improve people's understanding of beauty and enhance their creativity. The benefits of investment on arts are vital to the sustainable development of the society in the long term.

结尾段： "总结分论点 + 重申观点" 是非常推荐的收尾方式，按照这个思路可以对上文进行总结并有效呼应开头。日常练习注意开头和结尾的快速练习，争取考试的时候留更多时间给中间段落思考和展开。

Words

integrity *n.* 完整性，诚实

indispensable *adj.* 不可缺少的

pluralistic *adj.* 多元化的

inventive *adj.* 别出心裁的

Phrases

mainstream of arts spreading direction 艺术主流的发展方向

give a demonstration to 给予了解释

strengthen its function 加强了其功能性

Sentences

It comes with a heated controversy about...

伴随而来的一个具有争议性的探讨是有关……

Prompt 2

Imaginary Books and Stories

Many books and stories we read and hear are fictional; they talk about characters and events that are not real. Some people regard the fictions as purely entertainment, thinking they do not teach us anything useful about the real world. They may even argue books and stories about imaginary characters and events can even hinder clear thoughts. But can they be useful and teach us something about ourselves or the world around us? Given the divergent opinions, it is worth considering whether fictional books and stories can teach us anything useful?

Read and carefully consider these perspectives. Each suggests a particular way of thinking about the function of fictional books and stories.

Perspective One	Perspective Two	Perspective Three
Books and stories about characters and events that are not real would prevent the audience from having a clear understanding about the real world. They only mislead the audience and make them unrealistic.	Fictional characters and events can work as a medium to reflect real world and true self. Although they are unreal, they still come from life.	Although some events and stories seem unreal and even ridiculous on the surface, they can still convey abstract yet meaningful message.

Essay Task

Write a unified, coherent essay in which you evaluate multiple perspectives on the function of fictional books and stories. In your essay, be sure to:

- clearly state your own perspective on the issue and analyze the relationship between your perspective and at least one other perspective
- develop and support your ideas with reasoning and examples
- organize your ideas clearly and logically
- communicate your ideas effectively in standard written English

Your perspective may be in full agreement with any of those given, in partial agreement, or completely different.

Prompt Analysis

P1	✓ Even some fictions might express some unreliable stories, individuals who have the critical ability can absorb some meaningful information from them. ✓ 即使虚假的故事也会传递不真实的信息，但善于思考的人会从中悟出一些道理。 【Eg.】Marvel's superheroes, Chinese kung fu novels 漫威的超级英雄，中国的武侠小说
	✗ Unreliable stories might mislead individuals, hindering people from telling the difference between the reality and fantasy. ✗ 编造的故事本身就是虚假的、脱离现实的，所以会误导人们，使其无法区分虚拟的和真实的世界。 【Eg.】Marvel's superheroes, Chinese kung fu novels 漫威的超级英雄，中国的武侠小说
P2	✓ Fiction stories are sometimes based on reality, and they can, therefore, mirror the reality and bring us into deep thinking. ✓ 虚构的人物或故事很多时候是基于现实而创作的，所以可以反映很多现实的问题，并且为我们带来很多思考。 【Eg.】*The Great Gatsby, To Kill a Mockingbird*《了不起的盖茨比》，《杀死一只知更鸟》
	✓ Although many fictional figures and stories are based on reality, they are altered for the sake of art. Therefore, they benefit us in the form of entertaining rather than inspiring. ✓ 虽然虚构的人物和故事往往也是基于现实而创建的，但是它们会为了创造艺术效果而被篡改。所以，它们不会启发深刻的思考，只会带来艺术或娱乐效果。 【Eg.】Marvel's superheroes, Chinese kung fu novels 漫威的超级英雄，中国的武侠小说

	✓ Imaginary stories could help us to form some accurate social value. ✓ 有些故事和人物是完全虚构的，但是它们具有一些重要的社会价值，而且我们可以通过学习这些虚构的故事培养是非观。 【Eg.】*Aesop's Fables*《伊索寓言》
P3	✗ Imaginary stories function is entertainment, which might not give use social value instruction. ✗ 完全虚构的故事只能供人们娱乐，不会传递给我们有益的信息。 【Eg.】superficial or vulgar talk shows 肤浅的脱口秀

Model Essay 2

Reading is a habit for many people, and the books they read are not necessarily telling real events or stories. Some people tend to underestimate the value of fictional stories, thinking these stories will prevent the reader from having a clear understanding about the reality. However, as unreal as they are, they still teach us something useful about people and the society.

开头段： 本段采用经典的"话题引入 + 对立观点 + 自己观点"的模式展开。这三个步骤的展开不需要考生花费太多精力，从题目的提示语中可以提取"话题引入"的内容；而给出的三个 perspective 中也已经包括了对立的观点。考生只需稍微构思一下"自己观点"，使其清晰、明确、严谨即可。

Some books and stories about characters and events that do not really exist are, in fact, based on the reality. They are a mirror of the reality, and give the audience an opportunity to reflect on themselves and the society. Take the example of *The Great Gatsby*, by Fitzgerald as example. Fitzgerald set his story in the Roaring Twenties, telling a story about Jay Gatsby, who fell in love with Daisy, a typical flapper. In order to win over her love, he made fortune through bootlegging and throwing extravagant parties all nights. But in the end, not only did Daisy not love him back, but she also made him the scapegoat of a car accident. It is true that Gatsby and Daisy and other characters in the story are not real, but they symbolize the typical figures and decadent values of the Jazz Age. That is, the moral emptiness and hypocrisy beneath the material abundance. Reading this book propels people to contemplate their intrinsic defects and warns them to learn the lesson.

> **第一个主体段**：本段采用"主题句＋例证＋结尾"的方法展开，对应了题目中的 Perspective Two。前两句是一个因果关系，构成了该段的主题句（topic sentence），明确表明该段核心信息：即使有些故事或人物并非真实存在，但它们仍然源于生活，所以能引发人们对自己和对社会的思考，然后以《了不起的盖茨比》为例支撑该观点，最后一句话进行了总结。

Even though some stories and characters are purely made up, they still serve as the embodiment of the values and character that we want to inculcate in the young generations, so that the society runs under a consistent code of conduct. *The Body Who Cried Wolf*, one of the *Aesop's Fables*, is just a case in point. A shepherd boy, out of naughtiness, cried wolf twice when there was no wolf just to fool the villagers. But when there was actually a REAL wolf chasing the sheep, no body reacted to his cry. Though it is completely out of Aesop's imagination, it teaches the fundamental value about deception and honesty. All generations grow up hearing the recount of such enlightening fables.

> **第二个主体段**：该段继续使用第一个主体段的展开结构，对应了题目中的 Perspective Three，即一些完全虚构的故事或者人物也能传递一些重要的价值观。与第一个主体段的"do not really exist are, in fact, based on the reality（虽不忠实于生活，但是源于生活）"的故事不同，本段开始讨论一些"are purely made up（完全虚构的）"故事，然后用《伊索寓言》中"狼来了"的故事支持该观点。

Yet, some people are less enthusiastic about imaginary characters and stories; they regard them as unrealistic and perplexing so as to obstruct a clear understanding about the society. For example, some kids imitate Marvel's super heroes to teach bad guys a lessen using heroic yet illegal means. While it may be true, the value of such stories can yet not be denied. When immature kids and youth extract the wrong essence out of them, parents and teachers should take the responsibilities to guide them to distinguish the meaningful messages from the exaggerated and unreal portion.

第三个主体段：该段是让步段。先让步 Perspective One 中的观点 "Books and stories about characters and events that are not real would prevent the audience from having a clear understanding about the real world.（虚构的故事或人物阻碍我们对真实世界的认识和理解）"，然后进行转折，明确自己对对立观点的否定态度，即 "While it may be true, the value of such stories can yet not be denied.（虽然这些问题可能发生，但是我们也不能因此否定其意义）"。最后，给出避免这些问题的建议。

Some characters and events do not really exist but they can be a more effective medium to teach people something significant. Whether they are based on reality or entirely made up, they not only encourage the audience to have a better understanding about true selves and the world, but also help communicate positive values.

结尾段：该段重申主旨 + 总结两个分论点。

文娱艺术类作业

（一）完形填空练习：请在以下 **20** 个词组中找出合适的词组填入下面两段文字中

1. cultural needs 文化需求

2. echo 共识

3. achievements of art 艺术成就

4. national pride 民族自豪

5. adhere to the tradition 坚持传统

6. cultural diversity 文化多样性

7. edification 熏陶

8. artistic reflection 艺术反映

9. artistic standards 艺术水准

10. cultural insights 文化视角

11. eclipse 使……相形见绌

12. break with old customs 抛弃传统

13. enjoy great popularity 广受欢迎

14. pastimes 消遣方式

15. meditation 沉思

16. instructive 有启发性的

17. national identity and value 民族特性和价值观

18. cross-cultural communication 跨文化交流

19. adhere to the tradition 坚持传统

20. attach more importance to... 更重视……

完形填空一

The development of modern art could be （1） of the people, so that the audience can find （2） in the art appreciation. Art does not only belong to the people, but also to the nation.

完形填空二

Global economic integration promotes （1） to a great extent. （2） can not only （3）, but also bring different visual enjoyment to the world, which is an irresistible trend.

（二）汉译英练习

1. artistic value 艺术价值

   一部伟大的电影想要提名奥斯卡，不仅要有引人入胜的情节，还需要有很高的艺术价值。

2. the inherent advantages of...……的潜在好处

   隐私安全是比特币交易的潜在好处。

3. cultural diversity 文化多元化

   自从十八世纪开始，一波又一波的移民劳工为加州的文化多样性作出了重要贡献。

4. cross-cultural communication 跨文化交流

   有效的跨文化交流的关键是知识和理解。

5. achievements of art 艺术成就

   大英博物馆从世界各地收集了具有极高艺术成就的珍宝。

6. visual enjoyment 视觉享受

   每周末我都去看早场电影，享受视觉盛宴。

7. cradle of culture 文化摇篮

   大学是文化的摇篮，为文化产业提供了许多人才。

8. mainstream culture 主流文化

   这部在旧金山拍摄的新片，将把地下亚文化带到主流文化面前。

9. national pride 民族自豪

   这些巨大的成就极大地提高了中国人民的民族自豪感和自信心。

10. local customs and practices 风土人情

    这部电影为观众提供了一个全新的角度来了解四川的风土民情。

11. attract people's eyes 吸引人们的眼球

    有些事物可以一直吸引人们的眼球。

12. artistic taste 艺术品位

    总的来说，布朗夫妇的艺术品位和前任比起来相差很大。

13. adhere to the tradition 坚持传统

    艺术家的创作既不能完全坚守传统，也不能彻底打破时代的局限。

14. architectural vandalism 破坏建筑行为

    花费数月的技艺精湛的雕刻仅仅在几个小时内就被挥舞大锤的破坏建筑行为毁灭。

15. carry forward... 弘扬……

    我们必须弘扬我党实事求是的实践传统。

16. cultural needs 文化需求

满足人民日益增长的文化需求是我们政府的基本目标之一。

17. artistic reflection 艺术反映

它体现了唐代社会价值观的特有理想，是当时流行的艺术反映。

18. cause irreversible damage 造成不可逆转的损失

这个应用不被英特尔的芯片支持，将会对操作系统造成不可逆转的损失。

19. national identity and value 民族特性和价值观

爱国主义作为公民精神的核心，帮助强化我们的民族特性和价值观。

20. remove prejudice and misunderstanding 消除偏见和误解

跨文化交流有助于消除各国间的偏见和误解。

21. artistic standards 艺术水准

我校音乐课程的目的在于通过合唱和表演帮助孩子们全面提高艺术水准。

22. enjoy great popularity 广受欢迎

流行电视节目因为其娱乐性与大众文化保持一致而广受欢迎。

23. cultural devolution 文化退化

英国二十世纪后半叶的历史提醒我们文化退化先于政治，并迫使其随之变化。

24. cultural insights 文化视角

他们的作品体现出文学上的叛逆与激情，并成为一种独特的文化视角。

25. lasting artistic works 永恒的艺术作品

断臂维纳斯的美，使其成为美术史中永恒的艺术作品。

26. break with old customs 抛弃传统

自从新总裁上任以来，公司就打破了原有的管理模式。

27. carry down from generation to generation 代代相传

节俭作为一种优良的家风，可以代代相传。

28. echo 共识

他的话并没有在他们心中引起任何共识。

29. attach more importance to... 更重视……

在现代社会中，政府应当更加重视科技创新和技术进步。

30. spiritual enhancement 精神升华

如何实现大学生的精神升华已经成为高等教育中的一个热点问题。

31. eclipse 使……相形见绌

他的妻子比他更加聪明风趣，因此使他相形见绌。

32. pastimes 消遣方式

在英国，下班后去酒吧喝一杯是最流行的消遣方式之一。

33. meditation 沉思

在沉思中，我们让人与自然之间的和谐渗透到存在的每一层次。

34. an essence of immortality 永恒的精髓

书籍拥有永恒的精髓，是文明传承中人类创造的最持久的作品。

35. instructive 有启发性的

一个有启发性的导入活动会让学生更好地融入课堂。

36. edification 熏陶

艺术熏陶能让学生体验愉悦，培养自信，塑造健康的人格。

37. cultural differences 文化差异性

如何克服来自不同国家的职工之间的文化差异性，已经成为跨国公司人力资源管理中的严峻问题。

38. Time is fleeting and art is longlasting 时光飞逝，艺术永恒

一系列纪念莎士比亚逝世 400 周年的文化活动使人们意识到"时光飞逝，艺术永恒"。

（三）写作实操

Prompt 3

Influence of Music

It is undeniable that music plays an indispensable role in our culture, and music is needed throughout every period of history. Surely, music functions as a medium for musicians and singers to embed their thoughts and emotions in it. Some people also argue that music is more than just a reflection of thoughts; it can change how people think and what a society values. Is it simply a reflection of people's thoughts and social tendency, or is it powerful enough to actually make a change? Given the complexity regarding the influence of music, it is worth considering to what extent music affects the population.

Read and carefully consider these perspectives. Each suggests a particular way of thinking about the influence of music.

Perspective One	Perspective Two	Perspective Three
Music is a medium to reflect people's thoughts and feelings. Musicians create music for sharing their ideas and the audience listens to reinforce what they've already believed and feel.	Music can work on individuals. When one is sad, an upbeat rhythm can make him recover; when one is happy, blue music can depress him.	Music is not merely a mirror of social value but also an impetus for social change. Pioneering music can change a society or culture to a new direction.

Essay Task

Write a unified, coherent essay in which you evaluate multiple perspectives on influence of music. In your essay, be sure to:

- clearly state your own perspective on the issue and analyze the relationship between your perspective and at least one other perspective
- develop and support your ideas with reasoning and examples
- organize your ideas clearly and logically
- communicate your ideas effectively in standard written English

Your perspective may be in full agreement with any of those given, in partial agreement, or completely different.

Extended Reading

Reference Article: The Power of Music to Reduce Stress

The soothing power of music is well-established. It has a unique link to our emotions, so can be an extremely effective stress management tool.

Listening to music can have a tremendously relaxing effect on our minds and bodies, especially slow, quiet classical music. This type of music can have a beneficial effect on our physiological functions, slowing the pulse and heart rate, lowering blood pressure, and decreasing the levels of stress hormones.

As music can absorb our attention, it acts as a distraction at the same time it helps to explore emotions. This means it can be a great aid to meditation, helping to prevent the mind wandering.

Musical preference varies widely between individuals, so only you can decide what you like and what is suitable for each mood. But even if you don't usually listen to classical music it may be worth giving it a try when selecting the most calming music.

When people are very stressed, there is a tendency to avoid actively listening to music. Perhaps it feels like a waste of time, not helping to achieve anything. But as we know, productivity increases when stress is reduced, so this is another area where you can gain vast rewards. It just takes a small effort to begin with.

To incorporate music into a busy life, try playing CDs in the car, or put the radio on when in the bath or shower. Take portable music with you when walking the dog, or put the stereo on instead of the TV.

Singing (or shouting) along can also be a great release of tension, and karaoke is very enjoyable for some extroverts! Calming music before bedtime promotes peace and relaxation and helps to induce sleep.

Research on Music

Music has been used for hundreds of years to treat illnesses and restore harmony between mind and body. But recently, scientific studies have attempted to measure the potential benefits of music. They have found:

Music's form and structure can bring order and security to disabled and distressed children. It encourages coordination and communication, so improves their quality of life.

Listening to music on headphones reduces stress and anxiety in hospital patients before and after surgery.

Music can help reduce both the sensation and distress of both chronic pain and postoperative pain.

Listening to music can relieve depression and increase self-esteem ratings in elderly people.

Making music can reduce burnout and improve mood among nursing students.
Music therapy significantly reduces emotional distress and boosts quality of life among adult cancer patients.

Meditation

Certain music is appropriate for meditation as it can help the mind slow down and initiate the relaxation response. However, not all peaceful or "New Age" music works for everyone. Music with no structure can be irritating or even unsettling. Gentle music with a familiar melody more often is comforting. But search around to find what produces a sense of calm, familiarity, and centeredness for you as an individual.

The sounds of nature often are incorporated into CDs made specifically for relaxation. For example, the sound of water can be soothing for some people. It can help conjure up calming images such as lying beside a mountain stream on a warm spring day. Birdsong may also be of use as an aid to help your mind slow down and release stressful thoughts.

Music Therapy

Because music has the potential to influence us both psychologically and physiologically, it is an important area of therapy for stress management. Music therapy can make use of biofeedback, guided imagery, and other established techniques to play an important role in the treatment of people with stress-related disorders. But due to the dramatic effects music can have, a trained and knowledgeable music therapist always is required.

When used in combination with biofeedback techniques, music can reduce tension and facilitate the relaxation response. It may be more compatible with relaxation than verbal stimuli, which may be distracting—music is processed mainly in nonverbal areas of the brain.

Music may help people to identify and express the feelings associated with their stress. In a music therapy session, the client can express these emotions, providing an important cathartic release.

Producing music in an improvisational way, and discussing pieces of music and lyrics in a group, can also help us become more aware of our emotional reactions and share them constructively with the group.

Thinking More Clearly

Finally, listening to music can help the brain by improving learning and memory skills, always useful when we're under stress. This has come to be known as "The Mozart Effect." Experiments carried out by scientists at the University of California at Irvine found that students' test scores improved after listening to a recording of Mozart, compared with either a relaxation tape or silence. This may be because the processing of music shares some of the same pathways in the brain as memory.

(Excerpted from *https://psychcentral.com/lib/the-power-of-music-to-reduce-stress/*)

参 考 答 案

教育类作业

（一）完形填空练习

完形填空一

（1）active participation

（2）expand students' knowledge

（3）their academic performance

[翻译] 最近的一项哈佛研究表明，积极参与课外活动不仅可以使学生扩展课外知识，而且可以间接提升他们的学业表现。鉴于此，学校应该组织多样的校内和校外活动。

完形填空二

（1）Rote memorization

（2）represses students' individuality

（3）lateral thinking

（4）stifle their creativity

[翻译] 死记硬背对于学生而言不是一个可靠的学习方式，它极大地压抑了孩子们的个性；相反，老师们应该鼓励学生在课堂中运用学科间的横向思维，而不是把课堂变成老师的一言堂，压抑孩子们的创造力。

（二）汉译英练习

1. The mission of teachers is to impart knowledge and educate people.

2. Listening to academic lectures of the well-known experts and scholars can broaden your horizons and expand your knowledge.

3. They generally perform very well in school work and extracurricular activities.

4. A recent study has shown the importance of sleep to academic performance.

5. If you slack off, you will be highly likely to lag behind others.

6. With a positive outlook on life, people can overcome any obstacle.

7. Academic attainment demonstrates one's real level of knowledge and learning ability.

8. If you fail in compulsory courses, you will not be granted the graduation diploma.

9. Schools can promote the students' psychological well-being by organizing various volunteering activities.

10. This poverty program is designed to comprehensively cover all the poor villages in China.

11. Many people pursue self-paced education in spare time to promote career competency.

12. They are well-adjusted adults who are ready to surpass the achievement of previous generations.

13. The president calls all the men in the country to fulfill their responsibilities as citizens.

14. She concentrated her attention and study intensively in the research project, hoping to finish the task in an earlier time.

15. Demanding students to choose compulsory courses represses their individuality.

16. Rote memorization is never a way for students to learn efficiently.

17. The two parties should use lateral thinking to explore a better solution, so that everyone wins.

18. Since teachers in the past had authority that could not be challenged, students tended to follow whatever their teachers taught indiscriminately.

19. It's hard to choose to be a generalist or a specialist.

20. He is a very versatile actor who is capable in many fields.

21. People who lack self-discipline will come to nothing in life.

22. This job position requires a person proficient in English.

23. Our tour guide is well-acquainted with this city and leads us to a lot of places full of specialties.

24. A class where only teachers lecture will definitely stifle students' creativity.

25. The newly introduced robot program greatly sharpens students' intellect.

26. Successful high school education helps young students to develop expertise in problem-solving.

27. A good conscience is a soft pillow.

28. Learning superficially will help you nowhere; you should absorb the quintessence of every subject.

29. The psychologist felt emotionally detrimental when the customer accused her of cheating.

30. The business faces cut-throat competition in the market, thus it has to ensure super quality of its products.

31. Parents should teach children to differentiate virtue from evil to protect themselves from hurt.

32. His disrespectful and undisciplined behavior discourages everybody who wants to offer a hand.

33. The society attributes juvenile delinquency to young people's parents.

34. Living an indolent life can never guarantee you a rich life.

35. Only by maintaining the continuity of learning can you memorize knowledge for longer time.

36. As an adult, you should keep your mature and sustained commitment deep in heart.

37. Puberty means lots of rebellious and aggressive actions.

（三）实战篇

Model Essay 3

Education is the greatest twenty-first-century opportunity that equips every person for an equal start in life. Indisputably, the ever-accelerated updating of modern society has brought up a trend of demanding potential employees with professional skills before they enter the job market, thus many people believe that it is the responsibility of schools to prepare graduates for future employment. I concede that it is incumbent on the schools to train students with job skills and impart theoretical knowledge to them, but the priority of school education should go to cultivating students to be virtuous global citizens.

As perspective one states, it is the incompatibility between jobs and skills that leads to the high unemployment rate. It is true to some extent that if graduates are equipped well with job skills, they are more likely to find jobs. However, the crux of the high unemployment rate is more than whether schools prepare students well for the job market. According to Joseph E. Stiglitz, a Nobel Prize laureate in economics, "In a world of globalization, creating market value had become entirely separated from creating employment. Even when there is investment, it is not necessarily investment related to job creation: much of the investment is in machines designed to replace labor, to destroy jobs." Obviously, even when the graduates are equipped well with job skills before they enter into employment market, the unemployment rate will still remain high when there are a decreasing number of jobs available in the job market. No one would argue against that the development of technology and artificial intelligence is the determinant factor contributing to high unemployment rate. Thus, for the reasons listed above, I cannot agree with Perspective One.

Although job-related skills and theoretical knowledge are indispensable for graduates to seek for employment, the essence of school education should be the cultivation of qualified global citizens who have humanity's best interests at heart. Specifically, how to foster cosmopolitan global citizens? As for me, education is to pour out love into students regardless of their age, gender, race, intellect, and family background. Only when children grow up with love and respect can they become loving and kind. Education is to foster students with compassionate and tender hearts, because there is too much suffering and too many desperate people in the world, and only compassion can rescue people from their distress and help them to stand up again. Education is to build up students' character that will benefit them for their whole life. Education is to help students to be forgiving, understanding and less judgmental. No one can avoid being offended or hurt, and only forgiveness can set them and those who hurt them free, and only forgiveness can heal and help them to be stronger but remain tender. Being understanding and less judgmental is so essential to creating a harmonious human society because we live in such a diverse world with unique individuals. When education performs its duty to the full, there will be more qualified global citizens in the world to contribute to human society.

Needless to say, the primary purpose of education is to instill in students' fundamental values in addition to training them with academic skills. No one would argue against that education should cultivate students to be humane, to equip them with skills to contribute to the well-being of human beings and empower them to strive for the greater good of human society. It is no overstatement to say that every job desperately needs people with ethics. One can easily draw a conclusion that most of the tribulations, sufferings, and destructions in the human history have been created by those who did not and do not have morals. Regardless of the turbo-charged progress made in the science, technology, medicine, and education, the future of humankind is doomed on the self-destructive path without moral progress. I concede that it is the responsibility of schools to train students with skills; however, isn't clear that it is those skilled people who create destructive weapons massacring people brutally, stealing money from the poor, taking advantage of the holes in every system and destroying our human society? On the contrast, those who are uneducated are not able to do as much damage as those who are well-educated but with no ethics. It is self-evident that training students with skills alone without the integration of good values cannot cultivate qualified global citizens. Thus, I am in agreement with Perspective Three.

To conclude, although schools have the unshakable duty to equip students well with job skills and impart theoretical knowledge to them, school education should give priority to cultivating virtuous global citizens. Graduates with skills but with no ethics can only bring about destruction rather than construction to human society.

工作类作业

（一）完形填空练习

完形填空一

（1）creative work

（2）a sense of self-fulfillment

（3）cultivate one's independence and toughness

（4）balance work and life

[翻译] 创造性工作需要许多想象力，而且一旦完成就会给人一种成就感。同时，这种工作常常需要独立完成，所以能培养人的独立和坚强。另一方面，它有时候需要花费相当多的时间来设计和策划，所以难以令人平衡好工作与生活。

完形填空二

（1）workaholics

（2）work overtime

（3）seeking personal development

（4）promotion opportunities

[翻译] 工作狂们是指那些花费大量时间在工作上的人。通过加班加点工作，他们为了工作上寻求个人发展而牺牲个人生活。有时，疯狂工作是一种旨在获取更多晋升机会的行为。

（二）汉译英练习

1. Unfortunately, professionals from other fields, who make a much greater contribution to human society, are paid so much less.

2. The bonus that participants expect is closely linked to the competition they have to overcome in order to reach success.

3. It is an unfortunate fact that many employers may prefer to use the services of children simply to save money by paying them less than adults and it is this type of exploitation that should be discouraged.

4. Brain drain is an increasingly serious problem nowadays.

5. The difference in regional house prices acts as an obstacle to mobility of labor.

6. Whether one can give full play to his talents depends mostly on whether he has definite objectives or not.

7. Job hopping can be attributed to pursuing one's career goals.

8. Money is a recognition of the skills and dedication a person needs to be successful.

9. A sense of fulfillment is also encouraged if a worker feels the job is worth doing because it contributes to the society or the economy as a whole.

10. Factors like personal growth and sense of belonging can be keys to motivating employee's performance.

11. Women in modern times need to not only care for the family but also work, so it is important for them to learn how to balance work and life.

12. Nowadays, many people work hard all day long under the pressure of life and become a workaholic.

13. When looking for a job, candidates not only value salary, but also pay more and more attention to seeking personal development.

14. Experiencing setbacks is not necessarily a bad thing, and people can cultivate their independence and toughness.

15. In order to achieve greater development, we must not stick to the rules, but should actively carry out creative work.

16. Besides raising salary, promotion opportunities are also an effective mechanism for motivating employees.

17. Constantly challenging ourselves and breaking the limits can give us a great sense of accomplishment, which makes us feel that life is meaningful.

18. People's social class is relatively fixed. If you want to climb the social ladder, education is often an effective way.

19. Because of too many tasks, employees are often forced to work overtime, and their sleep and life will be negatively affected to a certain extent.

20. The bright prospect of the economy brings hope to society.

21. In modern society, electronic products are closely bound up with our life and work.

22. Traveling abroad can help expand our views and give us different perspectives to understand the world.

23. The from-nine-to-five has a fixed pace of life but tends to get bored and tired.

24. There is no denying that many people go to college just to get a well-paying job when they graduate.

25. Participating in social practice is very beneficial to personal growth, which can enrich one's social experience.

26. We should be brave to try and learn from it and accumulate experience.

27. There is no end to learning. We must keep forging ahead and improve our capabilities.

28. Many people who don't enter the workplace fantasize about an ideal workplace where relationships are simple. But the gap between reality and ideals can be found when you enter the workplace.

29. We cannot settle with the current situation, we must constantly meet new challenges and seek greater breakthroughs.

30. When planning for regional development, policy makers can not only consider the immediate material gains, but also build a blueprint for sustainable development.

Model Essay 3

Many students work very hard in the hope of finding desirable jobs after graduation, but the reality leaves them no glimpse of hope. The truth is that they are shut out from the door of the dream companies for the repeated reason of having no pertinent working experience, and companies have no intention to adopt apprentice programs to train students for fear of potential costs and risks. No matter what, companies should adopt apprenticeship even though there might be some costs in the short term.

Schools and universities alone can hardly get students fully prepared for future career and businesses should also take part in training students for certain skills and aptitudes. School education focuses primarily on academic and theoretical knowledge and information, which are not directly applicable to actual work. That helps explain today's increasing unemployment rate among newly graduates in the competitive workforce and gloomy economy. It is, therefore, imperative for businesses to function as a bridge between the tower of ivory and the workplace. After all, the newest and most advanced technologies are not in universities but rather in businesses because they have more incentive, better equipment, and more capital to make innovations in order to keep pace with and even lead the industry. So, only when businesses provide opportunities for future job seekers to learn necessary and advanced knowledge and skills, can they be really qualified when applying for an actual job.

Ironically, businesses are complaining the inadequacy of eligible employees while running strict systems to refuse anyone without working experience. If companies stick with such a short-sighted mindset, they are merely making troubles for themselves. The wise solution is not to compete only for experienced workers who know all the techniques and rules of a particular industry but also to train students of potentials for future use. Not only can young students infuse fresh blood into companies, but they are more likely to grow corporate loyalty than experienced and sophisticated workers. In the long run, apprentice programs will help enhance productivity and the apprentices can create more value for corporate culture.

Yet, it is stupid to say there is no cost for companies to adopt apprentice programs. It is, indeed, reasonable that some companies are afraid that the trainees may end up working for a competitor. While losing a former staff to a competitor can be a big threat for he or she may leak confidential information, it can also serve as an incentive for the company to enhance its security systems and relentlessly improve its technologies so that it can become safer and remain in the upper hand. For example, the fact that some used-to-be employees of the Apple Company eventually end up setting up their own firms spurs Apple to not rest on current success and continue to create miracles for the world. And across time, this is also beneficial for the industry as a whole.

Although it seems like an obstacle in the short term for businesses to develop apprenticeship, it will, in fact, benefit not only employees and employers but also the whole industry in the long run.

社会进步类作业

（一）完形填空练习

完形填空一

（1）is inextricably tied to

（2）at a turbo-charge rate

（3）polarization of the rich and the poor

[翻译] 随着全球化的发展，人类的命运被密不可分地捆绑在一起。尽管科技、教育、医学和农业正在以惊人的速度发展，但是穷人和富人的极化也加剧了。

完形填空二

（1）the hallmark of

（2）the socially and financially disadvantaged

（3）it is incumbent on

（4）eliminate poverty

（5）harmonious world

[翻译] 任何一个民主和文明的社会的标志是照顾那些社会上和经济上处于劣势的人群。因此，为了创建一个和谐的世界，政府有职责去消除贫困。

（二）汉译英练习

1. Private bankers and those who work in financial industry monopolize the financial market for their vested interests.

2. Those self-serving and corrupt politicians curry favor with bankers at the expense of the majority.

3. The region gained its independence from reign through civil disobedience.

4. Only when all citizens comply with laws can a society have order and stability.

5. This world would not be destroyed by the evilness of evildoers but by the appalling silence of good people.

6. The yawning gap of wealth would inevitably lead to social turmoil.

7. Technological advancement is fueled by innovation.

8. Those who indulge themselves in bestial behaviors will eventually lose their humanity.

9. People won their citizenship rights through nonviolent civil resistance.

10. The underprivileged are stripped of their dignity and identity by discriminatory social system.

11. Optimists never wallow in the valley of despair when confronted with daunting difficulties.

12. Arrogance would hamper one's development.

13. Knowledge is multiplying at a turbo-charged rate.

14. Joseph E. Stiglitz is a Nobel laureate in economics.

15. Environment contamination has long-lasting consequences on human society.

16. If technology fails to balance the economy and environment, a series of disasters will appear.

17. There is an increasing number of world-renowned scholars striving for the betterment of human society.

18. Helen Keller devoted herself to helping the socially and financially disadvantaged.

19. Perseverance and diligence can help people reach the full potential of their talents.

20. Mother Teresa cared, fed, and clothed the underprivileged in India.

21. Joseph E. Stiglitz along with other Harvard professors provide a penetrating analysis on the root cause of social problems in the US—private bankers issue the US dollars and hijack the government.

22. With the rapid pace of globalization, the fate of humanity is inextricably tied to each other.

23. The far-sighted economists' concern over economic collapse is substantiated by financial crisis in 2008.

24. Scholars with expertise and insights should shoulder their responsibility to serve their country rather than money.

25. Teachers should condemn rather than condone school bullying.

26. As evidenced by the fact that social inequality hampers economic development.

27. It is incumbent on educators to instill in the students noble values such as integrity, honesty, empathy and compassion.

28. The corrupt government and self-serving politicians would endanger social stability and safety.

29. Doctors are faced with a moral dilemma when they find out mad cow disease causing dementia.

30. Social justice should be prioritized over economic development.

31. In the modern world, many countries have to thwart terrorist attacks in order to protect their citizens.

32. Only by treating other nations and peoples with respect can a country truly have national security.

33. A government with integrity would never intrude on citizen privacy.

34. Government surveillance must be restricted by strict regulations and laws.

35. Taking care of the socially and financially disadvantaged is the hallmark of a civilized and democratic society.

36. Building a civilized and democratic society needs the best efforts of all citizens.

37. Governments should shoulder their responsibility to eliminate poverty inside and outside their countries.

38. Free health care for all citizens poses a significant financial burden on the government.

39. The social and economic inequality contributes to polarization of the rich and the poor.

40. All the scholars across the globe should foster a climate of peace and prosperity for all humanity.

41. Building up a fair social and economic system can help a country to get rid of poverty and backwardness.

42. Economic development and technological advancement can enhance comprehensive national strength of a nation.

43. Peaceful coexistence among countries would definitely lead to a harmonious world.

44. Tourism development can boost the local tertiary industry.

45. Governments need to strengthen the enforcement of laws to combat corruption.

46. Relying on science and technology to rejuvenate the nation is the surest way to prosperity.

47. Optimizing the distribution of resources can prevent unnecessary waste.

48. The revival of customs and traditions of a nation can attract more foreign tourists.

49. Science and technology constitutes a primary productive force for any nation.

50. In an era of globalization, it is crucial for all the nations to preserve their historical and cultural heritages.

（三）写作实操

Model Essay 3

Ever since the US mass surveillance revealed by Edward Snowden, a former contractor for NSA (National Security Agency) and CIA (Central Intelligence Agency), it has been the most debatable topic across the globe. Some people argue with indignation that government surveillance is by all means immoral because it violates their privacy and human rights, while others reason that privacy must be given up so that governments can ensure national security. Given the evil conspiracy of some foreign governments, surveillance is necessary, but it should be restricted only to the matter of national security and it should never violate its citizens' personal privacy and civil rights.

I partially agree with Perspective One because it is definitely unethical for any government to violate their citizens' human rights and privacy by surveillance. In the words of Noa Yachot, a communications strategist, at ACLU (American Civil Liberties Union)—American civil liberties union, "a legendary labor leader Cesar Chavez, who led farm workers' movement, was monitored by hundreds of FBI (Federal Bureau of Investigation) agents; and The NSA also tapped the phones of an esteemed list of Vietnam War critics, such as journalists, and even sitting senators." Obviously, government surveillance is immoral, because it not only violates people's civil rights and privacy, but also hampers social progress. However, considering the complicated and volatile political situations all over the world, sometimes it is necessary for governments to run surveillance to thwart any conspiracy of some evil foreign governments and their servants.

As Perspective Two states, national security must be prioritized over privacy because government surveillance is necessary to eliminate any potential threats from some foreign governments. Based on the bloody human history, many countries have been ravaged by the colonial power of some Empires. As we all know that one Empire once colonized one of the fourth land on the earth by slaughtering and robbing the wealth of the colonized. Likewise, in modern history, another Empire has been invading a startling number of countries on the earth, in the words of Jimmy Carter, "more than any other nation, my country has been almost constantly involved in armed conflict and, through military alliances, has used war as a means of resolving international and local disputes." In his book, 'A call to action: women, religion, violence and power', Jimmy Carter reflects on the devastation and mortality caused by the invasion of his nation on other sovereign nations. Considering that the political and economic climate determined by the private bankers issuing the dollars in Carter's nation, so in any near future it would be impossible for the congress to make any democratic and sensible decisions regarding international or domestic affairs. Consequently, other nations have to protect themselves from the destructive power of the warlike nation, then government surveillance can be used to deter or destroy its conspiracy. However, government surveillance should never violate their citizens' human rights and privacy. Therefore, I am partially in agreement with Perspective Two.

I unhesitatingly agree with Perspective Three that government surveillance should be regulated strictly by legislation and it must be restricted to matters of national security without violating citizens' privacy. According to the report released by United Nations High Commissioner for Human Rights, "Surveillance must be necessary and proportionate: The onus is on governments to demonstrate that their surveillance practices are not arbitrary or unlawful. That means governments must show that surveillance is both proportionate and necessary to a legitimate aim." Thus, it is essential for all the governments to honor and respect their citizens' right to privacy and other civil rights. History has revealed a simple truth that a government with no principle and morality will lose the support of its citizens. By the contrast, people-oriented governments that have their citizens' best interests at heart will be prosperous. It accords with common sense that unity makes a nation strong but internal division will ruin it. To illustrate this point, I can think of no better example than some foreign government—a government of the corporations, by the corporations and for the corporations that serves the private bankers and other corporate people at the expense of the majority of the citizens. Undoubtedly, only when the government surveillance is strictly regulated by legislation can the nation be unified and can the citizens' rights be protected.

To conclude, although mass surveillance is a fundamental threat to human rights, it is necessary given the complicated political situations across the globe. However, government surveillance should be regulated under strict legislation and it should never violate its citizens' civil rights, especially their rights to privacy.

个人选择类作业

（一）完形填空练习

完形填空一

（1）bold ambition

（2）sticking to

（3）come true

[翻译] 所有成功的人都拥有较强的意志力、自信心和对生活乐观的态度。以怀特·迪士尼为例，最初，没有人喜欢他的想法，但是他相信自己并且怀有去好莱坞发展的远大理想。他不断地提升和精进自己的想法。通过坚持自己的信念，怀特·迪士尼最终实现了他的梦想，并变成了世界上最著名的卡通制作巨匠之一。

完形填空二

（1）For the sake of

（2）cater to

（3）beyond dispute

（4）at the sacrifice/expense of

[翻译] 为了那些在不平等的法律下颤抖的不幸的人们，政府不应该只是去迎合富人的需求，而是应该投资更多在贫困项目上。如果以穷人的利益为代价，美国不会实现持久的国内发展，这一点是毋庸置疑的。

（二）汉译英练习

1. The president recently announced his intention to stand for re-election.

2. This American insurance company has targeted adults as its primary customers.

3. George's father implanted in him an ambition to obtain an education early in his childhood.

4. He is a man of extraordinary vitality, political vision, and ambitious dream.

5. Enthusiastic applause lent a sense of occasion to the volunteer activity.

6. She makes zealous efforts for charitable bodies.

7. The executive is respected as a very aggressive and competitive leader.

8. The college dropout leads a nonconformist life that arouses great attention.

9. We should stick to the issues and don't take it personally.

10. The engineering team encounter fierce resistance from their leaders.

11. People should not easily abandon their dreams but should strike hard and challenge themselves.

12. Most hopes came to nothing, and Gatsby was no exception.

13. Her wish to be a doctor has finally come true.

14. Your suggestion must be compatible with his personality and style.

15. Parents often try to rub into their children how much they owe to them.

16. Don't always attribute your failure to mere external factors.

17. It is worthwhile to struggle for freedom with improbable hope.

18. Successful people are those who are willing to take pains to achieve their dreams.

19. I am confident that you would succeed in this reform.

20. Our pioneers made their way hard through difficulties to fight for freedom.

21. The business demands all the workers to steadfastly adhere to the standard.

22. He distinguishes himself by committing himself to charity work.

23. Jimmy always thinks of his life and work schedule as too hard.

24. Each prioritized task should be carefully documented and taught to employees.

25. Even if you are reluctant to face the reality, you have to abide by the consequence.

26. She is engrossed in the book and didn't hear people arguing around her.

27. When asked for your views about your current job, on no account should you be passive.

28. Under no condition should we use the nuclear weapon first.

29. It will not take you very long to be accustomed to the way we do it.

30. Preparation from colleges can help graduates quickly adapt themselves to the new working environment.

31. His competitor has a sharp advantage over my cousin in terms of product quality.

32. Don't be anxious about the future too much; all you need to do is to focus on today.

33. The man is ashamed of betraying the nation by telling the military secret to the enemy.

34. The company is not capable of handling an order that large.

35. It is beyond dispute that the man should pay the monthly compensation for the old man.

36. This can be frustrating for someone eager for their voices to be heard.

37. Our team should economize on spending for we have limited budget.

38. Born with the musical talent, Alice was highly passionate on dancing.

39. People should have the dare to break through the confinement of custom and pursue freedom of life.

40. Never cater to others hastily; people should think before act.

41. As things turned the corner, my parents felt much relieved.

42. The liberty of this nation is at the expense of the lives of numerous soldiers.

43. A person cannot make history unless he or she makes significant contributions in the world.

44. Stagnation in business is holding back the country's economic recovery.

45. For the sake of these young students, the government should invest more for local education.

46. We must ascertain the responsibility in light of different situations.

47. The public looked down on the young woman for she refused to get married.

48. Your efforts will get nowhere if you have an unclear direction.

49. He succeeded in the experiment at the sacrifice of his health.

Model Essay 3

Since people step into a modern and civilized era, charity value has been the main ingredient of contemporary value. The undeniable influence of it on the construction of a harmonious society needs public attention. People cherish the relief to help others, but unfortunately, too generous help would have some negative results, because some people might become avaricious and ignore their social responsibility. Charity is critical in this society, yet the side effects of these benevolent behaviors needs attention.

What people have to admit is that citizens have the obligation to do the charity. Some people contend that it is individuals' responsibility to donate, as they conceive every citizen all gain his or her earnings from the society. The idea has been stated in Perspective One, which indicates that individuals who have gained the profits from the society need to face up to their social responsibility to help others. The blue fetches a job only if a construction project has been approved by the government; the white gets employed only if a company has been authorized to establish under the instruction of the government; the businessman can make their money only if the government gives proper regulation and opportunity for trades. It is logical and vital for those ones to pay back the society depending on their different profits. However, individuals have already supported the society by paying taxes to the government to a large extent; as a result, there is no need to do extra support to charity. If the society has transformed the obligation of helping the charity to the common residents, the citizens would feel burden in this society. The originally benevolent act transfers into another burden to bear besides the heavy tax. Placing the responsibility to the common individuals would not be the best solution to bridge the gap between the rich and poor, it is the government that should face up the obligation to diminish the conflict between the rich and poor, but not the common residents.

The side effects of doing charity on the poor also need consideration. The heated controversy is whether this kind of charity work is effective indeed in order to bridge the chasm between the rich and the poor. It seems that poor people are suffering from poverty, and free aid offered by the society is their last straw, which has been mentioned by Perspective Two. Nevertheless, never should those people overestimate the charity's capacity to help them at no cost forever as the poor might be totally dependent on the charity to help them out of indigence. Giving sufficient money or resources to support their lives may enhance their sense of dependence, which might stimulate them to form a habit of laziness. Consequently, the strong becomes the weak and the able becomes like paralysis. In contrast, those who are not given that much aid would try hard to stand on their own feet in this society, which is a virtuous cycle to promote them to build a good life on their own continuously. Spending endless but useless money on them would not be a wise option, because poor ones might form inaccurate attitudes towards the help from others, being too dependent on others.

The social welfare policies, such as the booming of job opportunities, might be an alternative solution to alleviate hardship. Sometimes, the direct help may not be the best one, while some other methods would help the ones who need help. The society needs a healthy and circulative economy to buttress developments and regular maintenance, which means stable and abundant employment. Perspective Three has given the right direction in helping the ones who need help. To be specific, the job provided for the poor would both diminish the poverty in short term and make benefits back to the society itself by achieving the economic necessities demonstrated above, as the poor ones might realize that they need to rely on themselves to make a living, not only hinge on others financial support. Thus, access to some delicately considered and planned charity aid instead of direct influence would expose the poverty to greater opportunities in a better situation and push forward the society in some ways.

Despite the increasing tension of poverty and urgency to alleviate it, it is highly worthy to contemplate this issue and come up with considerate, effective and profitable plans to render aid to the poor. As more people start to realize their duty to reward the society and aid the poor, millions of lenient people need to devote them to proper meaningful use. Individuals need to have the accurate attitude towards the way or method to help others.

科技创新类作业

（一）完形填空练习

完形填空一

（1）overdependence on electronic devices

（2）text back and forth

（3）plugged-in pursuits

[翻译] 现代社会中，智能手机、平板电脑、笔记本电脑随处可见，人们几乎很难不与电子产品打交道。然而，人们渐渐显示出对电子产品的过度依赖。他们不停地查看手机、发消息、更新社交网页，全情投入于各种令人上瘾的追求中。

完形填空二

（1）scientific and technological developments

（2）wonders of modern technology

（3）real-life communication

（4）online communication

[翻译] 从上个世纪下半期开始，我们的社会进入到了一个高科技产品迅速取代旧产品的新阶段。这些科技进步改变了人们的生活。虽然有非常多的好处，但是现代科技所创造的奇迹同样也有自身的问题。科技让我们更少关注现实生活中的交流，更多关注线上交流。

（二）汉译英练习

1. We live with an abundance of inventions and enhancements in technology and the creation of tablets is surely one of them.

2. We live in a time marked by technological advance.

3. A society cannot move forward without the technological innovation.

4. Scientific and technological developments come with their own set of problems.

5. With modern advancement, we do a lot of things that our ancestors could never do in the past.

6. Are all of these inventions and enhancements in technology making us less social?

7. Thanks to the wonders of modern technology, it is easier for people today to receive education than it was in the past.

8. The Internet makes everything more accessible.

9. The overloaded information, however, overwhelms people.

10. Internet shortens our attention span to certain things.

11. In a society characterized by Information Age, people today are much more informed.

12. In a time characterized by Big Bang Disruption in which products and ideas are exponentially replaced by newer and much advanced counterparts, people seem to evolve new strategies to acquire knowledge, probe the unknown world, and connect others.

13. Not only our cellphones but also our laptops, televisions, creations like Facebook and other social media platforms change people's lives.

14. They constantly monitor their phones, exchange texts and photos, and mind their social media pages.

15. People watch videos, play online games, and engage in countless other plugged-in pursuits.

16. Overdependence on electronic devices seems to be a new kind of addiction.

17. In today's society, we need some deliberate "tech-free" time.

18. Today, some technological gadgets fascinate people.

19. Young people today are fond of using social media sites.

20. Little by little, the cellphone and media usage seem to be subtly destroying the meaningfulness of interactions we have with others, disconnecting us from the world around us, and leading us to an immense sense of isolation in today's society.

21. The Internet seems to make people's communication fruitful.

22. Internet is the biggest game-changer in today's world.

23. In the end, people can communicate with people in the virtual world with ease, but they seldom communicate with people in the real world.

24. It seems that with technology, our lives become simpler, but we ultimately end up having less real-life communication.

25. There are many alternate forms of being social, as opposed to face to face.

26. We have multiple ways of communication.

27. During the lunch time, he texted back and forth.

28. Sometimes the "tech-free" time seems to disconnect people from the world around them.

29. We miss the face-to-face interaction with ear-splitting grin.

30. We miss the time when we grinned from ear to ear.

31. The recurring rumors on the Internet make the victim suffer a lot.

32. We need to prune the unnecessary costs.

33. The rumors on the Internet seem rampant.

34. Sometimes, compared with the online communication, we prefer face to face communication.

35. Sometimes people should stay focus on the real-world communication.

36. Sometimes people spend too much time on responding to a text.

37. This technological detachment has become today's reality.

38. The Internet seems intangible.

39. We care about obtaining supportive connections on the Internet.

40. If someone's posts get a ton of feedback, he or she will feel very happy.

41. The Internet often brings imminent sense of isolation.

42. Because of the obsession with the Internet, modern people are often deprived of important sense of well-being.

（三）写作实操

Model Essay 3

People seem to have an obsession with originality and creativity. Daniel Defoo was the first writer to use women protagonist in fiction-writing and became "the father of English novel". James Joyce created his "self-consciousness" approach in his novel *Dubliners*, establishing himself as a major American writer in the 20th century. Matthew Arnold devised and exploited "dramatic monologue", distinguishing himself from his contemporaries. Oftentimes we believe that new things to be original and many people claim to be original in their undertakings. In fact, people can hardly be original.

Originality is claimed most especially when something appears to be new. Admittedly, a great number of people do think in novel ways to accomplish their goals and make breakthroughs in their fields. With such novelty, we posit that people can truly be original in what they do. When it comes to drama, people would easily refer to Shakespeare and regard him as a much more innovative writer than his contemporaries—the University Wits. When people think about poetry-writing, no one can deny the significant role Walt Whitman played in experimenting the form for poems. For fiction writing, readers must be impressed by the unique style of Virginal Woolf in her novels marked by devoid of traditional elements in short stories or long stories. Aside from originality in the literature field, in a society characterized by "Big Bang Disruption" in which old products are exponentially replaced by newer products, innovation and imagination are indispensable. Chinese technological upstart Xiaomi manufacturing cellphones does not follow Steve Job's top-down pattern but encourages product managers and staff to provide their own creative ideas. Chinese social networking sites Renren.com and Weibo along with cellphone application WeChat allow people to post their feelings via texts and pictures online, reforming Chinese people's way of communicating with each other.

It seems that creativity serves quite well in every single aspect of our life, whether it is in an artistic kingdom or commercial world. However, when we examine the so-called creativity closely, we will find that the changes or reforms are neither truly new nor totally different from their older counterparts. Those adjustments or adaptions just draw on their predecessors' experience and are therefore strongly associated with what have been done. For example, Shakespeare got inspiration from some Greek mythologies in his own creation. What is more, his *King Lear* was published after Thomas Kyd's *King Leir* and probably adopted similar plots. It is true that Walt Whitman became one of the most frequently read poet for his free verse. His free verse, however, drew on blank verse as the free verse also abandoned rhymed metrical pattern. Also, British romantic poet William Blake was a major influence on Whitman. Although Virginia Woolf was famous for her distinguished modernist style, her self-conscious elements were originated from James Joyce who published his *Ulysses* eight years before Woolf published her *Jacob's Room*. James Joyce's Ulysses itself, in fact, was also Odysseus's modern parallel. Despite the fact that the cellphone provider Xiaomi did not follow Steve Job's top-down pattern, Xiaomi' extreme user experience can also be traced back to Job's consideration for iPhone users. Additionally, Xiaomi always incorporate some features of iPhone into its own products. Although Chinese social networking sites like Renren, Weibo, and WeChat revolutionized Chinese people's way of communication, they were close knockoffs of foreign social networking sites. To be more specific, Renren is Facebook's Chinese version, Weibo is the hybrid of Twitter and Instagram, and WeChat's moment features the characteristics of both Instagram and mobile Facebook.

Though originality does exist, and many people claim to be original in what they do, it is worth noting that with a thorough examination on their undertakings, one will surely find a link to what was already done by other people. Admittedly, there might seem to be worthy changes that might be contributed to innovation, but the meaning and essence of originality is still a myth as exhibited in such literature works of prominent and revered writers.

环保类作业

（一）完形填空练习

完形填空一

（1）sustainable development

（2）endangered species

（3）the overexploitation of resources

（4）enhance environmental awareness

[翻译] 日益严重的沙漠化问题威胁到了可持续发展，加剧了濒危物种的灭亡速度，造成大量的资源过度开发。因此，提高环保意识刻不容缓。

完形填空二

（1）advocate green

（2）disposable items

（3）reusable materials

（4）virtuous circle

[翻译] 我们需要倡导绿色活动，拒绝使用一次性物品，使用可回收材料，建立良性循环，保持生态平衡。

（二）汉译英练习

1. Pandas are an endangered species, and as a result, the government of China has placed attention on the protection of them.

2. Releasing excess carbon dioxide may cause adverse effect on global environment.

3. Scientists recently found a new kind of reusable material, which may be used in garment manufacturing industry.

4. There's no doubt that ecological degradation is, to some extent, one of the most serious problems people are facing.

5. His motor nerve was permanently damaged during the car accident, and as a result, he can never stand up again.

6. Thanks to everyone's sacrifice and perseverance, our country has made great progress in the battle against desertification.

7. Colliery, a kind of non-renewable resources, has been widely used to gain heat and electricity for hundreds of years.

8. My hometown is a peaceful village with limpid rivulet and fertile land.

9. Professor Yuan won worldwide respect and compliment for his incomparable achievement in studying how to boost crop yield.

10. According to the report, the waste water released from this factory contains multiple types of toxic chemicals, which may pollute the river and even poison citizens.

11. There's still a long way to go on waste disposal for China, first step of which is popularizing the knowledge of garbage classification.

12. The vegetation destruction in this area is so severe that government has to send a special team to handle it.

13. The first industrial revolution expedited the development of society, and at the same time, however, also led to the overexploitation of resources.

14. It's we students' duty to enhance environmental awareness and encourage people around us to do the same thing.

15. It's comforting to see more and more groups and organizations advocating green activities, like using public transport instead of driving private cars.

16. Not only the government but common people should make some efforts on redressing the ecological balance.

17. We should feel guilty for wreaking havoc on natural resources. Our disrespect to nature will finally ruin ourselves.

18. The whole country buried themselves into the fast progress in economy, ignoring the environmental deterioration happening at the same time.

19. The increasing number of population leads to human intrusion into animals' habitat, which may cause species extinction.

20. With the new full-automatic system, the disposal of municipal refuse has become much easier.

21. If we make full use of domestic sewage, the shortage of water resource will no longer be a harsh issue.

22. One of the steps of this experiment is to filtrate the suspended particles on the surface of water.

23. To raise people's consciousness about environmental protection, the government displayed public service advertising on TV and the Internet.

24. State intervention is essential when it comes to environment issues, since many companies do not obey the natural rules.

25. Planting trees helps reinforce the conservation of water and soil, especially in some regions like Shaanxi, China.

26. To protect pandas, Chinese government set a rare and endangered species breeding center in Chengdu, where thousands of pandas live comfortable life.

27. China keeps controlling its pace of economic development to avoid exceeding the carrying capacity of environment.

28. The reason why he and his company get praised is that he always remembers to comply with environmental regulations during manufacturing.

29. The new paper mill destroyed the forest and polluted the nearby river, which exacerbated local environmental problems.

30. It's common sense that the less disposable packaging we use, the better our environment will be.

（三）写作实操

Model Essay 3

Never before in history has the issue of global warming been more serious than today. However, no view is more dangerous than the one that there is no need for people to sacrifice their conveniences by reducing the greenhouse emission because the side effects of global warming are unsure in the unknown future. Scientifically speaking, if global warming is allowed to take its course, it will inevitably bring about more adverse effects on our living environments, and thereby both citizens and governments should work together to tackle global warming.

It is true to some extent that reducing energy consumption can eliminate the threat of global warming, but there are many other human activities such as industrial production, animal husbandry, using laundry dryer or even rice farming can all lead to greenhouse gases emission. According to the study by 'What is your impact', a non-profit organization, with more than 90% certainty, that this increase in overall temperatures is due to the greenhouse gases produced by humans. Activities such as deforestation and the burning of fossil fuels are the main sources of these emissions. Undoubtedly, when people choose green living lifestyle, using less energy can greatly reduce the release of greenhouse gas to save the earth. However, most of human activities unavoidably contribute to global warming. Therefore, it is essential for the environmental scientists to come up with a comprehensive plan to reduce greenhouse gases emission as much as possible. With the best efforts of all the scientists, engineers and agriculturists, we will have more environmentally-friendly products and fertilizers that would both efficiently and effectively reduce the emission of greenhouse gases, consequently eliminating the threat of global warming. Thus, I am partially in agreement with Perspective One.

I unhesitatingly agree with Perspective Two that it is urgent than ever before for both governments and individuals to work together to tackle global warming. According to NASA (National Aeronautics and Space Administration), "Since the Industrial Revolution began in about 1750, carbon dioxide levels have increased nearly 38 percent as of 2009 and methane levels have increased 148 percent." Are these scientific statistics shocking? Excessive emission of greenhouse gases is by all means detrimental to human society, which is totally different from the natural greenhouse effect that is beneficial for life on the earth. Also based on the study by 'What is your impact', a non-profit organization, "Global warming is affecting many places around the world. It is accelerating the melting of ice sheets, permafrost and glaciers, which is causing average sea levels to rise. These changes have affected both nature as well as human society and will continue to have increasingly worse effects if greenhouse gas emissions continue to grow at the same pace as today." While the human-released greenhouse gases are inevitable, one must make efforts to curb the ever-increasing temperature on the earth.

As for those who are in agreement with Perspective Three, they do not think it is necessary for them to sacrifice their conveniences for the unknown future because to them the adverse consequences of global warming are unsure. Or even if they understand and are sure about the repercussions of global warming, would they be willing to sacrifice their convenient but extravagant lifestyle? Needless to say that there are too many people who are accustomed to a lifestyle depending on energy-consumption—using laundry dyer when they can hang out their clothes to air dry them; using dishwashers when they can simply wash dishes by hands; driving the car when they can easily walk to the destination; turning up air conditioning to cool down their houses to be as cold as igloos built by Inuit people; burning candles during the daytime to create romantic atmosphere; using single-use dishes and cups on daily basis. Their way of life can shed some light on the point that choosing green living lifestyle would inconvenience those who are so used to their lifestyle relying on energy-consumption. To those people, why should they take into account the living environments of future generations? Obviously, this world would be a much better place if there are fewer of those irresponsible and self-centered people. Based on my own philosophy—the meaning of our life is to contribute to the betterment of human society, thus I cannot agree with those who hold Perspective Three.

To sum up, global warming is a determinant factor in causing natural disasters across the globe such as hurricanes, storms, snowstorms, draughts and floods. If the greenhouse gas emissions are still left unchecked, there will be more catastrophes threatening the existence of human beings. It is urgent and crucial for all the governments and people living on the earth to choose an environmentally-friendly lifestyle and make their best efforts to resolve global warming.

媒体类作业

（一）完形填空练习

完形填空一

（1）digital media

（2）illusion of free will and independence

（3）manipulated

[翻译] 一旦我们放松警惕，数字媒体和互联网将会对我们的生活甚至思想进行秘密控制。你可能会产生拥有<u>自由意志和独立</u>的错觉，但你已经被操纵了。例如，当你进行所谓令人满意的购买时，你甚至不知道产品的细节。当你坚定地相信转基因对健康有害时，你甚至不知道一些相关的科学。当你认为你以自己的利益投票给总统时，你甚至没有完全了解他的政策。

完形填空二

（1）vulnerable groups

（2）insulting

（3）freedom of speech

（4）conflict of opinions

[翻译] 审查制度虽然意在保护<u>弱势群体</u>免受<u>侮辱性的</u>或危险信息的侵害，但有时也会侵犯个人<u>言论自由</u>。每个人都有权利分享自己的想法，没有理由严格限制人们的想法和人们的信仰。一个多元化和民主的社会应该接受<u>意见冲突</u>。

（二）汉译英练习

1. I was browsing the rental postings online only to find out that my husband was one of the advertisers and wanted to sell our apartment.

2. It has become an open secret that an appealing advertisement is more useful than the high quality of products, which explains why brands distribute a huge amount of money in hiring superstars to endorse products.

3. Modern people are accustomed to digital media instead of printed media to derive or spread information.

4. Modern people are no longer limited to old media, such as newspaper, books, or televisions, to get information. Digital media serve as a more effective way for people to collect information and express their opinions.

5. Public-interest advertisements differentiate from commercial advertisements. The former serves to educate the public, while the ultimate goal of the latter is to promote products and services and make profits.

6. Children and youth are not intellectually mature yet and have no clear judgment about complicated issues; that is why they are easily manipulated by ill-intended people.

7. Some consumers think that they are immune to advertisements, but the reality is that advertisements have been constantly sending subliminal messages to control what they like and what they purchase.

8. In response to the decline in reading, the government has taken a series of measures to inculcate the irreplaceable value of reading into the citizens.

9. Schools' responsibility is not only to impart knowledge to students but also to help shape their values and character.

10. We must have a thorough research about the issue; otherwise, we may be misled by some plausible information.

11. The boy is mischievous and likes to exaggerate the description about his daily encounters.

12. A free society is willing to accept divergent opinions and encourage its citizens to express thoughts.

13. Although social media enable us to access information enormously, they also make it difficult for us to distinguish the truth from so much distorted information.

14. Censorship can sometimes become the legalized excuse for suppression of speech.

15. In a democratic society, one's freedom of speech should be respected and protected.

16. Freedom of speech is one of the constitutional rights. Only with this right can we fully express ourselves and create a society of diversity of thoughts and expressions.

17. Mainstream ideas on media stifle individualism in a way of imposing uniform ideas and values and discouraging uniqueness.

18. Conflict of opinions is common and helpful in the process of brainstorming. It encourages people to break stereotypes and biases, thus inspiring better ideas.

19. Young people, nowadays, are used to searching information online and seldom process any of it so that they are gradually converted into identical captives without opinions.

20. When expressing ideas in public we need to be politically correct, and it should not be treated as a restriction on us but a way of showing respect.

21. Air conditioners are very useful to especially vulnerable groups, such as the ill or old people.

22. Although the Internet users can pose opinions online anonymously, they should still behave themselves and show mutual respect.

23. Contents of perfume advertisements can be very provocative. They often feature a woman dressing sexily to seduce a handsome guy.

24. Women are thought to be more sensitive than men; they are susceptible to beautiful stories or miserable tragedies.

25. Throwing money in the face is definitely an insulting act. Few guys, no matter how poor they are, are able to take it.

26. The Internet is saturated with information both true and false, so we should be skeptical and selectively choose to believe.

27. The Internet, on one hand, brings about enormous convenience to us; on the other hand, it also pulverizes our privacy.

28. Some complain that censorship infringes on citizens' freedom of self-expression.

29. The rapid industrial development makes environmental protection a vexing issue.

30. Some radicals take advantages of social media to disseminate distorted and dangerous information to create fear and panic.

（三）写作实操

Model Essay 3

The advancement of contemporary society has expedited changes in various aspects of life, which also arouses a series of debates and issues. One of them concerns the public media. In order to attract more attention, new types of media, such as Twitter or Facebook, have exposed a mass of sandals concerning some personal information to fulfill people's curiosity. It is often cited that scandals are useful because they could help the society focus attention on some social problems in some way. However, spreading scandals is a double-edged sword, and the negative effects of scandals require more estimation.

Admittedly, scandals sometimes work as warning signs for the public, so that existing but ignored social issues are put on the table for discussion. This kind of ruthless exposure of negative behaviors, especially those conducted by celebrities, could arouse reflection on flaws of the society, and finally lead to overall promotion of social behaviors. For example, a piece of news saying that a man named Joe is doing drugs may not attract much attention, but the scandal of Iron Man, Robert Downey Jr., about his substance abuse and drug possession would be such a strike to fans of Tony Stark and Marvel. Potential causes behind drug abuse would be widely discussed and even researchers may devote more energy to studying the mechanisms behind addiction. In this scenario, the public media also act as the supervision force to oversee the behaviors of celebrities. Because of the existence of sandals, even popular figures and people with power should watch their behaviors all the time in case their faults get exposed.

Although scandals can bring about positive effects on the society, the endless curiosity of the public would sometimes turn the public characters involved in scandals into the victims. That is to say, even though some scandals are meant to expose negative behaviors of celebrities, including political figures, the public media may overuse their power to dig more about individuals of one scandal, and thus deprive these individuals of their rights to privacy, which is not fair. Take the example of Wang Baoqiang, a famous Chinese actor and director. The exposure of his wife's infidelity invited huge public curiosity and a sequent intrusion of pertinent events. Wang was then not only heartbroken by the loss of marriage but also tortured by the pressure of public opinion, and he had to postpone or even cancel most of the work and movies. The side effects of spreading scandals could be disastrous, especially in contemporary society where scandals travel fast on the Internet. As is advocated by Wang, what we need is a sensitive and more compassionate social media environment. Only in this environment can the side effects of scandals on people be minimized.

The purpose of the media that to produce and report scandals also needs more consideration, because scandals might act as the element to absorb the public attention on the specific media channel to gain the profits, as a result, it can be away from the truth by profit-mongers or eye-catchers. Especially for political scandals, one may utilize the strategy of exposing scandals of opponent's personal life to gain unfair advantages in a campaign. And as citizens, we need to tell from political lies and do not fall into traps of intentional scandals. To achieve this, questions such as "who discovered this scandal?" "who are the potential beneficiaries of this scandal?" "what's the influence of this scandal on the society?" should be asked frequently before we totally buy this kind of news. In show business, some movie stars might create sexual scandals for themselves in order to attract more attention. In this case, the public media are paid to broadcast the "false scandal". Consequently, if the purpose of the media is not to expose bad behaviors in the society, but to support or break down someone on purpose, the scandals they report will remain unreliable, thus bearing no positive social effects on improving people's behaviors.

To conclude, the public needs to have a critical judgment about scandals; besides that, government should tailor some regulation to monitor the media to diminish the negative consequence on these subjects of these scandals.

文娱艺术类作业

（一）完形填空练习

完形填空一

（1）cultural needs

（2）echo

[翻译] 现代艺术的发展可以很大程度上体现出人民群众的文化需求，让观众们可以在艺术观赏中找到共识。艺术不仅仅是人民群众的，更是民族的。

完形填空二

（1）cultural diversity

（2）Cross-cultural communication

（3）adhere to the tradition

[翻译] 全球经济一体化很大程度上促进了文化多元化。跨文化交流不仅可以坚持传统，还可以给全球带来不一样的视觉享受，是不可阻挡的发展趋势。

（二）汉译英练习

1. A great movie nominated for an Oscar requires not only attractive story-line, but also considerable artistic value.

2. Privacy security is the inherent advantage of Bitcoin trading.

3. Since the eighteenth century, waves of immigrant workers have contributed a wealth of cultural diversity to California.

4. The key to effective cross-cultural communication is knowledge and understanding.

5. The British Museum has collected treasures with high achievements of art from all over the world.

6. I catch the morning movies every weekend for my visual enjoyment.

7. University is the cradle of culture, which provides the cultural industry with a lot of talented people.

8. This new film, which was shot in San Francisco, will help place underground subculture into mainstream culture.

9. These tremendous achievements have greatly enhanced the Chinese people's national pride and confidence.

10. This movie provides the audience with a new angle to understand the local customs and practices of Sichuan.

11. Something can never fail to attract people's eyes.

12. All in all, the artistic taste of the Brown contrasts sharply with their predecessors.

13. It is neither possible for artists' creative work to adhere to the tradition entirely, nor can it completely break away from the constraints of eras.

14. Months of highly skilled hand carving were destroyed by a few hours of sledge hammer architectural vandalism.

15. We must carry forward the practice of seeking truth from facts, which is the tradition of our party.

16. Meeting the growing cultural needs of people is one of the fundamental goals of our government.

17. It contains the special ideality of social value of the Tang Dynasty, which shows the popular artistic reflection at that time.

18. This application is not supported by Intel chips and will cause irreversible damage to the operating system.

19. Patriotism, as the essence of civil spirit, helps to strengthen our national identity and value.

20. Cross-cultural communication helps to remove prejudice and misunderstanding among different countries.

21. The purpose of music lessons in our school is to help children to develop high artistic standards through choral singing and performance.

22. Popular TV plays enjoy great popularity, because their entertainment nature keeps consistence with mass culture.

23. The British history of the second half of the twentieth century indicated that cultural devolution preceded and indeed forced political changes.

24. Their works showed literary rebellion and passion, which made up a kind of distinctive cultural insight.

25. The beauty of the Venus de Milo makes it become artistic works in art history.

26. Since new CEO came into power, he has broken with old management of the company.

27. Thrift, as a fine family tradition, can carry down from generation to generation.

28. His words aroused no echoes in their hearts.

29. In modern society, the government should attach more importance to technological innovation and technical progress.

30. How to make the spiritual enhancement of college students has become a hot issue in higher education.

31. He is eclipsed by his wife, who is much cleverer and more amusing than he is.

32. In Britain, drinking in a pub after work is one of the most popular pastimes.

33. In meditation, we allow the harmony between men and nature to percolate to every layer of the existence.

34. Books possess an essence of immortality, which are the most lasting products of human effort in civilization heritage.

35. An instructive lead-in activity will enable students to integrate into the class better.

36. Art edification can allow students to experience joy, cultivate self-confidence and create healthy personalities.

37. How to overcome the cultural difference among the staff from different countries has become a serious problem in human resources management of multinational corporations.

38. A series of cultural events that were held to mark the 400th death anniversary of Shakespeare made people realize "time is fleeting, and art is longlasting".

（三）写作实操

Model Essay 3

Music, an important form of art, has been valued since forever, and the advancement of digital technologies today makes it possible for music to permeate every corner of society. With the prevalence of music comes the discussion about its influence and power in people's lives. A conservative view argues that music is merely a reflection of reality. However, music can actually give people certain subliminal messages and is a subtle yet powerful force to create new thoughts and values.

The composition of music and songs is often attributed to inspiration from life, and people hear more than once that many musicians relate their music to what they've heard, read, or experienced. Some people think that is all music is able to achieve—to reflect what have already been there. They would exemplify the concept through limited observation: the reason why some songs advocating gender equality come up is that people have already converted to an open mind due to the rising power and status of female group. But they've ignored a significant truth that some avant-garde singers, such as Helen Reddy, had already been communicating the idea back in their time. Nobody, of course, can say that music plays the only role in directing social value or creating certain thoughts, but it does make some contribution.

One of the most apparent contribution is that music works a magical way to influence the emotion or mind of individuals. As vehicles of ideas, songs and music get connected with listeners via shared feelings or thoughts. When immersed in the ambience, listeners will naturally be manipulated by the subliminal messages delivered by music. Thus, music is powerful enough to not only validate the existing thoughts but also forge new ones. Take the famous song, *Black Friday,* as an example. It is such a dismal piece of music that no one was able to laugh once finishing hearing it. But rather, thousands of people were condemned to schizophrenia or depression; hundreds of them even killed themselves. It was because of the destructive power of the song that the world even reached a unanimous agreement to ban it.

Since music can play individuals' sentiments in such a credible manner, it can also help create a social tendency when many individuals are subject to the same ideas embedded in music. Music can infiltrate people with some ideas or values to enhance or even create social tendencies. A recent incident of Chinese community protesting against racial discrimination in YG's song serves as very potent evidence. YG disseminates in his song *Meet the Flockers*, a very dangerous directions to rob the Chinese Americans. Surely, the song reflects crimes happening in Chinese community, but what's sinful about it is that the song turns what is a secret within some robbers into a public knowledge, which reinforces the stereotype about

Chinese Americans and encourages people, especially immature underage boys, to emulate the shameful deed. It is reported that the song has actually created a crazy trend to break in Chinese shops and houses. While this racial violence results from a series of factors, value-carrying music clearly plays a role in this.

Indeed, music comes from life; but it undoubtedly communicates thoughts among individuals and within a society with the help of digital technologies, which bring music to everywhere. Though it requires a whole package of factors to create certain social tendency, music with its powerful "brainwashing" ability certainly helps shape individual character and social values.